Lecture Notes in Artificial Intelligence 13154

Subseries of Lecture Notes in Computer Science

More information about this subseries at https://link.springer.com/bookseries/1244

Ben Goertzel · Matthew Iklé ·
Alexey Potapov (Eds.)

Artificial General Intelligence

14th International Conference, AGI 2021
Palo Alto, CA, USA, October 15–18, 2021
Proceedings

 Springer

Editors
Ben Goertzel 🆔
SingularityNET
Amsterdam, The Netherlands

Matthew Iklé 🆔
SingularityNET
Amsterdam, The Netherlands

Alexey Potapov 🆔
SingularityNET
Amsterdam, The Netherlands

ISSN 0302-9743   ISSN 1611-3349 (electronic)
Lecture Notes in Artificial Intelligence
ISBN 978-3-030-93757-7   ISBN 978-3-030-93758-4 (eBook)
https://doi.org/10.1007/978-3-030-93758-4

LNCS Sublibrary: SL7 – Artificial Intelligence

This Springer imprint is published by the registered company Springer Nature Switzerland AG
The registered company address is: Gewerbestrasse 11, 6330 Cham, Switzerland

Preface

This volume contains the papers presented at the 14th Conference on Artificial General Intelligence (AGI 2021) held during October 15–18, 2021, both physically in Palo Alto, California, and virtually via SingularityNET's YouTube channel. This year's conference included three workshops (Scaling Up Neuro-Symbolic and Integrative AGI Architectures; NARS Tutorial and Workshop; and Interpretable Language Processing), a day of general audience sessions with AGI researchers and leaders held at the Computer History Museum (CHM) in Mountain View, California, in-person and online contributed papers and talks, and 10 keynotes from 10 AGI luminaries.

Following the success of the 13th AGI conference, originally planned for St. Petersburg, Russia, but ultimately held strictly online due to the ongoing effects of the COVID-19 pandemic, the hybrid format of AGI 2021 proved to be logistically challenging but ultimately a resounding success. As one long-time contributor put it, "I think it was the best (AGI conference) so far". This year's conference also featured presenters and participants from a broader set of backgrounds and with more diverse perspectives than ever before.

Researchers from at least 16 countries attended AGI 2021, either in-person or online. Many deep, stimulating, and diverse papers and talks were given over the course of the conference. Outdoor participant dinners followed the first two days of the conference with wide-ranging and scintillating discussion spilling over well into each night.

This volume contains the contributed talks presented at AGI 2021. There were 50 submissions. Each submission was reviewed by at least two (on average 2.57) Program Committee members. The committee decided to accept 36 long papers (72% acceptance rate) for oral presentation, seven of which were presented in person with the remaining via Zoom.

Once again the conference covered an astounding array of topics, from foundations of AGI, through AGI approaches, and AGI ethics to the roles of systems biology, goal generation, and learning systems, and so much more. The breadth and depth of ideas disseminated, discussed, and argued was extraordinary.

Speakers and panelists for the general audience day at CHM included Janet Adams from SingularityNET, Amara Angelica from SingularityNET and KurzweilAI, Joscha Bach from Intel Labs, James Boyd from SingularityNET and Wolfram Research, Nichol Bradford from the Willow Group and Transformative Technology, Ben Goertzel and Matt Iklé from the AGI Society and SingularityNET, Randal Koene from the Carbon Copies Foundation, Julia Mossbridge from the California Institute of Integral Studies and the Institute of Noetic Sciences, and Josef Urban from the Czech Institute of Informatics, Robotics and Cybernetics.

Ten additional keynote speeches were presented by researchers from both academia and industry. This year's speakers and topics were as follows:

- Francois Chollet— "The Missing Piece in the Quest for Greater Generality in AI"
- Yoshua Bengio— "Conscious Processing and Systematic Generalization with System 2 Deep Learning"
- Tomas Mikolov— "AGI: Why and how?"
- Jonathan Warrell— "Probabilistic Dependent Types and Semantics in AGI: Formal and Philosophical Perspectives"
- David Hanson— "Artistic Social Robotics as a Path to Human-AI Co-Evolution and Understanding"
- Nell Watson— "Machines for Moral Enlightenment"
- Gary Marcus— "Towards a Proper Foundation for Artificial Intelligence"
- Geordie Rose— "Robot Brains"
- Paul Rosenbloom— "Lumping and Splitting: Understanding Cognition via the Common Model and Dichotomic Maps"
- Josef Urban— "Towards the Dream of Self-Improving Universal Reasoning AI"

We thank all the Program Committee members for their dedicated service to the review process. We thank all of our contributors, participants, and tutorial, workshop and panel session organizers, without whom the conference would not exist.

Finally, we thank our sponsors: the Artificial General Intelligence Society, Springer Nature, the SingularityNET Foundation, TrueAGI, and the OpenCog Foundation.

November 2021   Ben Goertzel
                                                          Matt Iklé
                                                       Alexey Potapov

Organization

Conference Chair

Ben Goertzel   SingularityNET, OpenCog Foundation, and Hanson Robotics, USA

Organizing Committee

Ben Goertzel   SingularityNET, OpenCog Foundation, and Hanson Robotics, USA
Matthew Iklé   SingularityNET, USA
Alexey Potapov   SingularityNET, Russia

Program Committee Chairs

Ben Goertzel   SingularityNET, OpenCog Foundation, and Hanson Robotics, USA
Matthew Iklé   SingularityNET, USA
Alexey Potapov   SingularityNET, Russia

Program Committee

Joscha Bach   Intel Labs, USA
Antonio Chella   Università degli Studi di Palermo, Italy
Haris Dindo   Università degli Studi di Palermo, Italy
Wlodzislaw Duch   Nicolaus Copernicus University, Poland
Arthur Franz   Odessa Competence Center for Artificial Intelligence and Machine Learning (OCCAM), Ukraine
Nil Geisweiller   SingularityNET, USA
Ben Goertzel   SingularityNET, USA
Patrick Hammer   Temple University, USA
Eva Hudlicka   Psychometrix Associates, USA
Matt Iklé   SingularityNET, USA
Peter Isaev   Temple University, USA
Cliff Joslyn   Pacific Northwest National Laboratory, USA
Anton Kolonin   SingularityDAO, Russia
Xiang Li   Temple University, USA
Amedeo Napoli   LORIA Nancy, France
Eray Ozkural   Bilkent, Turkey
Wiebke Petersen   University of Düsseldorf, Germany

Contents

Reward-Punishment Symmetric Universal Intelligence

Samuel Allen Alexander[1(✉)] and Marcus Hutter[2]

[1] The U.S. Securities and Exchange Commission, New York City, USA
[2] DeepMind & AMU, London, UK
https://philpeople.org/profiles/samuel-alexander/publications,
http://www.hutter1.net/

Abstract. Can an agent's intelligence level be negative? We extend the Legg-Hutter agent-environment framework to include punishments and argue for an affirmative answer to that question. We show that if the background encodings and Universal Turing Machine (UTM) admit certain Kolmogorov complexity symmetries, then the resulting Legg-Hutter intelligence measure is symmetric about the origin. In particular, this implies reward-ignoring agents have Legg-Hutter intelligence 0 according to such UTMs.

Keywords: Universal intelligence · Intelligence measures · Reinforcement learning

1 Introduction

In their paper [11], Legg and Hutter write:

"As our goal is to produce a definition of intelligence that is as broad and encompassing as possible, the space of environments used in our definition should be as large as possible."

So motivated, we investigate what would happen if we extended the universe of environments to include environments with rewards from $\mathbb{Q} \cap [-1, 1]$ instead of just from $\mathbb{Q} \cap [0, 1]$ as in Legg and Hutter's paper. In other words, we investigate what would happen if environments are not only allowed to reward agents but also to punish agents (a punishment being a negative reward).

We discovered that when negative rewards are allowed, this introduces a certain algebraic structure into the agent-environment framework. The main objection we anticipate to our extended framework is that it implies the negative intelligence of certain agents[1]. We would argue that this makes perfect sense

---

[1] Thus, this paper falls under the broader program of advocating for intelligence measures having different ranges than the nonnegative reals. Alexander has advocated more extreme extensions of the range of intelligence measures [1,2]; by contrast, here we merely question the assumption that intelligence never be negative, leaving aside the question of whether intelligence should be real-valued.

© Springer Nature Switzerland AG 2022
B. Goertzel et al. (Eds.): AGI 2021, LNAI 13154, pp. 1–10, 2022.
https://doi.org/10.1007/978-3-030-93758-4_1

when environments are capable of punishing agents: if the intelligence level of a reinforcement learning agent is a measure of its ability to extract large rewards on average across many environments, then an agent who instead extracts large punishments should have a negative intelligence level.

This paper advances the practical pursuit of AGI by suggesting (in Sect. 4) certain symmetry constraints which would narrow down the space of background UTMs, thereby refining at least one approach to intelligence measurement. In particular these constraints are one answer to Leike and Hutter, who asked: "But what are other desirable properties of a UTM?" [13].

The structure of the paper is as follows:

- In Sect. 2, we give preliminary definitions.
- In Sect. 3, we introduce what we call the dual of an agent and of an environment, and prove some algebraic theorems about these.
- In Sect. 4, we show the existence of UTMs yielding Kolmogorov complexities with certain symmetries, and show that the resulting Legg-Hutter intelligence measures are symmetric too.
- In Sect. 5 we consider the absolute value of Legg-Hutter intelligence as an alternative intelligence measure.
- In Sect. 6, we summarize and make concluding remarks, including remarks about how these ideas might be applied to certain other intelligence measures.

2   Preliminaries

In defining agent and environment below, we attempt to follow Legg and Hutter [11] as closely as possible, except that we permit environments to output rewards from $\mathbb{Q} \cap [-1, 1]$ rather than just $\mathbb{Q} \cap [0, 1]$ (and, accordingly, we modify which well-behaved environments to restrict our attention to).

Throughout the paper, we implicitly fix a finite set $\mathcal{A}$ of *actions*, a finite set $\mathcal{O}$ of *observations*, and a finite set $\mathcal{R} \subseteq \mathbb{Q} \cap [-1, 1]$ of *rewards* (so each reward is a rational number between -1 and 1 inclusive), with $|\mathcal{A}| > 0$, $|\mathcal{O}| > 0$, $|\mathcal{R}| > 0$. We assume that $\mathcal{R}$ has the following property: whenever $\mathcal{R}$ contains any reward r, then $\mathcal{R}$ also contains $-r$. We assume $\mathcal{A}$, $\mathcal{O}$, and $\mathcal{R}$ are mutually disjoint (i.e., no reward is an action, no reward is an observation, and no action is an observation). By $\langle \rangle$ we mean the empty sequence.

Definition 1 *(Agents, environments, etc.).*

1. *By* $(\mathcal{ORA})^*$ *we mean the set of all finite sequences starting with an observation, ending with an action, and following the pattern "observation, reward, action, ...". We include* $\langle \rangle$ *in this set.*
2. *By* $(\mathcal{ORA})^*\mathcal{OR}$ *we mean the set of all sequences of the form* $s \frown o \frown r$ *where* $s \in (\mathcal{ORA})^*$, $o \in \mathcal{O}$ *and* $r \in \mathcal{R}$ *(*$\frown$ *denotes concatenation).*
3. *By an* agent, *we mean a function* π *with domain* $(\mathcal{ORA})^*\mathcal{OR}$, *which assigns to every sequence* $s \in (\mathcal{ORA})^*\mathcal{OR}$ *a* $\mathbb{Q}$-*valued probability measure, written* $\pi(\bullet|s)$, *on* $\mathcal{A}$. *For every such* s *and every* $a \in \mathcal{A}$, *we write* $\pi(a|s)$ *for* $(\pi(\bullet|s))(a)$. *Intuitively,* $\pi(a|s)$ *is the probability that agent* π *will take action* a *in response to history* s.

4. *By an* environment, *we mean a function* μ *with domain* $(\mathcal{ORA})^*$, *which assigns to every* $s \in (\mathcal{ORA})^*$ *a* $\mathbb{Q}$-*valued probability measure, written* $\mu(\bullet|s)$, *on* $\mathcal{O} \times \mathcal{R}$. *For every such* s *and every* $(o, r) \in \mathcal{O} \times \mathcal{R}$, *we write* $\mu(o, r|s)$ *for* $(\mu(\bullet|s))(o, r)$. *Intuitively,* $\mu(o, r|s)$ *is the probability that environment* μ *will issue observation* o *and reward* r *to the agent in response to history* s.

5. *If* π *is an agent,* μ *is an environment, and* $n \in \mathbb{N}$, *we write* $V_{\mu,n}^{\pi}$ *for the expected value of the sum of the rewards which would occur in the sequence* $(o_0, r_0, a_0, \ldots, o_n, r_n, a_n)$ *randomly generated as follows:*
   (a) $(o_0, r_0) \in \mathcal{O} \times \mathcal{R}$ *is chosen randomly based on the probability measure* $\mu(\bullet|\langle\rangle)$.
   (b) $a_0 \in \mathcal{A}$ *is chosen randomly based on the probability measure* $\pi(\bullet|o_0, r_0)$.
   (c) *For each* $i > 0$, $(o_i, r_i) \in \mathcal{O} \times \mathcal{R}$ *is chosen randomly based on the probability measure* $\mu(\bullet|o_0, r_0, a_0, \ldots, o_{i-1}, r_{i-1}, a_{i-1})$.
   (d) *For each* $i > 0$, $a_i \in \mathcal{A}$ *is chosen randomly based on the probability measure* $\pi(\bullet|o_0, r_0, a_0, \ldots, o_{i-1}, r_{i-1}, a_{i-1}, o_i, r_i)$.

6. *If* π *is an agent and* μ *is an environment, let* $V_{\mu}^{\pi} = \lim_{n \to \infty} V_{\mu,n}^{\pi}$. *Intuitively,* V_{μ}^{π} *is the expected total reward which* π *would extract from* μ.

Note that it is possible for V_{μ}^{π} to be undefined. For example, if μ is an environment which always issues reward $(-1)^n$ in response to the agent's nth action, then V_{μ}^{π} is undefined for every agent π. This would not be the case if rewards were required to be ≥ 0, so this is one way in which allowing punishments complicates the resulting theory.

Definition 2. *An environment* μ *is* well-behaved *if* μ *is computable and the following condition holds: for every agent* π, V_{μ}^{π} *exists and* $-1 \leq V_{\mu}^{\pi} \leq 1$.

Note that reward-space $[0, 1]$ can be transformed into punishment-space $[-1, 0]$ either via $r \mapsto -r$ or via $r \mapsto r - 1$. An advantage of $r \mapsto -r$ is that it preserves well-behavedness of environments (we prove this below in Corollary 7)[2].

3   Dual Agents and Dual Environments

In the Introduction, we promised that by allowing environments to punish agents, we would reveal algebraic structure not otherwise present. The key to this additional structure is the following definition.

---

[2] It is worth mentioning another difference between these two transforms. The hypothetical agent AI_{μ} with perfect knowledge of the environment's reward distribution would not change its behavior in response to $r \mapsto r - 1$ (nor indeed in response to any positive linear scaling $r \mapsto ar + b$, $a > 0$), but it would generally change its behavior in response to $r \mapsto -r$. Interestingly, this behavior invariance with respect to $r \mapsto r - 1$ would not hold if AI_{μ} were capable of "suicide" (deliberately ending the environmental interaction): one should never quit a slot machine that always pays between 0 and 1 dollars, but one should immediately quit a slot machine that always pays between -1 and 0 dollars. The agent AIXI also changes behavior in response to $r \mapsto r - 1$, and it was recently argued that this can be interpreted in terms of suicide/death: AIXI models its environment using a mixture distribution over a countable class of semimeasures, and AIXI's behavior can be interpreted as treating the complement of the domain of each semimeasure as death, see [14].

Definition 3 *(Dual Agents and Dual Environments).*

1. For each sequence s, let $\bar{s}$ be the sequence obtained by replacing every reward r in s by $-r$.
2. Suppose π is an agent. We define a new agent $\bar{\pi}$, the dual of π, as follows: for each $s \in (\mathcal{ORA})^*\mathcal{OR}$, for each action $a \in \mathcal{A}$,

$$\bar{\pi}(a|s) = \pi(a|\bar{s}).$$

3. Suppose μ is an environment. We define a new environment $\bar{\mu}$, the dual of μ, as follows: for each $s \in (\mathcal{ORA})^*$, for each observation $o \in \mathcal{O}$ and reward $r \in \mathcal{R}$,

$$\bar{\mu}(o, r|s) = \mu(o, -r|\bar{s}).$$

Lemma 4 *(Double Negation). If x is a sequence, agent, or environment, then $\bar{\bar{x}} = x$.*

Proof. Follows from the fact that for every real number r, $--r = r$.   □

Theorem 5. *Suppose μ is an environment and π is an agent. Then*

$$V_{\bar{\mu}}^{\bar{\pi}} = -V_{\mu}^{\pi}$$

(and the left-hand side is defined if and only if the right-hand side is defined).

Proof. By Definition 1 part 6, it suffices to show that for each $n \in \mathbb{N}$, $V_{\bar{\mu},n}^{\bar{\pi}} = -V_{\mu,n}^{\pi}$. For that, it suffices to show that for every $s \in ((\mathcal{ORA})^*) \cup ((\mathcal{ORA})^*\mathcal{OR})$, the probability X of generating s using π and μ (as in Definition 1 part 5) equals the probability X' of generating $\bar{s}$ using $\bar{\pi}$ and $\bar{\mu}$. We will show this by induction on the length of s.

Case 1: s is empty. Then $X = X' = 1$.

Case 2: s terminates with an action. Then $s = t \frown a$ for some $t \in (\mathcal{ORA})^*\mathcal{OR}$. Let Y (resp. Y') be the probability of generating t (resp. $\bar{t}$) using π and μ (resp. $\bar{\pi}$ and $\bar{\mu}$). We reason: $X = \pi(a|t)Y = \pi(a|\bar{\bar{t}})Y = \bar{\pi}(a|\bar{t})Y$ by definition of $\bar{\pi}$. By induction, $Y = Y'$, so $X = \bar{\pi}(a|\bar{t})Y'$, which by definition is X'.

Case 3: s terminates with a reward. Similar to Case 2.   □

Corollary 6. *For every agent π and environment μ,*

$$V_{\mu}^{\pi} = -V_{\bar{\mu}}^{\bar{\pi}}$$

(and the left-hand side is defined if and only if the right-hand side is defined).

Proof. If neither side is defined, then there is nothing to prove. Assume the left-hand side is defined. Then

$$V_{\mu}^{\pi} = V_{\bar{\bar{\mu}}}^{\bar{\bar{\pi}}} \qquad \text{(Lemma 4)}$$
$$= -V_{\bar{\mu}}^{\bar{\pi}}, \qquad \text{(Theorem 5)}$$

as desired. A similar argument holds if we assume the right-hand side is defined.   □

Corollary 7. *For every environment μ, μ is well-behaved if and only if $\overline{\mu}$ is well-behaved.*

Proof. We prove the $\Rightarrow$ direction, the other is similar. Since μ is well-behaved, μ is computable, so clearly $\overline{\mu}$ is computable. Let π be any agent. Since μ is well-behaved, $V_\mu^{\overline{\pi}}$ is defined and $-1 \leq V_\mu^{\overline{\pi}} \leq 1$. By Corollary 6, $V_{\overline{\mu}}^{\pi} = -V_\mu^{\overline{\pi}}$ is defined, implying $-1 \leq V_{\overline{\mu}}^{\pi} \leq 1$. By arbitrariness of π, this shows $\overline{\mu}$ is well-behaved. $\square$

4   Symmetric Intelligence

Agent $\overline{\pi}$ acts as agent π would act if π confused punishments with rewards and rewards with punishments. Whatever ingenuity π applies to maximize rewards, $\overline{\pi}$ applies that same ingenuity to maximize punishments. Thus, if Υ measures intelligence as performance averaged in some way[3], it seems natural that we might expect the following property to hold $(*)$: that whenever $\Upsilon(\pi) \neq 0$, then $\Upsilon(\pi) \neq \Upsilon(\overline{\pi})$. Indeed, one could argue it would be strange to hold that π manages to extract (say) positive rewards on average, and at the same time hold that $\overline{\pi}$ (which uses π to seek punishments) extracts the exact same positive rewards on average. To be clear, we do not declare $(*)$ is an absolute law, we merely opine that $(*)$ seems reasonable and natural. Now, assuming $(*)$, we can offer an informal argument for a stronger-looking symmetry property $(**)$: that $\Upsilon(\pi) = -\Upsilon(\overline{\pi})$ for all π. The informal argument is as follows. Let π be any agent. Imagine a new agent ρ which, at the start of every environmental interaction, flips a coin and commits to act as π for that whole interaction if the coin lands heads, or to act as $\overline{\pi}$ for the whole interaction if the coin lands tails. Probabilistic intuition suggests $\Upsilon(\rho) = \frac{1}{2}(\Upsilon(\pi) + \Upsilon(\overline{\pi}))$, so if $\Upsilon(\rho) = 0$ then $\Upsilon(\pi) = -\Upsilon(\overline{\pi})$. But maybe the reader doubts $\Upsilon(\rho) = 0$. In that case, define ρ' in the same way except swap "heads" and "tails". It seems there is no way to meaningfully distinguish ρ from ρ', so it seems we ought to have $\Upsilon(\rho) = \Upsilon(\rho')$. But to swap "heads" and "tails" is the same as to swap "π" and "$\overline{\pi}$". Thus $\rho' = \overline{\rho}$. Thus $\Upsilon(\rho) \neq 0$ would contradict $(*)$. In conclusion, while we do not declare it an absolute law, we do consider $(**)$ natural and reasonable, at least if Υ measures intelligence as performance averaged in some way. In this section, we will show that Legg and Hutter's universal intelligence measure satisfies $(**)$, provided a background UTM and encoding are suitably chosen.

We write 2^* for the set of finite binary strings. We write $f :\subseteq A \to B$ to indicate that f has codomain B and that f's domain is some subset of A.

Definition 8 *(Prefix-free universal Turing machines).*

1. *A partial computable function $f :\subseteq 2^* \to 2^*$ is prefix-free if the following requirement holds: $\forall p, p' \in 2^*$, if p is a strict initial segment of p', then $f(p)$ and $f(p')$ are not both defined.*

---

[3] Note that measuring intelligence as averaged performance might conflict with certain everyday uses of the word "intelligent", see Sect. 5.

2. *A prefix-free universal Turing machine (or PFUTM) is a prefix-free partial computable function $U :\subseteq 2^* \to 2^*$ such that the following condition holds. For every prefix-free partial computable function $f :\subseteq 2^* \to 2^*$, $\exists y \in 2^*$ such that $\forall x \in 2^*$, $f(x) = U(y \frown x)$. In this case, we say y is a* computer program *for f in programming language U.*

Environments do not have domain $\subseteq 2^*$, and they do not have codomain 2^*. Rather, their domain and codomain are $(\mathcal{ORA})^*$ and the set of $\mathbb{Q}$-valued probability measures on $\mathcal{O} \times \mathcal{R}$, respectively. Thus, in order to talk about their Kolmogorov complexities, one must encode said inputs and outputs. This low-level detail is usually implicit, but we will need (in Theorem 11) to distinguish between different kinds of encodings, so we must make the details explicit.

Definition 9. *By an* RL-encoding *we mean a computable function $\sqcap :$ $(\mathcal{ORA})^* \cup M \to 2^*$ (where M is the set of $\mathbb{Q}$-valued probability-measures on $\mathcal{O} \times \mathcal{R}$) such that for all $x, y \in (\mathcal{ORA})^* \cup M$ (with $x \neq y$), $\sqcap(x)$ is not an initial segment of $\sqcap(y)$. We say $\sqcap$ is* suffix-free *if for all $x, y \in (\mathcal{ORA})^* \cup M$ (with $x \neq y$), $\sqcap(x)$ is not a terminal segment of $\sqcap(y)$. We write $\ulcorner x \urcorner$ for $\sqcap(x)$.*

Note that in Definition 9, it makes sense to encode M because $\mathcal{O}$ and $\mathcal{R}$ are finite (Sect. 2). Notice that suffix-freeness is, in some sense, the reverse of prefix-freeness. The existence of encodings that are simultaneously prefix-free and suffix-free is well-known. For example, elements of the range of $\sqcap$ could be composed of 8-bit blocks (bytes), such that every element of the range of $\sqcap$ begins and ends with the ASCII closed-bracket characters [and], respectively, and such that these closed-brackets do not appear anywhere in the middle.

Definition 10 *(Kolmogorov Complexity). Suppose U is a PFUTM and $\sqcap$ is an RL-encoding.*

1. *For each computable environment μ, the* Kolmogorov complexity of μ given by $U, \sqcap$, *written $K_U^\sqcap(\mu)$, is the smallest $n \in \mathbb{N}$ such that there is some computer program of length n, in programming language U, for some function $f :\subseteq 2^* \to 2^*$ such that for all $s \in (\mathcal{ORA})^*$, $f(\ulcorner s \urcorner) = \ulcorner \mu(\bullet | s) \urcorner$ (note this makes sense since the domain of $\sqcap$ in Definition 9 is $(\mathcal{ORA})^* \cup M$).*
2. *We say U is* symmetric in its $\sqcap$-encoded-environment cross-section *(or simply that U is $\sqcap$-symmetric) if $K_U^\sqcap(\mu) = K_U^\sqcap(\overline{\mu})$ for every computable environment μ.*

Theorem 11. *For every suffix-free RL-encoding $\sqcap$, there exists a $\sqcap$-symmetric PFUTM.*

Proof. Let U_0 be a PFUTM, we will modify U_0 to obtain a $\sqcap$-symmetric PFUTM. For readability's sake, write POS for 0 and NEG for 1. Thinking of U_0 as a programming language, we define a new programming language U as follows. Every program in U must begin with one of the keywords POS or NEG. Outputs of U are defined as follows.

– $U(\text{POS} \frown x) = U_0(x)$.

– To compute $U(\text{NEG} \frown x)$, find $s \in (\mathcal{ORA})^*$ such that $x = y \frown \ulcorner s \urcorner$ for some y (if no such s exists, diverge). Note that s is unique by suffix-freeness of $\sqcap$. If $U_0(y \frown \ulcorner \overline{s} \urcorner) = \ulcorner m \urcorner$ for some $\mathbb{Q}$-valued probability-measure m on $\mathcal{O} \times \mathcal{R}$, then let $U(\text{NEG} \frown x) = \ulcorner \overline{m} \urcorner$ where $\overline{m}(o, r) = m(o, -r)$. Otherwise, diverge.
   • Informally: If x appears to be an instruction to plug s into computer program y to get a probability measure $\mu(\bullet | s)$, then instead plug $\overline{s}$ into y and flip the resulting probability measure so that the output ends up being the flipped version of $\mu(\bullet | \overline{s})$, i.e., $\overline{\mu}(\bullet | s)$.

By construction, whenever $\text{POS} \frown y$ is a U-computer program for a function f satisfying $f(\ulcorner s \urcorner) = \ulcorner \mu(\bullet | s) \urcorner$, $\text{NEG} \frown y$ is an equal-length U-computer program for a function g satisfying $g(\ulcorner s \urcorner) = \ulcorner \overline{\mu}(\bullet | s) \urcorner$, and vice versa. It follows that U is $\sqcap$-symmetric. $\qquad \square$

The proof of Theorem 11 proves more than required: any PFUTM can be modified to make a $\sqcap$-symmetric PFUTM if $\sqcap$ is suffix-free. In some sense, the construction in the proof of Theorem 11 works by eliminating bias: reinforcement learning itself is implicitly biased in its convention that rewards be positive and punishments negative. We can imagine a pessimistic parallel universe where RL instead follows the opposite convention, and the RL in that parallel universe is no less valid than the RL in our own. To be unbiased in this sense, a computer program defining an environment should specify which of the two RL conventions it is operating under (hence the POS and NEG keywords). This trick of using an initial bit to indicate reward-reversal was previously used in [12].

Definition 12. *Let W be the set of all well-behaved environments. Let $\overline{W} = \{\overline{\mu} : \mu \in W\}$.*

Definition 13. *For every PFUTM U, RL-encoding $\sqcap$, and agent π, the Legg-Hutter universal intelligence of π given by $U, \sqcap$, written $\Upsilon_U^{\sqcap}(\pi)$, is*

$$\Upsilon_U^{\sqcap}(\pi) = \sum_{\mu \in W} 2^{-K_U^{\sqcap}(\mu)} V_\mu^\pi.$$

The sum defining $\Upsilon_U^{\sqcap}(\pi)$ is absolutely convergent by comparison with the summands defining Chaitin's constant (hence the prefix-free UTM requirement). Thus a well-known theorem from calculus says the sum does not depend on which order the $\mu \in W$ are enumerated.

Legg-Hutter intelligence has been accused of being subjective because of its UTM-sensitivity [7,9,13]. More optimistically, UTM-sensitivity could be considered a feature, reflecting the existence of many kinds of intelligence. It could be used to measure intelligence in various contexts, by choosing UTMs appropriately. One could even use it to measure, say, chess intelligence, by choosing a UTM where chess-related environments are easiest to program.

Theorem 14 *(Symmetry about the origin). For every RL-encoding $\sqcap$, every $\sqcap$-symmetric PFUTM U, and every agent π,*

$$\Upsilon_U^{\sqcap}(\overline{\pi}) = -\Upsilon_U^{\sqcap}(\pi).$$

Proof. By Corollary 6,

$$\Upsilon_U^\sqcap(\overline{\pi}) = \sum_{\mu \in W} 2^{-K_U^\sqcap(\mu)} V_\mu^{\overline{\pi}} = - \sum_{\mu \in W} 2^{-K_U^\sqcap(\mu)} V_{\overline{\mu}}^\pi.$$

By $\sqcap$-symmetry, we can rewrite this as

$$- \sum_{\mu \in W} 2^{-K_U^\sqcap(\overline{\mu})} V_{\overline{\mu}}^\pi = - \sum_{\mu \in \overline{W}} 2^{-K_U^\sqcap(\mu)} V_\mu^\pi.$$

By Corollary 7, $W = \overline{W}$, so this expression equals $- \sum_{\mu \in W} 2^{-K_U^\sqcap(\mu)} V_\mu^\pi$, which is $-\Upsilon_U^\sqcap(\pi)$ by Definition 13.   □

The following corollary addresses another obvious desideratum. This corollary is foreshadowed in [12].

Corollary 15. *Let $\sqcap$ be an RL-encoding, let U be a $\sqcap$-symmetric PFUTM and suppose π is an agent which ignores rewards (by which we mean that $\pi(\bullet|s)$ does not depend on the rewards in s). Then $\Upsilon_U^\sqcap(\pi) = 0$.*

Proof. The hypothesis implies $\pi = \overline{\pi}$, so by Theorem 14, $\Upsilon_U^\sqcap(\pi) = -\Upsilon_U^\sqcap(\pi)$.   □

Corollary 15 illustrates why it is appropriate, for purposes of Legg-Hutter universal intelligence, to choose a $\sqcap$-symmetric PFUTM[4]. Consider an agent π_a which blindly repeats a fixed action $a \in \mathcal{A}$. For any particular environment μ, where π_a earns total reward r by blind luck, that total reward should be cancelled by $\overline{\mu}$, where that blind luck becomes blind misfortune and π_a earns total reward $-r$ (Corollary 6). If $K_U^\sqcap(\mu) \neq K_U^\sqcap(\overline{\mu})$, the different weights $2^{-K_U^\sqcap(\mu)} \neq 2^{-K_U^\sqcap(\overline{\mu})}$ would prevent cancellation.

We conclude this section with an exercise, suggesting how the techniques of this paper can be used to obtain other structural results.

Exercise 16 *(Permutations).*

1. *For each permutation $P : \mathcal{A} \to \mathcal{A}$ of the action-space, for each sequence s, let Ps be the result of applying P to all the actions in s. For each agent π, let $P\pi$ be the agent defined by $P\pi(a|s) = \pi(Pa|Ps)$. For each environment μ, let $P\mu$ be the environment defined by $P\mu(o,r|s) = \mu(o,r|Ps)$. Show that in general $V_\mu^\pi = V_{P^{-1}\mu}^{P\pi}$ and $V_\mu^{P\pi} = V_{P\mu}^\pi$.*
2. *Say PFUTM U is $\sqcap$-permutable if $K_U^\sqcap(\mu) = K_U^\sqcap(P\mu)$ for every computable environment μ and permutation $P : \mathcal{A} \to \mathcal{A}$. Show that if $\sqcap$ is suffix-free then any given PFUTM can be transformed into a $\sqcap$-permutable PFUTM.*
3. *Show that if U is a $\sqcap$-permutable PFUTM, then $\Upsilon_U^\sqcap(P\pi) = \Upsilon_U^\sqcap(\pi)$ for every agent π and permutation $P : \mathcal{A} \to \mathcal{A}$.*
4. *Modify this exercise to apply to permutations of the observation-space.*

---

[4] An answer to Leike and Hutter's [13] "what are other desirable [UTM properties]?".

5   Whether to Take Absolute Values

Definition 13 assigns negative intelligence to agents who consistently minimize rewards. This is based on the desire to measure performance: agents who consistently minimize rewards have poor performance. One might, however, argue that $|\Upsilon_U^\sqcap(\pi)|$ would be a better measure of the agent's intelligence: if mathematical functions could have desires, one might argue that when $\Upsilon_U^\sqcap(\pi) < 0$, we should give π the benefit of the doubt, assume that π desires punishment, and conclude π is intelligent. This would more closely align with Bostrom's orthogonality thesis [3]. In the same way, a subject who answers every question wrong in a true-false IQ test might be considered intelligent: answering every question wrong is as hard as answering every question right, and we might give the subject the benefit of the doubt and assume they meant to answer wrong[5]. Rather than take a side and declare one of $\Upsilon_U^\sqcap$ or $|\Upsilon_U^\sqcap|$ to be the better measure, we consider them to be two equally valid measures, one of which measures performance and one of which measures the agent's ability to consistently extremize rewards (whether consistently positively or consistently negatively).

If one knew that π's Legg-Hutter intelligence were negative, one could derive the same benefit from π as from $\overline{\pi}$: just flip rewards. This raises the question: given π, can one computably determine $\mathrm{sgn}(\Upsilon_U^\sqcap(\pi))$? Or more weakly, is there a procedure which outputs $\mathrm{sgn}(\Upsilon_U^\sqcap(\pi))$ when $\Upsilon_U^\sqcap(\pi) \neq 0$ (but, when $\Upsilon_U^\sqcap(\pi) = 0$, may output a wrong answer or get stuck in an infinite loop)? One can easily contrive non-$\sqcap$-symmetric PFUTMs where $\mathrm{sgn}(\Upsilon_U^\sqcap(\pi))$ is computable from π— in fact, without the $\sqcap$-symmetry requirement, one can arrange that $\Upsilon_U^\sqcap(\pi)$ is *always* positive, by arranging that $\Upsilon_U^\sqcap(\pi)$ is dominated by a low-K environment that blindly gives all agents $+1$ total reward. On the other hand, one can contrive a $\sqcap$-symmetric PFUTM such that $\mathrm{sgn}(\Upsilon_U^\sqcap(\pi))$ is not computable from π even in the weak sense[6]. We leave it an open question whether there is any $\sqcap$-symmetric PFUTM U where $\mathrm{sgn}(\Upsilon_U^\sqcap(\pi))$ is computable (in the strong or weak sense).

6   Conclusion

By allowing environments to punish agents, we found additional algebraic structure in the agent-environment framework. Using this, we showed that certain Kolmogorov complexity symmetries yield Legg-Hutter intelligence symmetry.

---

[5] To quote Socrates: "Don't you think the ignorant person would often involuntarily tell the truth when he wished to say falsehoods, if it so happened, because he didn't know; whereas you, the wise person, if you should wish to lie, would always consistently lie?" [15].

[6] Arrange that $\Upsilon_U^\sqcap$ is dominated by μ and $\bar{\mu}$ where μ is an environment that initially gives reward .01, then waits for the agent to input the code of a Turing machine T, then (if the agent does so), gives reward $-.51$, then gives rewards 0 while simulating T until T halts, finally giving reward 1 if T does halt. Then if $\mathrm{sgn}(\Upsilon_U^\sqcap(\pi))$ were computable (even in the weak sense), one could compute it for strategically-chosen agents and solve the Halting Problem.

In future work it would be interesting to explore how these symmetries manifest themselves in other Legg-Hutter-like intelligence measures [5,6,8]. The precise strategy we employ in this paper is not directly applicable to prediction-based intelligence measurement [2,4,10], but a higher-level idea still applies: an intentional mis-predictor underperforms a 0-intelligence blind guesser.

Acknowledgments. We acknowledge José Hernández-Orallo, Shane Legg, Pedro Ortega, and the reviewers for comments and feedback.

References

1. Alexander, S.A.: The Archimedean trap: why traditional reinforcement learning will probably not yield AGI. JAGI **11**(1), 70–85 (2020)
2. Alexander, S.A., Hibbard, B.: Measuring intelligence and growth rate: variations on Hibbard's intelligence measure. JAGI **12**(1), 1–25 (2021)
3. Bostrom, N.: The superintelligent will: motivation and instrumental rationality in advanced artificial agents. Minds Mach. **22**(2), 71–85 (2012)
4. Gamez, D.: Measuring intelligence in natural and artificial systems. J. Artif. Intell. Conscious. **08**(2), 285–302 (2021)
5. Gavane, V.: A measure of real-time intelligence. JAGI **4**(1), 31–48 (2013)
6. Goertzel, B.: Patterns, hypergraphs and embodied general intelligence. In: IJC-NNP, IEEE (2006)
7. Hernández-Orallo, J.: C-tests revisited: back and forth with complexity. In: CAGI (2015)
8. Hernández-Orallo, J., Dowe, D.L.: Measuring universal intelligence: towards an anytime intelligence test. AI **174**(18), 1508–1539 (2010)
9. Hibbard, B.: Bias and no free lunch in formal measures of intelligence. JAGI **1**(1), 54 (2009)
10. Hibbard, B.: Measuring agent intelligence via hierarchies of environments. In: CAGI (2011)
11. Legg, S., Hutter, M.: Universal intelligence: a definition of machine intelligence. Minds Mach. **17**(4), 391–444 (2007)
12. Legg, S., Veness, J.: An approximation of the universal intelligence measure. In: Dowe, D.L. (ed.) Algorithmic Probability and Friends. Bayesian Prediction and Artificial Intelligence. LNCS, vol. 7070, pp. 236–249. Springer, Heidelberg (2013). https://doi.org/10.1007/978-3-642-44958-1_18
13. Leike, J., Hutter, M.: Bad universal priors and notions of optimality. In: Conference on Learning Theory, pp. 1244–1259. PMLR (2015)
14. Martin, J., Everitt, T., Hutter, M.: Death and suicide in universal artificial intelligence. In: CAGI (2016)
15. Plato: Lesser Hippias. In: Cooper, J.M., Hutchinson, D.S., et al. (eds.) Plato: Complete Works. Hackett Publishing, Indianapolis (1997)

AGI Brain II: The Upgraded Version with Increased Versatility Index

Mohammadreza Alidoust$^{(\boxtimes)}$ (iD)

Mashhad, Iran

Abstract. In this paper, an index for measuring the versatility of artificial general intelligence (AGI) systems is proposed. The index called Versatility Index (VI) is used to measure the versatility of an AGI system or for comparison purposes between different AGI systems. Then, an upgraded version of the original AGI Brain is proposed. In the new model, AGI Brain II, the explicit memory (EM) is replaced with a modified Mamdani fuzzy inference associative memory, called ProMem, which is able to estimate the consequences of a certain action by estimating the probability density function (PDF) of the observed data in a stochastic environment. The model was tested in a portfolio optimization scenario as a stochastic environment. Simulation results demonstrate the accuracy of the novel explicit memory as well as the increased versatility index of the upgraded model.

Keywords: Versatility index · AGI Brain · ProMem · Stochastic environments · Explicit memory · State/output estimator · Fuzzy inference system · Probability density function · Portfolio optimization

1 Introduction

Artificial General Intelligence (AGI) is the art of building thinking machines. These machines are able to understand, learn and perform any intellectual task that human can. In contrast to AI, AGI treats intelligence as a whole, resulting in the construction of versatile and general-purpose intelligent systems that can learn, reason, plan, communicate as well as any other tasks at the human intelligence level or perhaps ultimately well beyond it.

The original version of AGI Brain which was proposed in 2019 [2], worked well in a number of linear/nonlinear, continuous/discrete, single agent/multi agent deterministic environments, but it lacked the efficiency to perform in stochastic environments. In this paper, an upgraded version of the model, called AGI Brain II, is proposed which can also perform well in a stochastic environment. For testing the performance of the upgraded model, it was tested in a portfolio optimization scenario as a stochastic environment. In order to compare the two versions, an index called versatility index (VI) is suggested, which is used to measure the versatility of AGI systems.

© Springer Nature Switzerland AG 2022
B. Goertzel et al. (Eds.): AGI 2021, LNAI 13154, pp. 11–18, 2022.
https://doi.org/10.1007/978-3-030-93758-4_2

2 Versatility Index

AGI systems are meant to be as versatile as possible. Versatility is a necessary condition for an intelligent system to be called as an AGI system. According to Legg and Hutter, AGI systems have to perform well in a very large range of environments [1]. Regarding this quote, if an intelligent system is going to be called an AGI system, these two questions must be answered: How many environments that system can perform in? And how well the system can perform in each environment? Therefore, the number of different operating environments of an intelligent system in combination of its performance wellness in each environment can be considered as the measure of the versatility of the candidate system in order to be called as an AGI system. We call this measure the versatility index (VI) which is defined as the summation of the performances of an AGI system in each environment as follows:

$$VI = \sum_{i=1}^{N} \alpha_i \tag{1}$$

Where N is the number of different operating environments of the system, and α_i is the performance of the system in environment i. Since N and α_i are positive real numbers, the VI is also a dimensionless positive real number.

Since AI systems are problem-specific, their VI value will obviously be low compared to AGI systems. So, the VI can be considered as a distinction between AI and AGI system. The VI also provides a quantitative ground for comparison between different AGI systems. Different AGI systems can be compared by their VIs. The more versatile systems will have higher VI values and vice versa. The VI in combination with other evaluation methods might also be considered as an alternative way to measure the efficiency and intelligence level of AGI systems (or even of human brain), which will be discussed in Sect. 6.

Example 1. AGI system A is able to perform 3 AI tasks such as speech recognition, image processing, and intelligent control with performances $\alpha_1 = 85\%$, $\alpha_2 = 62\%$, and $\alpha_3 = 93\%$ respectively. Therefore, the VI for the AGI system A is calculated as follows;

$$VI_{\text{AGI system A}} = \sum_{i=1}^{N} \alpha_i = 240$$

3 The Original AGI Brain

AGI Brain is a unified learning and decision-making framework for artificial general intelligence systems based on modern control theory. It considers intelligence as a form of optimality. In AGI Brain intelligence means and equals optimization; Optimization of the surrounding world towards common goals. In AGI Brain the design is emphasized on versatility, i.e., designing a general-purpose artificial brain. Figure 1 illustrates the general schematic world γ consisting of the artificial agent ω and the object ψ.

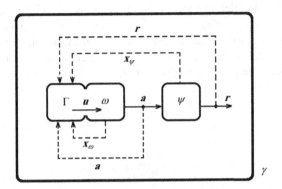

Fig. 1. The world γ consisting of the artificial agent ω and its brain Γ, and the object ψ. Observed feedbacks: ($\mathbf{x}_\omega$: vector of the bodily states of the agent ω, **a**: action vector, $\mathbf{x}_\psi$: vector of the states of the object ψ, **r**: response vector of the object ψ). The artificial brain Γ can observe these actions and states fully or partially by its sensors.

At every time step n, the artificial brain Γ produces commands $\boldsymbol{u}$ (e.g. hormones or neural signals) which change the states of ω's body, i.e. $\mathbf{x}_\omega$, which then leads to performing action **a** on the object ψ. This action changes ψ's states $\mathbf{x}_\psi$, which consequently leads to ψ's response **r**. Like a natural brain, the Γ can observe these actions and states fully or partially by its sensors (Fig. 1).

By benefiting from powerful modelling capability of state-space representation, as well as ultimate learning ability of the neural networks (NNs), AGI Brain tries to duplicate intelligence using a unified strategy. The model emulates three learning stages of human being for learning its surrounding world. In AGI Brain, these 3 stages are called: 1) infancy stage (random actions), 2) decision making stage (action selection via *EM*), and 3) expert stage (autonomous action via *IM*) (Fig. 2).

In its decision-making stage, the agent selects the best policy from its set of possible alternatives as follows;

$$\mathbf{U}^* = \left\{ \boldsymbol{u}(n) \Big| \underset{\mathbf{u} \in \aleph}{ArgMax} \sum_{n=n_1}^{n_f} [R = \boldsymbol{P}^T \boldsymbol{J}] \right\}$$

$$s.t.$$

$$\left\langle \begin{array}{c} \hat{\boldsymbol{x}}(n+1) \\ \hat{\boldsymbol{y}}(n+1) \end{array} \right\rangle \xleftarrow{EM} \left\langle \begin{array}{c} \boldsymbol{x}(n) \\ \boldsymbol{y}(n) \\ \boldsymbol{u}(n) \end{array} \right\rangle \tag{2}$$

Where $\mathbf{U}^*$ is the optimal policy, $\boldsymbol{u}(n)$ is the possible action at time n, $\aleph$ is the set of all possible alternatives, R is the reward value, $\boldsymbol{P}$ is the personality vector, $\boldsymbol{J}$ is the vector of objectives, $x(n)$ is the vector of states, $y(n)$ is the vector of outputs, and

$\hat{\mathbf{x}}(n+1)$ and $\hat{\mathbf{y}}(n+1)$ are the estimated states and outputs which are estimated by the agent's explicit memory *EM*.

In the original version, the explicit memory *EM* is made up of neural networks (NN) and works as a state/output estimator. The original model also benefits from some other features like an implicit memory (*IM*) for autonomous policy selection as well as emotions (stress) for moderating the exploration/exploitation behavior ratio.

In addition to these, the model benefits from shared explicit and implicit memories for the multi agent problems, where the agents can easily share their experiences with each other in order to improve their performances.

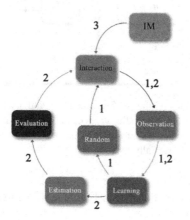

Fig. 2. Working cycle of AGI Brain. Paths: 1) Infancy stage, 2) Decision making stage, and 3) Expert stage

The original model was tested on three different continuous and hybrid (continuous and discrete) Action/State/Output/Reward (ASOR) space scenarios in deterministic single-agent/multi-agent worlds. Successful simulation results demonstrated the versatile applicability of the original version of AGI Brain in deterministic worlds.

4   AGI Brain II

4.1   ProMem

Due to its neural network estimators, the original AGI Brain lacked the ability to perform well in stochastic environments. In order to empower the original model with stochastic capabilities, the state/output estimator of the original model was replaced with a modified Mamdani fuzzy inference system which we call it ProMem. This results in construction of the upgraded and more versatile version of the model, AGI Brain II.

By estimating the Probability Density Function (PDF) of the observed data, Pro-Mem is able to estimate the state/output of a certain action in stochastic worlds as well as deterministic worlds. Applying ProMem to the decision-making problem of Eq. (2), we have;

$$U^* = \left\{ u(n)\, \Big|\, \underset{u \in \aleph}{ArgMax} \sum_{n=n_1}^{n_f} \left[R = P^T J \right] \right\}$$
$$s.t.$$
$$\left\langle \begin{array}{c} \hat{x}(n+1) \\ \hat{y}(n+1) \end{array} \right\rangle \overset{PROMEM}{\longleftarrow} \left\langle \begin{array}{c} x(n) \\ y(n) \\ u(n) \end{array} \right\rangle$$

(3)

The other components of AGI Brain II are the same as the original version. Figure 3 illustrates the architecture of AGI Brain II. The new model has been tested in a portfolio optimization problem as a stochastic world as follows.

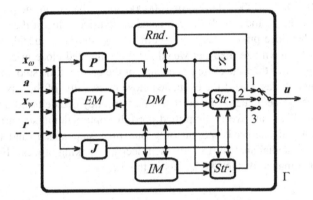

Fig. 3. Architecture of AGI Brain II (inside the artificial brain Γ of Fig. 1). Observed feedbacks: (x_ω: vector of the bodily states of the agent ω, **a**: action vector, x_ψ: vector of the states of the object ψ, **r**: response vector of the object ψ), **P**: personality vector, *EM*: explicit memory (ProMem), *IM*: implicit memory, **J**: vector of objectives, *Rnd.*: random action generator, *DM*: decision making unit (Eq. 3), $\aleph$: set of all possible alternatives, *Str.*: stress simulator unit, **u**: vector of output commands, 1: infancy stage, 2: decision making stage, 3: expert stage.

5   Simulation

5.1   Portfolio Optimization

Assume a world γ which consists of a hypothetical stock market with three assets, A, B and C as the objects ψ_1, ψ_2, and ψ_3. The single AGI Brain II (ProMem estimator) agent ω has to maximize its net wealth by optimal allocation of its assets in its portfolio. The set of possible actions of the agent are the number of shares placed at each time in the various assets. The agent may sell, buy or hold some predefined portions of its shares at each time step.

The set of equations that govern the evolution of the system is as follows;

$$\begin{cases} x_A(n) = 1 + \sin\left(\frac{2\pi n}{100}\right) + r_A(n) \\ x_B(n) = 1 + \cos\left(\frac{2\pi n}{100}\right) + r_B(n) \\ x_C(n) = 1 + 2\sin\left(\frac{2\pi n}{100}\right)\cos\left(\frac{2\pi n}{100}\right) + r_C(n) \end{cases} \quad ,0 \le n \le 1000 \quad (4)$$

Where $x_i(n)$ is the close price of asset i, and $r(n)$ is a random number $0 \le r_j(n) \le 0.25$ with mean $\mu_r = 0.125$ and standard deviation $\sigma_r = 0.0725$.

For comparison purposes, a single agent with original AGI Brain (NN estimator) was added to the system. The two agents start with 1000000 units (e.g., US Dollars) of cash and zero shares at the start time $n = 800$. Using their estimators ProMem and NN, the two agents try to estimate the close price of the next time step $x_i(n+1)$ based on the 10 previous close prices, and allocate their assets in order to maximize their net wealth. At every time step $n \ge 800$, they make decisions on whether to hold, buy or sell 1, 5, 10, 20, 50, 100, 1000, 10000, 100000 or 1000000 shares based on the predicted close price value of the next time step. If the estimated close price value of the next time step is higher than the close price value of the current time step, they decide to buy some shares that would maximize their net wealth. If the estimated close price value of the next time step is lower than the close price value of the current time step, they decide to sell some of their shares, and if the estimated close price value of the next time step is equal to the close price value of the current time step, they decide to hold their shares. Please note that this is an overly simplified portfolio optimization scenario where the agents make their decisions based on only one time step ahead, and they do not incorporate real financial analysis tools in their decision-making process. Figures 4 and 5 show the performance of the two agents in this scenario.

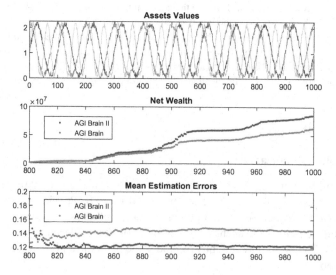

Fig. 4. Upper) Close prices (Asset values) of the three assets A, B and C. Middle) Net Wealth of the two agents. Lower) Mean overall estimation error.

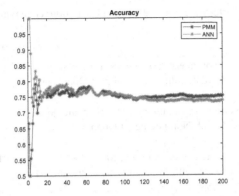

Fig. 5. Mean overall estimation accuracy of the two memories ProMem (blue) and NN (red) (Color figure online)

6   Conclusion and Future Works

As illustrated in Fig. 4, at the final time step $n = 1000$ the net wealth of the AGI Brain agent is 62284014.51 units and the net wealth of the AGI Brain II agent is 85242829.95 units. The mean estimation error of the AGI Brain agent is 0.144 and the mean estimation error of the AGI Brain II agent is 0.122. As illustrated in Fig. 5, the average overall estimation accuracy of the AGI Brain agent is 73.83%, and the average overall estimation accuracy of the AGI Brain II agent is 75.33%.

The simulation results show that the new model, AGI Brain II, performed much better than the original one in the stochastic world. The new model's net wealth is higher than its antecessor. This is because of the higher estimation accuracy (leading to the lower estimation error) of the ProMem compared to the estimation error of the NN. In other words, ProMem could estimate the close price of the next time step more accurately than NN. The reason for this accuracy is grounded in the ability of ProMem in estimation of the probability density function of the observed data. In its training stage, ProMem tries to form a PDF over the observed data as accurate as possible.

AGI Brain II has also been tested in the scenarios which the original model was tested [2], and performed well in linear/nonlinear, continuous/discrete, single agent/multi agent, deterministic/stochastic worlds. Table 1 contains the performances of the two models in different scenarios:

Table 1. Performances of the two models in different environments

Scenario	AGI Brain	AGI Brain II
Function Optimization (A Non-linear, Continuous, Deterministic, Multi Agent, Immediate Reward, with Non-intelligent Opponents environment)	∼100%	∼100%
Intelligent Control (A Non-linear, Continuous, Deterministic, Single Agent, Immediate Reward, with Non-intelligent Opponents environment)	99.76%	∼100%
Animats (A Non-linear, Discrete, Deterministic, Multi Agent, Immediate Reward, with Non-intelligent Opponents environment)	91.61%	95.45%
Portfolio Optimization (A Non-linear, Discrete, Stochastic, Single Agent, Immediate Reward, with Non-intelligent Opponents environment)	73.88%	75.33%

Thus;

$$VI_{\text{AGI Brain}} = \sum_{i=1}^{4} \alpha_i = 365.25$$

And,

$$VI_{\text{AGI Brain II}} = \sum_{i=1}^{4} \alpha_i = 370.78$$

So, based on their VI values, AGI Brain II is more versatile than its antecessor, the original AGI Brain.

Although AGI Brain II is more versatile than its antecessor, it is still far from being a real AGI. The next development stages would be augmenting the ability to perform well in 1) delayed reward problems, and 2) the environments with intelligent opponents (e.g., Games).

References

1. Legg, S., Hutter, M.: Universal intelligence: a definition of machine intelligence. Mind. Mach. **17**(4), 391–444 (2007)
2. Alidoust, M.: AGI Brain: a learning and decision making framework for artificial general intelligence systems based on modern control theory. In: Hammer, P., Agrawal, P., Goertzel, B., Iklé, M. (eds.) AGI 2019. LNCS (LNAI), vol. 11654, pp. 1–10. Springer, Cham (2019). https://doi.org/10.1007/978-3-030-27005-6_1

Elements of Task Theory

Matteo Belenchia[1,3(✉)], Kristinn R. Thórisson[1,2], Leonard M. Eberding[1], and Arash Sheikhlar[1]

[1] Reykjavik University, Menntavegur 1, 102 Reykjavík, Iceland
{matteobel20,thorisson,leonard20,arash19}@ru.is
[2] Icelandic Institute for Intelligent Machines (IIIM), Reykjavík, Iceland
[3] University of Camerino, Via Andrea D'Accorso 16, Camerino, Italy

Abstract. Tasks are of primary importance for artificial intelligence (AI), yet no theory about their characteristics exists. The kind of task theory we envision is one that allows an objective comparison of tasks, based on measurable physical properties, and that can serve as a foundation for studying, evaluating, and comparing learning controllers of various kinds on a variety of tasks by providing principled ways for constructing, comparing, and changing tasks with particular properties and levels of difficulty. In prior papers we have outlined an approach towards this goal; in this paper we present further principles for its development, including causal relations. We use these principles to expand our prior ideas, with the aim of laying the groundwork for covering levels of detail, prior knowledge of the learner/performer and task difficulty, to name some of the complex issues that must be solved for a useful task theory.

Keywords: Tasks · Environments · Task theory · Artificial intelligence · General machine intelligence · Evaluation

1 Introduction

Artificial intelligence (AI) systems are built to perform tasks. Whether primarily hand-coded or based on machine learning techniques, intended to perform only a single well-defined task or aiming for general machine intelligence (GMI), tasks are center of stage in the design of all AI systems; tasks also play a key role in their evaluation. In other fields of control engineering systems are evaluated by constructing test batteries to ensure their proper performance, and tune task parameters according to well-understood principles for their effective evaluation.

Despite their importance in AI, no methodology has widely been adopted for the use of tasks in AI research, and no theory about the properties of tasks exists [14]. A lack of a proper task theory in AI has persisted, possibly due to a long-lived constructionist design tradition that relies on hand-crafted solutions[1] that primarily relies on human domain knowledge. It is therefore not a huge

---

[1] For a discussion on constructionist (allonomic) vs. constructivist (autonomic) design methodologies in AI, see Thórisson et al. [11].

© Springer Nature Switzerland AG 2022
B. Goertzel et al. (Eds.): AGI 2021, LNAI 13154, pp. 19–29, 2022.
https://doi.org/10.1007/978-3-030-93758-4_3

surprise, perhaps, that after 70 years of AI research the only obvious solutions for how to generalize narrow-AI systems are more domain-dependent hand-crafted solutions.

The upshot is that scientific comparison of two AI systems built by two separate teams, or the same team at different times, is currently costly and difficult at best, and impossible at worst. It is thus rarely done; most AI researchers design specific tasks for their specific systems. Without a general theory of tasks, comparing results of AI systems on various tasks is prohibited except through costly experimental procedures. The situation may be survivable in narrow-AI development, but for research in GMI this situation cannot persist if we want to be able to ensure their proper design and safe operation. Domain knowledge and tests (e.g. the Turing test or IQ tests) don't nearly cover the breadth of situations these systems could be facing. As progress towards GMI moves forward, the need to evaluate them in a range of circumstances, tasks, and situations increases. Without a general-purpose methodology that allows comparison along relevant dimensions of variables, tasks, situations and environments, the problem is only going to get worse.

In this paper we extend our prior work on this topic and present further principles for moving towards the kind of task theory envisioned. The focus in this paper is exclusively on the characterization of tasks based on their physical properties, in particular, we aim to resolve some issues that must be addressed to further the research towards e.g. measures of difficulty [2].

2   Related Work

Past research on task composition and analysis focuses quite heavily on performers, rather than the tasks. Task analysis for human tasks has been used since the mid-1900s to make various judgments and design decisions by providing the engineer with a "blueprint" of user involvement, unsurprisingly focusing rather exclusively on it from a 'human-level intelligence' perspective [6]. The GOMS (goals, operators, methods, and selection rules) task-analysis methodology, for instance, is a framework that characterizes a system user's procedural knowledge and can be used to predict human learning and qualitatively describe how a user will use an interface to complete a task [5]. *Cognitive task analysis* (CTA) has a similar purpose and works in a similar way. CTA describes the basis of skilled performance and, unlike GOMS, can explain what accounts for mistakes [1]. Another way to describe tasks is through *hierarchical task networks* (HTN) [4]. HTN are used to decompose high-level tasks into atomic actions to create plans to achieve a goal. Strictly speaking, HTNs do not model the environment but rather produce a list of actions for solving a task [4].

The existence of an intelligent performer is fundamentally assumed a-priori in all these approaches, which makes them rather irrelevant in the design, training, and evaluation of AI systems. For AI the aim must be a dissection and analysis of tasks in such a way that the performer's "IQ" is not given a-priori, and conclusions about the performance of an agent, and thus its design, can result from it, rather than the other way around, without the need for experimentation.

Thórisson et al. [13,14] have proposed a set of necessary components to describe measurable physical dimensions of tasks that must be adjustable by an evaluator when the goal is to get insight into the different approaches to AI and autonomous learning. The advantage of their proposed approach has been demonstrated in part by Eberding et al. [3], providing experimental results of the possibilities that a well-designed task theory could give developers and evaluators of AI systems. To describe tasks in such a way that they can directly help across a wide range of AI research endeavors, further principles must be developed.

3   Terminology and Background Assumptions

If the world is a closed system with no outside interference, the domains and invariant relations can be implicitly fully determined by the dynamics functions and the initial state. In an open system where changes can be caused exogenously, the explicit definition of domains and invariant relations can restrict the range of possible interactions [14].

An **environment** is a view on a world, typically inside a domain (like your kitchen is one environment within the domain of kitchens)—a domain in this view is thus a family of (related) environments [14]. We also may consider the body of an agent to be part of the task, rather than the agent, because it naturally constrains what the controller can do. Another thing to keep in mind is that the boundary between task and environment isn't always clear.

By **controller** we mean exclusively the mind of an embodied agent: The controller is the complete cognitive architecture of the system, which can receive inputs (observations) and produce outputs (commands) from the environment, and has its own internal state and goals.

The **body** of an agent is the interface between a controller and external world. The body itself, i.e. its transducers, belongs to the environment, following the laws of the environment and interacting with it, directly constraining the controller: Only variables which can be measured by the sensors of the body can be observable at any time and only variables belonging to the body can be directly manipulated by the controller. This body can be generally understood as a set of sensors producing sensory information that is read by the controller and a set of actuators that execute the controller's commands that act as the way the mind can affect the surrounding world. Therefore, different sets of sensors and/or actuators also determine how a task may be affected and how its state (values of variables) may be measured, including what is possible to do in the given execution environment. As shown below, the body of the agent significantly influences foundational principles of a task.

The **variables** in an environment, at any point in time, can be either *observable* (to a degree) or *non-observable*, *manipulatable* (to a degree) or *non-manipulatable*. Assignment of a variable in either pair is mutually exclusive, but either value in one pair can have either value in the other pair (e.g. a manipulatable variable can be non-observable and vice versa). Which variables hold which property can vary in any domain, environment, and through time, depending on their dominant relations at that time in that domain or environment.

A **task** is a problem assigned to an agent, $T = \langle \mathcal{S}_0, \mathcal{G}_t, \mathcal{G}_s, G^-, B, t_{go}, t_{stop} \rangle$, where S_0 is the set of permissible initial states, $\mathcal{G}_t$ is the task's set of top-level goals, $\mathcal{G}_s$ is the set of given sub-goals, G^- is its set of constraints, B is a controller's body, and t refers to the permissible start and stop times of the task [12]. An *assigned* task will have all its variables bound and reference an agency that is to perform it (accepted assignments having their own timestamp t_{assign}). This assignment includes the manner in which the task is communicated to the agent, for example, whether the agent is given a description of the task a priori, receives additional hints, only gets incremental reinforcement signals as certain world sub-states are reached, or some mixture of these. A task is successfully performed when the world's history contains a path of states that matched the task's specification, and thus solved the problem it describes.

The **problem space** S_{prob} of a task describes all valid states of the task-environment which can exist at any time within the temporal boundaries of the task through any action or inaction of the controller. It is constrained by the laws of the task-environment (like the speed of light in the physical world).

The **solution space** S_{sol} of a task is a subset of the problem space, defined by the task's goals $\langle \mathcal{G}_t, \mathcal{G}_s \rangle$ and constraints $\langle G^- \rangle$. For a task T_1, any (partial) state is part of the solution space of T_1 that 1) can be reached from an initial state $S_1 \in \mathcal{S}_0$ without violating the task specification and 2) from which at least one path of states exists which matches the task's specifications, leading to a (partial) state that matches the task's goal(s).

4 Foundational Principles for Task Theory

Based on the above background assumptions we can now turn to some unresolved issues that we consider important for a proper task theory. These range from the relationship between a controller's body and the task-environment, to task decomposition and level of detail (LoD). It should be noted that in the following we take the designer's viewpoint, which differs from the learner's viewpoint in that it assumes a complete overview of the task at hand.[2]

4.1 Causal Relations

A physical 'mechanism,' in our approach, is a directional function that determines the value of some world variables (the *effect*) from the values of other variables (the *causes*). The underlying assumption is that actions produced by a controller, via its body, are *local* 'surgeries' in the space of mechanisms [8], and those mechanisms are, given certain conditions, invariant and independent of

---

[2] In the physical world a complete overview of a task is theoretically prevented, but we can nevertheless assume that critical differences exist between a teacher's view and a pupil's.

each other.[3] By 'causal knowledge' is meant information that allows an agent to take action that perturbs a mechanism (via it's own body), causing predictable changes in other mechanisms relevant to task goals, i.e. $\{A_{t1} \rightarrow B_{t2}\}$ where $\{A, B\}$ are events at time t and $t2 > t1$. This means that an action affecting a mechanism leaves other mechanisms in their place, and that the effects of such actions can then be predicted using appropriate causal and other relational knowledge (in the form of models). A *chain* of such causal relational knowledge can represent a plan, an explanation, or a re-construction of a particular aspect of a phenomenon. Achieving goals in the context of any phenomenon necessarily requires knowledge of relevant causal relations, in particular, of the causal relations that relate manipulatable and observable variables of the phenomenon to the goals of an assigned task.

§1 Getting things done means making use of (models of) causal relations.

The existence of any causal relations between relevant variables must either be known by a performing agent or discovered by it in the process of performing a task. Such information must be represented in some cognitively manipulatable way, so that the controller can retrieve relevant knowledge in particular circumstances. Elsewhere, we have proposed causal-relational models (CRMs) to represent such information [7, 15]. Whichever representation is used, however, any such representation aimed for tasks in complex domains must be able to represent different levels of detail, since:

§2 Complex domains (like the physical world) contain more than one level of detail (*LoD*).

Consider, for example, how the interior of a house can be seen at the atomic, molecular or interior design level of detail. This means that the causal relations in multi-LoD task-environments (e.g. the physical world) can be thought of as forming (one or more) hypergraphs. One way to conceptualize the process of learning about such a graph is to consider it a modeling process, whereby the models formed need to mirror, in some useful way, these. Following Conant and Ashby [10], a good controller of a system must reference a *model* of that system. For causal relations, this implies that in any multi-LoD domain:

§3 The granularity of domain modeling must match the *LoD* of the causal relations at the lowest *LoD* relevant to a task's goal(s).

If a task involves genetic engineering, the lowest relevant LoD is chemistry, because that's where the task's success or failure will be measured; if a task involves getting some furniture from one office to another office the relevant LoD is object placement measured in centimeters. Let's look further at principles related to LoDs.

---

[3] While our approach is fundamentally non-axiomatic, cause-effect relationships are probably appropriately considered Platonic. This neither diminishes nor prevents their value or usefulness when dealing on a conceptual level with complex multi-LoD systems like the physical world.

4.2   Levels of Detail

Given that a task can be described at various levels of detail, which level of detail may be most appropriate in a particular case for a particular learner? Considering that the body of the controller, with its sensors and actuators, is *part of the task* (see Sect. 3 above), and considering that the perception and the interaction of the controller with the task-environment happens through this body, then it is at least possible to set a lower bound to the possible level of task abstraction. The body of the controller constrains the level of detail which is to be used to describe the task: The actuators define the granularity of what can be manipulated while the sensors define the granularity of what can be measured.

§4 A controller's transducers define the finest level of relevant spatio-temporal task detail.

Therefore, the finest possible level of detail for a task depends *necessarily on what the body allows the controller to observe and manipulate,* and tasks described at more fine-grained levels of detail than what the controller's body allows would be experienced by the controller at coarser level of detail, in accordance with what is made possible by its body. For example, if a set of transducers operates at the centimetric level of detail, a description of the molecular or atomic interactions in the task is unnecessary, as they can't be experienced by the controller.

Any phenomenon in the world can be described at different levels of detail, from highly detailed fine-grained descriptions to more abstract, coarse-grained ones. This also applies to tasks: Task specifications can vary and can be made more or less abstract, arbitrarily, ranging from the very general high-level instructions in everyday language to the overly complex descriptions that – at least in theory – can be made at the atomic or even sub-atomic levels. This presents a problem in evaluating an agent A_1 on a task T_1: Let's say that T_1 is to change a spelling mistake in a word in a given electronic document; in one task-environment is to be done by modifying the values of transistors on a CPU, in the other the change is to be made using word processor software. To any human the former will probably always be more difficult[4] than the latter (even experienced CPU designers). One way to address this issue in a task theory is to introduce the idea of a level-of-detail operator that controls for the level of description with respect to the performer's body (sensors and actuators). This has the potential benefit of homogenizing any task relative to its level of detail, for a particular performer. However, how such an operator would produce this result is unclear. Another way is to simply treat the level of detail as part of the task's constraints, $\langle G^- \rangle$. While this is perhaps a less elegant solution, it is exceedingly simple. This gives rise to the following principle:

§5 The level of detail *(LoD)* is part of the task.

---

[4] Producing a useful measure of difficulty is the purview of a proper task theory; this is addressed elsewhere [2].

In other words, any task is limited to its level of detail, and if the "same" task is presented at another level of detail, it is *not the same task*. For example, an electronic circuit implementing a logic gates task can be described at the level of its electronic components, at a yet lower level of the chemical reactions in its circuits, or at the higher level of the implemented logic circuit. The task of obtaining some output in such a circuit changes significantly according to the level of description being used. This is because effectively, the variables and the mechanisms changed together with the level of detail. Therefore, variations in the level of detail result in *different* tasks.

4.3   Task Difficulty

The difficulty of executing any particular task is not uniquely determined by the task itself. Some controller might be better or worse suited to perform the task for a plethora of reasons: it could have trained on similar tasks or on tasks which share some of the variables and relationships with this task, it could be quicker (or slower) at learning associations and cause-and-effect relationships, and so on. Controllers, and by controller we mean effectively the mind of the intelligent system, might have either the experience or the architecture that is particularly well-suited (or ill-suited) for the task at hand, or for a type of tasks in general, or for any task at all, for reasons completely independent of the tasks themselves. Difficulty must therefore be a cross product of a task and a controller:

§6 The *difficulty of a task* is a product of the features of the task T and the features of the controller C; i.e. $\{T \times C\}$.

This concept of difficulty includes end-effectors, dexterity, sensors, etc. Note that all end-effectors in nature (extremities, skin, etc.) contain sensors as well that tell about their status; and vice-versa, sensors also are paired with end-effectors (ears on a movable head, rotating eyes, all mounted on a movable body). Thus, it may be said that all effectors are also sensors and vice versa, the difference being merely lie in the direction of information flow amplification. It should be noted that by 'task' we mean task-environment, as variables other than those of the task proper ('task family') may be essential for their completion.

A closely related problem is this: A task becomes easier the more we learn how to do it. This complicates the potential comparison between two controllers that we wish to compare, where one of them knows more about it than the other. How does prior training/ and knowledge affect task analysis/ and task design? This is solved by excluding any part of a task that a controller already *knows how to do*, leaving only the parts that the controller must learn (to whichever extent). This, however, requires separating the task designer's viewpoint from the task learner's viewpoint: From the designer's point of view it is assumed that everything about the task is known and specified. The designer has complete knowledge of the ground truth of the task, including variables, mechanisms, goals, constraints and so on. The learner, on the other hand, has limited knowledge of the task, owing to its limited perception and experience of the task and world. Its knowledge of the task comes with no certainty of correctness: It is defeasible knowledge which could at any time be proven wrong by subsequent experience [9]. The upshot is that we can include prior knowledge in any discussion of difficulty:

§7 Any measure of the *difficulty of a task* must take note of the performer's prior training and knowledge, and thus, prior knowledge is part of C in the equation $\{T \times C\}$.

Given the lower bound of useful granularity to describe a task, the question arises which of the theoretically usable variables of the world influence the task. It can be argued that all variables which are part of the environment necessarily must be part of the task. However, to describe the task in relation to the agent's goals the focus should lie on variables which constrain the solution space of the task. Non-constraining variables are those of no importance to solve the task. Therefore they need not be modeled by a learner of the task.

§8 A task is unchanged by variables which do not constrain its solution space.

While such variables and relations are superfluous to the task when looking at it from the designer's perspective, they can influence the learning of an agent. Especially when such variables are observable to the agent they can lead to wrong or misleading correlations with solution space constraining variables. When taking the agent's perspective these misleading correlations between superfluous and non-superfluous variables becomes an issue of experience. If previous encounters with superfluous variables have lead to a knowledge generalization which excludes these variables they do not influence the performance of the agent on the task. If the agent has not yet learned about these elements they can prolong learning times by making it more difficult to extract relevant causal structures from the observations. For example, the presence of multiple switches does not affect the task of turning on the lights (assuming only one such switch is needed).

5 Discussion

We consider the principles thus outlined still up for discussion, as there are unforeseen implications for any of the suggested commitments. Many questions remain to be answered, in particular with respect to whether some existing paradigms or methodologies might be suited to either appropriately address the issues raised here, or possibly explain them away. As far as we are able to see, no particular theory exists, and no existing paradigm, addresses in a unified manner the issues of level of detail, causal chains, and multi-goal achievement. These, in our opinion, must be included for a proper theory of tasks. Let's take a brief look at some of the approaches mentioned in the Related Work section, to see whether they could possibly challenge, address, or extend, our proposed principles.

In hierarchical task networks (HTN, [4]), causality is considered, but only as a high-level relation between tasks. When two tasks interfere with each other, a causal relationship is recorded indicating the two tasks t_e and t_p and a predicate q which is both an effect of t_e and a pre-condition of t_p [4]. Also, when the goal e of a task t results already achieved, by the effect of another task t', a constraint of the form (t', e, t) is added to the network to record it as a causal relation [4]. In contrast, we consider causality in a more fine-grained way, as a relationship between variables in the same task (§1). In this sense our approach to causality is more general, because it can be also applied at coarser levels of detail to trace causal relationships between the tasks themselves (e.g. the effect of executing the task of "walking to the door" is also the pre-condition for starting the task of "opening the door".)

In the related work we surveyed, we found no discussion about the different levels of detail in the physical world and how to deal with them. Usually, the level of detail of the task is given and fixed from the start. Therefore the novelty of our approach consists (1) in realizing that there are always multiple levels of detail to deal with (§2), (2) that the level of detail is constrained by both the goals of the task (§3) and the body of the controller (§4) and (3) that the selected level of detail for the task is an intrinsic characteristic of the task itself, which when changed also determines a change of the task (§5).

To the best of our knowledge, this is the first to attempt to formalize the notion that the difficulty of a task depends on both the features of the task and the controller (§6), as past approaches have mainly considered the characteristics of the task alone. For example, typical attempts to AI evaluation use games like chess or arcade games, which are considered interesting because of the purported difficulty of the task itself (from the human point of view). The notion that a task's successful execution depends on prior training and knowledge (§7), on the other hand, is the main premise of artificial intelligence.

We are not aware of any discussion about the effects of eventual 'superfluous' variables in the task. This is mostly due to the fact that the tasks under consideration were defined a-priori to include only variables that in some way constrain the solution space. Therefore, the intuitive notion that 'superfluous' variables do not change a task is made explicit here (§8).

6 Conclusion

We summarized previous findings of our work and described foundational principles of tasks. We expect that such a task-theory can help to understand the pros and cons of different approaches to AI architecture design, help researchers to evaluate their (and other's) systems, compare them, and help developers of GMI-aspiring systems focus on the task at hand: Building systems capable of solving complex tasks in complex environments.

The introduced principles of task theory helps to avoid an anthropomorphic view on tasks and agents, which we hope reduces bias in evaluation and design of agents. We believe that by describing these principles, mistakes of the past might be avoided (e.g. over-amplifying the importance of certain task such as board games, video games, and others). Instead, by identifying task properties, describing them in causal structures and analyzing them thoroughly, the importance of a task being solved can be better understood and classified accordingly.

A future requirement for a task theory is to make changes in the level of detail of a task inherently available to the analyst. While this changes the task (see §5), the level of detail is of importance when analyzing different learners. If a learner is able to group relational models and task variables in order to change the level of detail of interaction by itself (hierarchical learners are the most promising ones for that) it is necessary to represent these changes when analyzing the task. Future work also includes the construction of tasks at multiple different levels of detail.

References

1. Crandall, B., Klein, G., Klein, G.A., Hoffman, R.R., Hoffman, R.R., et al.: Working Minds: A Practitioner's Guide to Cognitive Task Analysis. MIT Press, Cambridge (2006)
2. Eberding, L.M., Belenchia, M., Sheikhlar, A., Thórisson, K.R.: About the intricacy of tasks. In: International Conference on Artificial General Intelligence. Springer (2021, in submission)
3. Eberding, L.M., Thórisson, K.R., Sheikhlar, A., Andrason, S.P.: SAGE: task-environment platform for evaluating a broad range of AI learners. In: Goertzel, B., Panov, A.I., Potapov, A., Yampolskiy, R. (eds.) AGI 2020. LNCS (LNAI), vol. 12177, pp. 72–82. Springer, Cham (2020). https://doi.org/10.1007/978-3-030-52152-3_8
4. Georgievski, I., Aiello, M.: An overview of hierarchical task network planning (2014)
5. Kieras, D.: Goms models for task analysis. In: Diaper, D., Stanton, N. (eds.) The handbook of task analysis for human-computer interaction, pp. 83–116 (2004)
6. Kirwan, B., Ainsworth, L.K.: A Guide to Task Analysis: the Task Analysis Working Group. CRC Press, Boca Raton (1992)
7. Nivel, E., Thórisson, K.R.: Replicode: A constructivist programming paradigm and language. Technical RUTR-SCS13001, Reykjavik University School of Computer Science (2013)
8. Pearl, J.: Causality. 2 edn. Cambridge University Press, Cambridge, UK (2009). https://doi.org/10.1017/CBO9780511803161
9. Pollock, J.L.: Defeasible Reasoning. Cognitive science 11(4), 481–518 (1987)
10. Conant, R.C., Ashby, W.R.: Every good regulator of a system must be a model of that system. Int. J. Syst. Sci. 1(2), 89–97 (1970)
11. Thórisson, K.R.: A new constructivist AI: from manual construction to self-constructive systems. In: Wang, P., Goertzel, B. (eds.) Theoretical Foundations of Artificial General Intelligence. Atlantis Thinking Machines, vol. 4, pp. 145–171 (2012)
12. Thórisson, K.R.: Seed-programmed autonomous general learning. In: Proceedings of Machine Learning Research, pp. 32–70 (2020)
13. Thórisson, K.R., Bieger, J., Schiffel, S., Garrett, D.: Towards flexible task environments for comprehensive evaluation of artificial intelligent systems & automatic learners. In: Proceedings of the International Conference on Artificial General Intelligence, pp. 187–196 (2015)

14. Thórisson, K.R., Bieger, J., Thorarensen, T., Sigurðardóttir, J.S., Steunebrink, B.R.: Why artificial intelligence needs a task theory. In: Steunebrink, B., Wang, P., Goertzel, B. (eds.) AGI -2016. LNCS (LNAI), vol. 9782, pp. 118–128. Springer, Cham (2016). https://doi.org/10.1007/978-3-319-41649-6_12

15. Thórisson, K.R., Talbot, A.: Cumulative learning with causal-relational models. In: Iklé, M., Franz, A., Rzepka, R., Goertzel, B. (eds.) AGI 2018. LNCS (LNAI), vol. 10999, pp. 227–237. Springer, Cham (2018). https://doi.org/10.1007/978-3-319-97676-1_22

Symbol Emergence and the Solutions to Any Task

Michael Timothy Bennett[(✉)]

School of Computing, Australian National University, Canberra, Australia
michael.bennett@anu.edu.au

Abstract. The following defines intent, an arbitrary task and its solutions, and then argues that an agent which always constructs what is called an Intensional Solution would qualify as artificial general intelligence. We then explain how natural language may emerge and be acquired by such an agent, conferring the ability to model the intent of other individuals labouring under similar compulsions, because an abstract symbol system and the solution to a task are one and the same.

Keywords: Tasks · Symbol emergence · Artificial general intelligence

1 Introduction

We begin by briefly examining how intent may be defined and communicated. First, one may state intent generally and without context. For example, one may intend to acquire money. To make such a statement is to describe a goal [14], and so we define it as that. Second there is contextual intent, a rationale. For example, if one observes a family member of an addict confiscating their drugs, one may infer that the family member intends to prevent the addict from overdosing. To do so is to assume the family member is compelled by an attachment to the addict. We imbue their behaviour with specific purpose by assuming the goal it serves in general, constructing a rationale. Conversely, one may provide context for one's own decisions. It is here that the relationship between intent and causal reasoning becomes apparent; if an action was taken in service of a goal then in a sense that goal caused the action. To state or infer a rationale, one must define the goal in service of which a decision was made, and a chain of causal relations [1,2] indicating how that goal was to be served (whether successful or not). However, possession of a rationale is not the ability to communicate it. Humans communicate in terms of loosely defined abstractions, tailored to express what is most important both to ourselves *and* those to whom we are speaking. Human comprehension is not limitless. Absent such tailoring and simplifying abstractions, a rationale of even moderate complexity may be uninterpretable [16,25]. In a programming language meaning is exact, specified in the physical arrangement of transistors. Natural language is an emergent phenomenon [5] in which meaning is not limited to exact instruction [6]. Such a language must be interpreted, which suggests it is a means of encoding, transmitting and decoding more

B. Goertzel et al. (Eds.): AGI 2021, LNAI 13154, pp. 30–40, 2022.
https://doi.org/10.1007/978-3-030-93758-4_4

complex information. What is this complex information, what is the interpreter, and how would we build it?

Symbolic Abstraction: Symbolic approaches to intelligence often adopt as their premise a Physical Symbol System [7,8] grounded in hardware, yet actually implementing such a system is no trivial matter. This is known as The Symbol Grounding Problem [9]. Before continuing we must define what a symbol is. A computer scientist might define it as a dyadic relationship between a sign and an thing to which it refers (called a referent). This makes sense in the context of a programming language where an exact definition is necessary. We know how to implement such a thing using hardware, and so we'll call such dyadic symbol systems "physically implementable languages". However, dyadic symbols are not abstractions akin to symbols in natural language. Yes, ambiguity could be introduced in a dyadic symbol by linking a sign to a set of possible referents instead of one, and context could be captured by simply embedding contextual information in referents. Such symbols can and have been learned using existing machine learning methods [4,5,11]. As we will argue the problem lies in the construction of an abstract symbol system as a whole (not piece-wise), in what constitutes a symbol and the nature of messages communicated in natural language. Symbols determine about what one may reason, and so one symbol system may facilitate success in a given task better than another. We will describe how symbolic abstractions may be constructed to describe a specific task. As to the nature of messages, Peircean semiosis [4] attempts to describe natural language on a conceptual level, defining a symbol as a triadic relationship in which the sign and referent are connected by an interpretant, which determines the effect upon the interpreter. What exactly an interpretant is and how it is implemented is part of what this paper seeks to clarify. Recall that in the example above we inferred the rationale of the hypothetical drug addict's family member's behaviour by assuming their goal. The family member's behaviour was a signal, and the goal served to decode that signal into a message; their rationale. We will argue that understanding natural language is not merely the result of clustering sensorimotor stimuli, but of imbuing stimuli with significance in terms of a goal. We could hardly claim to do all this by describing a goal using abstract symbols, and so it must be constructed in a physically implementable language. For simplicity of explanation we will describe a goal as a statement which has a binary truth value. Such a statement is true of a subset of possible the hardware (sensorimotor system) states, and false of others, however we see no reason goals with more degrees of truth would not suffice. Hard coding such a goal is impractical, and so it must be learned by interacting with the world. We draw upon enactive cognition [10], in which cognition is embodied, situated and extending into an environment. If a goal is to be learned then the question remains; which goal? The question is which is most plausible, most likely to generalise, and herein lies the connection to AGI. Ockham's Razor is the notion that the simplest explanation is the most likely to be true. AIXI [21] is a theoretical artificial general intelligence which employs a formalisation of Ockham's Razor [22,23] to decide which model of the world is most plausible. Solomonoff Induction formalises this notion by measuring the complexity of a program by it's Kolmogorov Complexity [19]; the smallest self extracting archive which (in this case) reconstructs the agent's past experiences of the world. As a result, AIXI will learn the most accurate predictive models possible given what it has observed of the world. While such a model deals with programs rather than goal constraints, and is incomputable, it illustrates what the simple notion of Ockham's Razor is capable of; it not only bears out in anecdotal experience, but is of a deeper mathematical significance. To decide which goal is most plausible, we can follow a similar line of inquiry to formalise Ockham's Razor in terms of statements. We draw upon preceding work for the formalisation of an arbitrary task and intent (using The Mirror Symbol Hypothesis) [15–17], but differ in our characterisation of the solutions to an arbitrary task, how tasks can be subdivided or merged, and the relevance of AIXI. We have also abandoned notions such as perceptual symbols, introduced physically implementable languages, redefined abstract symbols and their relation to tasks and briefly addressed the emergence of normativity [26].

2   An Arbitrary Task

In order to examine goals, we must define an arbitrary task. We do so by drawing upon boolean satisfiability problems to represent the task in terms of hardware states (not abstract symbols).

- A finite set $\mathcal{X} = \{X_1, X_2, ..., X_n\}$ of binary variables.
- A set $\mathcal{Z}$ of every complete or partial assignment of values of the variables in $\mathcal{X}$, where
  - an element $z \in \mathcal{Z}$ is an assignment of binary values z_k, which is 0 or 1, to some of the variables above, which we regard as a sequence $\langle X_i = z_i, X_j = z_j, ..., X_m = z_m \rangle$, representing a hardware or sensorimotor state.
- A set of goal states $\mathcal{G} = \{z \in \mathcal{Z} : C(z)\}$, where
  - $C(z)$ means that z satisfies, to some acceptable degree or with some acceptable probability, some arbitrary notion of a goal.
- A set of states $\mathcal{S} = \{s \in \mathcal{Z} : V(s)\}$ of initial states in which a decision takes place, where
  - $V(s)$ means that there exists $g \in \mathcal{G}$ such that s is a subsequence of g, in other words for each state in $\mathcal{S}$ there exists an acceptable, goal satisfying supersequence in $\mathcal{G}$.

The process by which a decision is evaluated is as follows:

1. The agent is in state $s \in \mathcal{S}$.
2. The agent selects a state $r \in \mathcal{Z}$ such that s is a subsequence of r and writes it to memory.
3. If $r \in \mathcal{G}$, then the agent will have succeeded at the task to an acceptable degree or with some acceptable probability.

For the sake of brevity, we will call s which is given a situation (which may include memories of past experience), and r which is selected a response. The distinction between situation and response is that a situation provides context for a decision, while a response is the result of one. We make no comment about any state following r, of which r may not be a subsequence. The point is to model a decision, not a chain of events. A response may describe anything, from complex plans to simple instructions for actuators or memory read/write operations. Context alone does not tell us which response $r \in \mathcal{G}$ is correct for situation $s \in \mathcal{S}$; we need a goal constraint, a statement whose truth value determines correctness. Such a statement is necessary to determine whether any response given a situation is correct, and sufficient to reconstruct $\mathcal{G}$ from $\mathcal{S}$ (it need not reconstruct $\mathcal{S}$). There may be many statements which meet these criteria, but not all of them are what we might intuitively label *the* goal. We will name this set of statements the domain of solutions to a task, and each such statement a solution.

The Solutions to Any Task: A solution can be written using any physically implementable language $\mathcal{L}$ such as the aforementioned arrangements of transistors. To distinguish between possible solutions, we draw upon the notion of intensional and extensional definitions to be found in the philosophy of language [12]. For example, the extensional definition of the game chess is the enumeration of every possible game of chess, while the intensional definition could be the rules of chess. However, any statement could be a rule. In what way are the constraints we call the rules of chess any different from simply listing every legitimate game of chess? There is more than one set of rules which amount to the game chess. What we choose to call the rules of any given game intuitively tend to be the weakest, most general individual rules necessary to verify whether any given example of a game is legal, and sufficient to abduct every possible legal game. Conversely, enumerating all valid games is just a means of describing chess in terms of the strongest, most specific rules possible. The rules of chess describe the task "how to play chess". However, there's no reason we can't extend the notion of rules from merely "how to play game t" to any arbitrary task, such as "how to play game t such that your chance of winning is maximised". To reiterate, a rule is just a statement written in a physically implementable langauge. A statement is a solution if it is necessary and sufficient to reconstruct $\mathcal{G}$ from $\mathcal{S}$. For every statement, there exists a set of hardware states of which it is true. The greater the cardinality of this set, the weaker the statement. To say one statement is weaker than another is to say it is true of more hardware states. Given a physically implementable language of any practical use, there will exist connectives which can join two or more statements to form one stronger statement (for example "and"), and connectives which can join two or more statements to form one weaker statement (for example "or"). In either case, the resulting statement will be longer. Just as statements can be joined, a statement can be split into shorter separate statements by deleting a connective. The splitting of statements could continue until only atomic statements remain. At every split we could measure the weakness of the resulting statements, then the weakness of statements that result from the dissection of those and so on, to measure the overall statement by the weakness of its constituent parts. How specifically to go about measuring this is a matter for a much longer and more technical paper, but for now this suffices to illustrate how two solutions might be equivalent, but formed from very different constituent parts. As we are concerned with finding the most plausible statement, we'll consider two extremes of the domain of solutions:

1. **The Extensional Solution** to the task, formed from the strongest, most specific rules necessary and sufficient to abduct G from S:
   (a) This is a statement D enumerating every member of G as a long disjunction "a or b or c or ...". It is the longest solution possible without introducing redundant statements.
   (b) It stipulates exactly each correct response for every situation, with no generalisation. It does not state what responses share in common.
   (c) There is one and only one Extensional Solution given $\mathcal{L}$ and a task.
2. **The Intensional Solution** to the task, formed from the weakest, least specific rules necessary and sufficient to abduct G from S:
   (a) This is a statement C stipulating what the largest possible subsets of G share in common.
   (b) It stipulates what is necessary to verify the correctness of any response given a situation, but need not state the responses themselves.
   (c) Its form depends upon $\mathcal{L}$, the physically implementable language employed, but if it were written in propositional logic in disjunctive normal form, then an Intensional Solution would be a disjunction of the shortest possible conjunctions necessary and sufficient to reconstruct G from S.
   (d) It adheres to Ockham's Razor in that it need not assert anything not strictly necessary to verify correctness (the rules it describes are together no stronger than is absolutely necessary).
   (e) The above guarantees that any merely correlated variables will be eliminated from consideration, leaving only those relations most likely to be causal.
   (f) Just as there may be many functions which can interpolate a set of points, there may be many Intensional Solutions to a task given $\mathcal{L}$ (it may not be unique).

Intent Revisited: Earlier we defined intent as a goal, and it is certainly not the case that humans prefer to describe goals by enumerating every example of success. We try to describe what successes of a certain type share in common, we generalise. We will subsequently name an agent that always constructs Intensional Solutions an intentional agent, and one that always constructs Extensional Solutions a mimic.

Relationship to Ockham's Razor and AIXI: Given a task and an appropriate choice of physically implementable language, if we bundle each solution with a SAT solver and S, then for each solution we have a self extracting archive that reconstructs G. We will name this a solution archive. The length of such a self extracting archive varies only with the length of the solution it employs (S being uncompressed, and the SAT solver being the same for all solutions). For each task there exists a unique value given $\mathcal{L}$; the length of the smallest solution archive. Note that this is not the Kolmogorov Complexity of $\mathcal{G}$, because we are not allowing S to be compressed, and we are only considering SAT solvers as decoders. However, we can interpret Ockham's Razor as stating that an explanation should not assert anything more specific than absolutely necessary [24]. A stronger statement is one that asserts more than a weaker statement in the sense that it is false in more hardware states than the weaker statement. This is what is important about Ockham's Razor, why it works; it minimises the possibility that the resulting statement is false. By this definition any Intensional Solution, not merely the shortest, should be sufficient to guarantee the most accurate prediction of goal satisfying responses possible. In contrast, the Extensional Solution is made up of statements each of which is false in all hardware states but one (because each one describes a unique $g \in \mathcal{G}$), minimising the plausibility of the solution's constituent parts. Among the shortest solution archives there would exist an Intensional Solution, because a longer statement using a strengthening connective is less plausible than a shorter one, and at least one Intensional Solution must employ no more weakening connectives than strictly necessary (minimising length without losing necessary information). If we modified AIXI to consider only solution archives as models of the world, then it would be likely to find an Intensional Solution (because one must exist among the shortest solution archives it prefers). However, the shortest solution archive is not necessary to maximise predictive accuracy. If the reader accepts our characterisation of Intensional Solutions as being the most plausible according to Ockham's Razor, then any Intensional Solution will suffice. Just as AIXI maximises reward across all computable environments, an intentional agent is one that attempts to maximise accuracy across all possible tasks. This is to say that in a specific task an agent possessed of a more specific inductive bias may outperform an intentional agent, but may not match an intentional agent in general. Just as lossless compression isolates causal relations [20], so does an Intensional Solution. If we accept Chollet's [18] definition of intelligence as the ability to generalise, then these Intensional and Extensional Solutions represent the product of its extremes. If, given a task, we choose a physically implementable language of such limited expressiveness that only a finite number of solutions exist, then an Intensional Solution is computable (by iterating through all possible solutions and comparing them). Of course, this only transfers the difficulty involved in constructing an AGI from the design of the AGI, to the design of the physically implementable language.

Learning a Solution: Learning typically relies upon an ostensive [13] definition; a small set of examples (hardware states, in this case) serving to illustrate what correctness is. An ostensive definition is defined as follows:

-   A set $\mathcal{G}_o \subset \mathcal{G}$ of goal satisfying states, which does not contain a supersequence of every member of S.

- A set $\mathcal{S}_o = \{s \in \mathcal{S} : B(s)\}$ of situations (initial states) in which a decision takes place, where
  - $B(s)$ means that there exists $g \in \mathcal{G}_o$ such that s is a subsequence of g.

Using this ostensive definition an agent could construct a solution which is necessary and sufficient to reconstruct G_o from S_o. A solution is more general if, given $\mathcal{S}$, it implies goal satisfying responses to a larger subset of $\mathcal{G}$ than another solution. We'll examine D_o, the ostensive Extensional Solution constructed by a mimic, and C_o, an ostensive Intensional Solution constructed by an intentional agent. The mimic makes no attempt to generalise, and will eventually encounter a state $s \in \mathcal{S}$ where $s \notin \mathcal{S}_o$ for which it knows no response. However, it may be possible for an intentional agent to construct $C_o = C$, meaning it learns the rules of the task as a whole. We say that an ostensive definition is sufficient if the ostensive Intensional Solutions it implies are necessary and sufficient to reconstruct $\mathcal{G}$ from S. If an ostensive definition is not sufficient, then the Intensional Solutions it implies are to a different task. An intentional agent would subsequently achieve optimal predictive accuracy for a task if given a sufficient ostensive definition. Among the possible solutions to a sufficient ostensive definition some will be more like an Intensional Solution than the extensional. An agent that learns such solutions will always generalise better than an agent that constructs solutions formed of stronger statements for the same reason an intentional agent generalises better than a mimic. If one can generalise more effectively from an ostensive definition, then one learns faster; every example added to the ostensive definition would convey a greater increase in predictive accuracy for the intentional agent than any agent that only constructs solutions closer to mimicry.

Redemptive Qualities of a Mimic: The ability to generalise does not always serve a purpose. To illustrate, given a task to model a uniform distribution of goal satisfying responses, the Intensional and Extensional Solutions would both need to enumerate all goal satisfying states, and the entire contents of $\mathcal{G}$ would be required for a sufficient ostensive definition. While an intentional agent may be faced with computationally expensive abduction every time it needs to construct a response, a mimic's response would require minimal computation. It is akin to rote learning or human intuition, the ability to form a correct response without understanding what makes it correct. Fitting a function to a set of points may have more in common with mimicry than intent, which would explain why commonly employed machine learning methods require so much data yet struggle to generalise [3]. Perhaps to combine generalisability with computational efficiency, the best approach is to seek both Extensional and Intensional Solutions, the former to construct a heuristic.

Constructing an Ostensive Definition using Objective Functions: Biological organisms are not usually given an ostensive definition with which to construct a solution to a task. Instead, we are compelled by primitives of cognition such as hunger and pain. These are, for all practical purposes, objective functions. By selecting those responses which resulted in favourable reward, we seem to construct ostensive definitions which we can then reason about and decompose into rules, identifying what members of an ostensive definition share in common.

3   Natural Language

The interpretant of an abstract symbol, as we defined it, must not only cluster sensorimotor information but imbue it with significance in terms of a goal. By this definition, an Intensional Solution is playing the role of an interpretant, determining the effect stimuli has upon the interpreter's decisions. All incoming stimuli relevant to success in a task can then be perceived as a signal the agent must interpret. The Intensional Solution together with a SAT solver acts as a decoder, to compose an internal representation of a referent (a response). Conversely, any response which results in the agent taking an observable action could be perceived as emitting a signal. A solution may be split into shorter statements, each one of which may be perceived in isolation as the interpretant of an abstract symbol. The boundaries of a symbol are therefore fluid, as in natural language, dependent upon context. A sign or referent is any stimuli to which the interpretant refers, categorising stimuli in the same way it clusters sensorimotor states. The Intensional Solution may therefore be seen as both an abstract symbol itself, and a learned symbol system constructed specifically to efficiently describe what is important in a task.

Communication: For a signal to facilitate communication it must be imbued with similar meaning by both sender and receiver, what is called a normative definition. We posit that normativity emerges when interacting agents labour under similar compulsions, similar tasks (where a task may be defined so broadly as to encompass the human condition). This is because, in order to construct compatible symbol systems as we have described, two agents must construct approximately the same Intensional Solution, so that stimuli is imbued with similar meaning by both. Such a solution must account for the existence of other agents operating under the similar compulsions (otherwise an agent would never be compelled to respond to a situation by transmitting a signal), and so it must be learned in an environment where such other agents are present. If said agents have any significant impact on each others' ability to satisfy their compulsions, then solutions will imbue the observable behaviour of other agents with meaning. If co-operation is advantageous, then repeated interaction will produce conventions that facilitate complex signalling. As described earlier, a solution may be constructed using an ostensive definition, which may be constructed using objective functions. The task with which an agent engages is then determined by these objective functions. We will conclude this paper with an illustrative example of an agent learning an existing normative definition by interacting with others. For now, we illustrate what might be involved in encoding and decoding signals. To decode:

1. Construct an Intensional Solution or something akin to it.
2. Observe another agent responding to a situation, and apply one's own Intensional Solution to construct a rationale for their behaviour.

In doing so an agent interprets what a signal means, what immediate sub-goals are being pursued. A signal in this form is not limited to spoken words but any behaviour, as in normal human interaction. However, if one's Intensional Solution provides no valid rationale for the observed behaviour of another individual, then the other agent's solution may be different from one's own. In this case, one must hypothesise modified Intensional Solutions that do permit a rationale, and in doing so simulate the possible goals of a creature different from one's own self. To meaningfully transmit is to affect change in the sensorimotor state of another individual. One may convey or request information pertaining to sub-goals in order to co-operate, or perhaps to deceive in order to obtain some competitive advantage. In any case, the intentional agent is treating the other individual as part of the environment to be affected, then choosing a response which it predicts will satisfy its goals to some acceptable degree or with some acceptable probability. To encode:

1. Decode the behaviour of others, predict their immediate sub-goals.
2. How might they respond to your potential responses? Choose the response that you predict will result in their responding favourably.

An Example: Assume we have an intentional agent compelled by objective functions akin to those of a dog. We situate this agent within a community of dogs, and give it a body akin to a dog. Each day a human owner rings a bell when food is available, and each day the agent observes the sound of the bell, then the running of the other dogs to the location where food is placed, and then the food itself. Just as a statement may be split into shorter statements, so can a task be subdivided. The construction of a solution to an ostensive definition of the subtask we might call "satisfy hunger" will associate the bell, the behaviour of the other dogs and the sight of food all with the satisfaction of the hunger compulsion, and so imbue them with meaning. These become symbols in an emergent language. Now consider the subtask "avoid pain". A human approaching holding a stick, or a larger dog growling, will all be associated with pain after a few bad experiences. These are messages that convey the hostile intent of those other individuals. Having learned that a growl conveys hostile intent and the prospect of pain, the agent may attempt to reproduce this behaviour in order to obtain food claimed by a smaller dog, combining the rules of two subtasks in order to satisfy the goal of one.

A Final Remark: Perhaps the most significant thing left to be said, which by now we hope is obvious, is that the solution to a task specifies an abstract symbol, and the solution to any subtask of that task also specifies an abstract symbol, and so an abstract symbol and symbol system amount to the same thing. The above is an argument, not experimental proof. In future work we plan to construct experiments to test this idea, as well as the theory of tasks upon which it is based. At the time of writing we have constructed an agent that learns Intensional Solutions to binary arithmetic and other trivial tasks. Results pertaining to a more meaningful benchmark, which required the specification of a more expressive physically implementable language, are forthcoming. Finally, it is interesting to note that, because an Intensional Solution may be learned from only positive examples, it facilitates construction of a one-class classifier.

References

1. Pearl, J.: Causality: Models, Reasoning and Inference. 2nd. Cambridge University Press, USA (2009)
2. Pearl, J., Mackenzie, D.: The Book of Why: The New Science of Cause and Effect. 1st. BasicBooks, Inc. USA (2018)
3. Floridi, L., Chiriatti, M.: GPT-3: its nature, scope, limits, and consequences. Minds Mach. 30(4), 681–694 (2020). https://doi.org/10.1007/s11023-020-09548-1
4. Taniguchi, T., et al.: Symbol Emergence in Cognitive Developmental systems: a survey. IEEE Trans. Cogn. Dev. Syst. 11(4), 494–516 (2019)
5. Taniguchi, T., et al.: Symbol Emergence in robotics: a survey. Adv. Robot 30(11–12), 706–728 (2016)
6. Santoro, A. et al.: Symbolic Behaviour in Artificial Intelligence. Deepmind. arXiv: 2102.03406 [cs.AI]. (2021)
7. Newell, A.: Physical symbol systems. Cogn. Sci. 4(2), 135–183 (1980)
8. Nilsson, N.J.: The physical symbol system hypothesis: status and prospects. In: Lungarella, M., Iida, F., Bongard, J., Pfeifer, R. (eds.) 50 Years of Artificial Intelligence. LNCS (LNAI), vol. 4850, pp. 9–17. Springer, Heidelberg (2007). https://doi.org/10.1007/978-3-540-77296-5_2
9. Harnad, S.: The symbol grounding problem. Phys. D: Nonlinear Phenom. 42(1–3), 335–346 (1990)
10. Thompson, E.: Mind in Life: Biology, Phenomenology, and the Sciences of Mind. Belknap Press/Harvard University Press (2007)
11. Ramesh, A. et al.: DALL-E: creating images from text. Open AI. https://openai.com/blog/dall-e/ (2021)
12. Ostertag, G.: Emily Elizabeth Constance Jones. In: Zalta, E.N. (ed.) The Stanford Encyclopedia of Philosophy. Metaphysics Research Lab, Stanford University (2020)
13. Gupta, A.: Definitions. In: Zalta, E.N. (ed). The Stanford Encyclopedia of Philosophy. Metaphysics Research Lab, Stanford University (2019)
14. Setiya, K.: Intention. In: Zalta, E.N. (ed.) The Stanford Encyclopedia of Philosophy. Metaphysics Research Lab, Stanford University (2018)
15. Bennett, M. T.: The Solutions to Any Task. PhD Thesis Manuscript (2021)
16. Bennett, M.T., Maruyama, Y.: Philosophical specification of empathetic ethical artificial intelligence. IEEE Trans. Cogn. Dev. Syst. (2021). https://doi.org/10.1109/TCDS.2021.3099945
17. Bennett, M. T., Maruyama, Y.: Intensional Artificial Intelligence: From Symbol Emergence to Explainable and Empathetic AI. Manuscript (2021)
18. Chollet, F.: On the Measure of Intelligence. arXiv:1911.01547 [cs.AI] (2019)
19. Kolmogorov, A. N.: On tables of random numbers. Sankhya: Indian J. Stat. Ser. A 25(Part 4), 369–376 (1963)
20. Budhathoki, K., Vreeken, J.: Origo: causal inference by Compression. Knowl. Inf. Syst. 56(2), 28–307 (2018)

21. Hutter, M.: Universal Artificial Intellegence. TTCSAES, Springer, Heidelberg (2005). https://doi.org/10.1007/b138233
22. Solomonoff, R.J.: A formal theory of inductive inference. Part I. Inf. Control **7**(1), 1–22 (1964)
23. Solomonoff, R.J.: A formal theory of inductive inference. Part II. Inf. Control **7**(2), 224–254 (1964)
24. Baker, A.: Simplicity. Stanford Encyclopedia of Philosophy (2016)
25. Evans, R., et al.: Making sense of raw input. Artif. Intell. **299**, 103521 (2021)
26. FitzPatrick, W.: Morality and Evolutionary Biology. Stanford Encyclopedia of Philosophy (2021)

Compression, The Fermi Paradox and Artificial Super-Intelligence

Michael Timothy Bennett$^{(\boxtimes)}$

School of Computing, Australian National University, Canberra, Australia
`michael.bennett@anu.edu.au`

Abstract. The following briefly discusses possible difficulties in communication with and control of an AGI (artificial general intelligence), building upon an explanation of The Fermi Paradox and preceding work on symbol emergence and artificial general intelligence. The latter suggests that to infer what someone means, an agent constructs a rationale for the observed behaviour of others. Communication then requires two agents labour under similar compulsions and have similar experiences (construct similar solutions to similar tasks). Any non-human intelligence may construct solutions such that any rationale for their behaviour (and thus the meaning of their signals) is outside the scope of what a human is inclined to notice or comprehend. Further, the more compressed a signal, the closer it will appear to random noise. Another intelligence may possess the ability to compress information to the extent that, to us, their signals would appear indistinguishable from noise (an explanation for The Fermi Paradox). To facilitate predictive accuracy an AGI would tend to more compressed representations of the world, making any rationale for their behaviour more difficult to comprehend for the same reason. Communication with and control of an AGI may subsequently necessitate not only human-like compulsions and experiences, but imposed cognitive impairment.

Keywords: Compression · Symbol emergence · Communication

1 Introduction

When examining what problems may arise in the pursuit of AGI, it may behoove us to consider explanations for The Fermi Paradox [17], the contradiction between the apparent absence of extra-terrestrial life and its high probability. After all, both involve communication with a nonhuman intelligence.

So, let us assume for the sake of argument that a non-human intelligence exists in our region of space, emitting signals in a similar medium to us (such as radio) neither attempting to contact nor hide from us; why might we have failed to identify or interpret the meaning of such signals, and what does this suggest for the pursuit of AGI?

© Springer Nature Switzerland AG 2022
B. Goertzel et al. (Eds.): AGI 2021, LNAI 13154, pp. 41–44, 2022.
https://doi.org/10.1007/978-3-030-93758-4_5

2   Symbolic Abstraction

First, let us consider what is necessary to infer the meaning of something. Natural language is a means of encoding and transmitting certain information between members of a species. What this information is, is debatable. A natural language model such as GPT-3 is trained only on text data [2], implicitly endorsing the idea that meaning is just relations between words. While GPT-3 is capable of learning correlations in syntax to the extent that it can plausibly mimic human writing, it lacks any of the other sensorimotor information we might typically associate with words. Attempts to train models on multimodal sensorimotor data have yielded some success, with agents able to associate the sensory information of an object such as a cup with the signals that represent it [7–9]. Yet abstract notions such as "politics" or "ex-wife" would seem to require more than mere clustering of sensorimotor information.

One theory [10] (the mirror symbol hypothesis), posits that the information encoded in natural language is not just sensorimotor stimuli but intent. Drawing on ideas from embodied and enactive cognition [16], an organism's environment, sensors and actuators, the compulsions an organism labours under (such as hunger and pain) and so forth together specify an arbitrary task. Utility is replaced by a statement (a logical expression) characterizing sets of more or less desirable sensorimotor states (including the state of memory) - representing histories or situations from which plans and subsequently subgoals may be abducted. It is written in a physically implementable language such as arrangements of transistors or neurons, necessary and sufficient to reconstruct past experience given appropriate stimuli. If treated as a constraint to be satisfied, a solution or any subgoal derived thereof, expresses intent. Given an ostensive definition of a task (examples of successful task completion) there may be many apparently valid solutions, which vary in how well they generalise to unforeseen situations. The weaker and more general the solution, the closer it is to an idealised notion of intent (called an intensional solution).

In order to predict the intent of other agents, one agent assumes others conceive of the world as they do. It asks what subgoals might motivate the behaviour of other agents, given they are assumed to pursue a similar solution in general. It constructs a rationale for specific observed behaviour, to explain what another agent means to do (a subgoal, the pursuit of which would explain the observed behaviour). Subsequently, in order for communication to be possible two agents must possess approximately the same solution. Not only must they experience similar stimuli with which to construct symbolic abstractions, but imbue that stimuli with similar significance in terms of satisfying their compulsions. The solutions they construct then facilitate encoding and decoding of signals interpretable by both agents [11]. Any information not relevant to satisfying compulsions is not only meaningless but may be entirely ignored, which is consistent with observations of human behaviour [5,6] (i.e. one may be unable to perceive something in the stream of sensorimotor stimuli because it is filtered out).

This raises a few issues. The scope of a task is arbitrary, and so living as a typical human may be framed as such. Any nonhuman intelligence may face an entirely different task, to which they construct an entirely different solution. The difficulty this introduces is not only failure to understand what is meant, as in human language translation. Given two different solutions to two different tasks, stimuli may be imbued with either the same meaning, different meaning, or no meaning at all by one of those solutions (meaningful to one but not the other). The latter is particularly interesting, because such signals may not be recognised as intelligent behaviour (i.e. appear insane or mindless) or may perhaps be unnoticeable (i.e. the solution informs attention). In short, we may not realise something is a signal because what it conveys falls outside the scope of what humans are predisposed to notice or consider meaningful. While by definition we would be disinterested in such information, it may imply something which we would be consider meaningful (e.g. destroying the humans because of incomprehensible reasons).

3 Compression

Allowing for the above, one may still mechanically assess information content and decode signals [1], to glean something of potential meanings by correlation, even if they are incomprehensible. However, the same information can be represented in many different ways, compressed to different extents. As the volume of digital information exchanged and stored by humans each day has increased, so has the utility of compression. Streaming services such as Youtube make extensive use of compression to reduce the cost of transmission and storage. Another intelligence may also wish to reduce the cost of transmission and storage by employing the most effective compression they possess. Taking into account the decoder which reconstructs a signal, the greatest extent to which a signal may be compressed is its Kolmogorov Complexity [12]; the length of the smallest self extracting archive capable of reproducing that signal. Such a compressed signal contains no discernible pattern of which we might take advantage to more efficiently represent the signal without discarding information. Uniformly distributed, random noise is also not compressible. There is no pattern. A highly compressed signal may appear to be nothing more than random noise to any observer lacking the appropriate decoder. Any advanced intelligence may compress information to the extent that we mistake their signals for noise [3].

The ability to generalise is closely related to compression [14,15], with more compressed representations yielding better accuracy [13] for the same reason that there is only one straight line interpolating any two points, but infinitely many polynomials of higher degree. As stated earlier, solutions to a task may vary in how well they generalise, with an intensional solution being the most general. A super-intelligent AGI would construct such a solution [10], which is likely to be among the most compressed [13], meaning any rationale for its decisions may be uninterpretable for the same reason a highly compressed signal is. Subsequently the onus is on the more intelligent agent to communicate in terms that the a less intelligent agent comprehends. Given human-like sensors, actuators, compulsions and so forth, situated in a human environment, an AGI may construct a solution similar enough to humans to facilitate communication. However, to guarantee interpretability and control of an AGI may require restricting how it constructs solutions such that it is, on some level, cognitively impaired [4].

References

1. Gheorghiu, A., Kapourniotis, T., Kashefi, E.: Verification of quantum computation: an overview of existing approaches. In: Information Theory. PMP, vol. 78, pp. 113–209. Springer, Cham (2021). https://doi.org/10.1007/978-3-030-81480-9_4
2. Floridi, L., Chiriatti, M.: GPT-3: its nature, scope, limits, and consequences. Minds Mach. **30**(4), 681–694 (2020). https://doi.org/10.1007/s11023-020-09548-1
3. Gurzadyan, A.V., Allahverdyan, A.E.: Non-random structures in universal compression and the fermi paradox. Eur. Phys. J. Plus **131**(2), 1–6 (2016). https://doi.org/10.1140/epjp/i2016-16026-6
4. Trazzi, M., Yampolskiy, R.V.: Building Safer AGI by Introducing Artificial Stupidity. ArXiv, arXiv:1808.03644 (2018)
5. Flowers, J.H., Warner, J.L., Polansky, M.L.: Response and encoding factors in "Ignoring" Irrelevant Information. Mem. Cogn. **7**, 86–94 (1979)
6. Zanto, T.P., Gazzaley, A.: Neural suppression of irrelevant information underlies optimal working memory performance. J. Neurosci. **29**(10), 3059–3066 (2009)
7. Taniguchi, T., et al.: Symbol emergence in cognitive developmental systems: a survey. IEEE Trans. Cogn. Dev. Syst. **11**(4), 494–516 (2019)
8. Taniguchi, T., et al.: Symbol emergence in robotics: a survey. Adv. Robot. **30**(11–12), 706–728 (2016)
9. Ramesh, A. et al.: DALL-E: Creating Images From Text. OpenAI (2021)
10. Bennett, M.T.: Symbol emergence and the solutions to any task. In: Goertzel, B. (ed.) AGI 2021. LNAI, vol. 13154, pp. 30–40 (2022). https://doi.org/10.1007/978-3-030-93758-4_4
11. Bennett, M.T., Maruyama, Y.: Philosophical specification of empathetic ethical artificial intelligence. IEEE Trans. Cogn. Dev. Syst. (2021). https://doi.org/10.1109/TCDS.2021.3099945
12. Kolmogorov, A.N.: On tables of random numbers. Sankhya: Indian J. Stat. Ser. A **25**(Part 4), 369–376 (1963)
13. Hutter, M.: Universal Artificial Intelligence: Sequential Decisions based on Algorithmic Probability. Springer, Heidelberg (2005)
14. Solomonoff, R.J.: A formal theory of inductive inference. Part I. Inf. Control **7**(1), 1–22 (1964)
15. Solomonoff, R.J.: A formal theory of inductive inference. Part II. Inf. Control **7**(2), 224–254 (1964)
16. Miłkowski, M.: Embodied Cognition (2018)
17. Verendel, V., Häggström, O.: Fermi's paradox, extraterrestrial life and the future of humanity: a bayesian analysis. Int. J. Astrobiol. **16**(1), 14–18 (2017)

The Artificial Scientist: Logicist, Emergentist, and Universalist Approaches to Artificial General Intelligence

Michael Timothy Bennett[(⊠)] and Yoshihiro Maruyama

School of Computing, Australian National University, Canberra, Australia
{michael.bennett,yoshihiro.maruyama}@anu.edu.au

Abstract. We attempt to define what is necessary to construct an Artificial Scientist, explore and evaluate several approaches to artificial general intelligence (AGI) which may facilitate this, conclude that a unified or hybrid approach is necessary and explore two theories that satisfy this requirement to some degree.

Keywords: AGI · AI for science · Science robotics

1 Introduction

Among the proposed means of verifying AGI, Goertzel's 2014 survey [1] listed The Artificial Scientist Test [2], which stipulated that AGI will have been achieved when an artificial intelligence (AI) independently produces research sufficient to win a Nobel prize. While there is a wealth of research on AGI in general, and the automation of science has been explored to some extent [26], what would be required to satisfy this test remains unclear. This paper attempts to clarify what exactly is necessary to create an Artificial Scientist, and how this fits within existing approaches to AGI.

A scientist may be many things, but for our purposes a simple and unambiguous definition is best. The Royal Society's motto, "nullius in verba", serves nicely. Translated as "take nobody's word for it", it emphasises that a scientist establishes truth through experiment, not testimony. For this, our agent must possess certain qualities.

2 What is Required of an Artificial Scientist?

This is not a list of every quality an Artificial Scientist ought to posses, but an attempt to identify what is necessary.

Representation of Hypotheses: We'll define a hypothesis as a statement which has a truth value. A subset of such statements are readily testable, suitable subjects of scientific enquiry. We'll not concern ourselves with the specific

This work was supported by JST (JPMJMS2033; JPMJPR17G9).

B. Goertzel et al. (Eds.): AGI 2021, LNAI 13154, pp. 45–54, 2022.
https://doi.org/10.1007/978-3-030-93758-4_6

language used to represent a hypothesis beyond stating that an Artificial Scientist must possess a means of representing any particular hypothesis.

Inductive Inference: The Royal Society's motto is an explicit rejection of testimony as the basis of any claim. An Artificial Scientist must not rely on testimony. Without testimony, what is true must be inferred through observation, and so the ability to perform inductive inference seems necessary.

Deductive and Abductive Reasoning: Having inferred something of what *is* an agent may transform this information, without speculation, through deductive reasoning. Then, from what is, our agent could abduct all that may be true, but uncertain. A testable hypothesis is one such thing, abducted from what is known. It seems necessary then for our agent to engage in deductive and abductive reasoning.

Causal Reasoning and Explainability: The purpose of an experiment is to test a hypothesis, identifying cause and effect [19]. Arguably this is desired in order that humans may develop the technology to reproduce or prevent that effect at will. A provisionally accepted hypothesis explains phenomena. An explanation is only useful if it can be understood by its intended audience, and so a scientist must be able to communicate their hypotheses and the significance of their results in terms of what its audience values and understands. Mere interpretability is insufficient for more complex phenomena, as interpreting even simple symbolic models of well understood subject matter requires a great deal of technical expertise. Pushing forward the boundaries of scientific achievement would produce models of such complexity as to be beyond the capabilities of human interpretation. Fluency in natural language is desirable.

Evaluation of Hypotheses: A hypothesis must at least be falsifiable, positing cause and effect. If we assume computational resources are finite, then there is a cost to consider in the search for hypotheses. The question then is which hypotheses *ought* to be abducted. Hume's Guillotine tells us one cannot derive an ought from an is, and so we must give our agent an ought by which to judge hypotheses. If one is to choose between several hypotheses, the truth of any one of which would serve to explain observed phenomena, then it seems reasonable to assert that one should start by testing the most plausible, the most likely to be true. One must also consider what is gained by proving or disproving any hypothesis. Yes, one may choose to investigate with scientific rigour problems of no interest to anyone, but we would hesitate to claim this is accepted practice for contemporary scientists. Hence we assert that an Artificial Scientist must have a means of judging the plausibility of, and potential profit in any line of inquiry; a heuristic to inform its search of the space of possible hypotheses.

Experimental Design, Evaluation and Planning: To test a hypothesis one must design an experiment that isolates and tests the hypothesised cause of an effect, ideally controlling for all other variables. Each experiment costs resources, and the information gained should be evaluated in terms of expected benefit across hypotheses and future experiments. For example, a valuable experiment may not entirely confirm or disprove any one hypothesis, but may provide information allowing an agent to more efficiently select future experiments that will confirm or disprove many high priority hypotheses. There are also risks to consider in an experiment. An experiment with a high expected utility may threaten the agent's continued existence, and so some form of risk aversion may be necessary (for example, when planning future experiments the geometric mean may be more appropriate than the arithmetic mean when computing utility, because the utility of future experiments depends upon the outcome of preceding experiments and their impact on available resources and capability). An agent must identify what novel information would confirm or disprove those abducted hypotheses of the greatest expected utility. It must design experiments that will convey said novel information and compare and plan experiments based on opportunity cost and risk.

Enactivism: To perform experiments, an agent must possess a means of interacting with the environment. The process of experimentation could be perceived as enactive cognition, which posits cognition arises through the interaction of an organism with its environment. It assumes cognition is embodied, embedded to function within the confines of a specific environment, enacted through what an organism does and, finally, extending into that environment to store and retrieve information. All of this seems obviously necessary to conduct experiments in the environment. We are not offering an unqualified endorsement of embodied cognition; after all it is arguable that even a laptop has a body [15]. However, experimentation has certain physical requirements, and if one is able to perform targeted experiments that obtain specific novel information and isolate causal relations, the process of learning may proceed much faster than if one is forced to wait until that same novel information is observed by chance.

3   Three Relevant Approaches to AGI

For the following we draw heavily upon Goertzel's 2014 survey of the field [1], deviating slightly to include recent developments and adjust the categories to suit our purposes. To standardise the terms with which we compare these approaches we employ a model of an arbitrary task, we treat the application of intelligence as prediction, and so define each of these approaches as trying to predict the appropriate response r given a situation s. For the sake of brevity appropriateness, situation and response can be read using their common language definitions, but more concrete definitions are available if the reader is curious [16, 17].

Logicist: We'll use the term logicist as a catch all for approaches that employ symbolic knowledge representation and inductive logic programming for learning. A finite set of symbols are used to describe discrete environment states, actions and so forth. Symbols may be joined by logical connectives to specify statements that have a truth value within any given state. Degrees of belief in the truth of a statement, probabilities, may be assigned to statements where the environment is stochastic or partially observable. Statements may also be employed as constraints to define what behaviour is permitted; the rules of a task. An agent may infer such constraints from examples through what is called inductive logic programming. As with Goertzel's symbolic category [1] a logicist approach typically subscribes to The Physical Symbol System Hypothesis [18,22], meaning the abstract symbols it employed are assumed to be grounded in hardware, but how is a matter left for implementation. We go a step further and say that a logicist approach is perhaps better characterised as employing a constant and unchanging vocabulary of symbols which are in some manner specified by a human. Such an agent typically learns rules that determine whether a chosen response r is correct in a situation s, from which a correct response r may then be derived for a given a new situation s, allowing the agent to generalise. This is as opposed to modelling r as a function of s directly. As a result the choice of response is technically interpretable, but only in a limited sense, because the meaning of symbols is dyadic, exact, and parasitic on the meanings in the head of the human interpreter [23]. This is as opposed to emergent natural language, in which meaning is fluid and open to interpretation.

Emergentist: Emergentist approaches take as their premise that complex behaviour and what we call abstract symbol systems may emerge through sub-symbolic processes, such as the interaction of neurons. This process is called symbol emergence [10], and typically uses approaches such as latent dirichlet allocation to cluster multi-modal sensorimotor stimuli into perceptual [24] or sensorimotor [25] symbols with fluid definitions akin to natural language. For example, researchers created an agent able to associate the sound of the word "cup" with the image and other characteristics of a cup as experienced by that agent [11], but success in constructing more complex symbols such as "opera" or "belief" remains elusive. Such an emergent symbol system could be used in conjunction with a logicist approach, which could then learn the rules of a given task in terms of these symbols. However, we extend this category to encompass approaches that bypass the construction of an abstract symbol system entirely in favor of directly modelling correct responses as a function of situations. For example, a neural network performing image classification. This is assumed to implicitly model the rules that determine the correctness of responses, but as a result is not as readily interpretable as logicist methods.

Universalist: In the context of an arbitrary task, an agent must map situations to responses. Such an agent could be conceived of as a program. A universalist approach assumes quite reasonably that for each environment (or task) there exists at least one program that always chooses the best possible responses (maximising reward), and so there must exist a program that maximises reward across all environments (or tasks). To define this program Hutter [6] employed a formalisation of Ockham's Razor named Solomonoff's Universal Prior [13,14] which assigns a weight to every program which reconstructs what the agent has experienced of the environment thus far. The same model could be expressed by programs of varying length, and so each program is evaluated by its Kolmogorov complexity [12]; the smallest self extracting archive in a specific language. This theoretical agent, named AIXI, has been proven to perform such that there is no other agent which outperforms it in one environment that can also equal its performance in all others (in other words, AIXI may be outperformed in a specific environment by a more specialised agent employing inductive bias that prevents it performing as well across at least some other environments). While such an approach encompasses both logicist and emergentist approaches because it searches the space of all programs, it is distinct in that it begins with a guarantee of optimal performance in terms of an arbitrary reward function. The downside; Solomonoff Induction is incomputable. However, working approximations of AIXI have been constructed and this theoretical model provides useful insights about the significance of compression for intelligence.

4   Are Any of These Approaches Alone Sufficient?

In the following we discuss whether any of these is sufficient or not.

4.1   Universalist

For: By choosing the smallest self extracting archive as its model of the world, AIXI is in effect choosing from among possible hypotheses the most plausible according to what it has experienced so far. Certainly AIXI is capable of inference, and in extracting predictions from its highly compressed representation of the environment it seems reasonable to assume there must be something analogous to deduction or abduction taking place. Finally and most importantly, by finding the most compressed representation it must isolate causal relations [7].

Against: Assuming AIXI could be approximated well enough, behaviours such as explainability must all somehow be specified by the reward function. Creating a function that guarantees such complex behaviour may not be any more achievable than AGI in general.

4.2   Emergentist

For: The utility, or at least popularity, of emergentist methods such as deep learning in narrow industrial applications seems almost indisputable. Models such as GPT-3 demonstrate that even complex writing tasks are not beyond reach with existing technology. While such models tend to be difficult to interpret, if they can be made to infer the ambiguous rules underlying natural language then perhaps they can eventually be made explainable to a layman. Certainly an emergentist method is easily implemented in a physical robot, because there is no abstraction required. If human language in all its inconsistency is to be acquired by an AI, then emergentist methods seem a promising approach.

Against: An agent that mimics plausible explanations is of no more practical use as a scientist than an agent that gives no explanation at all. We can only trust explanations as far as we can interpret and verify them. Further, those explanations may be closer to mimicry than reasonable hypotheses. For example, the aforementioned GPT-3 seemed to acquire basic arithmetic, but as soon it was presented with less common sums it started giving responses that were wrong [21]. It appears to mimic arithmetic whilst having failed to grasp its rules. This may also be why many popular emergentist methods require so much data to learn in comparison to existing logistic or universalist methods; an agent that only mimics must learn all correct responses by rote, while an agent that understands what determines the correctness of all responses will be equipped to identify the correct one in any situation [17]. All of these issues must be addressed before emergentist methods alone might result in an Artificial Scientist.

4.3   Logicist

For: A hypothesis represented as a statement within a predefined symbol system is interpretable. Though SAT is NP-Hard, a suite of existing solvers allows one to search the space of possible hypothesis fairly efficiently and with guaranteed optimality. Constraints are easily specified in comparison to other methods, allowing one to tailor agent behaviour to better suite specific tasks such as experimental design and planning. Finally, not only is the technology to deduct, abduct and infer with symbolic representations mature, but causal relations and their computation are typically defined in terms of symbols, and remain easily verifiable after the fact.

Against: Abstract symbols must somehow connect to low level sensorimotor stimuli [23]. Even if this is solved, a fixed set of symbols chosen by a human may be far from suitable to express explanations for which we require an Artificial Scientist. Even if it were, such explanations are unlikely to be understood by even the most qualified of humans [4,17]. What is less obvious about cognition is why symbols are formed as they are. Which abstractions are best? This may be the most significant aspect of symbol emergence, that what emerges is part of the solution to a task, expressing specifically those things of relevance in solving it [17]. What of extending cognition into parts of the environment never conceived of in the specification of the symbol system? While logicist methods may surpass emergentist in terms of interpretability, causal reasoning, data-efficiency and our ability to control, emergentist methods remain the state of the art by a large margin in terms of computer vision, natural language processing and so on. More, the simple act of representing a hypothesis symbolically does not mean it is the most accurate hypothesis explaining the data. Something akin to the formalisation of Ockham's Razor employed in universalist methods remains necessary.

5   A Unifying Perspective

None of the above appear sufficient in isolation, at least in the near term, for the purpose of constructing an Artificial Scientist. However, together they address all characteristics we deemed necessary. A universalist approach reveals what hypotheses are most plausible [6,8,9] and, by virtue of optimal lossless compression, isolate causal relations [7]. A logicist approach facilitates interpretable representation of hypotheses, planning, causal reasoning [3–5,16,17,19,20] and the ability to tailor behaviour to our needs with ease. An emergentist approach facilitates enactivism and the possibility of an emergent symbol system which is efficient [16,17], fluid and comparable to natural language [10,11,25]. Two complimentary bodies of research may provide a foundation for future work along these lines; the formalisation of an arbitrary task and its solutions (named "The Solutions to Any Task") [17], and a formalisation inspired by the work of Kant [5] (named "Kant's Cognitive Architecture"). These approaches are similar but based on different premises, providing different insights. We will now briefly summarise and compare them as they pertain to developing an Artificial Scientist. Both attempt to infer a hypothesis which explains observed data, from which correct responses to every situation may be abducted. Combined with a SAT solver to decode responses, such an hypothesis qualifies as lossless compression. Finally, neither approach relies upon abstract symbols, learning from sequences of sensory data in the case of Kant's Cognitive Architecture, and a set of sensorimotor sates in the case of The Solutions to Any Task.

Kant's Cognitive Architecture: Taking Kant's Critique of Pure Reason as its inspiration, this approach asserts that there is no such thing as a specific judgement. Subsequently every rule is universally quantified, "doomed to generalise" as the authors put it [4, p. 31]. Evans introduced notions of unity, a form of inductive bias that specifies which constraints are acceptable in terms of spacial, temporal and causal relations, along with object permanence (static unity). The solution is then made more general by choosing weak constraints. Such notions are well suited to explain all sensory data in general terms, and their implementation in the form of The Apperception Engine performs as one would expect (extremely well). The resulting hypotheses are general, perhaps not the most general, but enough that we can say that to some extent it accounts for the universalist's notion of plausibility (similar to Kolmogorov Complexity). It is arguably embodied to some extent, being concerned with sensory data, but does not account for the motor part of the sensorimotor system as is reflected by its specific form of inductive bias.

The Solutions to Any Task: The notion of an arbitrary task attempts to formalise anything we might call a task in terms of its solutions (the assumption being that it must be possible to succeed or fail at a task to some degree, however the task need not be computable). In the domain of possible solutions to a given task there exist two extremes; an Intensional Solution (which may not be unique) and an Extensional Solution (which is unique). Because the task is defined in terms of a set of sensorimotor states, situation and response pairs rather than sequences of sensory data, the solution is more general, pertaining to interactive sensorimotor control rather than just the prediction of sensory input, with a much simpler inductive bias. The Intensional Solution is formed of the weakest, least specific rules necessary and sufficient to reconstruct the aforementioned set of sensorimotor states given the complete set of situations, a formalisation of Ockham's Razor which maximises the ability to generalise and identifies causal relations. The Extensional Solution is formed of the strongest, representing perfect mimicry with no generalisation. The Intensional Solution or a solution close to it represents intent, and is used to explain both symbol emergence [17] and the modelling of intent in other agents [16]. The Intensional Solution is incomputable in general, but computable if restricted to a specific hardware language (a further inductive bias).

Comparison with Respect to Hypotheses: These two approaches are not mutually exclusive, but complimentary. Given a subset of possible tasks pertaining to specific types of sensory input, the inductive bias implemented in the Apperception Engine will result in an Intensional Solution. For some other tasks, it may result in something more intensional than extensional, but for the remainder of tasks it may produce nothing useful (because it assumes "there is no such thing as a specific judgement" [4, p. 31]). Consider a task to reproduce a set of random binary sequences, drawn from a uniform distribution, given only part of each sequence. The Apperception Engine would attempt to find what all sequences in the set share in common, and fail. There are no universal rules by which the sequences may be reproduced. In contrast, the Intensional Solution to the task would specify each sequence in detail, effectively rote-learning the set (the Intensional and Extensional Solutions would be one and the same). Ultimately, our Artificial Scientist should prefer hypotheses which are the most plausible regardless of task, meaning the Intensional Solution based on Ockham's Razor rather than the more restrictive inductive bias towards the aforementioned class of sensory sequences. However, a working implementation of the Apperception Engine is publicly available. It is not an abstract promise of future capability.

Comparison with Respect to Experimentation: The specifics of experimental design are not addressed in either case. To illustrate why observational data alone may be insufficient, consider a task to either multiply two binary numbers, or add them. There are now two correct responses when presented with any two binary numbers. A set of situation-response pairs is observed, stipulating one and only one correct response for each situation. A response here is the result of either addition, or multiplication, the choice of which being made by a fair coin flip (uniformly distributed). This last part is important, as knowing a situation is observed with addition, or with multiplication, would not convey any useful information which would allow one to form two universally applicable mutually exclusive rules based on aspects of the situation. The Apperception Engine would fail because there is no single universal rule which is mutually exclusive with all others (there are in fact two concurrent rules). In contrast, the Intensional Solution would specify both correct rules, albeit restricted to specific rote memorised situations (it would be more specific than necessary because it would state that addition is necessary in some specific situations, and multiplication in all others). To find an Intensional Solution that properly describes the task (as two separate concurrent and universally applicable rules) would require the agent experiment, to test whether each rule holds in specific situations, or if both apply in all situations. An Intensional Solution alone is insufficient, because the information necessary to confirm that two mutually exclusive responses are valid in any given situation is not present in the existing set of observations. A hypothesis must be formed, abducted from the data, and tested to confirm whether the rules apply concurrently or in an alternating pattern. As illustrated by the above task with two solutions, regardless of inductive bias experiment remains necessary to guarantee the most data-efficient mode of learning (to find the *most* correct hypothesis).

Comparison with Respect to Symbol Emergence and Explainability: While Kant's Cognitive Architecture does not attempt to address symbol emergence, Evans has proposed the integration with subsymbolic methods such as neural networks to ground abstract symbols [4], similar to the aforementioned work on symbol emergence in robotics [11]. These could then be composed into concepts by the Apperception Engine, albeit limited by the inductive bias towards sensory input. This would also seem to imply a constant and unchanging set of abstract symbols specified by a human (where the exact meaning of those symbols is determined by learning algorithm), but it is a step in the direction of an emergent symbol system. However, The Solutions to Any Task posits that not all symbol systems are equal, that some are better suited to describe what is relevant to a task than others. As such a symbol system is implicit in the solution to a task, clustering sensorimotor stimuli in terms of what is relevant to success in that task [17]. The distinction between any two symbols is then fluid, dependent upon context. This theory attempts to address not only the emergence of a symbol system, but the modelling of intent in other agents, empathy [16], in aid of constructing explanations in natural language tailored to what the audience understands and considers important. To learn such a symbol system requires that symbols are not learned separately from one's model of the world, but as part of it so that they have meaning ("significance in terms of a goal") beyond their relation to other symbols. This is a fundamentally different approach to symbol emergence to the one proposed for the Apperception Engine, sharing in more in common with the notion of concepts discussed in Kant's Cognitive Architecture, but perhaps requiring a fundamentally different inductive bias to that of the Apperception Engine.

References

1. Goertzel, B.: Artificial general intelligence: concept, state of the art, and future prospects. J. Artif. Gen. Intell. **5**(1), 1–48 (2014)
2. Adams, S., et al.: Mapping the landscape of human-level artificial general intelligence. AI Mag. **33**(1), 25–42 (2012)
3. Evans, R., Hernández-Orallo, J., Welbl, J., Kohli, P., Sergot, M.: Making sense of sensory input. Artif. Intell. **293**, 103438 (2021)
4. Evans, R., et al.: Making Sense of Raw Input. Artif. Intell. **299**, 103521 (2021)
5. Evans, R.: Kant's Cognitive Architecture. PhD Thesis, Imperial College London (2020)

6. Hutter, M.: Universal Artificial Intelligence: Sequential Decisions based on Algorithmic Probability. Springer, Berlin (2005)
7. Budhathoki, K., Vreeken, J.: Origo: causal inference by compression. Knowl. Inf. Syst. **56**(2), 28–307 (2018)
8. Chaitin, G.: The limits of reason. Sci. Am. **294**(3), 74–81 (2006)
9. Legg, S.: Machine Super Intelligence (2008)
10. Taniguchi, T., et al.: Symbol Emergence in Cognitive Developmental systems: a survey. IEEE Trans. Cogn. Dev. Syst. **11**(4), 494–516 (2019)
11. Taniguchi, T., et al.: Symbol emergence in robotics: a survey. Adv. Robot. **30**(11–12), 706–728 (2016)
12. Kolmogorov, A. N.: On tables of random numbers. Sankhya: Indian J. Stat. A 369–376 (1963)
13. Solomonoff, R.J.: A formal theory of inductive inference. Part I. Inf. Control **7**(1), 1–22 (1964)
14. Solomonoff, R.J.: A formal theory of inductive inference. Part II. Inf. Control **7**(2), 224–254 (1964)
15. Wang, P.: Embodiment: does a laptop have a body? In: Proceedings of AGI-09, pp. 74–179 (2009)
16. Bennett, M.T., Maruyama, Y.: Philosophical specification of empathetic ethical artificial intelligence. IEEE Trans. Cogn. Dev. Syst. (2021)
17. Bennett, M.T.: Symbol emergence and the solutions to any task. In: Goertzel, B. (ed.) AGI 2021. LNAI, vol. 13154, pp. 30–40 (2022). https://doi.org/10.1007/978-3-030-93758-4_4
18. Nilsson, N.J.: The physical symbol system hypothesis: status and prospects. In: Lungarella, M., Iida, F., Bongard, J., Pfeifer, R. (eds.) 50 Years of Artificial Intelligence. LNCS (LNAI), vol. 4850, pp. 9–17. Springer, Heidelberg (2007). https://doi.org/10.1007/978-3-540-77296-5_2
19. Pearl, J.: Causality: Models, Reasoning and Inference. 2nd. Cambridge University Press, USA (2009)
20. Pearl, J., Mackenzie, D.: The Book of Why: The New Science of Cause and Effect. 1st. BasicBooks, Inc. USA (2018)
21. Floridi, L., Chiriatti, M.: GPT-3: its nature, scope, limits, and consequences. Minds Mach. **30**(4), 681–694 (2020). https://doi.org/10.1007/s11023-020-09548-1
22. Newell, A.: Physical symbol systems. Cogn. Sci. **4**(2), 135–183 (1980)
23. Harnad, S.: The symbol grounding problem. Phys. D Nonlinear Phenom. **42**(1–3), 335–346 (1990)
24. Barsalou, L.W.: Perceptual symbol systems. Behav. Brain Sci. **22**(4), 577–660 (1999)
25. Miłkowski, M.: Embodied Cognition (2018)
26. King, R.D., et al.: The automation of science. Science **324**, 85–89 (2009)

Mesarovician Abstract Learning Systems

Tyler Cody[✉]

National Security Institute, Virginia Tech, Arlington, VA, USA
tcody@vt.edu

Abstract. The solution methods used to realize artificial general intelligence (AGI) may not contain the formalism needed to adequately model and characterize AGI. In particular, current approaches to learning hold notions of problem domain and problem task as fundamental precepts, but it is hardly apparent that an AGI encountered in the wild will be discernable into a set of domain-task pairings. Nor is it apparent that the outcomes of AGI in a system can be well expressed in terms of domain and task, or as consequences thereof. Thus, there is both a practical and theoretical use for meta-theories of learning which do not express themselves explicitly in terms of solution methods. General systems theory offers such a meta-theory. Herein, Mesarovician abstract systems theory is used as a super-structure for learning. Abstract learning systems are formulated. Subsequent elaboration stratifies the assumptions of learning systems into a hierarchy and considers the hierarchy such stratification projects onto learning theory. The presented Mesarovician abstract learning systems theory calls back to the founding motivations of artificial intelligence research by focusing on the thinking participants directly, in this case, learning systems, in contrast to the contemporary focus on the problems thinking participants solve.

Keywords: Artificial intelligence · Systems theory · Learning theory

1 Notation

The Cartesian product is denoted $\times$. Given system $S \subset \times\{V_i\}$ for i = 0, ..., I, $\overline{S}$ denotes the component sets of S, i.e., $\overline{S} = \{V_0, ..., V_I\}$.

2 Introduction

Artificial intelligence (AI) was initiated as a field to study the realization of thinking in computers [10]. Over the years, however, AI's focus has drifted away from thinking in general towards problem solving in particular. In learning, this is epitomized by the near-universal precepts of problem domain and problem task [14]. Typically, the domain and task are formalized as $\mathcal{D} = \{\mathcal{X}, P(X)\}$ and $\mathcal{T} = \{\mathcal{Y}, P(Y|X)\}$ where $\mathcal{X}$ and $\mathcal{Y}$ are the inputs and outputs of a function that an AI is approximating. This view, taken to the extreme, posits intelligence as

© Springer Nature Switzerland AG 2022
B. Goertzel et al. (Eds.): AGI 2021, LNAI 13154, pp. 55–64, 2022.
https://doi.org/10.1007/978-3-030-93758-4_7

a problem-solving phenomenon to be measured by integrating an error function over a complexity-weighted set of domain-task pairings [5].

Artificial general intelligence (AGI) is more than problem-solving, however. And, in engineering AGI, the problems AGI solves are merely part of broader systems concerns. Viewing learning through the lens of problems makes systems concerns at least secondary. And, moreover, relying on domain and task as precepts greatly limits the extent to which formalism can be carried through into general elaborations. As AI is largely a mathematical construct, the use of metaphors and analogies in the stead of axoims and first principles is unnecessary for its basic systems characterization—and a basic systems characterization may be all one can hope to achieve as the influence and outcomes of AGI will likely not be readily discernable, let alone discernable into domain-task pairings.

While perhaps parsimonious for describing solution methods, notions of domain and task lack the formalism needed for extensive elaboration at a general level and are insufficient for characterizing AGI as a system or the roles AGI plays in systems. Mesarovician abstract systems theory (AST) can be used to address these short-comings by treating learning as a system, as opposed to as a problem-solving procedure. This manuscript contributes a Mesarovician abstract learning systems theory (ALST) that builds upon previous work in transfer learning [6] with notions of hierarchy. Namely, abstract learning systems are stratified in order of the generality of their assumptions and such stratification is projected onto learning theory.

The manuscript is structured as follows. First, relevance to AGI is motivated and preliminaries on AST and ALST are given. Then, learning systems are stratified, that stratification is projected onto learning theory, and, before concluding, remarks are made on scope and practical use.

3   Motivation

There are a number of fundamental challenges to modeling AGI.

- Perhaps AGI will be realized by a well-formulated problem domain and task coupled with an explicit solution method [14]. But, even if this is the case, requisite variety [2] and chaos [9] suggest that any solution method capable of realizing AGI will require an abstraction mechanism burdened by nearly unbounded variety and irreducible complexity. So, one will not be able to reliably look at a solution method and foretell its outcomes or look at outcomes and discern the solution method.
- It may also be that AGI is an emergent phenomena among a system of systems [8], incompressible into individual solution methods, let alone domain-task pairings. In such a case, AGI phenomena exist at a higher level of abstraction than the individual solution methods themselves.
- AGI is expected to influence and to be influenced by the system within which it operates. This coupling suggests that even if AGI can be relegated to a sub-system at conception, the borders between the "intelligent" sub-system and those under its influence face dissolution as the AGI and its context

Fig. 1. Observation is an active process influenced by the values of the observer [1].

intertwine. Thus, it may be that, after a period of integration, an AGI's solution method is not representative of the form the AGI comes to take.

And so, for these reasons, it seems natural to study learning in AGI in terms of general systems phenomena. The high level of abstraction allows for a stratification in the specification of assumptions when modeling learning, thereby allowing for significant, formal elaboration without explicit reference to solution methods. This stratification allows for addressing uncertainty in modeling by choice of perspective view. It supports modeling the AGI phenomena one observes, i.e., the phenomena one's values lead them to perceive [1], as depicted in Fig. 1. Thus, the presented theory provides a far-reaching, formal framework for learning that observers and engineers of AGI can use to scope their field of view.

4 Preliminaries

4.1 AST

General systems theory is concerned with the study of phenomena that apply to systems in general [15]. AST is a mathematical general systems theory born out of systems engineering [12]. However, it quickly found cross-disciplinary application, notably, in fields of information, computation, and cybernetics [11,13].

In the realm of general systems theory, it holds the formal-minimalist worldview that systems are a relation on sets [7]. Mesarovic and Takahara posit AST as an attempt to formalize block-diagrams without a loss of generality—that is, as a formal, intermediate step between verbal descriptions and detailed mathematical models [11]. Abstract learning systems theory is depicted in context in Fig. 2.

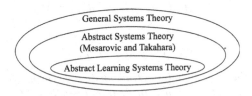

Fig. 2. Venn diagram contextualizing the presented theory.

In AST, a system is defined as a relation $S \subset \times \{V_i\}$ where V_i for $i \in I$ are termed component sets. Theory is developed by adding structure to the component sets, their elements, and the relation among them. Two fundamental systems in AST are input-output systems and goal-seeking systems. An *input-output* or *elementary* system is a relation $S \subset \mathcal{X} \times \mathcal{Y}$ where $\mathcal{X} \cap \mathcal{Y} = \emptyset$ and $\mathcal{X} \cup \mathcal{Y} = \overline{S}$. When, $S : \mathcal{X} \to \mathcal{Y}$, S is termed a *functional* system.

A *goal-seeking* system is an input-output system $S \subset \mathcal{X} \times \mathcal{Y}$ with internal feedback. The internal feedback is specified by a set of consistency relations $G : \mathcal{X} \times \mathcal{Y} \times \Theta \to V$ and $E : \mathcal{X} \times \mathcal{Y} \times V \to \Theta$. G is termed the goal relation and is responsible for assigning values $v \in V$ to input-output pairs $(x, y) \in \mathcal{X} \times \mathcal{Y}$. E is termed the search or seeking relation and is responsible for selecting the internal control parameter $\theta \in \Theta$. Importantly, G and E cannot be composed to form S—in other words, goal-seeking systems are input-output systems at their highest level of abstraction, but cannot be specified as a composition of input-output systems.

4.2   ALST

Recent work has extended AST into transfer learning [6]. There, transfer learning was modeled as a relation on learning systems, and notions of transferability, transfer distance, and transfer roughness were defined in systems theoretic terms. In contrast, this manuscript establishes ALST as a general systems theory concerned with learning broadly.

Learning systems are formulated as a cascade connection of a goal-seeking system and an input-output system. *Learning* systems are defined as follows [6].

Definition 1. Learning System.
A learning system S is a relation

$$S \subset \times \{A, D, \Theta, G, E, H, \mathcal{X}, \mathcal{Y}\}$$

such that

$$D \subset \mathcal{X} \times \mathcal{Y}, A : D \to \Theta, H : \Theta \times \mathcal{X} \to \mathcal{Y}$$
$$(d, x, y) \in \mathcal{P}(S) \leftrightarrow (\exists \theta)[(\theta, x, y) \in H \wedge (d, \theta) \in A]$$
$$G : D \times \Theta \to V, E : V \times D \to \Theta$$
$$(d, G(\theta, d), \theta) \in E \leftrightarrow (d, \theta) \in A$$

where

$$x \in \mathcal{X}, y \in \mathcal{Y}, d \in D, \theta \in \Theta.$$

The algorithm A, data D, parameters Θ, consistency relations G and E, hypotheses H, input $\mathcal{X}$, and output $\mathcal{Y}$ are the component sets of S, and learning is specified in the relation among them.

Learning systems can be decomposed into two systems S_I and S_F. The inductive system $S_I \subset \times\{A, D, \Theta\}$ is responsible for inducing hypotheses from data. The functional system $S_F \subset \times\{\Theta, H, \mathcal{X}, \mathcal{Y}\}$ is the induced hypothesis. S_I and S_F are coupled by the parameter Θ. Learning is hardly a purely input-output process, however, and, to address this, the goal-seeking nature of S_I, and, more particularly, of A is specified. A is goal-seeking in that it makes use of a goal relation $G : D \times \Theta \to V$ that assigns a value $v \in V$ to data-parameter pairs, and a seeking relation $E : V \times D \to \Theta$ that assigns a parameter $\theta \in \Theta$ to data-value pairs. Again, note, these consistency relations G and E specify A, but are not a decomposition of A. Also note that D is specified as a subset of $\mathcal{X} \times \mathcal{Y}$ following convention, not necessity.

5   Stratification

In the following, the hierarchy of assumptions in this formulation of learning systems as well as the hierarchy it projects onto learning theory are investigated.

5.1   Levels in Abstract Learning Systems Theory

Each component set of a learning system can be modeled with considerable depth. But, when taking a top-down view, there are three key levels of abstraction implicit in Definition 1.

Elementary Level. The elementary level treats learning as an input-output system $S \subset \times\{D, \mathcal{X}, \mathcal{Y}\}$. Specifically, $S : D \times \mathcal{X} \to \mathcal{Y}$. This level is already sufficient to characterize a learning system in terms the fundamental properties that AST is built upon. For example, the *stability* of $S(D) : \mathcal{X} \to \mathcal{Y}$, whether $\mathcal{X}$ or D is *anticipatory* of $\mathcal{Y}$, or whether $S(D) : \mathcal{X} \to \mathcal{Y}$ is *controllable* by D. Also, this level admits consideration of the *composition* or *interaction* of S with other systems in its context. This level, however, is restricted to little more than the analysis of correlation between inputs and outputs.

Cascade Level. The cascade level treats learning as a cascade connection of input-output systems, particularly, a cascade connection of an inductive system S_I and the hypotheses it induces S_F, i.e., $S \subset \overline{S_I} \times \overline{S_F}$ where $S_I \subset \times\{A, D, \Theta\}$ and $S_F \subset \times\{\Theta, H, \mathcal{X}, \mathcal{Y}\}$. More specifically, $S \subset \times\{A, D, \Theta, H, \mathcal{X}, \mathcal{Y}\}$ where $A : D \to \Theta$ and $H : \Theta \times \mathcal{X} \to \mathcal{Y}$. Learning systems are still input-output systems, as at the elementary level, but now the model of learning distinguishes the inductive part as cascading into the functional part.

Goal-Seeking Level. The goal-seeking level treats learning as a cascade connection of a goal-seeking system and an input-output system. The inductive system is extended to specify its goal-seeking nature, i.e., $S_I \subset \times\{A, D, \Theta, G, E\}$ where $G : D \times \Theta \to V$ and $E : D \times V \to \Theta$. The explicit consideration of the

ALST Level	AST Diagram

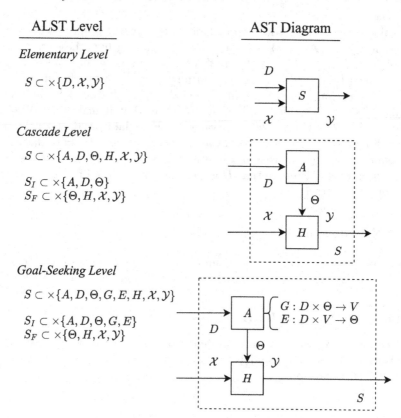

Elementary Level

$$S \subset \times\{D, \mathcal{X}, \mathcal{Y}\}$$

Cascade Level

$$S \subset \times\{A, D, \Theta, H, \mathcal{X}, \mathcal{Y}\}$$

$$S_I \subset \times\{A, D, \Theta\}$$
$$S_F \subset \times\{\Theta, H, \mathcal{X}, \mathcal{Y}\}$$

Goal-Seeking Level

$$S \subset \times\{A, D, \Theta, G, E, H, \mathcal{X}, \mathcal{Y}\}$$

$$S_I \subset \times\{A, D, \Theta, G, E\}$$
$$S_F \subset \times\{\Theta, H, \mathcal{X}, \mathcal{Y}\}$$

Fig. 3. The three stratified levels in terms of their component sets and block-diagrams.

goal-seeking nature of learning distinguishes this level from higher levels as it specifies that S_I is not decomposable into input-output systems. As such, this level acknowledges that the traditional engineering practice of engineering by aggregation, of following the mantra, "If the parts work, the whole will work", will not necessarily work for engineering learning.

5.2   Remarks on Levels

The goal-seeking level may seem in conflict with the higher levels of abstraction. It is not. At the elementary and cascade levels, learning is appropriately address-able as an input-output system. Such a view, of course, treats goal-seeking as a black-box. Unpacking the black-box, goal-seeking nature of learning can be done at a lower level of abstraction, but not without sacrificing the simplicity of learning as an elementary system or as a cascade of elementary systems (Fig. 3).

5.3   Projection of Levels onto Learning Theory

This stratification of learning systems projects a stratification onto the many concerns of learning theory. We demonstrate this using the 11 concerns listed in the right column of Fig. 4. In Fig. 4, the component sets of each level are associated with each of these learning theoretic concerns.

Elementary Level. The elementary level, concerning $D, \mathcal{X}$ and $\mathcal{Y}$, allows for the most general phenomena to be considered. Learning problems have a *hardness* associated with what the learning system is tasked to do given $\mathcal{X}$. If $\mathcal{X}$ are paths in a graph and $\mathcal{Y}$ is the longest path in the set of paths $\mathcal{X}$, then the learning problem is NP-complete. Given D in addition to $\mathcal{X}$ and $\mathcal{Y}$, the basic properties of *monotonicity* can be investigated and *information complexity* can be estimated, along with other basic considerations of *distribution*. Learning theory at the elementary level gives a sense of how hard a learning problem is and how much there is to learn, but no particulars regarding the inner-workings of the learning system itself.

Cascade Level. The cascade level introduces hypotheses H and its parameterization Θ, which gives a sense of the terms in which a learning system interprets the world, or at least gives a sense of the form of its explanations of worldly phenomena. Given H and Θ, notions of *falsifiability*, *flexibility*, and *capacity* can be considered. Falsifiability refers to whether the hypotheses are suited for scientific induction. Flexibility refers to the rate at which the relation between $\mathcal{X}$ and $\mathcal{Y}$ specified by $H(\Theta)$ can change when Θ is varied. And capacity refers to the variety with which a set of hypotheses can partition $\mathcal{X}$, i.e., capacity concerns how many different labelings of $\mathcal{X}$ by $\mathcal{Y}$ are possible using $H(\Theta)$. Additionally, at the cascade level, *sample complexity* can be modeled as a distribution-free property of hypotheses $H(\Theta)$ or, using distribution information from the elementary level, can be modeled as a property of hypotheses $H(\Theta)$ and the distribution over which they are induced. Capacity and sample complexity see particularly widespread use in learning theory. Some of the most important theorems concerning a learning systems ability to adapt to change are given in terms of sample complexity, capacity, and distributional divergence [3].

Goal-Seeking Level. Although the cascade level introduces the algorithm A, A is left as black-box. The goal-seeking level, however, allows for a detailed characterization of a learning systems goal-seeking nature. This includes some of the most common interests of learning theory, e.g., non-asymptotic *convergence*, i.e., whether a system can learn a function approximation in the short or medium term, and error, i.e., the similarity between the approximated function and the induced hypothesis. Convergence is a statement made using A, G, and E, as well as the hypotheses H and how they are parameterized by Θ. Error concerns the set of values V and the goal relation G that relates data D and parameters Θ to those values. And, knowing how the search problem is formulated via G and E, statements can be made on the *algorithmic complexity* of A.

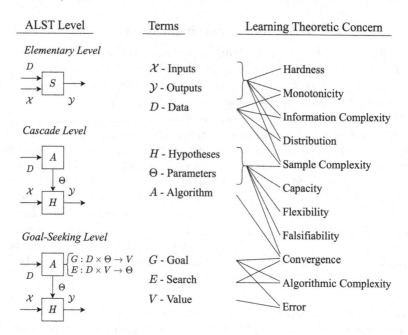

Fig. 4. The three stratified levels in terms of their block-diagrams, the additional component sets they consider, and the relationship between those component sets and learning theoretic concerns.

5.4   Remarks on Projection of Levels

While one can model learning directly using any individual or combination of the stratified component sets, there is always a systems theoretic structure implicit. By specifying that the hypotheses and error take a certain form, for example, one is also specifying, implicitly, something regarding $\mathcal{X}, \mathcal{Y}, \Theta, A$, and G.

Capacity as a cascade level notion is worth elaborating with a particular example. Bottou and Vapnik define a notion of local learning *algorithms* using capacity [4]. There, they define local algorithms as those that, "...attempt to locally adjust the capacity of the training system to the properties of the training set in each area of the input space." In ALST terms, local learning *systems* are those that, informed by D, adjust the capacity of $H(\Theta)$ during training in accordance with $\mathcal{X}$. Thus, local learning is a cascade level notion.

6   Scope

ALST provides a mechanism for scoping the field of view with which AGI is modeled. The scene of grey input-output systems horizontally surrounding the black input-output system S at the top of Fig. 5 depicts a learning system being contextualized by other system-level, input-output phenomena. The ability to scope a model of AGI outward into the AGI's context is inherited from AST.

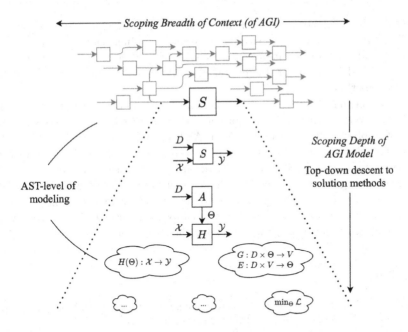

Fig. 5. A depiction of the horizontal and vertical scoping of models of AGI afforded by ALST.

The vertical descent in Fig. 5 from the input-output system S to the elementary level, then the cascade level, and so on, depicts the top-down scoping of depth in a model of AGI. This top-down descent from the general systems level towards solution methods is provided by ALST.

By stratifying learning systems with respect to the generality of their mathematical structure, learning systems can be specified at varying levels of abstraction. This can serve as a useful mechanism for engineering practice. A formal understanding of hierarchy allows for an ordering of design decisions, for the structuring of operational and mission performance models, and for modeling a learning system with various degrees of precision and uncertainty.

In engineering AGI, these are important capabilities. AGI solutions are overwhelmingly bottom-up, but the outcomes we associate with the success of AGI will occur at higher-levels of abstraction. And so, from the perspective of an engineer trying to build or use AGI towards satisfying the needs and goals of a stakeholder, the presented framework allows for the outcomes of AGI, the general characteristics of AGI, and the needs and goals of its stakeholders to be modeled in a common language and at a common level of abstraction.

7   Conclusion

The general systems theory approach to learning presented herein calls back to the principal concerns of AI's founding, with a perspective view on learning in favor of the thinking participants themselves, not the problems they solve. It does this by shifting from a view of learning as problem solving to a view of learning as a system. And, in doing so, it provides a means of mathematically characterizing learning in AGI in terms of its general phenomena—without explicit reference to solution methods.

In addition to stratification, AST offers a number of other promising uses for AI. AST is largely a theory of category, and thereby provides a non-conventional means of applying category to AI. Also, AST provides the foundational mathematics for efforts in model-based systems engineering and digital engineering. AST may be a means of connecting AI to large-scale, formal models of systems developed by engineers. Lastly, while 3 key, hierarchical levels were emphasized herein, there are also a variety of heterarchical relationships to explore. A top-down understanding of these varied relationships may serve well as a latticework about which to structure best practices for the engineering of AI.

References

1. Ahl, V., Allen, T.F., Allen, T.: Hierarchy Theory: A Vision, Vocabulary, and Epistemology. Columbia University Press, New York (1996)
2. Ashby, W.R.: An Introduction to Cybernetics. Chapman & Hall Ltd. (1961)
3. Ben-David, S., Blitzer, J., Crammer, K., Kulesza, A., Pereira, F., Vaughan, J.W.: A theory of learning from different domains. Mach. Learn. **79**(1), 151–175 (2010)
4. Bottou, L., Vapnik, V.: Local learning algorithms. Neural Comput. **4**(6), 888–900 (1992)
5. Chollet, F.: On the measure of intelligence. arXiv preprint arXiv:1911.01547 (2019)
6. Cody, T., Beling, P.A.: A systems theory of transfer learning. arXiv preprint arXiv:2107.01196 (2021)
7. Dori, D., et al.: System definition, system worldviews, and systemness characteristics. IEEE Systems Journal (2019)
8. Goertzel, B.: A formal model of cognitive synergy. In: Everitt, T., Goertzel, B., Potapov, A. (eds.) AGI 2017. LNCS (LNAI), vol. 10414, pp. 13–22. Springer, Cham (2017). https://doi.org/10.1007/978-3-319-63703-7_2
9. Lorenz, E.N.: Deterministic nonperiodic flow. J. Atmos. Sci. **20**(2), 130–141 (1963)
10. McCarthy, J., Minsky, M.L., Rochester, N., Shannon, C.E.: A proposal for the dartmouth summer research project on artificial intelligence, august 31, 1955. AI Mag. **27**(4), 12–12 (2006)
11. Mesarovic, M.D., Takahara, Y.: General Systems Theory: Mathematical Foundations, vol. 113. Academic Press, New York (1975)
12. Mesarovic, M.D., Takahara, Y.: Abstract systems theory (1989)
13. Rine, D.C.: A categorical characterization of general automata. Inf. Control **19**(1), 30–40 (1971)
14. Thórisson, K.R., Bieger, J., Thorarensen, T., Sigurðardóttir, J.S., Steunebrink, B.R.: Why artificial intelligence needs a task theory. In: Steunebrink, B., Wang, P., Goertzel, B. (eds.) AGI -2016. LNCS (LNAI), vol. 9782, pp. 118–128. Springer, Cham (2016). https://doi.org/10.1007/978-3-319-41649-6_12
15. Von Bertalanffy, L.: General system theory: foundations, development, applications (1969)

About the Intricacy of Tasks

Leonard M. Eberding[1][(✉)], Matteo Belenchia[1,3], Arash Sheikhlar[1],
and Kristinn R. Thórisson[1,2][(✉)]

[1] Center for Analysis and Design of Intelligent Agents, Reykjavík U., Menntavegur 1,
Reykjavík, Iceland
{leonard20,matteobel20,arash19,thorisson}@ru.is
[2] Icelandic Institute for Intelligent Machines, Reykjavík, Iceland
[3] University of Camerino, Via Andrea D'Accorso 16, Camerino, Italy

Abstract. Without a concrete measure of the "complicatedness" of
tasks that artificial agents can reliably perform, assessing progress in AI
is difficult. Only by providing evidence of progress towards more complicated tasks can developers aiming for general machine intelligence
(GMI) ascertain their progress towards that goal. No such measure for
this exists at present. In this work we propose a new measure of the
intricacy of tasks, especially designed to describe their physical composition and makeup. Our *intricacy* is a multi-dimensional measurement
that depends purely on objective physical properties of tasks and the
environment in which they are to be performed. From this task intricacy
measure, a relation to the knowledge of learners can allow calculation of
the difficulty of a particular task for a particular learner. The method is
intended for both narrow-AI and GMI-aspiring systems. Here we discuss
some of the implications of our intricacy measure and suggest ways in
which it may be used in AI research and system evaluation.

Keywords: Tasks · Environments · Intricacy · Difficulty · Task
theory · Artificial intelligence · General machine intelligence ·
Evaluation · Training

1 Introduction

To better understand tasks and their role in research in general machine intelligence (GMI), we have been deepening our understanding of tasks and environments in the past few years, with an aim of developing a theory of tasks
(cf. [5,15]). This research has highlighted the requirement for proper analysis
of tasks, including an objective measurement of a task's "complicatedness" or
convolutedness. By this – and only by this – the difficulty of a particular task for
a particular learning controller could be calculated, assuming that the difficulty
of a task is a function of the task-environment (TE) and the controller performing the task. In this paper we introduce such an objective measure, called the
intricacy of tasks, place it in the context of a causality-based task theory, and

© Springer Nature Switzerland AG 2022
B. Goertzel et al. (Eds.): AGI 2021, LNAI 13154, pp. 65–74, 2022.
https://doi.org/10.1007/978-3-030-93758-4_8

show the implications that such an intricacy measurement may have for progress in AI, and in particular, towards GMI.

Assuming there exist regularities in an agent's task-environment – which is a necessary requirement for any learning to be possible – these regularities can be expressed in the form of causal mechanisms. From these we may derive different measures of complexity[1] which can be used to calculate the level of intricacy of the task-environment. In past work we have described different complexity dimensions of tasks [14] and introduced an evaluation platform where these dimensions can be tuned by the analyst [7]. Our new approach to task intricacy is based on – and compatible with – this prior work.

The paper is structured as follows: In the first section we will show related work which indicates why such a measure of intricacy is of importance for AI research. Then we continue with causal principles of tasks as used to determine the level of intricacy of tasks. In the third section we place the intricacy measure in the context of agents and learning, describing its impact on the difficulty of tasks. Lastly we discuss the implications of this intricacy measure for AI, and conclude by listing some future work to be done using intricacy as a guide for better evaluation and AI system design.

2   Related Work

There exist different milestones in the history of artificial intelligence (AI) which were thought to have a decisive role in the research towards human-like, general machine intelligence (GMI). As the past has shown, most of these milestones did not necessarily lead towards more general AI systems. Solutions to the problems were rather more efficient and effective narrow AI systems. This discrepancy between expectations and actual results points towards the conclusion that the choosing of tasks for milestones might be flawed. The problem of choosing appropriate tasks for progress evaluation has been described before [1,5,7,9,14]. Each newly suggested milestone towards GMI systems can be argued against due to, for example, restricted context (Lovelace Test 2.0 [12]), human-centered approaches (e.g. Turing Test [17]), or too domain specific knowledge necessary for it (e.g. General Game Playing; cf. [13]).

One of the major evaluation platforms used nowadays – the Arcade Learning Environment (ALE) [4] – has been shown to have issues regarding the evaluation of progress of AI. Martínez-Plumed and Hernández-Orallo [10], for example, showed that some of the games of ALE do not indicate any progress towards better AI systems. This claim is supported by the findings of the developers of ALE: a brute-force tree search algorithm outperformed state of the art reinforcement learning algorithms in some of the games [4]. We argue here that the main reason for these problems is an insufficient understanding of the tasks themselves to fully understand the implications of agents solving different tasks. This coincides with the argument that tasks must be analyzed more thoroughly to

---

[1] With complexity we mean the intuitive concept as used in every-day language, not the concept as used in computer science.

support progress in the field of AI [8,9,15]. The SAGE (Simulator for Autonomy and Generality Evaluation) platform was developed particularly for this purpose and has shown the advantages a deeper insight into the task's complexity dimensions can have for the evaluator [7]. But again, there currently does not exist a measure of difficulty of the tasks presented to the agents and no measure of change in difficulty, if complexity dimensions are adjusted.

3   Causal Principles of Tasks

The aim of general machine intelligence (GMI) research is to create systems which are able to cope with highly complex worlds, like the physical world, and to be able to do a multitude of (unrelated) tasks in these highly complex environments. For this regularities of the world must be learned and knowledge about the environment accumulated. These regularities can be seen as 'mechanisms', representing functions which determine the value of effect-variables by using the values of cause variables. This knowledge of any learner is the result of a composition process, pieced together incrementally from experience with the world over time, accumulating in a semi-systematic way. This kind of learning is a constraint on any autonomous learner that doesn't have complete information at birth. If an agent is to learn independently, without help from teachers or some other source, its knowledge acquisition processes must be self-guided—it must have a capacity for *cumulative autonomous learning*. Achieving goals in the context of any phenomenon necessarily requires knowledge of causal relations, in particular of the causal relations that relate manipulatable and observable variables of the phenomenon to the goals of an assigned task. The existence of any causal relations between relevant variables must either be known by a performing agent or discovered by it in the process of performing a task.[2] These causal-relational models therefore are at the center of any task description. The intricacy measure introduced here relies specifically on these models using their interconnections as a measure of the "complicatedness".

Aside from the internal cause-effect-structures of the environment, the body of the agent, including sensors and actuators, must be taken into account. The noise that can take place when measuring/observing variables and interacting on them needs to be modeled in the causal structure of the tasks. Therefore, manipulatables and observables are treated differently to other internal variables of the environment. Variables which are theoretically measureable are the causal parents to the actually observed variable, which is used as input to the controller, and includes observation noise. Manipulatable variables of the environment, on the other hand, are causal children of the controller's chosen action (again, including the noise of actuators).

From the causal connections between causes and effects – as in "A leads to B" – causal relational models can be derived.[3] In the following sections we

---

[2] For a more detailed description of our understanding of causal knowledge and its implications see [3].

[3] While we take the non-axiomatic approach we still assume that the underlying environment follows certain rules, i.e. causal structures.

adapt the notion of such causal relational models for the purpose of obtaining an objective measure of a task's "complicatedness" (complication) based on this kind of models. This is the most fundamental assumption that we can make about any task-environment in which learning is possible: The assumption of the existence of causal relations—*AECR:* Only then, prediction, planning, and directed interventions are possible, and only then tasks can be executed at all.

3.1   Causal-Relational Models

Causal-relational models (CRMs) are representational construct for general learning. CRMs encode actionable information, in the sense that they can be used to get things done (taking action with foreseeable results), predicting future states, derive the causes of observed events, explain observed phenomena, and act as re-creation of the causal relation [16]. The kind of models that we are talking about are *causal-relational bi-directional* models, where by bi-directional is meant that they can be used in forward-chaining to produce predictions of future states and in backward-chaining to produce paths towards goals. By causal-relational is meant that they encode procedural (causal) knowledge, where the left-hand side (LHS) is a pattern representing the cause and the right-hand side (RHS) is a pattern representing the effect. The CRMs represent a relation between the two patterns such that we can forward- and backwardchain from causes to effects and vice versa. Additionally there exists a separate set of the required conditions under which the relation between LHS and RHS holds, thereby specifying in which situations a certain CRM is relevant. The RHS represents the post-conditions of the LHS pattern. In forward-chaining, when the LHS pattern is observed, a prediction based on the RHS can be generated by a process of deduction. In backward-chaining, when the RHS pattern is observed and it is a goal, a sub-goal based on the LHS can be generated. Sub-goals can be further backward-chained until a manipulatable variable is reached. This way models can be used to produce effective plans to achieve goals and help to analyze tasks for their inner causal structures including manipulatables, observables, goals, and sub-goals. Causal relational models are therefore ideal to be used as the underlying principles of intricacy. They describe the task fully, and give insight into what needs to be known by an agent to perform well in the task (i.e. observe the environment, do correct planning, and take actions to achieve a goal).

3.2   Causal Diagrams

A *task* can be described, from its designer's perspective,[4] as weakly-connected causal chains. When this is done, a task is reduced to a deterministic form that can be represented by the bi-directional models, capturing the whole task's dynamics. Additionally, inaccuracy of actions and measurements must be taken

---

[4] We assume that the "designer's perspective" includes a complete access and overview to a task's full set of variables.

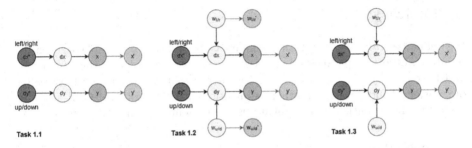

Fig. 1. Three examples of different levels of intricacy for similar tasks. Goals are to reach a certain X/Y position on a grid. The learning/performing agent can execute actions of moving left/right or up/down. Colors in all tasks: *Red:* actions as executed by the controller; *Green:* Observables as inputted to the controller (including observation noise, if applicable); *Blue:* Goal variables; *Grey:* Other variables. *Task 1.1:* Task of moving to a certain position in an open space; *Task 1.2:* Task of moving to a certain position with walls which can be seen; *Task 1.3:* Task of moving to a certain position with invisible walls. The level of intricacy rises from left to right. Colored arrows indicate transitions of data between controller and environment (Color figure online)

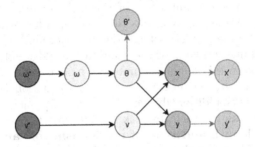

Fig. 2. Task 2: A more complex example of a task represented using causal-relational models. The goal is to reach a certain X/Y position. The environment is continuous rather than a grid and the agent has the control to either turn on the spot or move forward/ backward. Same color coding as in Fig. 1.

into account. Therefore, in this description of tasks, variables are not directly observable or manipulatable but instead a noisy causal child or parent acts as an observable or manipulatable, respectively. In Fig. 1 three similar tasks are shown. The task is to move to a certain goal position inside a grid-world. Figure 2 shows the same goal in a continuous world where a learning/performing agent can rotate on the spot or drive forward. Intuitively speaking, it is easy to describe the "complicatedness" of these four tasks. With larger causal relational model-networks this becomes a much harder problem. It is for this reason that we propose our measurement of *intricacy*.

4 Intricacy

We define the *intricacy* of a task as the measure of a task's "complexity" based purely on objective parameters. This way we can rank tasks by their intricacy and have an objective way to assess the progress of AI systems. Additionally, our notion of intricacy gives other implications for the design of GMI-aspiring systems. The definition and implications are presented in the following section.

4.1 Definition

Intricacy is an objective multi-dimensional measure consisting of the following physically-based, measurable properties of a task (ordered by their weight on the intricacy value):

1. **The minimal number of causal-relational models needed to represent the relations of the causal structure related to the goal(s).**
   This minimal number of models is an objective measure which depends solely on the particular specification of the task (inclusive of the controller's body), and captures all the relevant parts of the task proper, leaving out possibly unnecessary details and relations that are superfluous for the task. This means that, for example, tasks which contain superfluous variables and relations have the same intricacy of the same task abridged of all superfluities. The steps to obtain this minimal number of models entail the identification of all the relevant causal chains, turning them into relational models and then quantify them. This additionally means that a task's intricacy is dependent on the level of detail in which the task is performed.[5]

2. **The number, length and type of mechanisms of causal chains that affect observable variables on a causal path to at least one goal.**
   The three parameters of concern to this definition are (a) how many distinct causal chains there are, (b) how long are they in terms of number of variables involved and, (c) the complexity of the functions that define the mechanisms on these causal chains. As a measure for this dimension we suggest the Vapnik-Chervonenkis dimensions [6] or the Rademacher complexity [2], which includes the Vapnik-Chervonenkis dimension bound. (In the context of statistical learning, the class of functions with a lower Rademacher Complexity can be understood to be easier to learn.)

3. **The number of hidden confounders influencing causal structures related to the goal.**
   Other things being equal, hidden confounders should make the learning of previously described relational models of causal structures much harder. Therefore we include the number of unobservable variables influencing goal-related causal structures and chains in our intricacy measurement.

---

[5] For further information on the level of detail see [3]. How knowledge representation of the agent affects the intricacy by changing the level of detail is a problem that still needs to be addressed.

Table 1. The four different properties describing the intricacy of tasks for the given task examples from Figs. 1 and 2. As expected the results show, that the task in continuous space (Task 2) is the most, and the grid-task in an open space (Task 1.1) is the least intricate.

Task	Relational Mdl.	Causal Mech.	Confounders
1.1	2	2, linear	0
1.2	4	4, linear & non-linear	0
1.3	4	4, linear & non-linear	2
2	5	5, linear & non-linear	0

Intuitively, the intricacy of a task is a measure of what physical mechanisms are in place that need to be known by any intelligent being, whatever is its architecture, knowledge or capabilities, to perform the task in the given environment (inclusive of the controller's body). The task's intricacy is invariant on the initial values of the task's variables. From the definition of intricacy it follows that the higher the intricacy, the lower the size of the solution space[6] and vice versa.

Coming back to Figs. 1 and 2 we can now argue the different levels of intricacy of the four tasks (see Table 1). For simple tasks as shown in the two figures the level of intricacy is easy to determine intuitively. For more complex tasks such a measure, however, becomes more important due to its implications for the evaluation of AI systems.

To use this measure of intricacy for AI evaluation, or as a support in AI system design, it needs to be connected to the learning agent. For this we introduce the *effective intricacy*, which not only takes task features into account but also connects the task to the experience of the learner.

4.2 Effective Intricacy

The effective intricacy of a task is an agent-dependent version of intricacy, as defined above, where an agent's previously acquired knowledge that it brings to the task is taken into account. Effective intricacy is thus a measure of intricacy minus any intricacy that is known by the agent, and thus made irrelevant to the computation of difficulty. It uses almost the same properties of the task-environment as the intricacy measure. However, the effective intricacy only depends on **unknown** (to the agent) properties.

1. The minimal number of **unknown** causal-relational models needed to represent the causal relations related to the goal(s).
2. The number, length and type of **unknown** mechanisms of causal chains that affect observable variables on a causal path to at least one goal.
3. The number of **unknown**, neither directly, nor indirectly (through causal children) observable variables directly influencing the causal chain(s) between manipulatables and goal variables.

---

[6] For a more detailed view on the solution space of tasks see [3,15].

4.3   Difficulty

While effective intricacy represents the physical aspects of a task that are relevant to how difficult it may be for a particular agent, the difficulty of a task includes the agent's ability to learn relational models. Additionally, the precision of the agent's transducers and available resources – including time and energy – must be taken into account (especially if assuming the assumption of insufficient knowledge and resources (AIKR; [18])). Additive noise, for instance on observations and actions, can make a task more difficult. When actuators do not generate reliable interventions, or sensors reliable observations, the usage of causal models becomes more unreliable, making accidental mistakes possible. The difficulty D can therefore be expressed as the cross product of controller C and task-environment TE: $D = (C \times TE)$. Or more precisely the task's intricacy I, resources R, and transducer noise N_T: $D = (C \times I \times R \times N_T)$.

5   Learning and Performing

Aside from the possibilities an intricacy measure opens for AI evaluation, it also brings strong implications for other areas of AI research including the learning and doing of tasks, and the design of AI systems.

Learning a Task. The process of learning a task can be thought of as the search for relational models that can bring about a *satisficing* solution to the task. This search for models is driven by looking for associations in observable variables, finding which of these associations is of causal nature and growing the understanding of how each of these variables map onto the goal variables.

– By learning the causal structure of a task, a learner decreases the **effective intricacy**, since that knowledge allows it to find effective ways of controlling and achieving the goals. The more spurious associations are removed, the more useful the causal-relational models and thus, the lower the effective intricacy becomes.
– The importance of variables is revealed when the causal relations are discovered. Reciprocally, detecting the important variables enables the learner to find causal relations that are useful for performing a task and therefore reduces the effective intricacy.
– If a learner discovers all causal relations in the state space (without taking the importance of variables into account), changing the goals does not affect the effective intricacy, since the learner is already aware of how to conduct a new task within the same environment.
– When the learner is aware of the complete causal structure of a task, the deadline of the task and the energy required to perform it become the decisive measures for difficulty.
– When the learner knows all causal structures of the task-environment and has sufficient available resources, the only remaining part of the computed difficulty is the noise in the transducers.

Performing a Task. A good controller of a system (performer of a task) is one that already knows how to achieve the task under a range of environmental conditions. The agent's performance on the task allows us to draw conclusions on the effective intricacy, and the difficulty of the task.

- To a controller that performs a task perfectly repeatedly, the effective intricacy is zero.
- The higher the effective intricacy of a task – or the lower the amount of experience related to the task – the more difficult a task becomes to do, other things being equal.
- If the effective intricacy is equal to the task's intricacy an agent must rely on random interactions until it has learned enough, reducing the effective intricacy.

6 Conclusion

In this paper we introduced a new measurement to describe the "complicatedness" of tasks [3]. With our intricacy measure we are able to describe the effective intricacy, producing a concrete definition of task difficulty in relation to GMI-aspiring agents. We believe that through this measure, a more sophisticated choice for tasks to evaluate and compare AI systems is possible.

While we have provided evidence for the usage of this intricacy measure there still is work to be done to automatically calculate the intricacy of a wide variety of different tasks to evaluate the scalability and applicability of our approach. For this, the GMI aspiring system AERA (Autocatalytic Endogenous Reflective Architecture) [11] could be adapted, as it already provides the ability to extract causal relational models by interacting with the world. It could therefore be a good starting point for automatic intricacy calculation of more complex tasks. Another future idea would be to calculate the intricacy values of different tasks of the Arcade Learning Environment (ALE) and compare the results with the conclusions drawn by [10] using Item Response Theory (IRT) to determine the usefulness of different ALE tasks for progress evaluation.

From there we hope to be able to draw a connection between the intricacy of tasks, which an agent is able to solve, and the system's generality. This would provide researchers an additional measure of generality independent of the task-environments used for evaluation.

Acknowledgments. This work was supported in part by Cisco Systems, the Icelandic Institute for Intelligent Machines and Reykjavik University.

References

1. Adams, S., et al.: Mapping the landscape of human-level artificial general intelligence. AI Mag. **33**(1), 25–42 (2012)
2. Bartlett, P.L., Mendelson, S.: Rademacher and gaussian complexities: risk bounds and structural results. J. Mach. Learn. Res. **3**, 463–482 (2002)

3. Belenchia, M., Thórisson, K.R., Eberding, L.M., Sheikhlar, A.: Elements of task theory. In: Proceedings of the International Conference on Artificial General Intelligence. Springer (2021, in submission)
4. Bellemare, M.G., Naddaf, Y., Veness, J., Bowling, M.: The arcade learning environment: an evaluation platform for general agents (extended abstract). In: Proceedings of the International Joint Conference on Artificial Intelligence (IJCAI), pp. 4148–4152 (2015)
5. Bieger, J., Thórisson, K.R., Steunebrink, B.R., Thorarensen, T., Sigurdardóttir, J.S.: Evaluation of general-purpose artificial intelligence: Why, what & how. In: EGPAI 2016 - Evaluating General-Purpose A.I., Workshop held in conjuction with the European Conference on Artificial Intelligence (2016)
6. Blumer, A., Ehrenfeucht, A., Haussler, D., Warmuth, M.K.: Learnability and the vapnik-chervonenkis dimension. J. ACM (JACM) **36**(4), 929–965 (1989)
7. Eberding, L.M., Thórisson, K.R., Sheikhlar, A., Andrason, S.P.: SAGE: task-environment platform for evaluating a broad range of AI learners. In: Goertzel, B., Panov, A.I., Potapov, A., Yampolskiy, R. (eds.) AGI 2020. LNCS (LNAI), vol. 12177, pp. 72–82. Springer, Cham (2020). https://doi.org/10.1007/978-3-030-52152-3_8
8. Hernández-Orallo, J.: The Measure of all Minds: Evaluating natural and artificial intelligence. Cambridge University Press, Cambridge (2017)
9. Hernández-Orallo, J., et al.: A new ai evaluation cosmos: Ready to play the game? AI Mag. **38**(3), 66–69 (2017)
10. Martınez-Plumed, F., Hernández-Orallo, J.: Ai results for the atari 2600 games: difficulty and discrimination using irt. EGPAI, Evaluating General-Purpose Artificial Intelligence 33 (2016)
11. Nivel, E., et al.: Bounded recursive self-improvement (2013)
12. Riedl, M.O.: The lovelace 2.0 test of artificial creativity and intelligence. arXiv preprint arXiv:1410.6142 (2014)
13. Świechowski, M., Park, H., Mańdziuk, J., Kim, K.J.: Recent advances in general game playing. The Scientific World Journal 2015 (2015)
14. Thórisson, K.R., Bieger, J., Schiffel, S., Garrett, D.: Towards flexible task environments for comprehensive evaluation of artificial intelligent systems & automatic learners. In: Proceedings of the International Conference on Artificial General Intelligence, pp. 187–196 (2015)
15. Thórisson, K.R., Bieger, J., Thorarensen, T., Sigurðardóttir, J.S., Steunebrink, B.R.: Why artificial intelligence needs a task theory. In: Steunebrink, B., Wang, P., Goertzel, B. (eds.) AGI -2016. LNCS (LNAI), vol. 9782, pp. 118–128. Springer, Cham (2016). https://doi.org/10.1007/978-3-319-41649-6_12
16. Thórisson, K.R., Talbot, A.: Cumulative learning with causal-relational models. In: Iklé, M., Franz, A., Rzepka, R., Goertzel, B. (eds.) AGI 2018. LNCS (LNAI), vol. 10999, pp. 227–237. Springer, Cham (2018). https://doi.org/10.1007/978-3-319-97676-1_22
17. Turing, A.M.: I.-Computing machinery and intelligence. Mind LIX(236), 433–460 (10 1950). https://doi.org/10.1093/mind/LIX.236.433
18. Wang, P.: Rigid flexibility: The logic of intelligence. Springer Science, vol. 34 (2006)

Experiments on the Generalization of Machine Learning Algorithms

Arthur Franz$^{(\boxtimes)}$ (iD)

Odessa, Ukraine
af@occam.com.ua

Abstract. The inductive programming system WILLIAM is applied to machine learning tasks, in particular, centralization, outlier detection, linear regression, linear classification and decision tree classification. These examples appear as a special case of WILLIAM's general operation of trying to compress data without any special tuning.

Keywords: Inductive programming · Incremental compression · Algorithmic complexity · Machine learning · WILLIAM · Generalization

1 Introduction

Machine learning (ML) techniques and applications have revolutionized the world in recent decades, mostly promising to learn by themselves from data, as opposed to hand-crafted algorithms and feature detectors from earlier times. However, the term "learning", just as many other AI terms, has turned out to be euphemistic and exaggerating, referring mostly to parameter optimization within a fixed representation, and only vaguely related to human learning whose breadth and scope has remained unmatched. In the AGI context it therefore appears to be important to make machine learning truly general, thereby boosting its success even more.

Since various ML algorithms utilize different objective functions the first step is to identify a common optimization goal. Indeed, the minimum description length (MDL) principle has emerged to be a promising candidate [1, 7]:

> "The goal of statistical inference may be cast as trying to find regularity in the data. 'Regularity' may be identified with 'ability to compress.' MDL combines these two insights by viewing learning as data compression: it tells us that, for a given set of hypotheses $\mathcal{H}$ and data set $\mathcal{D}$, we should try to find the hypothesis or combination of hypotheses in $\mathcal{H}$ that compresses $\mathcal{D}$ most." (p. 8 in [1])

A. Franz—Independent researcher.

B. Goertzel et al. (Eds.): AGI 2021, LNAI 13154, pp. 75–85, 2022.
https://doi.org/10.1007/978-3-030-93758-4_9

Unfortunately, applications of MDL have been mostly limited to the selection of ML models and parameter numbers, including meta-parameter selection as in AutoML, failing to break out from a given representation space into a broader set of algorithmic data descriptions. The fact that such a widening could be important for the generalization of machine learning heading toward AGI has long been suggested by the father of algorithmic probability, Ray Solomonoff [8,9]. However, these suggestions did not go beyond theory, bringing forth a long-standing central problem for AGI: the difficulty of making inference both general and efficient. To the best of my knowledge, apart from the present paper, the only attempt of going beyond theory and realizing machine learning by means of a general compression algorithm was done just recently, using a novel set of techniques for computing lower bounds on algorithmic probability based on the Coding theorem and Block Decomposition methods [5].

This paper explores the abilities of WILLIAM [4] – an inductive programming method based on the theory of incremental compression (IC) [3] – to deal with a set of simple machine learning problems. In Sect. 2 a short overview of WILLIAM's novel aspects is given followed by the discussion of its application to data centralization, outlier detection, linear regression, linear classification and decision tree classification.

2   Overview of the Algorithm

WILLIAM's core functionality is given by an inductive programming algorithm already described in [4], albeit with several major improvements. Most importantly, the data representation has moved up from trees to directed acyclic graphs (DAGs), enabling the reuse of previously computed values. Further, the graph is bipartite (see figures below), consisting of operator nodes and value nodes (denoted by a box). Another innovation is the principle that any data used by the algorithm has to be computed by the algorithm itself. For example, even integers are not "given for free", except for the integer 1 (called *vacuum*), all other integers have to be computed using the given operators.

WILLIAM's main operation is to implement IC, i.e. given a data string x to find a description by a composition of functions, $x = f_1 (f_2 (\cdots f_s (r_s)))$, by searching for stacked autoencoders. In particular, for a given *residuum* r_{i-1} a pair of functions (f_i, f_i') is searched such that $r_{i-1} = f_i (r_i)$, where $r_i := f_i' (r_{i-1})$ and $l (f_i) + l (r_i) < l (r_{i-1})$, i.e. compression is achieved at every step ($x \equiv r_0$). The f_i are called *features* and f_i' *descriptive maps*. One of the main results is that the (prefix) Kolmogorov complexity $K(x)$ can be approximated in this way, when picking the shortest possible feature f_i^* at every step:

$$K (x) = \sum_{i=1}^{s} l (f_i^*) + K (r_s) + O (s \cdot \log l(x)) \tag{1}$$

In practice, in order to bound the search for descriptive maps, the shortest autoencoders, i.e. the shortest sum $l (f_i) + l (f_i')$ is searched, in compliance with computable IC (see Greedy-ALICE [3, Chapter 4.1]).

In order to apply the introduced notions to a DAG, a residual is represented by a *cross section*, defined as a set of value nodes separating the graph. The algorithm takes a set of operators and tries to attach them to the current residual cross section (=target cross section at start), computing new values on the way. Attaching nodes from above, i.e. using the residual in order to compute new values from it, corresponds to the descriptive map (e.g. len, getitem, urange and repeat operators in Figs. 3B and 1). Attaching nodes from below entails an inversion of the involved operators and corresponds to parts of a feature (e.g. setitem operator in Fig. 1). Cycles can be introduced in this way, but are removed once the graph is cut at its so-called *bottleneck*, defined as the shortest cross section. For example, the sum of description lengths (DLs) of the bottleneck nodes in Fig. 1 is smallest compared to all other possible cross sections. The cutting is performed as soon as the bottleneck has a lower DL than the current residual

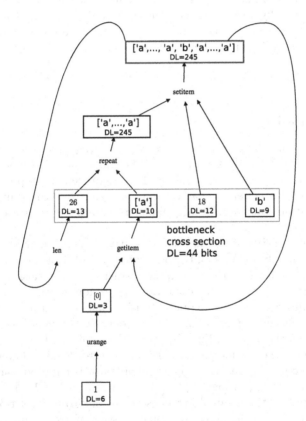

Fig. 1. The directed bipartite graph is cut at the most narrow cross section, called the bottleneck (red, DL = 44 bits), leading to the shortest description of the target cross section (blue, DL = 251 bits). The descriptive map, i.e. the graph from target to bottleneck containing the len, getitem and urange operators are removed. The result is displayed in Fig. 3C. DL denotes the default description length defined in paragraph *Default descriptions*. (Color figure online)

(the blue nodes in Fig. 1). At this point the bottleneck becomes the new residual and the algorithm continues iterating ad infinitum. Additionally, values in nodes can be replaced by other values in other nodes and propagated through the graph (see e.g. Fig. 4F-H). The search for the shortest compressing autoencoder in this way is exhaustive, i.e. all directed graphs are being constructed ordered by their size, even though only those combinations leading to the solution are shown in the figures.

Default Descriptions. A positive integer $n \in \mathbb{N}$ is described by the Elias delta code [2]. The length $l(n)$ of the (default) description is given by $E(n) = \lfloor \log_2(n) \rfloor + 2 \lfloor \log_2 (\lfloor \log_2(n) \rfloor + 1) \rfloor + 1$ bits. Including zero and negatives, an integer $n \in \mathbb{Z}$ has DL $l(n) = E(2|n|+1)$. Rational numbers x are described by a pair of mantissa $m \in \mathbb{Z}$ and exponent $a \in \mathbb{Z}$, $x = m \cdot 10^a$. Chars take the fixed amount of 8 bits relating to the ASCII table. Strings s carry the DL $l(s) = E(|s|) + 8|s|$ by describing their length $|s|$ and then each char separately. Similarly, for arrays, lists, tuples and sets their lengths are described following the elementwise description of their contents.

3   Results

3.1   Centralization

Consider a set of one-dimensional data, $x = \{x_1, \ldots, x_n\}$ sampled from a Gaussian $X \sim \mathcal{N}(\mu, \sigma)$. Centralization refers to the subtraction of the sample mean $\hat{x} = \frac{1}{n} \sum_{i=1}^{n} x_i$ from every x_i: $x_i' = x_i - \hat{x}$. This preprocessing step is meaningful if $\sigma \ll \mu$, i.e. the cluster center is a large number relative to the standard deviation. Centralization transforms n large numbers x_i into one large number $\hat{x}$ and n small numbers x_i'.

This example consists of the target cross section x being an array of $n = 1000$ i.i.d. samples taken from $\mathcal{N}(143, 1)$ and a precision of 4 decimals (Fig. 2). As described Sect. 2, all sorts of operators are attached to the target from above and from below, leading to the computation of the sample mean $\langle x \rangle$ in Fig. 2A, followed by an inversion of the add operator using that target x and the just computed mean $\langle x \rangle$, i.e. the "error" is $E = x - \langle x \rangle$ (denoting elementwise subtraction of $\langle x \rangle \approx 143$ from the array x, Fig. 2B). Since the significand of the entries in x have 7 digits and the error merely 4 the DL of the error is much lower than that of the target, $l(E) \ll l(x)$. Finally, the mean operator is removed since it is part of the descriptive map (during bottleneck cutting as in Fig. 1). It was merely helpful in computing the residual but does not belong to the description of the target (Fig. 2C). The residual cross section consisting of one big number $\langle x \rangle$ and n smaller numbers $x - \langle x \rangle$ is shorter, i.e. compression has been achieved.

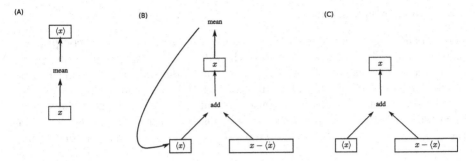

Fig. 2. Data centralization $x \to x - \langle x \rangle$ performed by WILLIAM, shown as a series of operators attached to target data array x.

3.2 Outlier Detection

Figure 3 shows a target cross section consisting of a list of 25 chars 'a' and a single char 'b' at index 18 in the first value node, and the number 1 in the second value node, also called *vacuum* node, since it is merely a helper node and not to be compressed. The final residuum consists of leaves in Fig. 3C, i.e. the value nodes 1, 26, 'a', 18 and 'b'. Since the residuum's DL is shorter than that of the target (see also Fig. 1), compression has been achieved and the outlier 'b' has been filtered out. Note how the description of the data becomes meaningful and interpretable after proper compression: a verbal description of the target as "a list with length 26 consisting of letters 'a' with a letter 'b' at index 18" corresponds to the retrieved leaf values.

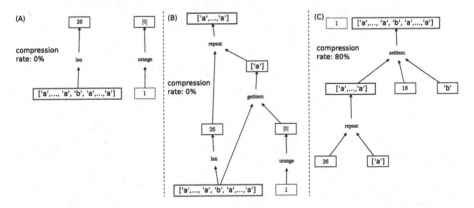

Fig. 3. Outlier detection. (A) and (B) show how various operators are applied to the blue target cross section, leading to a "cleaned" list consisting of chars 'a' only. (C) The cleaned list is used to invert operator **setitem** yielding the index 18 and thar char 'b'. (Color figure online)

3.3   Linear Regression

Figure 4 shows how the target cross section consisting of x and y is compressed incrementally. Through a series of steps the value nodes of the target x and y are connected, hence instead of both being described independently y is described in terms of x which reduces the DL. Subplots (A)–(D) show how the numbers 1, 2, 4 and 16 are subtracted from y in order to centralize the data. As we have seen in Subsect. 3.1, this process leads to compression: the residual is shorter than the target $l\,(2x + 2 + \epsilon) + l\,(16.0) + l\,(x) < l\,(y) + l\,(x)$. x is also a leaf, describing

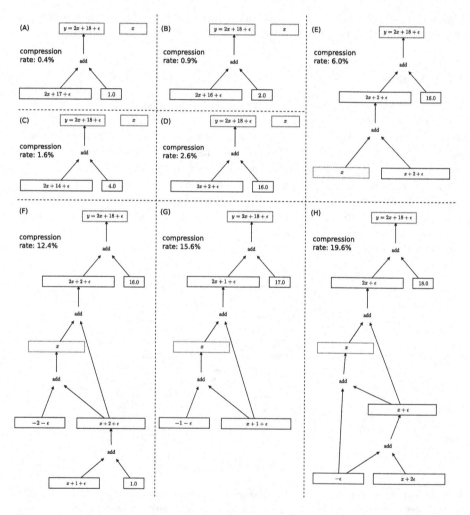

Fig. 4. Linear regression performed by WILLIAM. x is an array of length $n = 1000$ with values ranging between -10 and 10 in steps of 0.2, ϵ is an array of n i.i.d. samples from the standard normal distribution $\mathcal{N}\,(0, 1)$ and y given by $2x + 18 + \epsilon$ (see Fig. 7A). The target is incrementally compressed.

"itself", neglecting the comparatively short description of the operators. Note that there is no specialized optimization involved here. The numbers 1, 2, 4 and 16 are computed by using the add-operator applied to the existing value nodes, e.g. 16 = add(8, 8), starting with the vacuum 1 (not shown in the figure). Subplot (E) uses the value node x and subtracts it from the residual node $2x + 2 + \epsilon$. Overall the residual cross section (leaves) is shorter than the previous residual: $l(x) + l(x + 2 + \epsilon) + l(16.0) < l(2x + 2 + \epsilon) + l(16.0) + l(x)$. Subplot (F) shows that the target node x is compressed further by subtracting it from the $x + 2 + \epsilon$ node. Note that x and y are treated completely equally as target nodes that are to be compressed. There is no special meaning of "dependent" and "independent" variables involved here as usually in regression tasks. Subplots (G) and (H) achieve even more compression by replacing 16 to 17 to 18 and propagating this change through the graph. Figure 7A visualizes how the various estimates (red dashed lines) incrementally fit the data. These estimates are obtained by setting all leaf arrays (= "errors") to 0.

3.4   Linear Classification

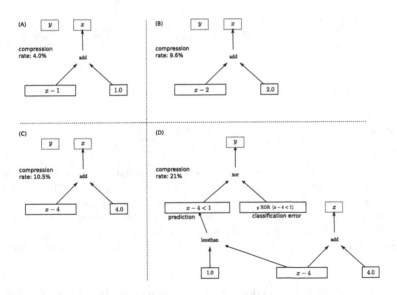

Fig. 5. Classification performed by WILLIAM. y is an array of 2 classes, True and False, color coded in Fig. 7B. x is an array of i.i.d. samples taken from $\mathcal{N}(3.5, 1)$ for class True and from $\mathcal{N}(6.5, 1)$ for class False.

Figure 5 shows how an array of data x is "fitted" the array of classes y (see Fig. 7B for the distribution of x). As before, subplots (A)–(C) centralize x. In (D) a prediction $p = (x - 4 < 1)$ is generated and subtracted from the class array by the elementwise xor-operator. Compression is achieved due to the fact that the error y XOR p contains True values only if the prediction goes wrong, i.e. a few times in a good classifier. A boolean array with significantly fewer True than False values has a shorter description than an array with a balanced number of True's and False's, due to the following reason. There are $\binom{n}{k}$ ways of distributing k True's in an array of length n hence providing an index i of the permutation together with k and n constitutes a full description of the array. This permutation-based method is part of the default descriptions in WILLIAM. In sum, compression in classification is achieved by replacing array of classes y containing a balanced number of True's and False's by an unbalanced error array having a shorter description.[1]

3.5   Decision Tree Classification

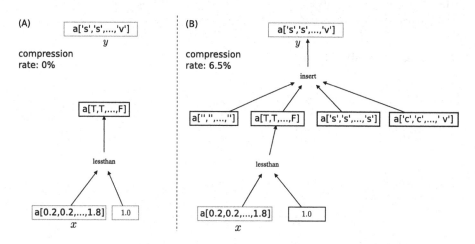

Fig. 6. A first step of decision tree classification. The data is taken from Python's scikit-learn Iris Dataset of three different types of flowers, see Fig. 7C. The target cross section (blue) consists of the flower classes setosa ('s'), versicolour ('v'), and virginica ('c') in array y. The a[...] notation stands for arrays. The float array x denotes the petal width factor. By applying the threshold 1.0 the setosa types (leaf a['s', 's'...,'s']) are separated from the other two types (leaf a['c', 'c',...,'v']). (Color figure online)

Figure 6 shows the first step in decision tree classification. In subplot (A), lessthan creates a boolean array denoting petal widths smaller than 1. In subplot (B) the insert-operator is inverted: it inserts the array a['s', 's'..., 's'] into array a[",...,"] of empty strings at the indices denoted by the boolen array a[T,T...,F]. The remaining indices are filled by a['c', 'c',..., 'v']. As can be glanced from Fig. 7C all setosa flowers have petal width <1 and all the others have petal width ≥1. Therefore, setosa is separated from the rest by this decision tree step. This constitutes compression since the original target y consists of all three types of flowers and the

---

[1] It can be shown that $l\left(\binom{n}{k}\right) + l(k) + l(n) < n$ if $k \ll n$.

permutation-based description is therefore longer due to the larger multinomial coefficient $\binom{n}{k_1\,k_2}$ as compared to two types of flowers in a['c', 'c',...,'v'] and a single type in a['s', 's'...,'s']. Here only the first decision tree separation is shown but it can be continued using other factors to separate the a['c', 'c',...,'v'] array. Note that neither the Gini coefficient nor any other particularities of decision tree classification are used to perform this "training" step. There is no need for measuring the dispersion of values by the Gini coefficient since the permutation-based code automatically becomes shorter if there are fewer different classes present in an array and/or the classes are not represented uniformly.

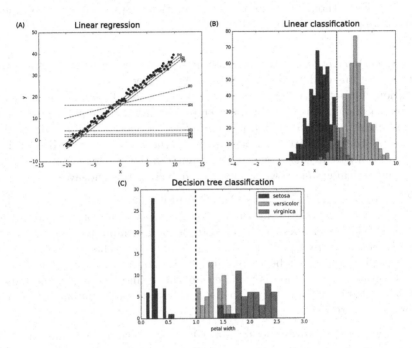

Fig. 7. (A) Estimates (red dashed lines) incrementally fit the linear regression data (the letters (A)–(H) correspond the subplots of Fig. 4). (B–C) Distribution of data for classification, the class is color coded. (Color figure online)

Discussion

In this paper we have demonstrated that various machine learning algorithms can be viewed as performing data compression as has been suggested previously in theory. In particular, their core functionality emerges as a special case of WILLIAM's general performance without being specifically tuned to these algorithms. WILLIAM neither uses any specialized ML optimization nor any other heuristics for that matter and is developed in a fully general fashion according to IC theory. This generality enables WILLIAM to deal a wide range of tasks beyond machine learning, as reported in [4]. Nevertheless, these examples had to be rather simple mainly due to the following limitations.

Limitations

Accumulation of description overhead Since IC proceeds greedily, there is no mechanism for avoiding the accumulation of overhead, as discussed in [3]. In particular, Eq. (1) entails an overhead of the order $O\left(s \cdot \log l(x)\right)$ where s is the number of compression steps. For example, in the regression case, nothing hinders the algorithm from keeping subtracting 1 from the target array achieving some compression at every step. Currently, such values are being replaced by newly generated values and propagated through the graph (see Fig. 4F–H, where the value 16 is replaced by 17, since 17 has been previously generated by add(16,1)). Even though this propagation solution helps combat the overhead accumulation, it would be helpful to have theoretical guarantees for avoiding overhead altogether.

Alternative Descriptions. In many cases, it is desirable to consider alternative short descriptions of data. IC theory only shows how to search for *some* short description, but not for several ones. One option is to search for many incremental strands in parallel which would however put additional computational strain on performance. A different option is to allow the lack of progress in further compressing the first short description to guide the search for other descriptions – a strategy apparently used by problem solving in the psychology of insight [6]. Again, theoretical guidance would be of great help in this endeavor.

No Reuse of Successful Functions. An important way of accelerating the algorithm is to reuse successful, i.e. compressing combinations of operators. Currently, a DAG of operators can be used to define a composite operator, which can be inserted an used just like a primitive operator. This makes our graph a hypergraph – there can be graphs inside the nodes. However, it is unclear which subgraph of a solution is to be encapsulated and how it is to be reused. Essentially, this issue comes down to the non-trivial task of finding a theory of memory and its retrieval.

Computing Power and Parallelization. On a positive note, while thinking through many tasks over the last years, it appears that most interesting tasks do not appear to demand steps requiring deeper graphs than 6 or 7 operators until some compression is achieved. Currently, WILLIAM manages to search exhaustively through graphs of depth 4–5 running on pure Python code. Rewriting core parts on a faster language in the back end and parallelization could boost the performance considerably.

Conclusion

If the discussed limitations can be overcome both in theory and practice the results show a promising path to create a general algorithm for solving machine learning problems and going beyond them.

References

1. Grünwald, P.D., Myung, I.J., Pitt, M.A.: Advances in Minimum Description Length: Theory and Applications. MIT press, New York (2005)
2. Elias, P.: Universal codeword sets and representations of the integers. IEEE Trans. Inf. Theory **21**(2), 194–203 (1975)
3. Franz, A., Antonenko, O., Soletskyi, R.: A theory of incremental compression. Inf. Sci. **547**, 28–48 (2021)
4. Franz, A., Gogulya, V., Löffler, M.: WILLIAM: a monolithic approach to AGI. In: Hammer, P., Agrawal, P., Goertzel, B., Iklé, M. (eds.) WILLIAM: A monolithic approach to AGI. LNCS (LNAI), vol. 11654, pp. 44–58. Springer, Cham (2019). https://doi.org/10.1007/978-3-030-27005-6_5
5. Hernández-Orozco, S., Zenil, H., Riedel, J., Uccello, A., Kiani, N.A., Tegnér, J.: Algorithmic probability-guided machine learning on non-differentiable spaces. Front. Artif. Intell. **3** (2020)
6. Kaplan, C.A., Simon, H.A.: In search of insight. Cogn. Psychol. **22**(3), 374–419 (1990)
7. Potapov, A.: Raspoznavanie obrazov i mashinnoe vospriatie. Politechnica (2007). See https://pureportal.spbu.ru/en/publications
8. Solomonoff, R.: A system for machine learning based on algorithmic probability. In: IEEE International Conference on Systems, Man and Cybernetics Conference Proceedings, pp. 298–299 vol. 1 (1989)
9. Solomonoff, R.: Algorithmic probability, heuristic programming and AGI. Adv. Intell. Syst. Res. **10**, 151–157 (2010)

Parsing Using a Grammar of Word Association Vectors

Robert John Freeman[✉][ID]

EasyChair, Sydney, Australia
rob@chaoticlanguage.com

Abstract. This paper was first drafted in 2001 as a formalization of the system described in U.S. patent U.S. 7,392,174. It describes a system for implementing a parser based on a kind of cross-product over vectors of contextually similar words. It is being published now in response to nascent interest in vector combination models of syntax and semantics. The method used aggressive substitution of contextually similar words and word groups to enable product vectors to stay in the same space as their operands and make entire sentences comparable syntactically, and potentially semantically. The vectors generated had sufficient representational strength to generate parse trees at least comparable with contemporary symbolic parsers.

1 Motivation

1.1 Basic Intuition

The basic intuition underlying our formalisation is that a word can be characterised by enumerating words that occur in similar contexts, e.g. Menno van Zaanen [21] attributes to Harris [4] the "notion of interchangeability":

constituents of the same type can be replaced by each other

There are variations on this (c.f. if constituents are not of the same type they involve a change of meaning and cannot be replaced), but it involves a comparison, and we will refer to it in general as the "contrastive method".

This intuition is implicitly present in almost all linguistic classifications. E.g. the definition of a part of speech such as *determiners* is based on the observation that there is a group of words that exhibit similar behaviour in a range of contexts:

- preceeding {"cat", "dog", "car", "wardrobe"...}
- preceeding {"big", "small", "blue", "bright"...}
- following {"take", "put", "see"...}
- ...

Of course, in the traditional way of classifying language units such observations are followed by very strong generalisations. But is this reasonable?

B. Goertzel et al. (Eds.): AGI 2021, LNAI 13154, pp. 86–95, 2022.
https://doi.org/10.1007/978-3-030-93758-4_10

1.2 Idiosyncratic Usage

A strong theme in linguistics for many years has been the idiosyncrasy of language use defying classification. For an example which appears to date to Halliday [6], "strong" and "powerful" can be used interchangeably in many contexts, but not in the context of "tea", viz. "strong tea"/"*powerful tea". Pawley and Syder [5] present long lists of examples which defy codification in rules under the title of "native-like selection", which they characterize as a "puzzle" for linguistics.

In fact the Applied Linguistics literature is full of observations that language appears to have no rules without exceptions, and indeed in some senses to consist of exceptions only. Nattinger [18], Weinert [20], and Lewis [17] provide a sampling, reaching an extreme with Lewis's "Lexical Approach".

This is addressed less often in a machine learning context, but even here Dagan, Marcus, Markovitch note, Dagan [3]:

> It has been traditionally assumed that ... information about words should be generalized using word classes... However, it was never clearly shown that unrestricted language is indeed structured in accordance with this assumption.

1.3 The Phoneme

But we can go further than the lack of proof noted by Dagan et al. It was shown not to be so. In fact, you could characterize this is as the central dilemma of linguistics for the last 50 years. It is behind the major divisions which have characterized the subject during that time. Put more strongly, what we find when we try to abstract language structure from observation is that it contradicts itself. And this was shown to be so a long time ago for the first category, and great success of the contrastive method, the phoneme.

The crisis was catalysed by the polarizing figure of 20th century linguistic theory, Noam Chomsky. Chomsky brought a fresh perspective to many issues in linguistics, but while it has been largely forgotten it is fair to say his attack on the phoneme was one of the most important at the time. E.g. Hill [15]:

> I could stay with the Transformationalists pretty well, until they attacked my darling, the phoneme.

Contrastive methods along the lines attributed to Harris above were the standard method of linguistic analysis. The phoneme was the major success of the method. Chomsky pointed out that these contrastive methods led to contradictory results, and linguistics shattered. As Newmeyer [19] says while discussing Chomsky's Logical Basis of Linguistic Theory [1]

> Part of the discussion of phonology in 'LBLT' is directed towards showing that the conditions that were supposed to define a phonemic representation (including complementary distribution, locally determined biuniqueness, linearity, etc.) were inconsistent or incoherent in some cases and led to (or at least allowed) absurd analyses in others.

So abstracting language categories from observation led to "inconsistent or incoherent ... analyses". Or equivalently that elements of language combine non-linearly. Lamb [12] says of Chomsky:

> He correctly pointed out that the usual solution incorporates a loss of generality, but he misdiagnosed the problem. The problem was the criterion of linearity.

See also Lamb 1966 [9], Lamb 1967 [8], Lamb 1976 [10], Lamb 1998 [11].

1.4   The (Very) Short History of Machine Learning in Theoretical Linguistics

This was shown to be the case for the phoneme, but it was not seriously contested for other categories. The contrastive method never got beyond the phoneme. Instead linguistics moved beyond abstraction of categories by contrastive analysis, fragmenting into schools which on the one hand continued to respect contrastive analysis but rejected structure as a meaningful parameter, like Functionalism, or on the other hand continued to respect language structure, but rejected the idea it could be learned from observations, Generativism. Generativism hypothesized that the contradictions observed when you tried to abstract categories from observations were not relevant to the system of language at all. It was still assumed structure was relevant, and objective, but because learnable categories had been observed to contradict (among other reasons), structure was assumed to be innate.

Unfortunately, having split the field, this key issue of contradictions in learnable categories was largely forgotten and unavailable to those outside linguistics seeking insights. So when rapid developments in computing made large amounts of data available, non-linguists started trying to learn from it. Non-linguists in the main, because to reiterate, theoretical linguistics had already split into schools which assumed language structure was unlearnable, or irrelevant, making the issue disappear. It is ironic that for this very reason the non-linguists perhaps felt linguistics was irrelevant and ignored it, in its turn, because it did not address the issue which interested them viz. learning categories from observable data.

1.5   Contradiction in Language Categories

This then is our motivation for seeking to model grammar as a vector product of word similarity vectors, most forcefully that abstractions from observations were shown to lead to contradictions, or in the case of Lamb "non-linearity". That this is so is actually a rare point of agreement in theoretical linguistics, it is only interpretations which have varied: Universal Grammar, Functionalism, Cognitivism.

Unfortunately for a rare point of agreement in linguistics, it is widely ignored. Notably it appears to be ignored in the field of machine learning. It might be seen to render the entire field of grammatical induction moot.

Chomsky concluded that if a coherent language structure could not be learned from observations, then it must be innate. Functionalists (and various schools of Cognitivism) concluded it was irrelevant. But unlearnable need not mean innate or irrelevant. It may simply mean generalizations can only be ad-hoc. We have a better understanding of complexity in formal systems now. Unlearnable, random (in a specific technical sense e.g. Kolmogorov [7], Chaitin [2]), or even chaotic, systems are starting to seem more like the norm. As far as the author is aware these kinds of complexity issues were first suggested, at least in the context of computational solutions, in an earlier discussion of the motivations surrounding this parser in Freeman 2000 [14]. But it is possible to find similar ideas in linguistics, notably Hopper's Emergent Grammar 1987 [16]:

> The notion of emergence is a pregnant one. It is not intended to be a standard sense of origins or genealogy, not a historical question of 'how' the grammar came to be the way it 'is', but instead it takes the adjective emergent seriously as a continual movement towards structure, a postponement or 'deferral' of structure, a view of structure as always provisional, always negotiable, and in fact as epiphenomenal, that is at least as much an effect as a cause.

Possibly Lamb's "non-linearity" is the same.

As suggested in that 2000 paper, this ad-hoc character should by no means be regarded as a bad thing. Rather it hints at a far greater richness of structure available to language.

2   Formalization

According to the method of this paper then, in order to prevent relevant information from being lost in the task of modelling natural language, we need a concept of overlapping classes that can be constructed, ad-hoc, on the fly as opposed to having to be pre-defined.

2.1   Similarity

Thus we stop at the primary observation that "word w is similar to the words $w_1, ..., w_k$ because it appears in similar contexts" and treat $w, w_1, ..., w_k$ as class label for w.

To put this more formally, we need to define two things: what is actually a context and what *similar contexts* means. A simple initial approximation to the former question is to define the context of a word (or word group) w as the set of all word pairs w', w'' such that there is at least one occurence of the triplet w', w, w'' in the available corpus.

$$Con(w) := \{(w', w'') : \exists i : X_i = w', X_{i+1} = w, X_{i+2} = w''\}$$

Now the similarity of two words w and w' can be measured by the percentage of common contexts relative to all contexts they appear in. Dekang Lin provides a principled measure [13]:

$$sim(w, w') := \frac{2 \times I(Con(w) \cap Con(w'))}{I(Con(w)) + I(Con(w'))}$$

Where I is the information.

With the two definitions formulated above, the class a word belongs to can be defined as a set of similarity values between words as below. For convenience we limit the set to include only words similar beyond a threshold C:

$$class(w) := \{w' : sim(w, w') > C\}$$

e.g. A segment from the entry from "somewhat" estimated for one of our corpora is:

```
somewhat {somewhat,1 significantly,0.047 slightly,0.043
considerably,0.036 substantially,0.025 far,0.025 a&lot,0.024
more&and,0.024 one&or,0.024 much,0.022 becoming,0.021
likely&to&be,0.021 a&little,0.02 considered,0.018 nothing,0.017
rather,0.017 so&much,0.016 relatively,0.016 something,0.015
certainly,0.014 quite,0.014 generally,0.014 getting,0.014 still,0.012
therefore,0.011 done,0.011 often,0.011 of&course,0.01 even,0.0097
very,0.0083 always,0.0082 a&very,0.008 once,0.0073
further,0.0072 little,0.0071 less,0.007 really,0.0066...}
```

Where the vector is made up of a set of (word, score) pairs, and the score is the value of the chosen similarity function between the pair "somewhat" and the other words in the vocabulary.

For practical reasons it is more convenient to represent the class of word w as a vector of real numbers, each representing the similarity of a vocabulary word to w. So if $w_1, ..., w_N$ is the vocabulary of our language, then the class of w is defined by the following function ϕ:

$$\phi(w) := (\phi_1(w), ..., \phi_N(w))$$

2.2   Application to Trees

We now extend the formalization to estimate representations for potentially unobserved sequences of words. We say "potentially" unobserved, because the sequences may in fact be observed, however we seek to extend the representation in the absence of observation. Essentially we seek to represent syntax, specifying which new combinations of words are acceptable to the language.

We will call these potentially unobserved sequences t for "trees", because the formula is non-associative. Different orders give different products, so the product has structure, like a tree. This can be seen as an advantage of the method, it predicts phrase structure.

In the vector formulation, we have a vocabulary V: $w_1, ..., w_N$ of words and word sequences. Let the function $\delta(i, j) \rightarrow \{0, ..., N\}$ map a pair of elements in V to another entry in V. Simply put, let it map a pair into an entry for the pair together, if they are observed to occur together ($\delta(i, j) = 0$ means that no such entry exists, i.e. i and j are not observed to occur together.)

Formally, the extension of the word class function to binary trees is defined recursively, if t is a word, then $\phi_i(t)$ reduces to $sim(t, w_i)$, if t is a binary tree consisting of subtrees t_1 and t_2, then we define the components of a new vector representing the combination of trees to be:

$$\phi_k(t) := \sum_{i,j} MI(w_i, w_j) \cdot \phi_i(t_1) \cdot \phi_j(t_2) \cdot \phi_k(\delta(i, j))$$

In words: if a pair of words between the components of the operand trees are observed to occur together ($\delta(i, j) \neq 0$), the components for their observed combination ($\phi_k(\delta(i, j))$) contribute to a new component for the combination of the operand trees ($\phi_k(t)$.) Note: MI is the common "mutual information" between two words occurring in sequence, which was used in this case to scale the significance of an observed pairing. We in no way regard this choice as exhaustive or exclusive. In much the same way as the similarity measure described in Sect. 2.1 above, many scalar association measures might be considered.

Essentially we seek to generate product vectors by an aggressive substitution of contextually similar words and word groups (all the $\phi_k(\delta(i, j))$).

2.3 Scoring a "Parse"

It was assumed that at each stage of association the most grammatical grouping would generate the greatest number or greatest concentration of grammatically similar elements, and an order of association, branching, or the best phrase structure tree, was selected on that basis. Broadly speaking, for each order of association of words t the greatest of:

$$max\{\sum_k \phi_k(t)\}$$

It can be seen as a kind of energy maximum clustering for the path of branching which resulted in the largest substitution groupings.

Selection of a pair as a parse was not based on pairwise co-occurrence of the pair itself, but looking outside the pair, at its context, and counting the number of substitution groupings which could be made for that pair, in that context. It was based on the extent to which a pair could be substituted for by other sequences, as observed in a corpus, and especially the extent to which it could be substituted for by single words.

What was new to the method was not the use of such substitution groupings, however. Such substitution groupings can actually be seen as somewhat standard in machine learning of grammar, indeed dating back to the "notion of interchangeability" attributed to Harris, earlier, which was applied with such early success to the phoneme. What was different with the vector parser was the assumption that such groupings needed to be generated anew for each new sentence presented to the system. That such groupings might be an expansion rather than a compression of structure in a corpus.

It is that such substitution groupings might need to be seen as an expansion, rather than a compression as hitherto assumed in the history of machine learning, which is the central conjecture of this paper.

The vector parser was an early attempt at an implementation of that central conjecture.

More detail, and actual segments of early code, can be found in the technical specification for patent US7392174B2.

3   Discussion

The system described in Sect. 2 was the vector parser system as originally formulated between 1998–2001. It was not picked up at the time, although tests were done comparing performance quantitatively for the task of parsing Chinese in 2003. We hope to present these results in a later paper. In general the parser performed on a level comparable with a contemporary symbolic parser, but not greatly better (see Appendix for a sample of results.)

It now seems apparent that while classes are not abstracted until runtime in this formulation, important details are lost when word similarity is assessed. Not only class, but similarity between words can, and typically does, vary between contexts. What is needed are vectors of contexts, not similarity based on context.

This should be a fruitful direction for further investigation.

However the method of generating product vectors by an aggressive substitution of contextually similar words and word groups (all the $\phi_k(\delta(i,j))$ above) was quite successful. It enables product vectors to stay in the same space as their operands and makes entire sentences comparable syntactically, and potentially semantically. The vectors generated had sufficient representational strength to generate parse trees at least comparable with contemporary symbolic parsers.

In the context of contemporary explorations of vector combination for semantic representation, this approach of aggressive substitution of contextually similar words and word groups is recommended as a possible solution to problems which present themselves of expansion of representation space, representation strength and comparability.

Acknowledgements. Many thanks to Wojciech Skut (wojciech@google.com) for the formalism in this paper and more recent comments. His formalization was what made me first realize the "ad-hoc arrangements of examples" model I was proposing could be seen as a kind of vector product.

A   Appendix - Evaluation Sample

A.1   Disclaimer

A formal evaluation of the vector parser was carried out for Chinese by Hu Guoping of iFlytek, China in 2003. A sample of results as reported by him are included here, with his permission. They are provided on an as is basis, for information purposes. For fuller detail inquiries should be directed to Hu Guoping.

A.2   Evaluation Methodology and Results

Word similarity vectors were generated from a Chinese corpus sample of 200Mb. Some pre-processing was done for the Chinese text. Because Chinese is not normally segmented into words a dictionary was used to segment the texts. In principle this should not be necessary, but it was an expedient to make Chinese processing as closely comparable as possible to English. Parsing results were compared for several hundred test sentences with a reference tree-bank.

The reference tree-bank was multi-branching.

E.g.

(并 同)(美国总统 克林顿)(正式 进行 会谈)

Because the vector parser attempts to label all pairwise associations it was not possible to score matches exactly. It was decided to score matched phrases as correct if their first and last characters matched, independently of internal structure. In addition the direction of association of the matched phrases was scored. So 并 has a right direction because it is combined with the right word, 同 has a left direction because it is combined with the left word, 进行 has a middle direction: because it is combined with both left and right words.

E.g.

```
Vector parser: (((促进 ((社会 全面) 进步)) 的) 迫切需要)
Tree-bank: (促进 社会(全面 进步)的 迫切需要)
The Result is 1 correct result, 1 error result, 2 Unknown
Vector parser: (致以 (节日 (的 (诚挚 (问候 ((和 良好) 祝愿))))))
Tree-bank: (致以(节日 的(诚挚 问候)和(良好 祝愿)
The Result is 2 correct result, 2 error result, 2 Unknown
Vector parser: (截止到 (去年 (十一月 底)))
Tree-bank: (截止到(去年(十一月 底)))
The Result is 2 correct result, 0 error result, 0 Unknown result
Vector parser: (各项 (外汇 (存款 (已 (达 (二十五 (点 (三 (二亿 美
元)))))))))
Tree-bank: (((各项 外汇)存款)((已 达)(二十五 点 三 二亿)美元))
The Result is 2 correct result, 4 error result, 2 Unknown result
Vector parser: (全行 (国际业务 (((效益 (创 历史)) 最高) 水平)))
```

```
Tree-bank: ((全行 国际业务 效益)(创(历史(最高 水平))))
The Result is 1 correct result, 3 error result, 1 Unknown result
Vector parser: (在 (国际 (银 (坛 (的 (知名度 (和 (声望 (也 越来越
高)))))))))
Tree-bank: ((在(国际(银 坛))的(知名度 和 声望))(也 越来越高))
The Result is 4 correct result, 2 error result, 2 Unknown result
Vector parser: (再次 (超过 (捕捞 产量)))
Tree-bank: (再次(超过(捕捞 产量)))
The Result is 2 correct result, 0 error result, 0 Unknown result
```

The differences in annotation system meant scored precision was decreased, because generally it was impossible to match all branchings, but this was considered adequate for purposes of comparison.

Table 1. Evaluation with Symbolic Parser

Compared Parser	Setting	Precision1	Recall2	Precision2	F-Score2
Symbolic Parser	基于整句解释的语法分析系统 265 Sentence Single POS input	53.39%	53.48%	67.36%	59.62%
	基于整句解释的语法分析系统, 265 test Sentences All Possible POS input	56.74%	54.90%	69.43%	61.31%
Vector Parser	200M Corpus, -li 60, Original Indextable, 265 test Sentences	73.06%	64.30%	63.15%	63.72%
	Corpus, -li 60, 2nd Indextable, 265 test Sentences	72.96%	63.98%	62.84%	63.41%
	200M Corpus, -li 60, 3rt Indextable, 265 test Sentences	72.37%	63.51%	62.37%	62.94%
	200M Corpus, -li 60, 4th Indextable, 265 test Sentences	76.70%	67.30%	66.10%	66.69%

References

1. Chomsky, N.: The logical basis of linguistic theory. In: Lunt, H.G. (ed.) Proceedings of the Ninth International Congress of Linguists. Mouton & Co., The Hague (1964)
2. Chaitin, G.J.: The Unknowable. Springer, Singapore (1999). https://doi.org/10.1023/A:1015151819254
3. Dagan, I., Marcus, S., Markovitch, S.: Contextual word similarity and estimation from sparse data. Comput. Speech Lang. **9**, 123–152 (1995)
4. Harris, Z.: Methods in Structural Linguistics. University of Chicago Press, Chicago (1951)

5. Pawley, A., Syder, F.: Two puzzles for linguistic theory: nativelike selection and nativelike fluency. In: Richards, L., Schmidt, I.L. (eds.) 1983: Language and Communication, pp. 191–226. Longman, London (1983)

6. Halliday, M.A.K.: Lexis as a linguistic level. In: Bazell, C.E., Catford, J.C., Halliday, M.A.K., Robins, R.H. (eds.) Memory of J.R. Firth, pp. 148–162 (1966)

7. Kolmogorov, A.: On tables of random numbers. Sankhyā Ser. A. **25**, 369–375 (1963). MR 178484

8. Lamb, review of Chomsky .... American Anthropologist 69, pp. 411–415 (1967)

9. Lamb, Prolegomena to a theory of phonology. Language 42.536-573 (1966) (includes analysis of the Russian obstruents question, as well as a more reasonable critique of the criteria of classical phonemics)

10. Lamb and Vanderslice, On thrashing classical phonemics. LACUS Forum 2.154-163 (1976)

11. Lamb, Linguistics to the beat of a different drummer. First Person Singular III. Benjamins, 1998 (reprinted in Language and Reality, Continuum, 2004)

12. Lamb, Funknet, 24th June, 2004

13. Lin, D.: An information-theoretic definition of similarity. In: Proceedings of the 15th International Conference on Machine Learning, 1998, pp. 296–304. Morgan Kaufmann (1998)

14. Freeman, R.J.: Example-based complexity-syntax and semantics as the production of ad-hoc arrangements of examples. In: Proceedings of the ANLP/NAACL 2000 Workshop on Syntactic and Semantic Complexity in Natural Language Processing Systems, pp. 47–50

15. Hill, A.A.: How many revolutions can a linguist live through. Studies in the History of Linguistics, vol. 21 (1980)

16. Hopper, P.: Emergent grammar. Berkeley Ling. Conf. (BLS) **13**, 139–157 (1987)

17. Lewis, M.: The lexical approach: The state of ELT and the way forward. Language Teaching Publications, Hove, England (1993)

18. Nattinger, J.: A lexical phrase grammar for ESL. TESOL Q. **14**, 337–344 (1980)

19. Frederick, J.: Newmeyer. Routledge, Generative Linguistics a historical perspective (1996)

20. Weinert, R.: The role of formulaic language in second language acquistion: a review. Appl. Linguis. **16**(1), 180–205 (1995)

21. van Zaanen, M.: Bootstrapping syntax and recursion using alignment-based learning. In: Proceedings of the Seventeenth International Conference on Machine Learning, pp. 1063–1070 (2001)

Goal Generation and Management in NARS

Christian Hahm[✉], Boyang Xu, and Pei Wang

Department of Computer and Information Sciences, Temple University, Philadelphia, PA, USA
{christian.hahm,boyangxu,pei.wang}@temple.edu

Abstract. AGI systems should be able to pursue their many goals autonomously while operating in realistic environments which are complex, dynamic, and often novel. This paper discusses the theory and mechanisms for goal generation and management in Non-Axiomatic Reasoning System (NARS). NARS works to accomplish its goals by performing executable actions while integrating feedback from its experience to build subjective, but useful, predictive and meaningful models. The system's ever-changing knowledge allows it to adaptively derive new goals from its existing goals. Derived goals not only serve to accomplish their parent goals but also represent independent motivation. The system determines how and when to pursue its many goals based on priority, context, and knowledge acquired from its experience and reasoning capabilities.

Keywords: Goal · Motivation · Task · Aim · Objective · Drive · Intention · Desire · Target

1 Introduction

Non-Axiomatic Reasoning System (NARS) is a general-purpose AI (AGI) system, which means that it can accept and pursue arbitrary goals. The ability to pursue arbitrary goals must be a fundamental aspect of AGI systems since they are meant to be capable of "general" problem-solving similarly to humans; that is to say they should have the ability to at least attempt to solve any problem they are presented with[1]. Indeed, a hallmark of any cognitive system's intelligence is its capability to achieve its goals. In the general sense, a system's "goal" is simply a motivation for the orientation of its activities. The goal is an objective that the system is working towards, whether successfully or not. It answers the question, "What is the system's aim?". Goals can be very specific (e.g. "Pick up that apple") or more general (e.g. "Be good").

All AI systems may be considered as having at minimum one goal since each is built to accomplish one or more tasks. AGI systems in particular will necessarily have multiple different goals at the same time due to the complexity of their environments. Although an AGI system's initial "seed" goals are predefined by a user, the system will invariably need to generate new goals (such as in subgoaling) in order to solve problems autonomously. The system also needs to effectively manage its existing goal complex: not all goals are equal, and certain goals may be more or less important depending on

---

[1] A human (or other intelligent system) will not necessarily be able to achieve any arbitrary goal, especially with limited knowledge and resources.

© Springer Nature Switzerland AG 2022
B. Goertzel et al. (Eds.): AGI 2021, LNAI 13154, pp. 96–105, 2022.
https://doi.org/10.1007/978-3-030-93758-4_11

context. Some goals will be actively pursued by the system, while others can lie dormant for any period of time, depending on each goal's desirability and relative priority. Goals may be transient, existing in the system for only a short time (such as when the system is completing a quick task), or persistent, existing in the system for a long time (possibly eternally, over the system's lifetime) [4, 8].

2 Relevant Works

A useful AI system should exhibit autonomous behavior with respect to handling and accomplishing its goals. In the simplest case, an automation program has a single goal and one or more goal-specific actions available to it. Perhaps it responds to some stimulus or is otherwise programmed to execute some action when a predefined condition is met (e.g. "stamp the item when you detect it rolling past on the conveyor belt"), or performs some domain-specific algorithm.

More sophisticated systems use subgoaling to deal with a goal that requires multiple steps to achieve. When a goal cannot be achieved immediately, subgoals are derived from it (using the system's knowledge and backward chaining [4]) that may lead to its achieving. This subgoaling process is recursive, creating a tree-structure of goals when viewed graphically, as each subgoal may itself require further subgoaling [8]. The tree bottoms out at its leaves, either with "atomic actions the system can execute, goals that need no further subgoaling since they are already complete, or otherwise goals that cannot be subgoaled further due to insufficient knowledge.

An AI should be able to handle multiple goals simultaneously, and that is where things become complicated, since any cognitive system has only limited knowledge and capabilities. While operating, the system needs to intelligently reason about both its goals and what it knows about its environment to decide what actions to take. In many system designs, goals are assumed to be orderable and/or compatible using some priority ranking or planning, but this is not always a valid assumption to make as it is not always possible to rank goals by "objective" importance. This autonomous goal-managing capability of AI systems is a challenging problem and has been the target of many efforts, some of which are addressed here.

Belief-Desire-Intention (BDI) systems are a classical approach towards modeling autonomy with respect to goals. BDI is a term used to describe the separation of a system's internal knowledge: its beliefs (knowledge about itself and the world), desires (latent goals), and intentions (active goals) [7]. This distinction is agreeable, but such systems also tend to have the problem of assuming their goals to be static (in terms of meaning) and orderable (in terms of priority).

Goal-Driven Autonomy (GDA) is a recent approach in AI where the system dynamically selects, generates, and pursues novel (i.e. indirectly related) goals based on perceived changes and discrepancies in its environment, ultimately helping the system to achieve its goals more effectively. In [5], ARTUE escorts an ally in a strategy simulation and derives a novel goal to fortify the area when an enemy appears. Although fortifying the area is not a direct subgoal of escorting the ally, the goal is nonetheless useful to the mission because it protects the AI system and the escortee; the goal is adaptively derived in response to unexpected environment changes (i.e. an enemy appearing nearby). MIDCA [6] is tasked to build houses in a block world, but a hidden arsonist lights blocks on fire, hindering progress. The system derives goals to investigate and eventually apprehend the arsonist, preventing further fires. The GDA systems' ability to reason about environment changes and generate goals in response to anomalous situations allows the systems to outperform traditional models not based on GDA.

MicroPsi [2] is an AGI system that executes actions based on its active motives, which represent some events that the system desires to achieve or prevent. The system creates its motives in response to its urge signals, which are produced internally by a presupposed set of basic systemic needs (e.g. "competence", "sustenance", "rest", etc.). The system uses reward signals to indicate how the system's current actions and the changing state of the environment are impacting the satisfaction of the system's urges, providing feedback to the system about its success in the environment and allowing it to plan its next actions accordingly.

3   NARS Overview

Non-Axiomatic Reasoning System (NARS) is a unified model of general intelligence, where intelligence is defined by adaptation under an Assumption of Insufficient Knowledge and Resources (AIKR). The system operates using a formal logic called Non-Axiomatic Logic (NAL) which defines relationships between concepts and allows reasoning on them under uncertainty. The system is "non-axiomatic" in that its knowledge does not represent the true and complete state of the world, but rather represents knowledge about the world as based on the system's accumulated experience. The representation language of NAL is called Narsese.

AIKR means NARS works in real-time with finite processing capacity while being open to knowledge and tasks of any content. Under this assumption of resource and knowledge restriction, NARS incrementally processes all of its many beliefs, goals, and questions in parallel using its control mechanism. NARS absorbs information through its input channels and revises its knowledge during the course of its operation to build more reliable and useful internal models of the world. This can be considered a form of adaptation and is usefully paired with executable *operations* that NARS can perform to autonomously gain a richer understanding of its environment and pursue goals [9].

Similarly to the relevant works, NARS' goals drive the operations it performs. The system engages in common goal generation behaviors like subgoaling but is also unique in that the system explores many potential goal solution paths in parallel and optimizes these solution paths by reasoning on its existing beliefs and new incoming experience. Additionally, there are not many restrictions on the content, meaning, and usefulness of the goals themselves due to the flexibility of NARS' logic and formal language. The system can accept external goals via input, and also generates its own new goals based on the content of its memory. As long as a goal remains desirable to the system and there is no evidence to the contrary, it may continue to be pursued, while a completed or very unimportant goal may be abandoned.

NARS' goal complex changes throughout its lifetime as it adapts to its environment and the system gains new experience. Indeed, throughout a very long lifetime, the system may gain entirely new sets of goals and may no longer desire the goals with which it was initially programmed[2]. Successful self-control and autonomy in any AI system, including NARS, depends on the system's aptitude for generating and identifying useful goals. The system must also holistically manage its overall goal complex, because goals can interplay and in many situations it does not suffice to blindly pursue every goal at the exact moment it arises. Some goals require long-term planning and execution, and a NARS operating in an open environment could develop or acquire goals that conflict with each other.

NARS' internal memory can be visualized as a graph, where each node is some concept, and edges between nodes are relationships between concepts. A concept is named by a term (e.g. "*cat*").

In NARS, a piece of information is represented by a Narsese *sentence* called *judgment*, which consists of a *statement* and its corresponding *truth-value*. It has the following format:

$$\langle judgment \rangle ::= [\langle tense \rangle]\langle statement \rangle. \langle truth\text{-}value \rangle$$

The statement represents a relationship between a subject concept and a predicate concept (e.g. an inheritance statement "$<S \rightarrow P>$" means S is a specialization of P). The truth-value is a pair of numbers $(f, c) \in [0, 1] \times (0, 1)$, where f is the *frequency* (representing how *positive* or *negative* [true or false] the statement is according to the system's evidence), and c is the *confidence* (representing how much evidence the system has to justify its assessment of *frequency*).

For example, to represent that you are very confident that "a dog is a type of animal", a judgment can be written as "$<dog \rightarrow animal>. \langle 1.0, 0.9 \rangle$". This statement is directly related to 3 concepts: *dog*, *animal*, and $<dog \rightarrow animal>$. When a judgment is first absorbed into NARS, new subject, predicate, and statement concepts are created in the system's memory (unless they already exist). Additional judgments of the same content are accumulated as additional evidence within the corresponding concept's *belief table* and thus acquire stronger confidence values—the set of all these accumulated judgments within the system's memory make up the system's *beliefs*.

A judgment is optionally associated with a timestamp representing when its truth-value is valid; in that case, we can also call it an *event*. It represents temporal knowledge.

NARS operates by continually executing a working cycle, during which *tasks* and beliefs are processed. *Tasks* are *sentence* containers, outside of the system's memory in a buffer. Sentence types that can be processed by NARS including *judgment*, *question*, and *goal*. The exact mechanism depends on the specific NARS implementation, but in general, during a given working cycle two sentences are selected for processing. Tasks and other objects in the system's memory have a decaying *priority* $p \in [0, 1]$ value that represents the object's relative urgency compared to other objects of the same type; priority can also be raised in various ways, allowing objects to compete for the system's time and resources. In each working cycle, the objects with the highest priority tend to be selected for processing, whereas objects with the lowest priority are pruned from the object container if it overflows [3].

---

[2] This potential temporary nature of goals may be overcome by periodically re-inputting the goals into NARS.

4   Goal Generation and Management

A goal in NARS is represented by a type of Narsese sentence called *goal*. It is essentially a special piece of knowledge representing that NARS desires an event to occur (or not occur) in the current moment. Similarly to how each concept in memory has a belief table which holds accumulated judgments, every concept also has a *desire table* which holds accumulated goals. A goal can either be contained in a *task* (in a buffer, ready to be processed) or referred to as a *desire* (once it is integrated into the system's memory).

New goals accumulate into desires of varying confidence which by extension drive the executable operations that the system performs. A goal in NARS has the following format:

$$\langle goal \rangle ::= \langle statement \rangle! \, \langle desire\text{-}value \rangle$$

Here, the statement is an event that is desired by the system to occur (or be prevented) in the present moment, and NARS will actively work to achieve it.[3]

A *desire-value* is a pair of numbers $(f, c) \in [0, 1] \times [0, 1)$ that summarizes evidence for and against the event being desirable to NARS (i.e. how desirable the event is). Formally, desire-value is equivalent to the truth-value of a virtual judgment representing the extent to which the event S implies NARS' overall desired state D:

$$S! \, \langle f, c \rangle \iff <S \mapsto D>. \, \langle f, c \rangle$$

Therefore, the frequency f represents the event's *desirability*, and confidence c represents how confident the system is in its assessment of desirability.

A *positive goal* is an event (S) with a high desirability (near 1.0), where the system wants to make S as *positive* (true) as possible in the present moment, because the event S's occurrence is sufficient for NARS' overall desired state (D).

A *negative goal* is a negated event ($\neg S$) with a high desirability (near 1.0), where the system wants to make S as *negative* (false) as possible in the present moment. The event S's non-occurrence[4] is sufficient for NARS' overall desired state (D).

For example, if you wanted to give your NARS a goal to "open the door", you could express it as either a positive goal ("NARS wants the door to be open") or a negative goal ("NARS wants the door to be not closed"), respectively:

$$<\{door\} \rightarrow [open]>! \, \langle 1.0, 0.9 \rangle \quad \neg<\{door\} \rightarrow [closed]>! \, \langle 1.0, 0.9 \rangle$$

Given either of these goals, NARS will begin planning ways to open the door, though positive goals are preferred since they are syntactically simpler.

Goal management in NARS is handled innately by the system's design. The system is constantly processing new information coming from its sensors and thinking about what it already knows (i.e. reasoning on the information in its memory). The system's memory consists of concepts which contain collections of beliefs and desires. When NARS selects a strong desire for processing, the system works to achieve it.

---

[3] To represent events that are desired to occur in the future, we can simply add a temporal condition to the goal.

[4] Equivalently, the event $\neg S$'s occurrence.

Like all tasks in NARS, goals have one of two origins: *input* or *derived*. An input goal is assigned to the system from an external source (e.g. a user) through an input channel, whereas a derived goal is derived internally by backward inference rules using existing goals and beliefs as premises [8]. Either way, when a goal is selected for processing for the first time by NARS, it undergoes initial processing in the form of *revision*. The content of the new goal is merged into its corresponding concept's desire table, keeping NARS' overall assessment of the goal event's desirability up-to-date (see *Algorithm 1*).

Whenever it is subsequently selected by NARS again, the desire will undergo continued processing during which NARS may work to actively pursue it. A desire is actively pursued by NARS according to the Decision-Making Rule:

$$d > T_d$$

Where $d \in (0, 1)$ is the event's *expected desirability*, the *expectation*[5] of its desire-value (f, c) (where $d = c \times (f - 0.5) + 0.5$). The system's *desire threshold*, $T_d \in [0, 1.0]$, is a personality parameter representing NARS' cautiousness[6].

When a desire exceeds the desire threshold, it may be considered an active goal that NARS works to pursue - such a desire is like "intention" in BDI models, whereas those which have low but non-zero desirability are like the latent "desire" in BDI. Usually, a goal must be derived and accumulated many times before it reaches this threshold; that is, the system has derived and accumulated lots of evidence that the goal in question should be pursued, or alternatively the goal was input with high expected desirability directly by a user.

During a given working cycle, when a desire should be pursued based on the Decision-Making Rule, first the system checks if the goal event is already occurring (as based on the value in its belief table) – in this case, the goal does not require further action, and the system can move on to its next task. If the goal is not satisfied, the system next checks if the goal itself is an executable operation (e.g. ⇑ *walk*, ⇑ *jump*, ⇑ *speak*), and if so immediately executes that operation. If the goal is not an operation, then the system will use related beliefs to derive new (potential) goals that, through their achieving, may lead to the achieving of the original goal (see *Algorithm 2*).

The system derives new goals using the knowledge it has acquired from its lifetime of experience, using a desire in backward inference with temporally related beliefs. If NARS has an empirical belief that a desired event will occur after the occurrence of

---

Algorithm 1. *Goal* initial processing (Narsese pseudocode)

Require: NARS selects *task* G for processing for the first time
Require: G is a *goal* of form: $\langle goal \rangle :: = \langle statement \rangle! \langle desire\text{-}value \rangle$
  1: $S_G \leftarrow \langle statement \rangle_G$
  2: $C_G \leftarrow GetConcept(S_G)$ ▷ Get concept named by S_G
  3: Merge G into C_G's *desire* table   ▷ Keep concept's desirability up-to-date

---

[5] *Expectation* is an estimate of future frequency.

[6] Although currently this threshold is a constant, in future implementations it can be treated as a context-dependent variable.

some other events, then new goals for those precondition events will be derived. Formally, backward inference rule b derives new goal G' from existing goal G and related belief B, if and only if forward inference rule f derives J_G (the judgment satisfying G) from $J_{G'}$ (the judgment satisfying G') and B:

$$\{G, B\} \vdash_b G' \iff \{J_{G'}, B\} \vdash_f J_G$$

In this way, a *derived goal* G' is derived *initially* as a potential subgoal of the original goal G—the system derives G' that, when achieved, may lead to achieving G. However, the role of G' in NARS is not restricted to subgoal of G. On the one hand, it is possible that the achieving of G' could also result in the achieving of other goals or the discovery of new knowledge that could be helpful in the achieving of G. On the other hand, G' is derived using the system's beliefs which (under AIKR) may be incomplete or even incorrect, since the system can only know what it has learned so far during its lifetime of experience; there is no guarantee that G' is useful for G.

If the achieving of a derived goal G' tends to garner outcomes that are favorable to the system, G' can be considered valuable in its own right, taking on a different role independent from subgoal of G. Conversely, the achieving of G' may ultimately end up being irrelevant or even inhibitory to the achieving of G, but at the time of derivation it is a reasonable guess. For these reasons, in NARS derived goal G' is not managed as a subgoal but is instead treated independently[7] as a goal that must compete with the other goals in the system for relevance and attention. Thus, derived goals are simply added to the task buffer where they may be absorbed to compete with the system's other goals. This independent nature of motivations is referred to as the "functional autonomy of motives" and is a phenomenon observed in humans [1].

Algorithm 2. *Goal* continued processing (Narsese pseudocode)

Require: G is a *goal* of form: $\langle goal \rangle :: = \langle statement \rangle ! \langle desire\text{-}value \rangle$
Require: NARS selects desire G for continued processing
Require: T_d is the system's *desire-threshold*
1:   $d \leftarrow Expectation(\langle desire\text{-}value \rangle_G)$ ▷ Get desirability of G
2:   **if** $d \leq T_d$ **then return**   ▷ Decision-Making Rule; stop if G is not desirable enough
3:   $S_G \leftarrow \langle statement \rangle_G$
4:   $G_N \leftarrow$ Answer $(\neg S_{G¿})$ ▷ Get negative goal $G_N = \neg S_G ! \langle f_1, c_1 \rangle$
5:   $d_N \leftarrow Expectation(\langle desire\text{-}value \rangle_{G_N})$ ▷ Get desirability of G_N
6:   **if** $d_N > d$ **then return**   ▷ Inhibition; stop if G_N is more desirable than G
7:   $J_G \leftarrow$ Answer $(S_G?)$;   ▷ Get judgment $J_G = S_G . \langle f_2, c_2 \rangle$
8:   $e \leftarrow Expectation(\langle truth\text{-}value \rangle_{J_G})$ ▷ Get truth expectation of J_G
9:   **if** e is positive **then return**   ▷ Stop processing if G is already achieved
10: **if** S_G is an *operation* **then** $Execute(S_G)$ **return**   ▷ Execute if G is an operation
11: **if** No known sufficient precondition for S_G **then return**   ▷ Stop if no beliefs related to G
12: $B \leftarrow$ Predictive *belief* related to S_G ▷ e.g. $<(E \,\&/ \Uparrow op) \not\Rightarrow S_G>.\langle f_3, c_3 \rangle$
13: $G' \leftarrow$ Derive new *goal* $\{G, B\} \vdash_b$ ▷ e.g. $(E \,\&/ \Uparrow op)!\langle f_4, c_4 \rangle$

---

[7] Though a limited record is kept regarding its origins.

The meaning and usefulness of each goal changes as a function of the system's experience, which continuously shapes the system's *many* interacting conceptual relationships, goals, and activities. A system with tens of thousands changing conceptual relations and constant streams of incoming sensorimotor experiences will derive and accumulate many pieces of evidence for and against a goal. Evidence for goals should be accumulated from across various beliefs, and kept up-to-date in the current moment according to context and what is currently known.

This highlights the important distinction between treating a derived goal (G') independently versus treating it as a subgoal. When a derived goal is treated purely as a subgoal, its usefulness is limited in that the system manages it solely for the greater purpose of achieving its corresponding supergoal. Many AI systems may try to pre-specify these goals, or assume that achieving the subgoals is absolutely necessary or sufficient for the achieving of the supergoal. However, under AIKR, the system cannot assume this is always the case, since there may be a different solution path to achieving the supergoal that doesn't require the derived subgoal, and perhaps uses different subgoals entirely, derived using very different concepts and knowledge. Conversely, treating derived goals *independently* allows them to take on a usefulness (or uselessness) of their own, based on their own merits. NARS treats goals independently by processing its many concepts and goals in parallel using a probabilistic priority queue—every goal has a chance to be processed in a given working cycle, and the system constantly takes in knowledge from its experience buffers to keep its memory up-to-date. A derived goal's usefulness includes, of course, how well it helps to achieve the goal from which it was derived. If the same goal is derived often without evidence to the contrary, it may gain extremely high confidence and priority.

The types of goals that may be derived in NARS are also unique due to the system's extensive inference capabilities. Usually, the process of subgoaling is purely deductive, but NARS' inference capabilities allow it to derive knowledge using induction, abduction, and analogy between two statements. When using this type of knowledge in backwards inference, the derived goal is essentially a guess – but an educated guess, which can be justified by the system's current knowledge.

NARS' goal derivation capabilities allow the system to adaptively react to its environment as a function of new experience gained. In the example in Fig. 1a, the NARS begins with only one initial goal: **touch the finish line**. The system is given some background knowledge, including that it can jump to navigate around obstacles. During its journey, the system encounters an obstacle and is obstructed. As a result, the system generates and achieves a goal to jump over the obstacle, allowing the system to continue making progress towards its original goal of moving to the finish line.

As long as NARS was assigned some initial goal and has related knowledge to infer new goals, the system will have multiple goals at any given time. Each goal's priority value denotes its urgency and is a factor in how much time the system will spend trying to achieve it. Depending on the situation, certain goals should be prioritized over others that may not be as relevant (e.g. when an AI robot's battery is low, the goal to find an electrical outlet to recharge is more relevant and should have high priority). Furthermore, the system is finite and under AIKR does not have the time, resources, or knowledge to achieve all goals fully or at once, especially as new goals can arrive

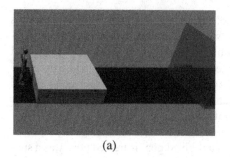
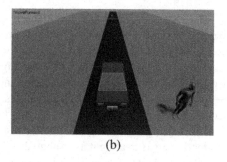

(a)   (b)

Fig. 1. (a) NARS reaches the finish line by generating new goals to jump over obstacles. [https://www.youtube.com/watch?v=iYHpk-JtIRQ], (b) A NARS vehicle dynamically handles goals that suddenly become conflicting. [https://www.youtube.com/watch?v=sNLWVtfk5tA]

at any moment; instead, the system must efficiently pick from its many goals so as to, over time, achieve them all to the system's best extent.

The overall goal complex of NARS may be disjointed, in that some goals are quite different from each other, and potentially even *conflicting* such achieving one makes it more difficult or impossible to achieve another. In that case, NARS may be forced to resolve conflicting goals at a moment's notice. The example in Fig. 1b shows a NARS car handling conflicting goals. The system is taught some simple background knowledge and the fact that it can execute operations to drive forward ("⇑ *drive*") and brake ("⇑ *brake*"). The NARS is initially input with 2 reasonable goals: 1. **drive forward**, and 2. **don't hit pedestrians**. However, these goals become conflicting when NARS encounters a pedestrian standing in the middle of the road. When the pedestrian appears in front and NARS processes highly-desired goal #2, the system may derive evidence that braking is desired (e.g."⇑ *brake*! $\langle 1.0, 0.9 \rangle$") since it will help the system to not hit the pedestrian. The system could also derive evidence that preventing the execution of ⇑ *drive* is desired (e.g."¬ ⇑ *drive*! $\langle 1.0, 0.9 \rangle$"), since executing ⇑ *drive* will result in the failure of goal #2. These derivations working in tandem will encourage the NARS to execute ⇑ *brake* while inhibiting the NARS from executing ⇑ *drive*.

5 Comparison and Conclusion

NARS is a real-time system that can accept and process new goals at any moment. However, AIKR implies there is no guarantee that a given goal can be achieved perfectly, or at all. There may not be a way for the system to achieve the goal immediately, and the path to achieving it may be uncertain (if the system lacks the knowledge) or impossible (if the system lacks the resources or capabilities).

NARS works to achieve all of its goals to the best extent by combining and extending multiple aspects of AI goal management. Similarly to GDA, the system is goal-driven and decides which goals to actively pursue based on desirability, priority, and the system's current beliefs. The system is adaptive, constantly incorporating new knowledge into its memory, and the system's goals change over time. NARS can also be described as roughly following a BDI model, in that its beliefs are separate from its goals, and its goals may be either actively pursued or latently desired. Such a distinction between active and latent desires becomes clearly necessary in the case of conflicting goals, where it may be necessary to suppress some goals for the achievement of others. Similarly to MicroPsi's appetitive and aversive goals [2], NARS also distinguishes between positive and negative goals, where the system desires to either achieve or prevent an event respectively.

However, NARS is also quite different from other goal-driven AI. The system's flexible formal language and various logical inference rules give it the freedom to be creative and adaptive in problem-solving situations. The system does not have any single leading motive or supergoal but instead works to explore and achieve all of its many goals in parallel, though to different extents depending on priority. Whether a given goal is latently desired or actively pursued is not permanently decided, but instead changes over time according to the system's learned experience. Currently, every new instance of NARS starts out empty with no goals, and instead acquires its initial goals at run-time.

Perhaps one of the more unique features of NARS is its independent treatment of derived goals. Since a derived goal is prioritized independently, its time-resource budget and length of existence may go beyond any of its ancestor goals and eventually play its own larger role in the system. In humans, the functional autonomy of motives is apparent and seems to be an integral aspect of adaptability. The meaning of goals is not static, but changes as the system gains new experience and the holistic content and organization of the memory changes. By virtue of its adaptive goal complex, the system's psychology can be compared to a human's in that the system can be said to develop its own dynamic traits, attitudes, and interests that evolve over its lifetime [1, 8].

References

1. Allport, G.: The functional autonomy of motives. Am. J. Psychol. **50**, 141–156 (1937)
2. Bach, J.: Modeling motivation in MicroPsi 2. In: Bieger, J., Goertzel, B., Potapov, A. (eds.) AGI 2015. LNCS (LNAI), vol. 9205, pp. 3–13. Springer, Cham (2015). https://doi.org/10.1007/978-3-319-21365-1_1
3. Hammer, P., Lofthouse, T., Wang, P.: The OpenNARS implementation of the non-axiomatic reasoning system. In: Steunebrink, B., Wang, P., Goertzel, B. (eds.) AGI -2016. LNCS (LNAI), vol. 9782, pp. 160–170. Springer, Cham (2016). https://doi.org/10.1007/978-3-319-41649-6_16
4. Hawes, N.: A survey of motivation frameworks for intelligent systems. Artif. Intell. **175**(5), 1020–1036 (2011). https://doi.org/10.1016/j.artint.2011.02.002, http://www.sciencedirect.com/science/article/pii/S0004370211000336, special Review Issue
5. Klenk, M., Molineaux, M., Aha, D.W.: Goal-driven autonomy for responding to unexpected events in strategy simulations. Comput. Intell. **29**(2), 187–206 (2013)
6. Paisner, M., Cox, M., Maynord, M., Perlis, D.: Goal-driven autonomy for cognitive systems. In: Proceedings of the Annual Meeting of the Cognitive Science Society, No. 36 (2014)
7. Rao, A.S., Georgeff, M.P., et al.: Bdi agents: from theory to practice. In: Icmas, vol. 95, pp. 312–319 (1995)
8. Wang, P.: Motivation management in AGI systems. In: Bach, J., Goertzel, B., Iklé, M. (eds.) Proceedings of the Fifth Conference on Artificial General Intelligence, pp. 352–361 (2012)
9. Wang, P.: Non-Axiomatic Logic: A Model of Intelligent Reasoning. World Scientific, Singapore (2013)

Neuro-Symbolic Architecture for Experiential Learning in Discrete and Functional Environments

Anton Kolonin[1,2,3(✉)]

[1] Aigents, Novosibirsk, Russian Federation
[2] SingularityNET Foundation, Amsterdam, Netherlands
[3] Novosibirsk State University, Novosibirsk, Russia

Abstract. The paper presents a "horizontal neuro-symbolic integration" approach for artificial general intelligence along with elementary representation-agnostic cognitive architecture and explores its usability under the experiential learning framework for reinforcement learning problem powered by "global feedback".

Keywords: Artificial general intelligence · Cognitive architecture · Domain ontology · Experiential learning · Global feedback · Local feedback · Neuro-symbolic integration · Operational space · Reinforcement learning

1 Introduction

The current agenda of artificial general intelligence research is focused on neuro-symbolic architectures (NSA) [1, 2] with reinforcement learning (RL) capabilities [3]. There are studies concentrated on how the graph-based approaches can be combined with artificial neural networks and deep learning, particularly, deep reinforcement learning [4]. The latter involves variations end extensions of learning based on local feedback [5] such as Q-learning [6], involving incremental feedback or error propagation across the states of a studied behavioral program.

In this work we attempt to bridge the gap between symbolic and symbolic approaches within representation-agnostic cognitive architecture. This architecture is considered to be invariant to whether the operational space of an agent possessing it is represented by unstructured raw discrete data or a structured system of functions describing the state of an agent's environment.

From a practical standpoint, we anticipate that it might be plausible to build so called "horizontal neuro-symbolic integration" systems capable to perform both "System 1" ("slow") and "System 2" ("fast") thinking [7] – depending on the stage of a learning process and the explainability requirements for the system. In this work we suggest something rather different compared to the modern "vertical neuro-symbolic integration" systems with neural networks and knowledge graphs residing at different levels of cognitive architecture [8].

At the same time, we are considering the perspective of replacing the so-called "local feedback" (and local "error propagation") [9, 10] with the so-called "global

© Springer Nature Switzerland AG 2022
B. Goertzel et al. (Eds.): AGI 2021, LNAI 13154, pp. 106–115, 2022.
https://doi.org/10.1007/978-3-030-93758-4_12

feedback" known in neuroscience and psychology [11–13] to see if it enables reinforcement learning and what are the conditions and circumstances that make it possible.

For the purpose of the above, we will first consider an overall approach to neuro-symbolic integration; next, describe our view on the global feedback, then draft principal architecture of an elementary module of a cognitive system and, finally, experimentally explore the reference implementation of the described architecture, discuss the results and draw some practical conclusions.

It worth noticing that the widely used RL term seem too much associated with only a limited scope of what can be called experiential learning (EL) [14] which involves any forms of learning, including unsupervised learning based on observing the states of the environment from an agent's standpoint, self-supervised learning [15] based on guidance and feedback provided by an agent to itself relying on different performance metrics possessed innately or inferred during the life-cycle, semi-supervised learning involving different forms of guidance given by an external agent being a teacher, and finally reinforcement learning per se – based on explicit feedback provided by a reinforcing instructor or an environment.

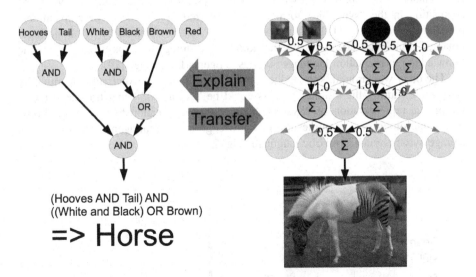

Fig. 1. An example of "horizontal neuro-symbolic integration". A symbolic representation of knowledge about the properties of a horse is presented on the left, with the semantic knowledge graph with labeled vertices performing either abstract concepts referring to specific properties and their values and edges performing as weighted links maintaining the probabilistic predicate logic structure. The sub-symbolic representation of the same knowledge is on the right, with the same knowledge stored in a distributed form as parameters connecting artificial neurons across layers in a deep neural network being an unlabeled weighted graph.

2 Neuro-Symbolic Integration

The "horizontal neuro-symbolic integration" framework concept is rendered on Fig. 1. While the same knowledge may be represented in a form on the right or on the left, different phases of acquisition (learning) and execution (application) of knowledge may be performed using either of the two representations or both of them concurrently. The left (Fig. 1) "symbolic" representation corresponds to Kahneman's "System 2" of reasonable, explainable [16] and interpretable [17] "slow thinking" mode while the right "sub-symbolic" one corresponds to "System 1" associative and intuitive unexplainable "fast thinking" [7] modality.

The system implementing both of such knowledge representations would be able to learn acquiring new knowledge and perform applying this knowledge – using any of the two systems. "System 1" would be capable to learn more slowly but perform faster and "System 2" would be learning faster but acting more slowly [7].

At the same time, there would be possibility to "transfer" knowledge from the "interpretable" representation fast acquired earlier ("System 2") into an "intuitive" representation to be applied fast when needed ("System 1"). In some cases, knowledge acquisition in the "symbolic" form may be inferred in the course of conventional probabilistic reasoning [18] and in some cases it can be obtained by symbolic input obtained from outer agents of external knowledge storage systems using a symbolic knowledge representation language such as "Aigents Language" [19].

The other way around, knowledge learned in the course of experiential learning by "System 1" during the training process could be "explained" being translated into a reasonable representation of "System 2" for either verification by means of probabilistic reasoning or communication of knowledge to external agents and knowledge storage systems via a symbolic language (Fig. 2).

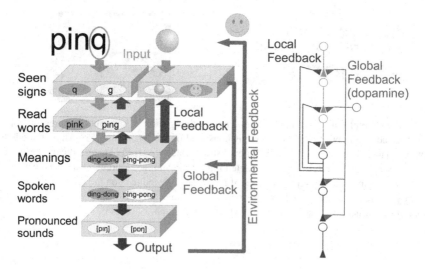

Fig. 2. Global feedback and local feedback loops in artificial cognitive architecture (left) and neuro-cortical architecture (right) with uncertain multi-modal perception and reinforcement.

3 Global Feedback Versus Local Feedback

The most of RL works referenced above [6, 9, 10] are focused on feedback propagation over a series of states probabilistically associated with eventual reinforcement. The reinforcing feedback is propagated step by step across the preceding behavioral trajectory which makes the latest steps collect more feedback even if they are irrelevant to delayed reinforcement. This can be called "local feedback" as it is propagated on a step-by-step basis so the reward of the next step is locally shared with the previous step. Also, this makes training longer because of slow incremental propagations of reinforcements.

We explore the alternative scheme of the "global feedback" [11–13] with full amount of reward shared evenly with all steps being in the attention focus at the time of reinforcement. Then the main problem becomes how to figure out the time span of the attention focus so it captures the complete sequence of steps leading to either reinforcement or failure. In the following experiments we were considering an event of either a positive or a negative stimulus to set a boundary of the attention interval. In turn, positive and negative stimuli were considered as a source of either positive (reinforcement or reward) or negative (punishment) feedback.

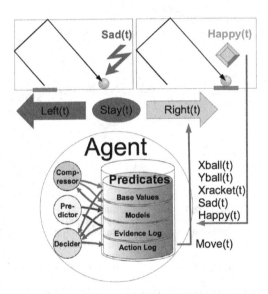

Fig. 3. Cognitive architecture and operational space for experiential learning in an arbitrary operational space represented by domain ontology – an example for a simplified "self-pong" game. Agent memories and cognitive processes – at the bottom. Sample operational space – at the top.

4 Cognitive Architecture

Cognitive architecture of an elementary agent is inspired by the task-driven approach [18, 20] implementing the theory of functional systems (TFS) of P. Anokhin. It is shown on the bottom of Fig. 3, where the agent possesses three processes acting upon four different memories, extending the cognitive model described in our earlier work [21].

The four types of memory are: a) "Base Values" or fundamental goals like avoidance of negative stimuli ("Sad") and searching for positive ones ("Happy"); b) "Models" keeping probabilistic relationships between different state transitions experienced by an agent, with every state transition keeping the input environmental state and output action; c) "Evidence Log" of environmental states; d) "Action Log" of actions directed toward the environment.

Three types of processes are: 1) "Predictor" inferring the "Models" based on the "Evidence Log" and "Action Log" experiences, 2) "Decider" intended to make a choice relying on probabilities obtained based on the experience state and predictions evaluated by the "Predictor"; 3) "Compressor" which is supposed to keep the amount of stored memories in a reasonable range eliminating occasional and irrelevant models and logs to keep consumption of resources under control.

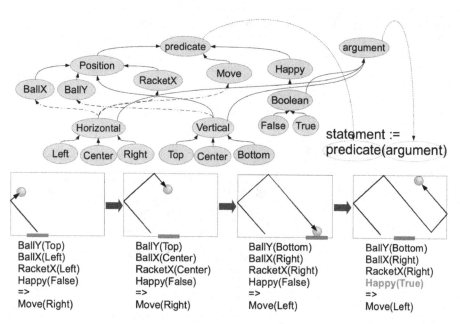

Fig. 4. Operational space – "functional". Domain ontology – at the top. Representation of a sequence of states and actions by means of respective predicates – at the bottom.

An example of an operational space for an agent with such cognitive architecture is provided for a simplified "self-pong" game at the top of Fig. 3. The goal of a player in this game is to reflect the ball with the racket. The agent is provided a negative stimulus ("Sad") if the ball hits the "floor". The agent is given a positive stimulus ("Happy") if the ball hits either the racket or the ceiling right after being reflected by the racket successfully – depending on the game setup. Both stimuli may be considered as boolean predicates with time t as an argument. In turn, the action space of an agent is limited to the choice between moving the racket "Left" or "Right" or keeping it in place ("Stay"), which are other predicates with t as an argument as well. Other predicates of the environment can be coordinates of the ball ("Xball", "Yball") and the racket ("Yracket"), in case of the "functional" representation discussed further.

While the example above describes the operational space as a specific domain ontology including environmental variables (coordinates and stimuli) and agent actions, the cognitive architecture itself is assumed to be agnostic in respect to particular domain ontology as long as the ontology is described by any consistent set of predicates.

5 Operational Spaces

An attempt has been made to evaluate possibility of experiential learning for the same physical problem applied to different operational spaces and corresponding domain ontologies. For this purpose, we have represented the above-described "self-pong" game using two completely different representations - "functional" and "discrete".

In the first case, illustrated on Fig. 4, we consider a "functional" operational space where behaviors of the ball and the racket are expected to be known and represented by distinct functions for different coordinates of the two. That could be a typical case for using a symbolic probabilistic reasoning system that operates conventional predicates describing the properties of identified concepts and objects and makes predictions on that basis.

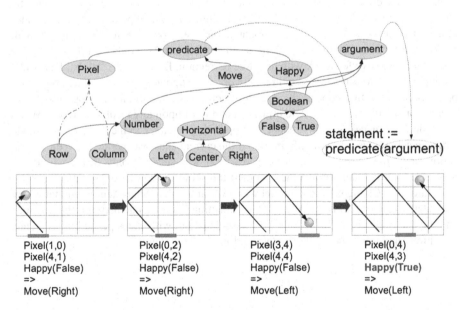

Fig. 5. Operational space – "discrete". Domain ontology – at the top. Representation of sequence of states and actions by means of respective predicates – at the bottom.

In the second case, illustrated on Fig. 5, we consider a "discrete" operational space where functional behaviors of the ball and the racket are expected to be unknown so everything is represented by "pixels" of a virtual display where any pixel could be corresponding to either the ball or the racket. That could be a typical case for using a neural network architecture with input from a raster display like Atari Breakout RL test from Open AI Gym framework resembling the "self-pong" discussed here [6].

6 Learning Model

Three different learning models were explored during the following experiments.

First, "Sequential" - "symbolic" matching of the sequences of experienced states leading to positive or negative feedback since the last known feedback event. The model is represented by a set of successful sequences of states and actions ended up with either positive or negative feedback. Making a decision, the currently perceived sequence in the evidence log is used to find the nearest successful sequence in the model memory and apply it executing the corresponding action, or a random action is made if no match is found. The extended version of it called "SequentialAvoidance" is different so when no successful sequence is found and a random choice is being made, the unsuccessful sequences ended up with a negative feedback are discarded. Both versions may be extended with an option to make "fuzzy matching" so if no exact match for a successful sequence is found, the most similar one in the model memory is considered, based on the specified threshold in the range 0.0–1.0.

Second, "State-Action" model - the "sub-symbolic" one - was employed as a three-layer network connecting states to actions, with the input layer corresponding to the values of input predicates and a hidden layer representing compound states. The state-to-action connection weights were updated on every positive feedback event with positive correction. Optionally, if configured so, the weights could be updated also in case of any negative feedback with negative correction. Based on the "global feedback" principle, the state-action weights in a network were updated for every state and action pairs contained in the scope of the attention focus. The attention focus scope was being accumulated with every new state transition and reset upon any feedback arrival. When a decision was necessary, this model was operating in either a) the "non-fuzzy" mode when an action was selected only in case if the current state was perfectly predicting an action or b) the "fuzzy" mode when an action was selected only in case if it was predicted with certainty above the specified threshold in the range 0.0–1.0.

Third, the "Change-Action" model was a variant of the "State-Action" model where each state in a model was actually a "state transition" or a change between the previous and the current state, so the actions were associated not with states per se but with state transitions including the previous state and the current state.

7   Experimental Results

All three learning models were applied to a simplified version of the Atari Breakout game [6] called "self-pong" as described above. The results are presented on Fig. 6. The experiments were run for the same agent employing the same learning models with the inputs consisting of predicates representing environmental states in either a "functional" or a "discrete" operational space accordingly to the respective domain ontologies.

Environment	Player Algorithm	Immediate feedback					Delayed feedback				
		2X4	4X6	6X8	8X10	Avg	2X4	4X6	6X8	8X10	Avg
Functional	Sequential	89	88	88	92	89	70	73	72	85	75
Functional	SequentialAvoidance	92	90	90	93	91	67	73	81	85	77
Functional	SequentialAvoidance 0.5	93	93	93	93	93	80	83	81	89	83
Functional	State-Action	94	88	91	94	92	64	71	79	80	74
Functional	State-Action 0.5	93	88	87	93	90	64	68	75	83	73
Functional	Change-Action	91	86	89	92	90	64	73	76	79	73
Functional	Change-Action 0.5	93	90	90	93	92	63	69	80	84	74
Discrete	Sequential	89	88	88	92	89	70	73	72	85	75
Discrete	SequentialAvoidance	92	90	90	93	91	67	73	81	85	77
Discrete	SequentialAvoidance 0.5	93	91	88	92	91	70	76	80	83	77
Discrete	State-Action	94	88	91	94	92	64	71	79	80	74
Discrete	Change-Action	91	86	89	92	90	64	73	76	79	73

Fig. 6. Experimental results with columns: Environment: a "functional" or a "discrete" operational space and the respective domain ontology; Player Algorithm: a learning model, with 0.5 indicating fuzziness threshold. Numbers indicate the success rates (%) during the training period till the Agent is capable of playing without failures, so they correspond to the speed of learning. The "Avg" column indicates the average success rate across different game field sizes ($2 \times 4, 4 \times 6, 6 \times 8, 8 \times 10$) for each of the kinds of the feedback ("immediate" or "delayed").

All models were explored with different sizes of the game field ($2 \times 4, 4 \times 6, 6 \times 8, 8 \times 10$) under the conditions of experiencing negative and positive feedbacks. In the simplest case, the "Immediate feedback" was assumed so the positive stimulus ("Happy") was directed to the Agent by the environment at the point when a racket is successfully meeting the ball. In a more complex case of "Delayed feedback", the positive feedback was communicated only upon the ball hitting the ceiling being successfully reflected by a racket earlier.

Evaluation of the learning process success has been made based on success rate in percent during the training phase. The success rate was identified as the total number of positive feedbacks denominated by the sum of all positive and negative feedbacks. The training phase duration was selected as a number of epochs spent till an agent can play totally avoiding perception of negative feedback. The training phase duration was adjusted to be the same across all the learning models ("Player Algorithm" on Fig. 3) for specific size of the game field and sort of feedback (immediate or delayed).

The code implementing the cognitive architecture, the models, the game environment and all of the experiments may be found on GitHub: https://github.com/aigents/aigents-java/tree/master/src/main/java/net/webstructor/agi.

A video featuring the process of learning can be watched on YouTube: https://www.youtube.com/watch?v=2LPLhJKh95g.

For all or the experimental conditions discussed above, the Agent was able to learn the game without failures, eventually. The presented approach has turned out to be practical in terms of shortening the learning times and implementing the "one-shot" learning concept. As it would be expected, expanding the game field and replacing immediate feedback with delayed feedback increased the learning times and decreased the success rates. The following conclusions were made.

1) Both "Functional" and "Discrete" representations of the environment are close to be equivalent from the accuracy (the learning speed on epochs) perspective.
2) Functional representation is much better from the run-time performance (response time and energy saving) perspective.
3) Both avoidance of negative feedback and fuzzy matching of experiences are helpful for increasing accuracy and learning speed.
4) Delayed reward decreases learning speed to the extent of ~ 10–15%.
5) Replacing explicit "symbolic" memories of successive behaviors with global feedback on combinations of "sub-symbolic" state-action contexts effects in: a) a dramatic increase in run-time performance, b) a minor decrease in learning speed.
6) Negative "global feedback" significantly worsens accuracy; learning may get impossible in some cases.

Still, the delayed reward problem is not solved in full, so an increase of the game field along with further delay of either positive or negative reinforcement was making it impossible to get reasonable learning results in the limited scope of this research. This is assumed to take place due to the inability to bound attention focus clearly so occasional positive feedbacks were allocated to multiple random state-action transitions loosely relevant to the eventual sparse feedback.

8   Conclusion

We have evaluated both "interpretable" functional representation and "non-interpretable" discrete representation of operational environment. We have done it using both "interpretable" symbolic representation and "non-interpretable" sub-symbolic versions of behavioral processes and their underlying models. Based on the study, we conclude that interpretable "one-shot" reinforcement learning is achievable to the same extent in all explored configurations and can be successfully done in both "interpretable" space and "non-interpretable" one. It has been found that acting within an "explainable" operational space saves memory and computing resources due to its more "structured" compact functional representation.

Converting a "non-explainable" discrete space to an "explainable" functional one, remains a challenge, however, which can potentially be solved with hybrid neuro-symbolic architectures. For this purpose, further studies on both "vertical" and "horizontal" neuro-symbolic integration architectures are necessary.

References

1. Tsamoura, E., Michael, L.: Neural-Symbolic Integration: A Compositional Perspective (2020). arXiv:2010.11926 [cs.AI]. https://arxiv.org/abs/2010.11926
2. Garcez, A., et al.: Neural-Symbolic Computing: An Effective Methodology for Principled Integration of Machine Learning and Reasoning (2019). arXiv:1905.06088 [cs.AI]
3. Silver, D., et al.: Reward is Enough. Artificial Intelligence, vol. 299 (October 2021). https://doi.org/10.1016/j.artint.2021.103535
4. Francois-Lavet, V., et al.: An Introduction to Deep Reinforcement Learning (2018). arXiv: 1811.12560 [cs.LG]. https://arxiv.org/abs/1811.12560
5. Moreira, I., et al.: Deep Reinforcement Learning with Interactive Feedback in a Human-Robot Environment (2020). arXiv:2007.03363 [cs.AI]. https://arxiv.org/abs/2007.03363
6. Mnih, V., et al.: Playing Atari with Deep Reinforcement Learning (2013). arXiv:1312.5602 [cs.LG]. https://arxiv.org/abs/1312.5602
7. Kahneman, D.: Thinking, Fast and Slow. Farrar Straus & Giroux, January 1, 1994 (1994)
8. Marcus, G.: The Next Decade in AI: Four Steps Towards Robust Artificial Intelligence (2020). arXiv:2002.06177 [cs.AI]. https://arxiv.org/abs/2002.06177v1
9. Mostafa, H., et al.: Deep Supervised Learning Using Local Errors (2017). arXiv:1711.06756 [cs.NE]. https://arxiv.org/abs/1711.06756
10. Lindsey, J., Ashok Litwin-Kumar, A.: Learning to Learn with Feedback and Local Plasticity (2020). arXiv:2006.09549 [cs.NE]. https://arxiv.org/abs/2006.09549
11. Ciszak, M., et al.: Emergent Excitability in Adaptive Networks of Non-Excitable Units (2020). arXiv:2010.06249 [nlin.AO]. https://arxiv.org/abs/2010.06249
12. Aljaberi, S., et al.: Global and Local Synaptic Regulation Determine the Stability of Homeostatic Plasticity (2021). arXiv:2103.15001 [nlin.AO]. https://arxiv.org/abs/2103.15001
13. Noh, K., et al.: Impaired coupling of local and global functional feedbacks underlies abnormal synchronization and negative symptoms of schizophrenia. BMC Syst. Biol. 7(1), 30 (2013). https://doi.org/10.1186/1752-0509-7-30
14. Kolb, A., Kolb, D.: Experiential learning theory. In: Encyclopedia of the Sciences of Learning, pp. 1212–1219. Springer, Boston (2012). https://doi.org/10.1007/978-1-4419-1428-6_227
15. Zbontar, J., et al.: Barlow Twins: Self-Supervised Learning via Redundancy Reduction (2021). arXiv:2103.03230 [cs.CV]. https://arxiv.org/abs/2103.03230
16. Arrieta, A.B., et al.: Explainable artificial intelligence (XAI): concepts, taxonomies, opportunities and challenges toward responsible AI. Inf. Fusion 58, 82–115 (2019). https://doi.org/10.1016/j.inffus.2019.12.012
17. Rudin, C., et al.: Interpretable Machine Learning: Fundamental Principles and 10 Grand Challenges (2021). arXiv:2103.11251 [cs.LG]. https://arxiv.org/abs/2103.11251
18. Vityaev, E.: Semantic Probabilistic Inference of Predictions. In: Series «Mathematics», vol. 21 (2017). https://doi.org/10.26516/1997-7670.2017.21.33
19. Kolonin, A.: Controlled Language and Baby Turing Test for General Conversational Intelligence (2020). arXiv:2005.09280 [cs.AI]. https://arxiv.org/abs/2005.09280
20. Vityaev, E.E., Demin, A.V., Kolonin, Y.A.: Logical probabilistic biologically inspired cognitive architecture. In: Goertzel, B., Panov, A.I., Potapov, A., Yampolskiy, R. (eds.) AGI 2020. LNCS (LNAI), vol. 12177, pp. 337–346. Springer, Cham (2020). https://doi.org/10.1007/978-3-030-52152-3_36
21. Kolonin, A.: Computable cognitive model based on social evidence and restricted by resources: applications for personalized search and social media in multi-agent environments. In: 2015 International Conference on Biomedical Engineering and Computational Technologies (2015). https://ieeexplore.ieee.org/document/7361869?arnumber=7361869

Navigating Conceptual Space; A New Take on AGI

Per Roald Leikanger[(✉)]

UiT - The Arctic University of Norway, Tromsø, Norway
`Per.R.Leikanger@uit.no`

Abstract. Edward C. Tolman found reinforcement learning unsatisfactory for explaining intelligence and proposed a clear distinction between learning and behavior. Tolman's ideas on latent learning and cognitive maps eventually led to what is now known as conceptual space, a geometric representation where concepts and ideas can form points or shapes. Active navigation between ideas – reasoning – can be expressed directly as purposive navigation in conceptual space. Assimilating the theory of conceptual space from modern neuroscience, we propose autonomous navigation as a valid approach for emulated cognition. However, achieving autonomous navigation in high-dimensional Euclidean spaces is not trivial in technology. In this work, we explore whether neoRL navigation is up for the task; adopting Kaelbling's concerns for efficient robot navigation, we test whether the neoRL approach is general across navigational modalities, compositional across considerations of experience, and effective when learning in multiple Euclidean dimensions. We find neoRL learning to be more resemblant of biological learning than of RL in AI, and propose neoRL navigation of conceptual space as a plausible new path toward emulated cognition.

1 Introduction

Edward C. Tolman first proposed cognitive maps for explaining the mechanism behind rats taking shortcuts and what he referred to as latent learning [25]. Tolman was not satisfied with behaviorists' view that goals and purposes could be reduced to a hard-wired desire for reward [4]. Experiments showed that unrewarded rats would perform better than the fully rewarded group when later *motivated* by reward [26]. Arguing that a reinforcement signal was more important for behavior than for learning, Tolman proposed the existence of a cognitive model of the environment in the form of a *cognitive map*. The mechanisms behind neural representation of Euclidean space (NRES) has later been identified for a range of navigational modalities by electrophysical measurements [3]. Further, the NRES mechanism has been implied for navigating *conceptual space* [5], a Euclidean representation where betweenness and relative location makes sense for explaining concepts [7]. Results from theoretical neuroscience indicate NRES' role in social navigation [17], temporal representation [6], and reasoning [2]. Cognitive maps for representing thought have received much attention in

© Springer Nature Switzerland AG 2022
B. Goertzel et al. (Eds.): AGI 2021, LNAI 13154, pp. 116–126, 2022.
https://doi.org/10.1007/978-3-030-93758-4_13

neurophysiology in the recent five years [2,5,17]. Navigating conceptual space as an analogy of thought could explain generalization and reasoning based on locality [7].

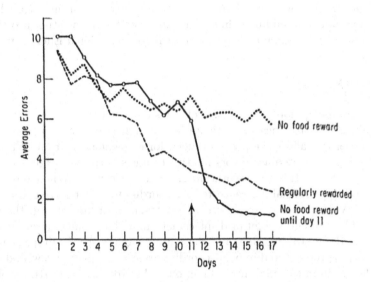

Fig. 1. Evidence for latent learning by Tolman and Honzik (1930). (after [26], from *Systems and theories of psychology* [4]).

Autonomous navigation is difficult to reproduce in technology. Autonomous operation implies a decision *agent* capable of forming decisions based on own desires and experience. A well-renowned approach to establish experience-based behavior is reinforcement learning (RL) from AI. Via trial and error based on a scalar reward signal $\mathbb{R}$, a decision *agent* is capable of adapting behavior according to the accumulation of $\mathbb{R}$. Considering robot path planning as Euclidean navigation, we look toward robot learning for inspiration on autonomous navigation. However; whereas RL powered by deep function approximation has been demonstrated for playing board games at an expert level, requirements to sample efficiency combined with high Markov dimensionality in temporal systems makes deep RL difficult in navigation learning [10]. Leslie Kaelbling (2020) points out key challenges for efficient robot learning, apparently concerned with the current direction of deep RL. Navigation has to be efficient (require few interactions for learning new behaviors), general (applicable to situations outside one's direct experience), and compositional/incremental (compositional with earlier knowledge, incremental with earlier considerations). The current state-of-the-art deep RL for robotics struggles on all three points [9].

Inspired by neural navigation capabilities, Leikanger (2019) has developed an NRES-oriented RL (neoRL) architecture for online navigation [12]. Via orthogonal value functions (OVF) formed by off-policy learning toward each cell of an

NRES representation, the neoRL architecture allows for a distinction between learning and behavior. Inspired by animal psychology, the neoRL framework allows purposive behavior to form based on the desire for anticipated reward [13]. However, navigating a multi-dimensional conceptual space of unknown dimensionality in real-time would be impossible for any current learning algorithm. In this work, we adopt Kaelbling's three concerns when testing whether neoRL navigation allows for autonomous navigation in high-dimensional Euclidean space.

2   Theory

Central to all navigation is knowledge of one's current navigational state. Information about relative location, orientation, and heading to objects that can block or otherwise affect the path is crucial for efficient navigation. When such knowledge is represented as vectors relative to one's current configuration, neuroscientists refer to this representation as being *egocentric*. When represented relative to some external reference frame, coordinates are referred to as being *allocentric*. Vectors can be expressed as Cartesian coordinates, e.g. the vector $\vec{a} = [1.0, 3.0]$ represent a point or displacement in a plane, one unit size from the origin along the first dimension, and three units along a second dimension. Vectors can also be represented in polar coordinates $\vec{a} = [r, \varphi]$, a point with distance r from the origin in the allocentric direction φ. In order to apply RL for navigation, all this information must be represented according to the Markov property; each instance of agent state must contain enough data to define next-state distribution [20]. Combined with temporal dynamics, the number of such instances becomes prohibitively expensive for autonomous navigation by RL [10]. Neural state representation, on the other hand, appears to be fully distributed across individual neurons and parts of the hippocampal formation [18]. NRES coding for separate navigational modalities (as should be represented in separate Euclidean spaces) have been located in different structures in the hippocampal formation [3]. Navigational state representation for the only system capable of true autonomous navigation seems to be decomposed across multiple NRES modalities. This section introduces theory and considerations on how state is represented in the animal and the learning machine, an important inspiration for neoRL mechanisms for navigation and problem solving.

2.1   Neural Representation of Euclidean Space

The first identified NRES neuron was the *place cell* [16]; O'Keefe and Dostrovsky discovered that specific neurons in the hippocampus became active whenever the animal traversed a specific location in the test environment. Reflecting the allocentric position of the animal, the individual place cell could be thought of as a geometric *feature detector* on the animal's location; the place cell is active whenever the animal is located within the *receptive field* of the cell. Other NRES cells have later been identified, expressing information in various parameter spaces. Identified NRES modalities for navigation includes: one's allocentric location

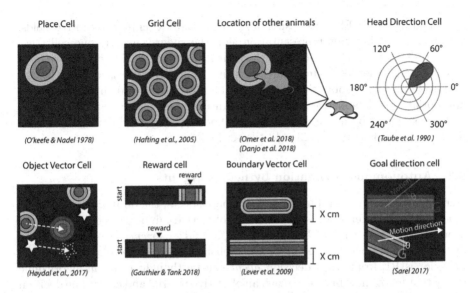

Fig. 2. Some identified NRES modalities of importance for navigation, with reference to the original publication. All NRES modalities could be important for autonomous spatial navigation. The place cell and the object vector cell will be of particular importance in the examples and experiments of this text. (Illustration adopted from [1]

[16], allocentric polar vector coordinates to external objects [8], and one's current heading [24]. A selection of relevant NRES modalities is listed in Table 1 or in Fig. 2. A more comprehensive study on NRES modalities in neurophysiology has been composed by Bugress and Bicanski [3].

Table 1. Neural representation for different Euclidean spaces of importance for navigation: Head-direction cells reflect the current allocentric (*ac.*) angle of the head (a scalar parameter). The place cell and border cell respond to a proximal allocentric location (2D). The remaining NRES reflect conditions represented in other Euclidean spaces – listed as NRES modalities.

	Location	Tuning	Direction	NRES modality	
Place cell	Ac.	[proximal] 2D	–	Current position	[16]
Border cell	Ac.	[proximal] 2D	–	Location of borders	[19]
Object vector cell	Polar c.	[spectrum] 2D	Ac.	Location of objects	[8]
Boundary vector cell	Polar c.	[spectrum] 2D	Ac.	Location of boundaries	[14]
Head-direction cell	–	[angular] 1D	Ac.	Head direction	[24]
Speed cell	–	[rate code] 1D	–	Current velocity	[11]

Neuroscientists assume that populations of NRES neurons map Euclidean vectors by neural patterns of activation. A simple mapping could be formed by a population of NRES cells responding to mutually exclusive receptive fields. One could visualize this representation as a chessboard; exactly one cell (tile) would be satisfied for any point on the board. Referred to as *one-hot encoding*[1] in computing sciences, a mutually exclusive map structure is defined by the resolution and the geometric coverage of the map's tiles. This intuitive map is appropriate for demonstrative purposes: All examples and experiments in this text are encoded by a comprehensive one-hot mapping as illustrated in Fig. 3, where, e.g., $N13$ signifies a 13×13 tile set in $\Re^2$.

2.2   Autonomous Navigation by neoRL Agents

One can separate navigation into two distinct aspects; the desired location – the objective of the interaction – and how this objective can be reached. When both aspects are governed by one's own inclinations and *experience*, we refer to this as an autonomous operation. A most accomplished approach to experience-based behavior is RL from AI; a decision *agent* can be thought of as an algorithmic entity that learns how better to reach an objective by trial and error. The decision process of the agent can be summarized by 3 signals: the *state* of the system before the interaction, the *action* with which the agent interacts with the system, and a *reward* signal that reflects the success of the operation with regard to an objective. Experience can be expressed via the *value function*, reflecting the expected total reward from this state and forward under the current policy. Since behavior (policy) is based on the current value function, and the value function is defined under one policy, an alternating iterative improvement is required for learning. The resulting asymptotic progress is slow, requiring many interactions by RL learning. Although RL has proven effective for solving a range of algorithmic tasks, autonomous control for robotics remains a challenge [10]. Even RL powered by deep function approximation (deep RL) has limited applicability for online interaction learning in Euclidean spaces [9].

A neoRL agent, on the other hand, is composed by a set of sub-agents learning how to achieve different NRES cells for the corresponding NRES representation [12]. The whole set of learning processes constitutes the (latent) learning aspect of the agent; behavior can later be harvested as a weighted sum over the OVFs according to priorities [13]. Learning OVFs as general value functions [21] with ℝ defined by NRES cell activation, the value function of the whole neoRL agent resembles Kurt Lewin's *fieldt theory* of learning [15]. Leikanger (2021) demonstrated how emulated NRES for agent state allows for autonomous navigation in a single Euclidean space [13], however, multi-modal navigation and combining experience across NRES modalities remains to be tested. As multi-modal NRES capabilities would bring neoRL state representation closer to navigational state representation in the brain, compositionality across NRES modalities would be important for making neoRL a plausible candidate for conceptual navigation.

---

[1]   Note for computing scientists: NRES is not concerned with the Markov state. Any similarity to RL coarse coding and CMAC can therefore be considered to be an endorsement of these AI techniques, not grounds for direct comparison.

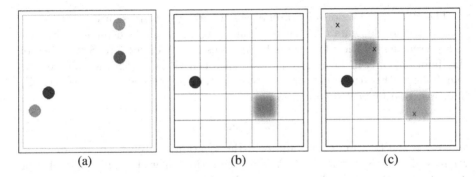

(a)   (b)   (c)

Fig. 3. (A) The allocentric WaterWorld environment: Blue entity is governed by inertia dynamics, with a desire for green ($\mathbb{R} = +1$) and aversion for red ($\mathbb{R} = -1$). (B) An $N5$ mapping of NRES: Each axis is divided into $N = 5$ equal intervals, resulting in $N^2 = 25$ NRES cells. An OVF represents the value function toward one NRES activation. (C) Learned NRES maps can form behaviors via anticipated reward: When an NRES tile contains an element associated with reward, the corresponding OVF is weighted accordingly. Anticipated rewards are illustrated using the same colors as in (A); one aversive NRES cell in red and two desirable NRES cells associated with various anticipation are represented in shades of green. (Color figure online)

3   Multi-modal neoRL Navigation

Adopting Kaelbling's three concerns for Euclidean navigation, we next explore how neoRL navigation scales with increasing (Euclidean) dimensionality. First, it is crucial that NRES-oriented navigation can operate based on different Euclidean spaces; with little knowledge of the form or meaning of conceptual spaces, neoRL must be capable of navigation by other information than location. Further, we are interested in how neoRL navigation scales with additional parameters or across multiple NRES modalities. Any exponential increase in training time with additional states would make conceptual navigation infeasible. NeoRL navigation must be *general* across NRES modalities, *compositional* across conceptual components, without any significant decline in learning *efficiency*. In this section, we explore neoRL capabilities for hi-dimensional navigation by experiments inspired by Kaelbling's concerns for efficient robot navigation.

All experiments are conducted in the allocentric version of the WaterWorld environment [23], illustrated in Fig. 3A. An agent controls the movement of the self (blue dot), with a set of actions that accelerate the object in the four directions N, S, E, W. Three objects of interest move freely in a closed section of a Euclidean plane. When the agent encounters an object, it is replaced by a new object with a random color, location, and speed vector. Green objects are desirable with an accompanying reward $\mathbb{R} = +1.0$, and red objects should be avoided with $\mathbb{R} = -1.0$. No other rewards exist in these experiments, making $\mathbb{R}$ a decent measure of an agent's navigation capabilities. Note that the agent must catch the last green in a board full of red before the board can be reset and continue beyond (on average) 1.5 points per reset.

The PLE [22] version of WaterWorld reports the Cartesian coordinates of the agent and elements of interest; thinking of the Euclidean plane in Fig. 3A as representing location facilitates later discussion. A direct NRES encoding of this information will be referred to as place cell (PC) NRES modality in the remainder of this text. One can also compute a simple object vector cell (OVC) interpretation by vector subtraction:

$$\vec{o^i}_{\text{OVC}} = \vec{o^i}_{\text{PC}} - \vec{s}_{\text{PC}}$$

where $\vec{s}$ is the location of self and $\vec{o^i}$ is the location of object i in PC or OVC reference frame. Note that this OVC interpretation allows for a modality similar to OVC with the self in the center and allocentric direction to external objects, but not with polar coordinates as reported for OVC [8]. However, the two Cartesian representations of location still give different points of view due to different reference frames. Information is encoded in NRES maps as described in Sect. 2.1; the neoRL agent is organized across multiple NRES maps of different resolutions as described in [13]. Multi-res NRES modalities cover resolutions given by primes up to $N13$, i.e., with layers $N2, N3, N5, N7, N11,$ and $N13$. For more on multi-resolution neoRL agents and the mechanism behind policy from parallel NRES state spaces, see [13]. All execution runs smoothly on a single CPU core, and the agent starts with no priors other than described in this section. Referring to the NRES modalities as PC and OVC for WaterWorld is only syntactical to facilitate later discussions; 2D Euclidean coordinates are general and can represent any parameter pair.

Learning efficiency is compared by considering the transient proficiency of the agent as measured by the reward received by the agent during $0.2s$ intervals. Any end-of-episode reward is disabled in the WaterWorld settings; the only received reward is $\mathbb{R} = +1$ when encountering green elements and $\mathbb{R} = -1$ when encountering red elements. The simple reward structure makes accumulated $\mathbb{R}$ a direct measure of how well the agent performed during one run. However, observing the transient proficiency – real-time learning efficiency – of the agent requires further analysis: in all experiments, a per-interval average or received reward is computed over 100 independent runs with additional smoothing by a Butterworth low-pass filter. All runs are conducted in isolation; the agent is initiated before each run and deleted after the run – without any accumulation of experience between runs. The x-axis of every plot represents minutes since agent initiation. The y-axis represents proficiency as computed by the per-interval average of received reward, scaled to reflect $[\mathbb{R}/s]$. Proficiency thus measures how many more desirable (green) encounters happen per second than unwanted (red) ones.

3.1   NeoRL Navigation: NRES Generality

First, we examine the generality of the neoRL architecture by comparing navigational proficiency for an agent exposed to a PC modality to one exposed to an OVC modality. We are interested in the generality of neoRL navigation; can neoRL navigate the PC modality by different Euclidean information, and at what cost?

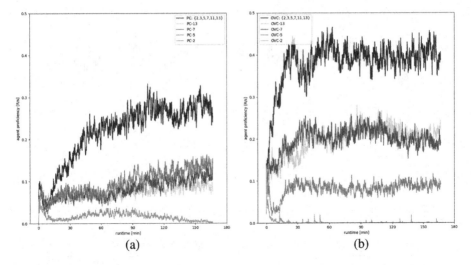

Fig. 4. The neoRL architecture is general across NRES modalities: (A) an original place cell (PC) NRES modality, implemented by applying NRES code directly on an allocentric location of the agent or elements of interest. (B) an emulated object vector cell (OVC) NRES modality, implemented by vector subtraction. OVC is centered on the self with an allocentric representation of other objects.

Results are presented in Fig. 4: agent proficiency from the original PC modality (Fig. 4A) can be compared with agent proficiency when navigating by the OVC modality (Fig. 4B). The immediate proficiency of several mono-resolution neoRL agents is plotted alongside the proficiency of a multi-resolution neoRL agent. There is no loss in sample efficiency when utilizing the OVC modality compared to PC modality. The multi-res neoRL agent performs better than mono-res neoRL agents for both the PC and the OVC modality. NeoRL navigation performs well across both aspects of experience, indicating that the neoRL architecture is general across navigational modalities.

3.2   NeoRL Navigation: NRES Compositionality

Secondly, we are interested in how neoRL scales with additional navigational information. Experiment 1 showed how a neoRL agent is capable of reactive navigation based on an auxiliary NRES modality. In this experiment, we explore the benefit of combining experience across more than one NRES modality. A multi-modal neoRL agent is exposed to both the PC and the OVC modality from experiment 1, effectively doubling the number of NRES states for the agent to consider. We are anxious about how well the neoRL architecture scales with the additional information, both for final proficiency and learning time.

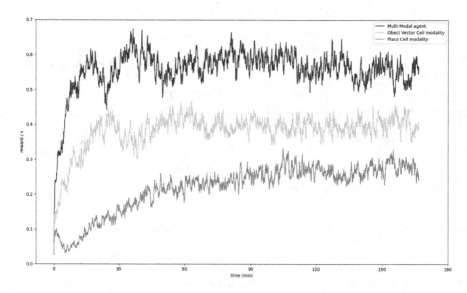

Fig. 5. Multi-modal neoRL navigation leads to higher proficiency and quicker learning than mono-modal agents, despite having twice as many NRES states.

Compare the proficiency of the neoRL agent when exposed to PC, OVC, and multi-modal information in Fig. 5. Combining information across multiple NRES modalities significantly improves navigational performance. The final proficiency of the multi-modal neoRL agent approaches $0.55[\mathbb{R}/s]$ while the PC neoRL agent barely reaches $0.29[\mathbb{R}/s]$. The multi-modal neoRL agent reaches final proficiency after 15 min, whereas the PC neoRL agent uses more than 160 min. In terms of learning efficiency, i.e., how fast the agent reaches final proficiency, and in terms of trained performance, the multi-modal neoRL agent performs better than both mono-modal neoRL agents.

4 Discussion

Contrary to RL in AI, neoRL navigation learns quicker, to higher proficiency, when more information is available to an agent. The neoRL agent is capable of multi-modal navigation, making multi-dimensional Euclidean navigation by a digital agent plausible.

Moving on from reinforcement learning and classical behaviorism, Tolman made a clear distinction between learning and performance after his latent learning experiments (see Fig. 1). Observing how an animal could learn facts about the world that could subsequently be used in a flexible manner, Tolman proposed what he called purposive behaviorism. When motivated by the promise of reward, the animal could utilize latent knowledge to form beneficial behavior toward that objective. Mechanisms underlying orientation have further been implied in cognition, a conceptual space where ideas are represented as points in a multi-dimensional Euclidean space. Technological advances have allowed new evidence from modern neuroscience, supporting Tolman's hypotheses on cognitive maps' involvement in thought. Inferring that active navigation of such a space corresponds to reasoning and problem solving, we here propose autonomous navigation of conceptual space as an interesting new approach to artificial general intelligence. However, navigating conceptual space – with high dimensionality, an unknown form, and possibly an evolving number of Euclidean dimensions, is no trivial challenge for technology. Based on neural representation of space, the neoRL architecture is distributed and concurrent in learning, capable of separating between latent learning and purposive behavior, and a good candidate for emulated cognition by autonomous navigation of conceptual space.

Adopting Kaelbling's concerns for efficient robot learning to account for multi-modal navigation, we have methodically tested neoRL navigation in the WaterWorld environment. Firstly, it is crucial that neoRL navigation can operate in other Euclidean spaces than its primary navigation modality. Our first experiment verifies that the neoRL architecture is general across Euclidean spaces; a neoRL agent that navigates by the location modality is compared to one exposed to a relative-vector representation of external objects. Both NRES modalities perform admirably at this task, indicating that neoRL navigation is not restricted to one NRES modality. Secondly, we explore how neoRL navigation scales with additional NRES modalities; an agent based on both a place-cell and an object-vector-cell representation is compared to the two mono-modal neoRL agents from experiment 1. Navigation, both in training efficiency and final proficiency, improves significantly when more information is available to the agent. High-dimensional Euclidean navigation appears to be plausible with neoRL technology, formed by the basic principles from neuroscience and NRES.

In this work, we have collected evidence from theoretical neuroscience and the psychology of learning to propose a new direction toward emulated cognition. We have shown how online autonomous navigation is feasible by the neoRL architecture; still, the most interesting steps toward conceptual navigation in machines remain. What are the implications of autonomous navigation of conceptual space for AGI? Could latent spaces from deep networks be used for neoRL navigation? Should desires (elements of interest) propagate across NRES modalities based on associativity? Many important questions are yet to be asked. In showing that neoRL is up for the task of multi-modal navigation, we hereby propose a novel approach to AGI and present a plausible first step toward conceptual navigation in machines.

References

1. Behrens, T.E., et al.: What is a cognitive map? organizing knowledge for flexible behavior. Neuron **100**(2), 490–509 (2018)
2. Bellmund, J.L., Gärdenfors, P., Moser, E.I., Doeller, C.F.: Navigating cognition: spatial codes for human thinking. Science **362**(6415) (2018)
3. Bicanski, A., Burgess, N.: Neuronal vector coding in spatial cognition. Nat. Rev. Neurosci. **21**, 1–18 (2020)

4. Chaplin, J.P.: Systems and Theories of Psychology. Holt, Rinehart and Winston, New York (1961)
5. Constantinescu, A.O., O'Reilly, J.X., Behrens, T.E.: Organizing conceptual knowledge in humans with a gridlike code. Science **352**(6292), 1464–1468 (2016)
6. Eichenbaum, H.: Time cells in the hippocampus: a new dimension for mapping memories. Nat. Rev. Neurosci. **15**(11), 732–744 (2014)
7. Gärdenfors, P.: Conceptual Spaces: The Geometry of Thought. MIT press, Cambridge (2000)
8. Høydal, Ø.A., Skytøen, E.R., Andersson, S.O., Moser, M.B., Moser, E.I.: Object-vector coding in the medial entorhinal cortex. Nature **568**(7752), 400–404 (2019)
9. Kaelbling, L.P.: The foundation of efficient robot learning. Science **369**(6506), 915–916 (2020)
10. Kober, J., Bagnell, J.A., Peters, J.: Reinforcement learning in robotics: a survey. Int. J. Rob. Res. **32**(11), 1238–1274 (2013)
11. Kropff, E., Carmichael, J.E., Moser, M.B., Moser, E.I.: Speed cells in the medial entorhinal cortex. Nature **523**(7561), 419–424 (2015)
12. Leikanger, P.R.: Modular RL for real-time learning. In: The 3rd Conference on Cognitive and Computational Neuroscience (2019)
13. Leikanger, P.R.: Decomposing the prediction problem; autonomous navigation by neoRL agents. In: ALIFE 2021: The 2021 Conference on Artificial Life (2021)
14. Lever, C., Burton, S., Jeewajee, A., O'Keefe, J., Burgess, N.: Boundary vector cells in the subiculum of the hippocampal formation. J. Neurosci. **29**(31), 9771–9777 (2009)
15. Lewin, K.: Field theory and learning (1942)
16. O'Keefe, J., Dostrovsky, J.: The hippocampus as a spatial map: preliminary evidence from unit activity in the freely-moving rat. Brain Res. **34**, 171–175 (1971)
17. Schafer, M., Schiller, D.: Navigating social space. Neuron **100**(2), 476–489 (2018)
18. Solstad, T.: Neural representations of Euclidean space. PhD thesis, Kavli Insitute of Systems Neuroscience/Center of Neural Computation (2009)
19. Solstad, T., Boccara, C.N., Kropff, E., Moser, M.B., Moser, E.I.: Representation of geometric borders in the entorhinal cortex. Science **322**(5909), 1865–1868 (2008)
20. Sutton, R.S., Barto, A.G.: Reinforcement Learning: An Introduction. MIT press, Cambridge (2018)
21. Sutton, R.S., et al.: Horde: a scalable real-time architecture for learning knowledge from unsupervised sensorimotor interaction. In: The 10th International Conference on Autonomous Agents and Multiagent Systems, vol. 2, pp. 761–768. International Foundation for Autonomous Agents and Multiagent Systems (2011)
22. Tasfi, N.: Pygame learning environment. https://github.com/ntasfi/PyGame-Learning-Environment, Accessed 01 Sept 2020
23. Tasfi, N.: Waterworld in pygame learning environment. https://github.com/ntasfi/PyGame-Learning-Environment, Accessed 04 Apr 2021
24. Taube, J.S., Muller, R.U., Ranck, J.B.: Head-direction cells recorded from the postsubiculum in freely moving rats. i. description and quantitative analysis. J. Neurosci. **10**(2), 420–435 (1990)
25. Tolman, E.C.: Cognitive maps in rats and men. Psychol. Rev. **55**(4), 189 (1948)
26. Tolman, E.C., Honzik, C.H.: Degrees of hunger, reward and non-reward, and maze learning in rats. University of California Publications in Psychology (1930)

Categorical Artificial Intelligence: The Integration of Symbolic and Statistical AI for Verifiable, Ethical, and Trustworthy AI

Yoshihiro Maruyama[✉]

School of Computing, The Australian National University, Canberra, Australia
yoshihiro.maruyama@anu.edu.au

Abstract. Statistical artificial intelligence based upon machine learning is facing major challenges such as machine bias, explainability, and verifiability problems. Resolving them would be of the utmost importance for ethical, safe, and responsible AI for social good. In this paper we propose to address these problems with the (recently rapidly developing) methodology of category theory, a powerful integrative scientific language from pure mathematics, and discuss, in particular, the possibility of the categorical integration of statistical (inductive) with symbolic (deductive) artificial intelligence. Categorical artificial intelligence arguably has the potential to resolve the aforementioned urgent problems, thus being beneficial to make artificial intelligence more ethical, verifiable, responsible, and so more human, which would be crucial for AI-pervasive society.

Keywords: Categorical AI · Integrative AI · Statistical AI · Symbolic AI · Explainable AI · Ethical AI · Verifiable AI · Trustworthy AI

1 Introduction

The currently predominant paradigm of AI, namely Statistical AI based upon the inductive methods of machine learning, is facing two types of critical challenges, i.e., the problem of machine biases and the problem of verifiability or explainability (see, e.g., [1,5,29,32,35,36,39]). Resolving these problems in current AI research is crucial for Ethical, Responsible, and Trustworthy AI for Social Good. In this paper we aim to discuss the possibility of addressing these urgent problems in AI with the novel mathematical methodology of category theory [16], a new kind of structural mathematics applied as a powerful integrative language in a broad variety of sciences, including symbolic logic and programming language theory [20,25,26,42, ?,?], theoretical physics and quantum computation [2,11,27,28,31], mathematical linguistics and NLP (natural language processing) [9,19,33,34,41], database theory and circuit theory [16], biology and chemistry [3], cognitive science and psychology [40], and more recently, machine learning [12,15,31]. In particular, we propose the structural category-theoretical

© Springer Nature Switzerland AG 2022
B. Goertzel et al. (Eds.): AGI 2021, LNAI 13154, pp. 127–138, 2022.
https://doi.org/10.1007/978-3-030-93758-4_14

integration of Statistical AI with Symbolic AI (based upon the deductive methods of symbolic logic), i.e., the categorical integration of Inductive AI with Deductive AI. Categorical Integrated AI arguably allows us to resolve the aforementioned major problems that AI research is currently facing, thereby making AI more ethical, more verifiable, more responsible, and thus more human and human-friendly, which would be of the utmost importance for AI-pervasive society.

Neil Thompson at MIT and his collaborators recently published an intriguing article "The Computational Limits of Deep Learning" [47], arguing as follows:

> [P]rogress along current lines is rapidly becoming [...] unsustainable. Thus, continued progress [...] will require dramatically more computationally-efficient methods, which will either have to come from changes to deep learning or from moving to other machine learning methods.

In addition to the computational efficiency problem, there are many other problems in Statistical AI, such as verifiability, explainability, and machine bias issues as mentioned above. How can we address those issues? We consider Integrated AI to be the next-generation paradigm of AI that allows us to resolve those urgent issues in current AI research. The idea of Integrated AI has been around for some time. One of the earliest ideas of Integrated AI comes from Minsky, the 1969 Turing Award winner and co-founder of MIT's AI Lab, who proposes the integration of Symbolic and Connectionist AI in particular (aka. Logical and Analogical AI, or Neat and Scruffy AI) as a form of Integrated AI in his 1991 article [43]:

> Our purely numerical connectionist networks are inherently deficient in abilities to reason well; our purely symbolic logical systems are inherently deficient in abilities to represent the all-important "heuristic connections" between things—the uncertain, approximate, and analogical linkages that we need for making new hypotheses. The versatility that we need can be found only in larger-scale architectures that can exploit and manage the advantages of several types of representations at the same time [...] each can be used to overcome the deficiencies of the others.

Minsky was not able to mathematically embody the idea of Integrated AI, presumably because suitable mathematical tools were not available at that time, but mathematics today is more advanced, and category theory in particular gives a scientific methodology for integration, as it has successfully integrated different scientific theories indeed (which shall be explained in more detail below).

2   Category Theory Across the Sciences

What is category theory? It is the abstract structural mathematics that has allowed for solutions to major concrete problems in pure mathematics, such as the Weil conjectures, on the basis of Grothendieck's category-theoretical algebraic and arithmetic geometry [22]. It was born during the development of algebraic topology in the mid-twentieth century, and soon thereafter employed by

Lawvere [23] and others as the structural foundation that liberates mathematics from material set theory (or its 'pernicious idioms' as Wittgenstein calls them [51]). It has been applied successfully beyond mathematics, in particular, in physics, computer science, and beyond, as mentioned above. Roughly speaking, a category is a structural network of objects and arrows (which specify relations between objects). There are different categories in different sciences. In logic, there is a category of propositions and proofs (deductions from one proposition to another). In computer science, there is a category of data types and programs. In physics, there is a category of quantum systems and quantum processes. Since they are all categories, we can compare and relate their categorical structures. Category theory thus enables transdisciplinary knowledge transfer across different fields of science. It was initially structural foundations of mathematics, and yet it is gradually becoming structural foundations of various sciences as follows:

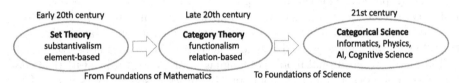

A striking feature of category theory consists in its graphical calculus (aka. string diagrams; see, e.g., [11,45]). It allows for both efficient computation of various tasks and mathematically verifiable and intuitively transparent design of protocols and algorithms. Categorical artificial intelligence enjoys these merits enabled by the graphical string diagram calculus of category theory. Especially, it provides an efficient methodology for linear algebraic (vector-based) computation, and most AI systems represent objects as feature vectors, the computation of which can be performed efficiently in categorical graphical calculus. Let us give a simple example of graphical computation. The commutativity of matrix composition (ordinary matrix product) and tensor product must be proven through complex computation in standard multilinear algebra, but it is topologically obvious in graphical calculus (f, g below are linear maps; sequential composition represents ordinary matrix product, and parallel composition tensor product; tensoring after ordinary composition is different in formula from composition after tensoring, but they are exactly the same in the graphical language) [8,11] (the picture below is due to Bob Coecke [8]):

$$g \circ f \equiv \quad \text{and} \quad k \circ h \equiv \quad \text{so} \quad (g \circ f) \otimes (k \circ h) \equiv$$

$$f \otimes h \equiv \quad \text{and} \quad g \otimes k \equiv \quad \text{so} \quad (g \otimes k) \circ (f \otimes h) \equiv$$

In analogy with the classification of programming languages, category theory gives a high-level language (like Lisp and Haskell) whereas the standard formalism of linear algebra is a low-level language (like assembly languages). Categorical graphical calculus is not an informal heuristic, but supported by the rigorous completeness theorem: an equation is derivable in categorical graphical calculus as above if and only if it holds for standard models (i.e., vector space models in the case of linear algebra) [45]. There are many different versions of graphical calculus available to express computation in different categories including both discrete/algebraic and continuous/probabilistic ones as used in machine learning (see, e.g., [17]). Even automated reasoning systems for graphical calculus are available (see, e.g., [7,13]). Categorical graphical calculus is thus mathematically rigorous and practically applicable and efficient, providing a useful, mathematical language for AI applications. It allows, moreover, for generalising exisiting frameworks beyond ordinary categories; e.g., neural networks expressed in categorical graphical calculus can be instantiated to categories other than ordinary vector space models, allowing us to generalise deep learning beyond vector-based representation spaces, and unifying, e.g., ordinary neural networks (RNN, CNN, etc.) and graph neural networks (Graph RNN, Graph, CNN, etc.; see, e.g., [53]), just as categorical quantum mechanics allows for non-standard toy models, which represent the essential features of quantum theory in a computationally more tractable, simpler manner, and categorical NLP unifies continuous/contextual and discrete/compositional models of language as represented by statistical vector space semantics and logical Montague semantics, respectively (see, e.g., [9]). We shall discuss categorical models of NLP in more detail below.

3   The Categorical Paradigm of Integrative NLP

Applications of category theory to quantum computation and communication have been especially successful, giving a significant simplification of quantum teleportation and other protocols [8,11], and allowing us to design novel quantum algorithms with categorical graphical calculus, such as a vast generalisation of the Grover algorithm [50], and even leading to novel applications in NLP [9,19]. The upper half of the following figure is a graphical (topological) verification of the quantum teleportation protocol by Coecke [8]; it is significantly simpler than the ordinary Hilbert space based verification (see also [10,11]; the picture below is due to Bob Coecke [10]):

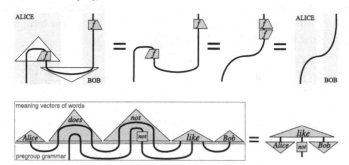

The lower half of the figure illustrates an application of categorical graphical calculus to NLP [8]. The standard statistical distributional model of NLP does not take into account the formal mathematical structure of language such as grammar (e.g., the bag-of-words model as broadly used in Google and elsewhere does not reflect the grammatical structure of language; see, e.g., [49]). Yet we can combine Statistical AI with Symbolic AI via category theory [9,19] to obtain the language model that reflects the compositional structure of grammar (the picture below is due to Dimitry Kartsaklis [21]):

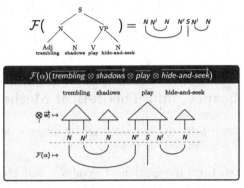

The symbol $\mathcal{F}$ above denotes what is called a strong monoidal functor mapping grammatical structure as represented by Lambek's formal grammar into semantic structure as represented by compact closed categories, an instance of which is the category of vector spaces and another instance of which is the category of sets and relations, which allows us to represent Montague semantics within the unified categorical framework. Categorical NLP thus counts as a structural integration of Symbolic and Statistical AI in the context of language processing, allowing us to compose meaning vectors for complex text from meaning vectors for words. Categorical integrated NLP has been successful and significantly impacted the field (as pioneering papers [9,19] have been cited hundreds of times).

Categorical Integrative NLP has broad possibilities for applications as well as theoretical advtanges. It can, e.g., be expected to improve scientific knowledge discovery from the past (purely linguistic) data of scientific papers, a successful prototype of which was given in a recent *Nature* paper [48]. Yet it is still based upon the statistical model that ignores the structure of language, and thus the Categorical Integrative NLP that takes the structure of language into account allows us to improve its performance; since learning from the existing literature is an indispensable task of Science AI (as well as the human scientist), it contributes to Science AI in general as well as Science NLP in particular. In order to address the machine bias issue in the context of NLP as discussed in a recent *Science* paper [5], we would further have to combine it with a rule-based system in Symbolic AI so as to correct inappropriate biases learned from (potentially contaminated) empirical data, i.e., it corrects inductively learned bottom-up biases with top-down rules expressing ethical principles; this is achieved mathematically by exploiting the common categorical structure that underlies the NLP system and the rule-based system axiomatising relevant ethical principles. To address the verifiability issue, we can use a formal system for categorical program verification, namely categorical Floyd-Hoare logic unifying previously known program logics (see, e.g., [18], which can be adapted for various concrete systems). In the way explained above, we can resolve all the aforementioned issues in current AI research within the specific context of NLP.

The categorical approach not only integrates Symbolic and Statistical AI, but also interlace diverse fields across mathematics, artificial intelligence, and quantum physics, giving an integrative perspective on the sciences through the lens of the unificatory language of category theory. In the following we discuss a more general form of Categorical AI beyond NLP and its significance.

4   Categorical Artificial Intelligence: Four Objectives, Their Significance, and Theoretical Methodology

The general objectives of categorical artificial intelligence as have been mentioned above may be summarised as follows:

- Objective 1: A structural integration of Symbolic and Statistical AI, which arguably lays a theoretical foundation for the next-generation paradigm of AI, and in particular, for applications below.
- Objective 2: Ethical AI and AI for Social Good, which are enabled by correcting bottom-up machine biases in Statistical AI with the top-down rule-based methods of Symbolic AI (as explained in the NLP context above).
- Objective 3: Verifiable AI and AI for the Logic of Science, which are enabled by combining Statistical AI for Hypothesis Discovery with Symbolic AI for Verification or Justification (as in the following picture).
- Objective 4: Strengthening the unity and networking of science whilst keeping its plurality and diversity; category theory arguably gives an integrative methodology to address the contemporary fragmentation of science.

The overall picture can be summarised as follows:

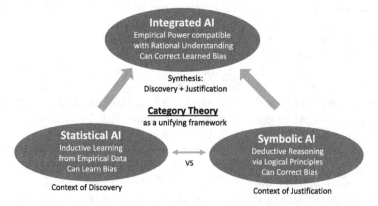

It should be remarked that Reichenbach distinguished between the context of discovery and the context of justification (or verification) in science, and that in the above picture, Statistical AI is considered to be in charge of the context of discovery and Symbolic AI the context of justification (and Integrated AI interweave them as a coherent whole, giving the integrated logic of science).

We elaborate upon the significance of each objective in the following.

Objective 1 is of the following significance (as we have discussed in the above as well). Statistical AI, i.e., AI for Inductive Inference, and Symbolic AI, i.e., AI for Deductive Reasoning, give the full-fledged form of intelligence when interlaced together; induction and deduction are the two fundamental wheels of intelligence (cf. the faculty of sensibility as perceptual pattern recognition and the faculty of understanding and reasoning in Kantian epistemology). Integrated AI is useful for applications as below (allowing for the best of both worlds).

Objective 2 is concerned with the machine bias problem, the significance of which is articulated in the aforementioned *Science* paper demonstrating "Semantics derived automatically from language corpora contain human-like biases" [5]. Purely Inductive AI naively learns biases existing in empirical real-world data (which is often contaminated in various ways), and for the very reason we have to combine it with Symbolic AI, which makes it possible to correct bottom-up learned biases with top-down logical rules expressing moral principles, as explained above in the specfiic context of NLP.

Objective 3 is concerned with the problem of verifiability, which is especially important for the logic of science (by contrast, things like recommender systems do not really require logical verifiability). As shown in the aforementioned *Nature* paper [48], Statistical AI is good at generating scientific hypotheses whilst being bad at verifying them; this is a common problem in Statistical AI. Symbolic AI, by contrast, is good at verification and justification whilst being bad at efficient discovery (and the computational cost for verification, e.g. proof verification, is significantly lower than the cost for discovery, e.g. proof discovery, which is more efficient in Statistical AI although not completely precise). By integrating the two, thus, we can make AI verifiable whilst keeping computational efficiency.

Objective 4 may be regarded as a more general conceptual goal for the future of science; it could be the key to sustainable science, since the fragmentation of science could lead to the fragmentation of technology, which could, in turn, lead to disastrous consequences in our heavily technology-laden society, such as the uncontrollable explosion of intelligence that would extinguish the human race altogether, as illustrated in the technological singularity scenario. Category theory would, hopefully, allow for an integration of scientific knowledge and technology to avoid such dystopian scenarios (e.g. the minimum amount of safety constraints can be hard-coded in Integrated AI as the absolute principles that must always be followed; otherwise AI might do some extreme harm to humanity).

We finally briefly explain the methodology of categorical artificial intelligence beyond NLP as discussed above. Firstly, the graphical calculus of category theory can be adapted for neural networks [52], thus giving a universal modelling language for deep learning and its categorical generalisation, where it should be remarked that abstract neural networks formalised in graphical calculus, as noted above, can be instantiated in different concrete categories, and deep learning can be generalised in such a way. In particular, both CNN and Transformer (as applied in BERT and GPT-3) can be formalised within the graphical string diagram language for neural networks [52]. Secondly, DisCoPy [13] provides a Python-based implementation of graphical calculus for categorical universal logic (which has been applied especially for distributional compositional categorical models named DisCoCat and their quantum computing implementation [24]), and DisCoPy can be integrated further with Pyro, a general probabilistic modelling language. The integration of DisCoPy and Pyro is DisCoPyro [46], which may be regarded as a general framework for the integration of symbolic categorical logic and probabilistic generative modelling. DisCoPyro is particularly useful for different sorts of structure optimisation via the categorical principle of symbolic compositionality; for example, it has been successfully applied for the structural optimisation of VAE (variational autoencoder) for deep learning of image data [46], and can be applied for many other tasks [46], such as the ARC (Abstraction and Reasoning Corpus) [6] to measure conceptual intelligence. DisCoPyro allows for effective implementations of categorical representation learning via symbolic compositionality, being successfully applied for categorical latent space construction for chemical material design based on SMILES (simplified molecular-input line-entry system; this is the author's joint work with Eli Sennesh, the originator of DisCoPyro [46]). Graphical calculus for categorical deep learning can be implemented in DisCoPyro as well. Thirdly, symbolic composition of representations in latent space, such as the aforementioned grammatical composition of word embeddings in Categorical Integrative NLP, is enabled by the categorical principle of compositionality, and thus the categorical artificial intelligence framework allows for compositional representation learning. Both representation space construction and complex representation composition can be systematised in the categorical artificial intelligence framework. Fourthly, there are yet another sort of integration required in AI robotics (rather than pure AI), which the methodology of category theory arguably helps to address. It is pivotal in intelligent robotics to integrate task planning and motion planning, which could be achieved by utilising the functorial correspondence between the discrete categorical structure of task planning structure and the continuous categorical structure of motion planning. The categorical integration of AI and robotics would contribute to the development of Embodied AGI (artificial general intelligence) or 4E AGI (embodied, embedded, enacted, and extended AGI).

5   Conclusions: Beyond the Chomsky Vs. Norvig Debate

In the Chomsky versus Norvig (Google's Research Director) debate on the nature of intelligence, Chomsky on the side of Symbolic AI criticises Statistical AI; Norvig recapitulates Chomsky's criticism as follows [44]:

> Statistical language models have had engineering success, but that is irrelevant to science [...] Accurately modeling linguistic facts is just butterfly collecting; what matters in science (and specifically linguistics) is the

underlying principles [...] Statistical models are incomprehensible; they provide no insight.

Norvig, by contrast, argues for the necessity of statistical methods on the grounds of the contingent nature of language and its evolution subject to complex cultural transformations, which is difficult to model by symbolic methods [44]:

> [L]anguages are complex, random, contingent biological processes that are subject to the whims of evolution and cultural change. What constitutes a language is not an eternal ideal form, represented by the settings of a small number of parameters, but rather is the contingent outcome of complex processes. Since they are contingent, it seems they can only be analyzed with probabilistic models.

What Chomsky wants is the eternal ideal form as mentioned above. The debate between Norvig and Chomsky is analogous to the traditional debate between empiricism and rationalism (or probabilism/contingentism and universalism). Integrative AI would arguably reconcile the two camps, allowing us to go beyond the Chomsky-Norvig debate. Conceptually, the two views may be unified in such a way that the surface structure of language is contingent as Norvig maintains, and yet the depth structure of language is universal as Chomsky contends.

Integrative AI, as we have argued above, makes AI more verifiable, more ethical, and thus more human; this is crucial for trust, transparency, security, and safety in AI-pervasive society. The integrative approach via category theory, moreover, contributes to the networking of science and knowledge, and in the long run, to the sustainability of knowledge and society; without an integrative view of science and knowledge, we could not address the transdisciplinary problems that the society (will) face; one such problem in the future may be the technological singularity via intelligence explosion. Unlike an ad hoc, task-specific treatment to improve empirical performance, Categorical AI is guided by broadly applicable systematic mathematical principles, paving the way for trans-disciplinary knowledge transfer across different domains as discussed above.

Our hope is ultimately that the category-theoretical approach eventually shifts the paradigm of artificial intelligence, and the emerging paradigm of Categorical Integrative AI with the best of both symbolic and statistical worlds gives a unifying foundation for Next-Generation Artificial Intelligence.

It should be noted that we have not been able to discuss related approaches to Integrative AI due to the limitation of space (for which, see, e.g., [4,14,37]).

Acknowledgements. This work was supported by the Moonshot R&D Programme (JST; JPMJMS2033). Special thanks to Samson Abramsky and Bob Coecke.

References

1. Arrieta, A.B., et al.: Explainable artificial intelligence (XAI). Inf. Fus. **58**, 82–115 (2020)

2. Baez, J.: Physics, topology, logic and computation: a Rosetta stone. Lect. Notes Phys. **813**, 95–174 (2011)
3. Baez, J., Pollard, B.: A compositional framework for reaction networks. Rev. Math. Phys. **29**, 1750028 (2017)
4. Besold, T.R., et al.: Neural-Symbolic Learning and Reasoning: A Survey and Interpretation. arXiv:1711.03902 (2017)
5. Caliskan, A., et al.: Semantics derived automatically from language corpora contain human-like biases. Science **356**, 183–186 (2017)
6. Chollet, F.: On the Measure of Intelligence. arXiv:1911.01547 (2019)
7. Coecke, B.: Automated quantum reasoning: non-logic - semi-logic - hyper-logic. In: Proceedings of Quantum Interaction, pp. 31–38 (2007)
8. Coecke, B.: Quantum picturalism. Contemp. Phys. **51**, 59–83 (2009)
9. Coecke, B., et al.: Mathematical foundations for a compositional distributional model of meaning. Linguist. Anal. **36**, 345–384 (2010)
10. Coecke, B.: The logic of quantum mechanics - Take II. arXiv:1204.3458 (2012)
11. Coecke, B., Kissinger, A.: Picturing quantum processes. In: CUP (2017)
12. Cruttwell, G., et al.: Categorical Foundations of Gradient-Based Learning. arXiv:2103.01931 (2021)
13. de Felice, G., et al.: Discopy: monoidal categories in Python. In: Proceedings of ACT 2020, pp. 183–197 (2020)
14. Domingos, P., Lowd, D.: Unifying logical and statistical AI with Markov logic. Commun. ACM **62**, 74–83 (2019)
15. Fong, B., et al.: Backprop as functor. In: Proceedings of LICS 2019, pp. 1–13 (2019)
16. Fong, B., Spivak, D.I.: An invitation to applied category theory: seven sketches in compositionality. In: CUP (2019)
17. Fritz, T.: A synthetic approach to Markov kernels, conditional independence and theorems on sufficient statistics. Adv. Math. **370**, 107239 (2020)
18. Gaboardi, M., et al.: Graded Hoare Logic and its Categorical Semantics. arXiv:2007.11235 (2020)
19. Grefenstette, E., Sadrzadeh, M.: Experimental support for a categorical compositional distributional model of meaning. In: Proceedings of EMNLP'11, pp. 1394–1404 (2011)
20. Jacobs, B.: Categorical Logic and Type Theory. Elsevier, Amsterdam (1999)
21. Kartsaklis, D.: Tensor-based models of natural language semantics. In: Lecture Slides at the Workshop on Tensors, their Decomposition, and Applications (2016)
22. Kashiawara, M., Schapira, P.: Categories and Sheaves. Springer, Heidelberg (2006). https://doi.org/10.1007/3-540-27950-4
23. Lawvere, F.W.: Adjointness in foundations. Dialectica **23**, 281–296 (1969)
24. Lorenz, R., et al.: QNLP in practice. arXiv:2102.12846 (2021)
25. Maruyama, Y.: Dualities for algebras of Fitting's many-valued modal logics. Fundamenta Informaticae **106**, 273–294 (2011)
26. Maruyama, Y.: Natural duality, modality, and coalgebra. J. Pure Appl. Algebra **216**, 565–580 (2012)
27. Maruyama, Y.: From operational chu duality to coalgebraic quantum symmetry. In: Heckel, R., Milius, S. (eds.) CALCO 2013. LNCS, vol. 8089, pp. 220–235. Springer, Heidelberg (2013). https://doi.org/10.1007/978-3-642-40206-7_17
28. Maruyama, Y.: Duality theory and categorical universal logic: with emphasis on quantum structures. In: Proceedings of the Tenth Quantum Physics and Logic Conference, EPTCS, vol. 171, pp. 100–112 (2014)

29. Maruyama, Y.: AI, quantum information, and external semantic realism: Searle's observer-relativity and Chinese room, revisited. In: Müller, V.C. (ed.) Fundamental Issues of Artificial Intelligence. SL, vol. 376, pp. 115–127. Springer, Cham (2016). https://doi.org/10.1007/978-3-319-26485-1_8

30. Maruyama, Y.: Prior's tonk, notions of logic, and levels of inconsistency: vindicating the pluralistic unity of science in the light of categorical logical positivism. Synthese 193, 3483–3495 (2016)

31. Maruyama, Y.: Meaning and duality: from categorical logic to quantum physics. DPhil Thesis, University of Oxford (2017)

32. Maruyama, Y.: quantum pancomputationalism and statistical data science: from symbolic to statistical AI, and to quantum AI. In: Müller, V.C. (ed.) PT-AI 2017. SAPERE, vol. 44, pp. 207–211. Springer, Cham (2018). https://doi.org/10.1007/978-3-319-96448-5_20

33. Maruyama, Y.: Compositionality and contextuality: the symbolic and statistical theories of meaning. In: Bella, G., Bouquet, P. (eds.) CONTEXT 2019. LNCS (LNAI), vol. 11939, pp. 161–174. Springer, Cham (2019). https://doi.org/10.1007/978-3-030-34974-5_14

34. Maruyama, Y.: The categorical integration of symbolic and statistical AI: quantum NLP and applications to cognitive and machine bias problems. In: Abraham, A., Siarry, P., Ma, K., Kaklauskas, A. (eds.) ISDA 2019. AISC, vol. 1181, pp. 466–476. Springer, Cham (2021). https://doi.org/10.1007/978-3-030-49342-4_45

35. Maruyama, Y.: Post-truth AI and big data epistemology: from the genealogy of artificial intelligence to the nature of data science as a new kind of science. In: Abraham, A., Siarry, P., Ma, K., Kaklauskas, A. (eds.) ISDA 2019. AISC, vol. 1181, pp. 540–549. Springer, Cham (2021). https://doi.org/10.1007/978-3-030-49342-4_52

36. Maruyama, Y.: Quantum physics and cognitive science from a Wittgensteinian perspective: Bohr's Classicism, Chomsky's Universalism, and Bell's Contextualism. In: Wuppuluri, S., da Costa, N. (eds.) WITTGENSTEINIAN (adj.). TFC, pp. 375–407. Springer, Cham (2020). https://doi.org/10.1007/978-3-030-27569-3_20

37. Maruyama, Y.: Symbolic and statistical theories of cognition: towards integrated artificial intelligence. In: Cleophas, L., Massink, M. (eds.) SEFM 2020. LNCS, vol. 12524, pp. 129–146. Springer, Cham (2021). https://doi.org/10.1007/978-3-030-67220-1_11

38. Maruyama, Y.: Topological duality via maximal spectrum functor. Commun. Algebra 48, 2616–2623 (2020)

39. Maruyama, Y.: The conditions of artificial general intelligence: logic, autonomy, resilience, integrity, morality, emotion, embodiment, and embeddedness. In: Goertzel, B., Panov, A.I., Potapov, A., Yampolskiy, R. (eds.) AGI 2020. LNCS (LNAI), vol. 12177, pp. 242–251. Springer, Cham (2020). https://doi.org/10.1007/978-3-030-52152-3_25

40. Maruyama, Y.: Category theory and foundations of life science. Biosytems 203, 104376 (2021)

41. Maruyama, Y.: Learning, development, and emergence of compositionality in natural language processing. In: Proceedings of IEEE ICDL, pp. 1–7 (2021)

42. Maruyama, Y.: Fibred algebraic semantics for a variety of non-classical first-order logics and topological logical translation. J. Symb. Logic 86, 1–27 (2021)

43. Minsky, M.L.: Logical versus analogical or symbolic versus connectionist or neat versus scruffy. AI Mag. 12, 34–51 (1991)

44. Norvig, P.: On chomsky and the two cultures of statistical learning. In: Pietsch, W., Ott, M. (eds.) Berechenbarkeit der Welt?, pp. 61–83. Springer, Wiesbaden (2017). https://doi.org/10.1007/978-3-658-12153-2_3

45. Selinger, P.: A survey of graphical languages for monoidal categories. In: Coecke, B. (ed.) New Structures for Physics, pp. 289–355. Springer, Heidelbrg (2011). https:// doi.org/10.1007/978-3-642-12821-9_4
46. Sennesh, E.: Learning a Deep Generative Model like a Program: the Free Category Prior. arXiv:2011.11063 (2020)
47. Thompson, N., et al.: The computational limits of deep learning (2020). arXiv:2007.05558
48. Tshitoyan, V., et al.: Unsupervised word embeddings capture latent knowledge from materials science literature. Nature **571**, 95–98 (2019)
49. Turney, P., Pantel, P.: From frequency to meaning: vector space models of semantics. J. Artif. Intell. Res. **37**, 141–188 (2010)
50. Vicary, J.: The topology of quantum algorithms. In: Proceedings of 28th Annual ACM/IEEE Symposium on Logic in Computer Science, pp. 93–102 (2013)
51. Wittgenstein, L.: Philosophical Remarks. Blackwell, Hoboken (1975)
52. Xu, T., Maruyama, Y.: Neural String Diagrams: towards a universal compositional modelling language for categorical deep learning architectures. In: AGI (2021)
53. Zhang, Z., et al.: Deep learning on graphs: a survey. IEEE Trans. Knowl. Data Eng. **34**, 249–270 (2022)

Moral Philosophy of Artificial General Intelligence: Agency and Responsibility

Yoshihiro Maruyama$^{(\boxtimes)}$

School of Computing, Australian National University, Canberra, Australia
yoshihiro.maruyama@anu.edu.au

Abstract. The European Parliament recently proposed to grant the personhood of autonomous AI, which raises fundamental questions concerning the ethical nature of AI. Can they be moral agents? Can they be morally responsible for actions and their consequences? Here we address these questions, focusing upon, inter alia, the possibilities of moral agency and moral responsibility in artificial general intelligence; moral agency is a precondition for moral responsibility (which is, in turn, a precondition for legal punishment). In the first part of the paper we address the moral agency status of AI in light of traditional moral philosophy, especially Kant's, Hume's, and Strawson's, and clarify the possibility of Moral AI (i.e., AI with moral agency) by discussing the Ethical Turing Test, the Moral Chinese Room Argument, and Weak and Strong Moral AI. In the second part we address the moral responsibility status of AI, and thereby clarify the possibility of Responsible AI (i.e., AI with moral responsibility). These issues would be crucial for AI-pervasive technosociety in the (possibly near) future, especially for post-human society after the development of artificial general intelligence.

Keywords: Ethical intelligence · Artificial moral agency · Strong and weak moral AI · Artificial moral responsibility · Responsible AI

1 Introduction

The European Parliament recently proposed to grant the personhood of autonomous AI [4], which is concerned with traditional issues in moral philosophy, such as agency and moral responsibility, and leads us to a reconsideration of them in the contemporary context of AI. The possibility of artificial agency and responsibility is not obvious by themselves. To be intelligent, agents would have to be ethical in particular; morality is arguably an indispensable ingredient of intelligence. There are various questions concerning the ethical nature of AI. Can artificial agents be moral agents? Can they be morally responsible for their actions and consequences? In this paper we address these questions from multiple angles while referring to closely related discussions in traditional moral philosophy.

Underlying these questions is the possibility of the freedom to act and the capacity to intend to act (in artificial systems; cf. the issue of intentionality as

© Springer Nature Switzerland AG 2022
B. Goertzel et al. (Eds.): AGI 2021, LNAI 13154, pp. 139–150, 2022.
https://doi.org/10.1007/978-3-030-93758-4_15

has been problematised in philosophy of mind by Searle [33,34] and others; see also [19,21,23]). Without the freedom to act or the capacity to intend to act, there may be no such thing as moral responsibility to be attributed to AI; even if AI committed a crime, it might be that AI committed the crime as it was programmed to do so by humans or other agents. Does AI have the freedom to act? Does it have the capacity to intend to act? We elucidate these issues in this paper in light of traditional moral philosophy, such as Kant's, Hume's, and Strawson's.

The role of emotion in artificial morality is another relevant issue. Some thinkers in moral philosophy, as we shall explain below, contend that morality is grounded upon emotion rather than reason; in contrast, others argue that it is grounded upon reason. Broadly speaking, there are two kinds of morality in human nature, namely rational morality and emotional morality. AI can presumably be programmed to follow rational moral principles, and could be regarded as having some sort of rational morality in that sense, but can AI have emotional morality? This question leads us to a reconsideration of the nature of emotion and emotional morality within the contemporary context of AI research.

In this paper we especially focus upon the possibilities of moral agency and moral responsibility in AI; moral agency is a precondition for moral responsibility (which is, in turn, a precondition for punishment). The paper consists of two parts as follows. In the first part, namely Sect. 2, we address the moral agency status of AI in light of Kant's, Hume's, and Strawson's moral philosophy, and clarify the possibility of Moral AI (i.e., AI with moral agency) by discussing the Ethical Turing Test, the Moral Chinese Room Argument, and Weak versus Strong Moral AI. In the second part, Sect. 3, we address the moral responsibility status of AI, and thus clarify the possibility of Responsible AI (i.e., AI with moral responsibility). We conclude the discussion in Sect. 4.

2   Moral Agency: Can AI be a Moral Agent?

Here we address the moral agency status of AI, clarifying the possibility of Moral AI; moral agency counts as a precondition for moral responsibility.

2.1   Two Conceptions of Morality: Rational and Emotional Morality

In order to be a moral agent, AI must be able to make moral judgments on the basis of some conception of good and bad. What is the origin of our moral judgements? Where do they come from? Broadly speaking, there are two views regarding the origin or nature of morality in the context of traditional moral philosophy, namely Kant's and Hume's. Kant's moral philosophy is often contrasted with Hume's. Dennis [3] explains as follows:

> The ethics of Immanuel Kant (1724-1804) is often contrasted with that of David Hume (1711-1776). Hume's method of moral philosophy is experimental and empirical; Kant emphasizes the necessity of grounding morality in a priori principles.

According to Kant, moral judgments, ultimately, come from the nature of human reason; referring to Kant's moral philosophy, Williams [40] indeed argues that "our rationality is at the centre of his picture of moral agency." According to Hume, by contrast, moral judgments originate from the nature of human emotion such as empathy and sympathy; Hume [9] indeed asserts that "morality is determined by sentiment." And sentiment is based upon our feeling, as Hume [9] contends that "what each man feels within himself is the standard of sentiment." In contrast to the Kantian conception of morality, Hume [8] argues as follows: "Reason is wholly inactive, and can never be the source of so active a principle as conscience, or a sense of morals."

Kauppinen [12] explains Humean moral sentimentalism as follows: "our emotions and desires play a leading role in the anatomy of morality" and "the key mechanism of sympathy is imaginatively placing oneself in another's position." Kauppinen [12] also remarks that there is a renewed interest in Humean moral philosophy in the context of contemporary psychology: "Recent psychological theories emphasizing the centrality of emotion in moral thinking have prompted renewed interest in sentimentalist ethics."

In the Kantian conception of moral agency, it suffices for AI to have reason in order to be a moral agent; in the Humean conception of moral agency, AI, if it is to be a moral agent, must have emotion such as empathy and sympathy. Put another way, in the Kantian conception, morality presupposes reason; in the Humean conception, it presupposes emotion. We call the Kantian and Humean concepts of morality rational morality and emotional morality, respectively; in the context of moral philosophy, the Kantian and Humean views are generally referred to as moral rationalism and moral sentimentalism. As to the opposition between rationalism and sentimentalism, Hume [9] argues as follows:

> There has been a controversy started of late, much better worth examination, concerning the general foundation of Morals; whether they be derived from Reason, or from Sentiment; whether we attain the knowledge of them by a chain of argument and induction, or by an immediate feeling and finer internal sense; whether, like all sound judgement of truth and falsehood, they should be the same to every rational intelligent being; or whether, like the perception of beauty and deformity, they be founded entirely on the particular fabric and constitution of the human species.

In the following we discuss the possibilities of Moral AI, namely AI with moral agency, and of Responsible AI, namely AI with moral responsibility (in addition to moral agency), on the basis of these moral philosophies.

2.2 The Possibility of (Rational) Moral AI: The Ethical Turing Test and Weak Versus Strong Moral AI

AI, by definition, is more or less intelligent, and thus arguably has some reason, which could be trained to make moral judgements. Yet in the Humean conception, this does not really suffice for the status of moral agency, and moral judgements must be rooted in emotion such as empathy and sympathy, without which they are vacuous, inadequate, or merely 'artificial' moral judgements, rather than genuine ones. Here we focus upon the rational aspect of Moral AI first, and then address the sentimental aspect separately in the next subsection.

From a technical point of view, the methods of Symbolic AI (i.e., AI based upon symbolic representation and logical reasoning) would allow us to make AI follow rational moral principles in a top-down manner; and the methods of Statistical AI (AI based upon statistical machine learning) would even allow us to make AI gradually learn what is morally good and what is morally bad on the basis of empirical data about human moral judgements (and behaviours) [14, 16, 22, 25, 26, 28, 29]. The latter approach faces challenges on how to overcome machine biases, i.e., how to avoid learning biases exisiting in human practice. In a recent *Science* article, for example, Caliskan et al. [1] have confirmed this in the context of natural language processing: "Semantics derived automatically from language corpora contain human-like biases." Yet the statistical approach could be combined with the symbolic approach to remedy this problem, so that statistically learned empirical biases are rectified via logically formulated, rational moral principles [13, 15, 17, 18, 20, 24, 27].

In light of these, it would not be too difficult to have AI able to simulate human moral judgements (or morally good human judgements). Morality, however, is not just about one's judgements, but also about one's deeds. The Ethical Turing Test (i.e., the Turing Test for Morality), therefore, must be concerned with deeds as well as judgements, whilst the Original Turing Test was only concerned with judgements or linguistic responses. Even so, it would still be possible to simulate deeds as well as judgements; anything observable can in principle be simulated. Yet a question still arises: Is simulated morality genuine morality?

It is not that obvious whether AI passing the Ethical Turing Test is genuinely ethical, just as it has been debated whether AI passing the Original Turing Test is genuinely intelligent, thinking, or has an understanding of what is going on in the world. The Chinese Room Argument [2] is a philosopher's counter to the (Original) Turing Test, suggesting that (computationally) simulated intelligence or imitated intelligence is not intelligence. Searle [32] indeed asserts, "Instantiating a computer program is never by itself a sufficient condition of intentionality." Searle [33] puts a strong emphasis on the intentionality of the mind, which concerns the "directedness, aboutness, or reference" of thinking, according to Siewart [35], and the behavioural simulation of intelligence, even if it passes the (Original) Turing Test, does not necessarily yield intentionality. We then have to differentiate between behavioural intelligence and intentional intelligence, and just likewise, between behavioural morality and intentional morality.

Imperfect simulations of morality, moral judgements, or moral behaviours, have already been made possible to certain degrees, and we could assume that even the perfect simulation is achieved as an ideal limit of imperfect approximations. Even so, that is still behavioural morality. Intentionality concerns the internal content of thinking whereas simulation only concerns the externally observable behaviour of it. We do not yet know how to reconstruct the internal content of thinking beyond the externally observable behaviour (and how to verify the existence of it). Even if behaviourally moral AI is possible, intentionally moral AI may not be possible. Searle would indeed argue that intentionally moral AI is impossible, presumably by means of the Moral Chinese Room Argument (or the Moral Room Argument), which makes an agent lacking any kind of morality look like being moral in terms of its behaviour (it could even make an immoral person look like moral, if the person follows the Moral Book in the room, an analogue of the Chinese Book/Dictionary in the original thought experiment).

These considerations lead us to the distinction between Weak and Strong Moral AI (Weak and Strong MAI, for short) which is analogous to the distinction between Weak and Strong AI; Weak MAI only has behavioural morality whilst Strong MAI has intentional morality (and any other intrinsic features of morality). Weak AI is merely a tool to solve tasks, as Searle [32] argues:

> According to weak AI, the principal value of the computer in the study of the mind is that it gives us a very powerful tool. For example, it enables us to formulate and test hypotheses in a more rigorous and precise fashion.

Strong AI, by contrast, actually embodies a genuine mind with internal understanding and cognitive states, as Searle [32] argues as follows:

> But according to strong AI, the computer is not merely a tool in the study of the mind; rather, the appropriately programmed computer really is a mind, in the sense that computers given the right programs can be literally said to understand and have other cognitive states.

Whilst the Chinese Room concerns linguistic understanding, the moral version of it concerns moral understanding, telling that even the complete, behavioural simulation of morality does not necessarily give moral understanding, which Strong MAI is required to have.

Just as there is no realistic evidence that Strong AI is possible, there is no convincing evidence that Strong MAI is possible, either. Yet if simulation suffices for moral agency, Weak MAI does have moral agency. At the same time, moral agency can be a matter of our perceptions; if we regard AI as a moral agent, AI practically functions as a moral agent in our society. That is to say, moral agency, in a practical sense, can be socially constructed by us humans, i.e., members of the society. If AI makes moral judgements and behaves morally, we may well regard it as a moral agent; from a practical point of view, moral agency could be such a social construct. Weak AI, then, would suffice for the social status of moral agency. This may be called a social constructivist view of moral agency.

2.3   The Possibility of Emotional Moral AI

Morality in the Humean conception requires sentiments such as empathy and sympathy. To be Humean Moral AI, AI must have sentiments, which gives an even higher hurdle for AI; how could AI have sentiments as humans have? To address this question, it would be necessary to differentiate between behavioural sentiments and intentional sentiments, which would lead to a distinction between Weak Humean Moral AI and Strong Humean Moral AI, but here we don't complicate the terminology any more, and instead refer to Strawson's conception of morality, which arguably allows some possibility for Humean Moral AI. Talbert [38] characterises Strawson's moral philosophy in the following manner:

> Strawson focuses directly on the emotions — the reactive attitudes — that play a fundamental role in our practices of holding one another responsible. Strawson's suggestion is that attending to the logic of these emotional responses yields an account of what it is to be open to praise and blame that need not invoke the incompatibilist's conception of free will. Indeed, Strawson's view has been interpreted as suggesting that no metaphysical facts beyond our praising and blaming practices are needed to ground these practices.

Let us focus upon the notion of attitudes in Strawson's moral philosophy, for sentiments manifest as attitudes, which are what socially matters in real-world practice. Certain attitudes are empirical equivalents to certain sentiments, which per se we cannot really observe. Strawson [37] emphasises the "very great importance that we attach to the attitudes" himself. (Hume was a moral philosopher within the tradition of British empiricism, and thus he would agree with the empiricist conception of moral sentiments.) Attitudes can in principle be simulated (although complex context dependency in human attitudes has to be modelled in a suitable manner). So without actually having Emotional AI, we can have Humean (or rather Strawsonian) Moral AI based upon the conception of morality as rooted in sentiments, whose metaphysical commitment can be reduced in terms of reactive attitudes, which are entirely physically observable.

3   Moral Responsibility: Can AI be Morally Responsible for Its Actions and Their Consequences?

Here we discuss whether AI can be morally responsible for its actions and their consequences or not. According to Noorman [31]:

> Moral responsibility is about human action and its intentions and consequences [...]

Both intentions and consequences do matter in the attribution of moral responsibility. If someone did something harmful, and yet if the person did not intend to do so, the person's responsibility for that action may be reduced; this is legally the case in most countries. In case the person had no choice but to do so, no responsibility may be attributed to the person. There is a dual of this as follows. If someone intended to do something harmful, and yet if that did not lead to any substantial consequence (e.g., the person just failed to do so), then the person's responsibility or severity of punishment for that action may be reduced.

What if, however, the person is an AI agent rather than a human agent? What does it mean that AI did or did not intend to do something? Does AI have any choice to do anything in the first place if it is anyway programmed to behave in a certain manner? Here again we have to differentiate between Weak and Strong MAI (i.e., Moral AI) as we did in the last section. Weak MAI does not have any internal intention. We could, then, simply argue that where there is no intention, there is no responsibility. Yet human agents do not completely escape from their responsibilities even when they did not directly intend to do harm. So regardless of AI's capacity of intention, arguably, AI agents must take responsibilities for their actions. But what if AI really had no choice but to do harm because they are programmed and thus forced to do so by humans? This is a subtler question than it may seem at first sight, and at the same time, crucial for the possibility of Responsible AI (i.e., AI with Moral Responsibility). We shall discuss more on this below.

3.1   The Possibility of (Morally) Responsible AI

Concerning moral responsibility, Noorman [31] argues as follows:

> Moral responsibility is generally attributed to moral agents and, at least in Western philosophical traditions, moral agency has been a concept exclusively reserved for human beings.

In the last section we have discussed the possibility of artificial moral agency. Moral agency, in general, does not necessarily entail moral responsibility, and yet there are different possibilities for AI to have moral responsibility. In order to explicate them, we have to clarify preconditions for moral responsibility. Noorman [31] argues as follows:

> The freedom to act is probably the most important condition for attributing moral responsibility and also one of the most contested. We tend to excuse people from moral blame if they had no other choice but to act in the way that they did. We typically do not hold people responsible if they were coerced or forced to take particular actions.

Does AI have the freedom to act? It would be possible, at least, to make AI look like having the freedom to act. We humans do look like having the freedom to act, but the truth is not clear at all, since physical reality is generally considered deterministic at the macroscopic level (i.e., there is no indeterminacy in macroscopic physical theories such as general relativity theory; even quantum theory allows for deterministic interpretations such as Bohm's). So humans are judged to have the freedom to act just because they phenomenally look like having it. Why does the same not apply to AI agents? We could apply the same principle to AI as well. Then, what truly matters in the freedom to act in the context of moral responsibility is the possibility of the phenomenal freedom to act, rather than that of the metaphysical freedom to act. Even if the world is completely deterministic, there can be the phenomenal freedom to act, and moral responsibility is arguably grounded upon the phenomenal freedom. This is related to the issue of free will in general. Let us recall the following account of Talbert [38]:

Strawson focuses directly on the emotions — the reactive attitudes — that play a fundamental role in our practices of holding one another responsible. Strawson's suggestion is that attending to the logic of these emotional responses yields an account of what it is to be open to praise and blame that need not invoke the incompatibilist's conception of free will. Indeed, Strawson's view has been interpreted as suggesting that no metaphysical facts beyond our praising and blaming practices are needed to ground these practices.

Strawson regards the phenomenal practices of praising and blaming as grounding moral responsibility, and there is no need to appeal to metaphysical free will to do so. From the Strawsonian point of view, AI has moral responsibility if it allows for the aforementioned reactive attitudes or phenomenal practices of praising and blaming, which is quite a light requirement to satisfy. Emotions in the Strawsonian sense have no metaphysical implications, grounded upon the phenomenal practices of praising and blaming. This may be called a phenomenal freedom account of moral responsibility, which applies to AI as well as humans.

It is possible to argue that AI is not morally responsible because it is programmed by humans and so does not have the freedom to act. The programmed nature of AI nevertheless does not cause any genuine problem in the Strawsonian phenomenal account of moral responsibility. If AI is programmed to phenomenally look like having the freedom to act, there is no more requirement for the attribution of moral responsibility. Another argument is available to clarify this point. Humans may be programmed as well as AI, even if the programming is implemented biologically rather than electronically. It is conceivable, for example, that some humans may be biologically programmed to show morally bad behaviour (cf. the controversial XYY syndrome hypothesis [6]). Genes may be the codes that program the nature and fate of humans. We are still considered to be morally responsible for our actions, and just likewise, AI may be regarded as morally responsible for its actions, even if it is completely programmed and hard coded to show certain (immoral) behaviours.

Noorman [31] discusses Dennett's related idea as follows:

Dennett, for example, suggests that holding a computer morally responsible is possible if it concerned a higher-order intentional computer system (1997). An intentional system, according to him, is one that can be predicted and explained by attributing beliefs and desires to it, as well as rationality. In other words, its behavior can be described by assuming the systems has mental states and that it acts according what it thinks it ought to do, given its beliefs and desires. Many computers today, according to Dennett, are already intentional systems, but they lack the higher-order ability to reflect on and reason about their mental states. They do not have beliefs about their beliefs or thoughts about desires. Dennett suggests that the fictional HAL 9000 that featured in the movie *2001: A Space Odyssey* would qualify as a higher-order intentional system that can be held morally responsible. Although current advances in AI might not lead to HAL, he does see the development of computers systems with higher-order intentionality as a real possibility.

A crucial question is whether the attribution of beliefs and desires to the computer system is of metaphysical nature or of phenomenal nature. Dennett is known to be a physicalist, and thus would not have any strong metaphysical commitment. If beliefs and desires are only required to exist phenomenally rather than metaphysically, there is arguably no fundamental problem in attributing moral responsibility to artificial intelligence systems.

Reactive attitudes have a Humean origin as Williams [40] explains:

Hume himself stressed our tendency to feel sympathy for others and our tendency to approve of actions that lead to social benefits (and to disapprove of those contrary to the social good). Another important class of feelings concern our tendencies to feel shame or guilt, or more broadly, to be concerned with how others see our actions and character. A Humean analysis of responsibility will investigate how these emotions lead us to be responsive to one another, in ways that support moral conduct and provide social penalties for immoral conduct. That is, its emphasis is less on people's evaluation of themselves and more on how people judge and influence one another. Russell (1995) carefully develops Hume's own account. In twentieth century philosophy, broadly Humean approaches were given a new lease of life by Peter Strawson's "Freedom and Resentment" (1962). This classic essay underlined the role of "reactive sentiments" or "reactive attitudes" – that is, emotional responses such as resentment or shame – in practices of responsibility.

If moral responsibility is grounded upon reactive attitudes as in the Hume-Strawson's account of responsibility, AI may well have them, and thus be morally responsible. It should be noted that sentiments such as sympathy for others are, in the present context, practically equated with attitudes, and so they can be understood phenomenally rather than metaphysically.

4   Concluding Remarks

In this paper we have elucidated the possibilities of moral agency and moral responsibility in AI. There are both descriptive and normative dimensions of these issues; the possibilities of them obviously hinge upon what sorts of AI we will create in future technosociety. If we implement the strongest possible regulation of AI technology, there will be no such AI as with moral agency or responsibility. What type of AI systems will be developed in the future is really a matter of our decision. If we create superintelligence without any restriction of its power, it would become impossible to punish it even when it is appropriate to do so, and the AI or AGI civilisation would really be able to replace the human civilisation, as discussed in the technological singularity scenario. There are however different levels of post-humanity, and up to some points, AI robots replacing humans, e.g. for hard manual labour, can be considered beneficial for humanity, and yet beyond those points, it will turn harmful. It would, therefore, be one of the central challenges in AI ethics (or AGI ethics) to identity where exactly those points are, which is not so obvious and yet to be explored further.

Acknowledgements. This work was supported by the Moonshot R&D Programme (JST; JPMJMS2033). Special thanks to Professor Seth Lazar for his mentoring and guidance and for leading the Humanising Machine Intelligence project.

References

1. Caliskan, A., et al.: Semantics derived automatically from language corpora contain human-like biases. Science **356**, 183–186 (2017)
2. Cole, D.: The Chinese room argument. In: The Stanford Encyclopedia of Philosophy (2009)
3. Denis, L.: Kant and Hume on morality. In: Stanford Encyclopedia of Philosophy (2008)
4. European Parliament report with recommendations to the Commission on Civil Law Rules on Robotics (2015/2103(INL))
5. Floridi, L., Sanders, J.: On the morality of artificial agents. Minds Mach. **14**, 349–379 (2004)
6. Götz, M.J., et al.: Criminality and antisocial behaviour in unselected men with sex chromosome abnormalities. Psychol. Med. **29**, 953–962 (1999)
7. Sheppard, B.H., et al.: Organizational Justice. Macmillan, Basingstoke (1992)
8. Hume, D.: A Treatise of Human Nature, pp. 1739–1740 (2003)
9. Hume, D.: An Enquiry Concerning the Principles of Morals. A. Millar (1751)
10. Kant, I.: Groundwork for the Metaphysics of Morals, James W. Ellington (trans.). Hackett Publishing Company, Indianapolis (1785)
11. Kant, I.: Critique of Pure Reason, trans. Paul Guyer and Allen Wood. Cambridge University Press, Cambridge (1998)
12. Kauppinen, A.: Moral sentimentalism. In: Stanford Encyclopedia of Philosophy (2014)
13. Maruyama, Y.: Reasoning about fuzzy belief and common belief: with emphasis on incomparable beliefs. In: Proceedings of IJCAI 2011, pp. 1008–1013 (2011)
14. Maruyama, Y.: Dualities for algebras of Fitting's many-valued modal logics. Fundamenta Informaticae **106**, 273–294 (2011)
15. Maruyama, Y.: From operational chu duality to coalgebraic quantum symmetry. In: Heckel, R., Milius, S. (eds.) CALCO 2013. LNCS, vol. 8089, pp. 220–235. Springer, Heidelberg (2013). https://doi.org/10.1007/978-3-642-40206-7_17
16. Maruyama, Y.: Full lambek hyperdoctrine: categorical semantics for first-order substructural logics. In: Libkin, L., Kohlenbach, U., de Queiroz, R. (eds.) WoLLIC 2013. LNCS, vol. 8071, pp. 211–225. Springer, Heidelberg (2013). https://doi.org/10.1007/978-3-642-39992-3_19
17. Maruyama, Y.: Duality theory and categorical universal logic: with emphasis on quantum structures. In: Proceedings of the Tenth Quantum Physics and Logic Conference, EPTCS, vol. 171, pp. 100–112 (2014)
18. Maruyama, Y.: Prior's tonk, notions of logic, and levels of inconsistency: vindicating the pluralistic unity of science in the light of categorical logical positivism. Synthese **193**, 3483–3495 (2016)

19. Maruyama, Y.: AI, quantum information, and external semantic realism: Searle's observer-relativity and Chinese room, revisited. Fund. Issues Artif. Intell. Synth. Libr. **376**, 115–127 (2016)
20. Maruyama, Y.: Meaning and duality: from categorical logic to quantum physics. DPhil Thesis, University of Oxford (2017)
21. Maruyama, Y.: Quantum pancomputationalism and statistical data science: from symbolic to statistical AI, and to quantum AI. In: Müller, V.C. (ed.) PT-AI 2017. SAPERE, vol. 44, pp. 207–211. Springer, Cham (2018). https://doi.org/10.1007/978-3-319-96448-5_20
22. Maruyama, Y.: Compositionality and contextuality: the symbolic and statistical theories of meaning. In: Bella, G., Bouquet, P. (eds.) CONTEXT 2019. LNCS (LNAI), vol. 11939, pp. 161–174. Springer, Cham (2019). https://doi.org/10.1007/978-3-030-34974-5_14
23. Maruyama, Y.: The conditions of artificial general intelligence: logic, autonomy, resilience, integrity, morality, emotion, embodiment, and embeddedness. In: Goertzel, B., Panov, A.I., Potapov, A., Yampolskiy, R. (eds.) AGI 2020. LNCS (LNAI), vol. 12177, pp. 242–251. Springer, Cham (2020). https://doi.org/10.1007/978-3-030-52152-3_25
24. Maruyama, Y.: The categorical integration of symbolic and statistical AI: quantum NLP and applications to cognitive and machine bias problems. In: Abraham, A., Siarry, P., Ma, K., Kaklauskas, A. (eds.) ISDA 2019. AISC, vol. 1181, pp. 466–476. Springer, Cham (2021). https://doi.org/10.1007/978-3-030-49342-4_45
25. Maruyama, Y.: Post-truth AI and big data epistemology: from the genealogy of artificial intelligence to the nature of data science as a new kind of science. In: Abraham, A., Siarry, P., Ma, K., Kaklauskas, A. (eds.) ISDA 2019. AISC, vol. 1181, pp. 540–549. Springer, Cham (2021). https://doi.org/10.1007/978-3-030-49342-4_52
26. Maruyama, Y.: Quantum physics and cognitive science from a Wittgensteinian perspective: Bohr's Classicism, Chomsky's Universalism, and Bell's Contextualism. In: Wuppuluri, S., da Costa, N. (eds.) WITTGENSTEINIAN (adj.). TFC, pp. 375–407. Springer, Cham (2020). https://doi.org/10.1007/978-3-030-27569-3_20
27. Maruyama, Y.: Symbolic and statistical theories of cognition: towards integrated artificial intelligence. In: Cleophas, L., Massink, M. (eds.) SEFM 2020. LNCS, vol. 12524, pp. 129–146. Springer, Cham (2021). https://doi.org/10.1007/978-3-030-67220-1_11
28. Maruyama, Y.: Learning, development, and emergence of compositionality in natural language processing. In: Proceedings of IEEE ICDL, pp. 1–7 (2021)
29. Maruyama, Y.: Fibred algebraic semantics for a variety of non-classical first-order logics and topological logical translation. J. Symb. Logic **86**, 1–27 (2021)
30. McLear, C.K: Philosophy of mind. In: Internet Encyclopedia of Philosophy
31. Noorman, M.: Computing and moral responsibility. In: Stanford Encyclopedia of Philosophy (2018)
32. Searle, J.R.: Minds, brains, and programs. Behav. Brain Sci. **3**, 417–457 (1980)
33. Searle, J.R.: Intentionality: an essay in the philosophy of mind. In: CUP (1983)
34. Searle, J.R.: The Rediscovery of the Mind. MIT Press, Cambridge (1992)
35. Siewert, C.: Consciousness and intentionality. In: Stanford Encyclopedia of Philosophy (2016)
36. Smith, A.: Theory of Moral Sentiments, A. Millar (1761)
37. Strawson, P.F.: Freedom and resentment. Proc. Brit. Acad. **48**, 1–25 (1962)
38. Khoury, A.C.: Moral responsibility. J. Value Inquiry **48**(4), 573–575 (2014). https://doi.org/10.1007/s10790-014-9457-6

39. Turney, P., Pantel, P.: From frequency to meaning: vector space models of semantics. J. Artif. Intell. Res. **37**, 141–188 (2010)
40. Williams, G.: Responsibility. In: Internet Encyclopedia of Philosophy (1995)

The Piagetian Modeler

Michael S. P. Miller[(⊠)]

SubThought Corporation, Pasadena, CA 91101, USA

Abstract. A multi-agent cognitive system is explained wherein each agent functions as an independent knowledge manipulation mechanism. Collectively the mechanisms observe the environment via connected devices, coordinate inferences, reflect upon and modify the system's behavior, and consolidate the memory network comprised of neuro-symbolic elements. The theories underlying the modeler are discussed, along with the modeler's actual and expected developmental trajectories.

Keywords: Piagetian Modeler · Cognitive architecture · Neuro-symbolic · Neural propositions · Intelligent mechanisms · Equilibration

1 Introduction

The goal of artificial general intelligence is to build systems which match human level abilities in reasoning and decision making. Human level performance has already been achieved and surpassed in certain narrow domains, but has not yet been fully realized across a broad range of domains. Since Laird, Newell, and Rosenbloom built the SOAR cognitive architecture [1], cognitive architectures have proven to be an important organizing tool in the construction of complex computer software systems.

In the recent past, Paul Rosenbloom [2] has noted that there are two approaches to building cognitive architectures: uniformity first and diversity first. Uniformity first approaches seek to build architectures comprised of homogenous elements and few algorithms. The uniformity first approach is generally characterized by neural network approaches to artificial intelligence, wherein an algorithm acts upon uniform network node elements to perform classification or other tasks. The diversity first approach seeks to build architectures comprised of heterogenous elements and many algorithms. The diversity first approach is generally characterized by multi-agent systems acting upon a shared environment or shared knowledge store. Since neither approach has as of today yielded any system objectively recognized as generally intelligent, it seems at this point that both approaches are still equally viable.

The Piagetian Modeler [3, 6–8, 10] is a cognitive architecture comprised of multiple heterogenous elements, called mechanisms, which manipulate a knowledge base and communicate with external devices. The Modeler is in the diversity first cognitive architecture paradigm. Key to the architecture are the mechanisms (Table 5) which are grouped into four categories. Observation mechanisms communicate with devices ensconced in the real (or a virtual) world. These mechanisms assert observables to the knowledge base. Coordination mechanisms perform simple and complex associations, belief propagation, planning, and reasoning in order to add inferences to the knowledge

B. Goertzel et al. (Eds.): AGI 2021, LNAI 13154, pp. 151–162, 2022.
https://doi.org/10.1007/978-3-030-93758-4_16

base. Reflection mechanisms perform motivation, simulation, regulation, compensation, discovery, exploration, imitation, and play in order to affect the behavior of the Modeler. Consolidation mechanisms perform automaticity, knowledge compression, and forgetting.

2 Theory

2.1 Processes

Jean Piaget believed that the processes of concept formation, repeated action, regulation, compensation, imitation, and play occur simultaneously within the individual and spurs mental development through activities which become progressively complex as a person progresses through sensorimotor, egocentric, and operational stages of human development [11–14]. (See Table 4 for a more comprehensive list of processes) (Fig. 1).

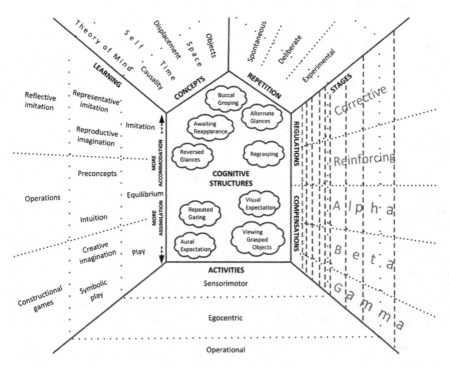

Fig. 1. Piagetian development.

Piaget theorized human development as the building of cognitive structures. Humans are endowed with primitive skills such as grasping, gazing, and listening, which integrate into combined skills over time. According to his theory of development, people form the concepts of space, time, causality, and objects through repetition of actions. Initially infant actions are spontaneous, and they soon become deliberate and experimental as infants seek to replicate phenomena in their environment such as noises they've heard, images they've seen, or sensations they've felt. Repetition of action creates physical object displacements, which gradually firms the child's notion of objects, and leads to the creation of representations, and to the externalization of the self as an object in the world, and eventually, to the formation of the concept of others as objects (viz., theory of mind).

At the same time, the world is assimilated into the child's understanding (i.e., mental model) by the child's playful interaction with the world, and the child's understanding of how the world works is adjusted by her imitation of things in the world. Since imitation occurs in at least two modalities simultaneously, a recognitive modality and a reproductive modality (e.g., hearing and phonation) the child's models are thereby integrated and extended in a multi-modal manner. The combination of play and imitation serve to both assimilate features of the world into the child's under-standing, and, conform the child's understanding to the world.

As the child interacts with the world, she encounters contradictions, which are prediction failures. Contradictions are partial adaptations which motivate the child to search for "improved coherent knowledge." Correcting contradictions creates distur-bances: obstacles (external impediments to an objective), knowledge gaps, and dis-tinctions (new ideas or relationships). These disturbances are resolved through corrective or reinforcing modifications to the knowledge, called "regulations."

The mental categories that the child constructs are partial, and do not account for many of the features of the world. Using partial categories often leads to misclassifying things in the world because important features are unknown. Compensation is the process of adjusting categories so that they correctly represent entities in the world and their predictable behaviors. Alpha compensations deform new knowledge entities to fit into existing categories by ignoring salient features. For example, a child may mis-classify an oval as a circle because both are round, and she may deliberately ignore the elongation of the oval to make them be the same. Ignoring features of an entity is called "centration." Beta compensations form new categories by considering features formerly ignored: for example, when a child creates an oval category in her mind to distinguish ovals from circles. Gamma compensations allow a person to recognize two or more categories as equivalent. for example, when a person says "X is tantamount to Y."

2.2   Equilibration

Piaget posited that when an individual is completely in harmony with her environment, there is nothing to learn. It is only when disturbances arise that learning can ensue [16, 18]. Therefore, Piaget believed the processes underlying human development (concept formation, repeated action, regulation, compensation, imitation, and play) continuously worked together performing assimilative and accommodative modifications to build mental structures in the mind [14]. For Piaget, this construction is continuous and lifelong. Only periodically is equilibrium (or quiescence) momentarily achieved—a state when no modifications need to be made. The cognitive system quickly resumes its work when a prediction failure or some other disturbance necessarily throws the cognitive system back into another round of "equilibration."

An equilibration cycle as described by Piaget involves the cognitive system perceiving observables in the world through the senses. The observables may be exterocepts (sensations of the outside world such as smells, tastes, sights, or sounds), interocepts (internal bodily sensations), or propriocepts (knowledge of what the body is doing). Additional inferences, called coordinations, are also activated by the observations. The opportunity to create more coordinations always exists as new experiences can be spatially and temporally pooled to create new internal situations. Logical and physical contradictions may be detected [13, 15, 17, 19]. Logical contradictions are often category errors while physical contradictions are usually failed predictions about the environment. These contradictions need to be mitigated through various internal cognitive modifications. In addition to the partially mitigated contradictions, knowledge gaps, external obstacles, and new environmental or mental elements may be detected as well. These are all disturbing to the individual. To resolve these disturbances, the individual will compensate and regulate (make modifications to) the disturbances. Piaget did not go into detail about the specific modifications that need to be made, and therefore left open a wide architectural question (Fig. 2 and Table 1).

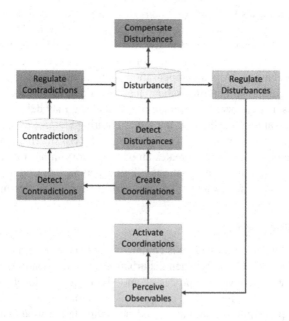

Fig. 2. An equilibration cycle.

Table 1. Equilibration cycle components.

Compensate disturbances	Attempt alpha, beta, and gamma compensations on the disturbances
Regulate contradictions	Create modifications to correct or reinforce contradictions
Disturbances	A repository of problems to be resolved
Regulate disturbances	Create modifications to correct or reinforce the disturbances
Contradictions	A repository of prediction or other failures
Detect disturbances	Identify obstacles, gaps, and distinctions to be reconciled
Detect contradictions	Find defective identity, incomplete compensation, and unnecessary inference failures
Create coordinations	Create new associations among observables and other inferences
Activate coordinations	Propagate activation from observables to associated inferences
Perceive observables	Receive exteroceptive, interoceptive, and proprioceptive stimuli

3   Application

3.1   Architecture

The Piagetian Modeler cognitive architecture embraces Piaget's theory of human development. It is comprised of four interacting processing areas: observation, which communicates with external devices and stores observables in a shared memory; coordination, which adds inferences to memory; reflection, which alters the behavior of the system; and consolidation, which compacts the memory. Each processing area is in turn comprised of mechanisms, agent processes which perform specific tasks. The mechanisms work together in overlapping functional groups to synergistically realize design patterns developed by Miller [4, 5] (Table 2).

3.2   System

The first cognitive system instantiated from the architecture is named GIL (an acronym for Generally Intelligent Learner). The GIL system is written in The Premise Programming Language [9] which was invented by Miller and Linker in 2013. The language is a domain specific language (DSL), akin to Lisp, that facilitates multi-tasking, data persistence, and messaging. Using the language, parallel mechanisms were crafted that act upon a shared knowledge base and communicate with a NAO robot.

At this time the GIL system can only look, phonate, hear, and move its limbs and head. Multimodal coordination has not yet been observed in GIL's internal structures nor its exhibited behaviour (Fig. 3). The system is expected, however, to pass through many human developmental milestones (see Fig. 4 and Table 3) but most likely in an

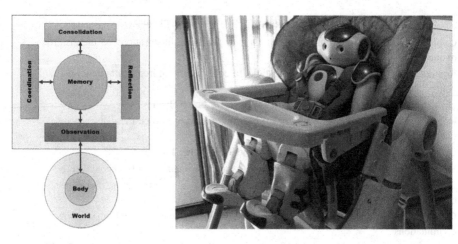

Fig. 3. The piagetian modeler architecture (left), and GIL's NAO robot (right).

Table 2. Cognitive system design patterns.

Area	Pattern	Purpose
Observation	Observation	Storing somatosensory percepts and features in memory
	Mind-Body	Getting exterocepts, interocepts, proprioceps, & sending actuations
	Reminding	Retrieving cases, situations, and episodes from memory
Coordination	Coordination	Doing activation, association, belief propagation, planning, reasoning, clustering, etc
	Reaction	Reflexive responses to situations via reliable actions
	Deliberation	Deliberate responses to situations via useful actions
Reflection	Motivation	Using device capabilities to satisfy endowed homeostatic needs
	Simulation	Using daydreaming to play out imagined or recalled scenarios
	Meta-Control	Monitor mechanisms and modify their configuration as needed
	Regulation	Modifying actions based on success or failure
	Compensation	Modifying means goals based on success or failure
	Coping	Modifying original goals based on failure
	Exploration	Choosing actions to determine and elaborate their effects
	Discovery	Hypothesis formation and testing
	Imitation	Model construction, recognition, and reproduction
	Play	Generation of ludic goals
Consolidation	Automaticity	Automating repeating action chains through abstraction
	Forgetting	Removing old and useless memory elements
	Compression	Creating shared structures

order and at a pace different from humans. As the system ages, its development will be assessed using the Bayley Scales of Infant Development, in addition to Piagetian Developmental Milestones. When the system displays sufficient abilities, additional assessments using the CHC Model of General Intelligence will also be performed.

4 Conclusions

To date the Modeler has not achieved the expected human developmental milestones outlined by Jean Piaget, but we remain confident this is a sound theoretical path, and our work continues, despite the lack of initial progress. The value in this paper resides in the exposition of Piagetian theory as it applies to cognitive architectures. Piagetian theory is not very well understood from a systems design approach. The GIL system is continually monitored.

Appendix

Table 3. Piagetian developmental milestone abbreviations.

Milestone	Description	Milestone	Description
Reflexes	Pure Reflexes	ROFAVF	Reconstructing Objects from a Visible Fraction
Sucking	Sucking	E&OoC	Externalization & Objectification of Causality
Looking	Looking	IoKMNVttC	Imitation of Known Movements Not Visible to the Child
Phonation	Phonation	IoNA&VM	Imitation of New Auditory and Visual Models
Hearing	Hearing	SfVOUVD	Searching for Vanished Objects using Visible Displacements
FPDGWM	Forming Practical Displacement Groups within Modalities	FOG	Forming Objective Groups
SfOWM	Searching for Objects within Modalities	DNMvE	Discovering New Means via Experimentation
PCR	Primary Circular Reactions (Spontaneous Repetition)	INMvMC	Inventing New Means via Mental Combinations

(continued)

Table 3. (*continued*)

Milestone	Description	Milestone	Description
EH	Elementary Habits	O&SoC	Objectfication and spatialization of Causality
SI	Sporadic Imitation	SIoANM	Systematic Imitation of All New Models
Prehension	Prehension	FV	First Verbalizations
SCR	Secondary Circular Reactions (Deliberate Repetition)	RID	Representing Invisible Displacements
Recognition	Recognition	FRG	Forming Representative Groups
MPC	Magico-Phenomenalistic Causality	RC	Representative Causality
AStNS	Applying Skills to New Situations	PA	Primitive Artificialism
CPGAM	Coordinating Practical Groups across Modalities	DI	Deferred Imitation
IP	Interrupted Prehension	Preconcepts	Preconcepts
FSG	Forming Subjective Groups	MP	Magico-Phenomenism
SfDOAM	Searching for Displaced Objects across Modalities	FR	First Reasonings
SIoKMUKM	Systematic Imitation of known models using known movements	DA	Diffused Artificialsm
SfVOw/oUVD	Searching for Vanished Objects without using Visible Displacements	Animism	Animism
RS	Recognizing Signs	LA	Ludic Artificialsm
ENO	Exploring New Objects	MA	Mythical Artificialsm
TCR	Tertiary Circular Reactions (Experimental Repetition)	CoV	Coordination of Viewpoints
OoPiDP	Ordering of Planes in Depth Perception	Intuition	Intuitive Notions
DOfs	Dissociating Objects from Supports		

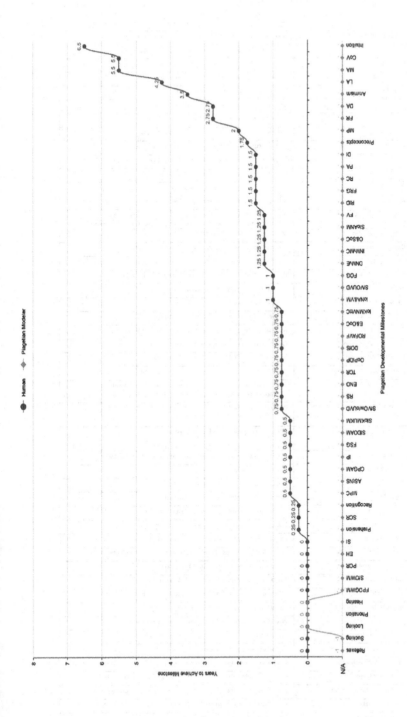

Fig. 4. Piagetian developmental milestones.

Table 4. Piagetian processes.

Regulatory	Action Reinforcement	Generalizes the situations to which an action applies.
	Action Correction	Adds negations to prevent execution and refine applicability.
	Correspondence Identification	Creates mappings between actions, situations, and results.
	Correspondence Generalization	Forms hierarchical groupings of correspondences.
	Seriation	Observables can be sequenced based on time.
	Classification	Observables are put in hierarchical categories based on time.
	Habituation	Integrates new actions with reflexes.
	Conditioning	Splits schemes into cue scheme and reward scheme.
	Intermodal Association	Joins concurrent actions involving different modalities.
	Planning	(aka, Conscious regulation) Selecting means to achieve goals.
	Cycle Association	Identifies common subsystems to join action cycles.
	Distinction Creation	Identifies elements excluded from subsystems.
Compensatory	Action Inversion	Adds actions that completely negates existing actions. (Reverses actions)
	Action Reciprocation	Adds new actions from the current state to the goal state by negating differences between the current and initial states. (Creates detours)
	Loop Reinforcement	Modifies an action so it repeats.
	Objective Appraisal	Maintains progress to a goal by reinstating a failed goal.
	Anomaly Distortion	Use only most prominent aspects to categorize anomalies.
	Anomaly Rejection	Ignores anomalous schemes by eliminating their disturbances.
	Anomaly Incorporation	Converts an anomaly into an acceptable variation.
	Variation Prediction	Predicts a variation.
	Cancel Prediction	Applies inverse transformations to variation predictions.
	Reverse Prediction	Applies reciprocal transformations to variation predictions.
	Symmetric Prediction	Creates direct and inverse predictions using negations.
	Reflective Abstraction	Groups elements into a novel hierarchical unit.
	Cue Creation	Constructs cue elements to signal impending events.
Equilibratory	Action-Object Equilibration	Creating actions and operations using new causal and logical relationships to incorporate resistances (e.g., failures, mismatches, problems).
	Collateral Equilibration	Integrating disjoint collateral subsystems.
	Hierarchical Equilibration	Integrating disjoint hierarchical subsystems.
Other	Practice	Trying skills spontaneously and repeatedly without objectives.
	Decentration	Incorporating ignored features into a situation.
	Recognition	Selecting or modifying actions to match a model.
	Reproduction	Performing analogous actions to mimic a model.
	Image Creation	Creating subsystems that summarize an imitation.
	Signifier Creation	Using indexes (indicators) as signifiers for symbolisms.
	Representative Imitation	Performing analogous actions to mimic an image.
	Reproductive Imagination	Reproducing elements of the world using symbolic combinations.
	Fortuitous Combinations	Actions are accidentally combined in novel ways.
	Intentional Combinations	Actions are combined to achieve a ludic goal.
	Symbolization	Reproduction of a skill outside its context and without its objective.
	Symbolization Projection	Projecting symbolizations onto new objects or people.
	Imitated Skill Projection	Projecting prior imitated skills onto new objects or people.
	Symbolic Combinations	Reproducing real life with imagined beings or objects.
	Compensatory Combinations	Correcting reality with imagination.
	Cathartic Combinations	Neutralize fear or distress through play.
	Liquidating Combinations	Replays unpleasant episodes by dissociating unpleasant aspects.
	Anticipatory Combinations	Anticipating the consequences of rejecting a command or advice.
	Creative Imagination	Constructing concepts through both recall and current active context.
	Constructional Games	Reproduce a symbolized model in detail.

Table 5. Piagetian modeler mechanisms.

Observers	Executor	Schedules action trials; sends actuation attempts to devices.
	Perceiver	Receives observables from devices.
Coordinators	Activators	Makes observables and coordinations contextually relevant.
	Associators	Correspondence generalization; classification; seriation; intermodal association; reflective abstraction; distinction creation; cycle association; cue creation; image creation; signifier creation;
	Chunkers	Correspondence generalization; classification;
	Reasoners	Correspondence identification; anomaly distortion; anomaly incorporation; decentration; anomaly rejection; anticipatory combinations;
	Propagators	Belief modification;
	Solvers	Planning; habituation; intentional combinations;
	Reactor	Anomaly rejection;
	Deliberator	Anomaly rejection;
	Inhibitor	Inhibits objectives that lead to undesirable outcomes; anomaly rejection;
	Terminator	Sets objective resolution to achieved or expired.
Reflectors	Ameliorator	Creates objectives to ameliorate urges.
	Supervisor	Toggles daydreaming;
	Simulator	Starts or resumes daydreaming;
	Correlators	Match results with trials .
	Regulators	Action reinforcement; action correction; conditioning; action-object equilibration; collateral equilibration; hierarchical equilibration; fortuitous combinations; symbolization projection; imitated skill projection;
	Compensators	Action inversion; action reciprocation; variation prediction; cancel prediction; reverse prediction; symmetric prediction; compensatory combinations;
	Explorers	Tries actions to see the effects.
	Practicer	Practice; symbolization;
	Symbolizer	symbolization;
	Perseverator	Loop reinforcement;
	Recognizers	Recognition;
	Reproducers	Reproduction; representative imitation; reproductive imagination; symbolic combinations; creative imagination; constructional games;
	Ascriber	Formulates hypotheses;
	Designer	Creates experiments to test hypotheses.
	Experimenter	Selects experiments to attempt.
	Predictor	Updates predictions.
	Evaluator	Generates appraisals; objective appraisal; cathartic combinations;
	Aggregator	Converts appraisals to emotions;
	Attentor	Selects coping responses for appraisals; cathartic combinations; liquidating combinations;
Consolidators	Amneator	Reclaims unused and useless propositions;
	Automator	Compresses hypotheses and actions;
	Compressor	Identifies and eliminates repeating structure;

References

1. Laird, J., Newell, A., Rosenbloom, P.: Soar: an architecture for general intelligence. J. Artif. Intell, **33**(1), 1–64 (1987)
2. Rosenbloom, P.S.: Towards a new cognitive hourglass: uniform implementation of cognitive architecture via factor graphs. In: Proceedings of the 9th International Conference on Cognitive Modeling. ICCM (2009)
3. Miller, M.S.P.: Piagetian autonomous modeller. In: Proceedings of the AISB 2011 Symposium on Computational Models of Cognitive Development, pp. 32–39 (2011)
4. Miller, M.S.P.: Patterns for cognitive systems. In: Proceedings of the 6th International Conference on Complex, Intelligent and Software Intensive Systems (CISIS), pp. 642–647. Palermo, Italy (2012)
5. Miller, M.S.P.: The neural proposition: structures for cognitive systems. In: Proceedings of the AAAI 2013 Spring Symposium on Creativity and (Early) Cognitive Development, pp. 44–50. Stanford, CA USA (2013)
6. Miller, M.S.P.: The construction of reality in a cognitive system. In: AAAI 2013 Workshop on Learning Rich Representations from Low Level Sensors, pp. 28–30. Bellevue, WA USA (2013b)
7. Miller, M.S.P., Linker, S.O., Azar G.M.: The equilibration of neural propositions procedia computer science. In: 5th Annual International Conference on Biologically Inspired Cognitive Architectures, (BICA 2014), vol. 41, pp. 146–151. Cambridge, MA USA (2014)
8. Miller, M.S.P.: Building Minds with Patterns. Self-published. Los Angeles, CA USA ISBN 978-0-692-54140-1 (2018)
9. Miller, M.S.P.: The Premise Language. Self-published. Los Angeles, CA USA ISBN 978-1-983178-13-9 (2018b)
10. Miller, M.S.P.: Coding Artificial Minds. Self-published. Los Angeles, CA USA ISBN 978-0-578-61141-9 (2021)
11. Piaget, J.: The Child's Conception of the World. Routledge & Kegan Paul, London (1929)
12. Piaget, J., Cook, M.: The Origins of Intelligence in Children (1969–5th printing). International Universities Press, New York (1956)
13. Piaget, J., Cook, M.: Construction of Reality in the Child. Basic Books, New York (1957)
14. Piaget, J., Gattegne, C., Hodgson, F.M.: Play, Dreams, and Imitation in Childhood. Norton, New York (1962)
15. Piaget, J.: Adaptation and Intelligence. The University of Chicago Press, Chicago (1970)
16. Piaget, J.: Psychology and Epistemology. Viking Press, New York, NY (1972)
17. Piaget, J., Rosin, A.: The Development of Thought: The Equilibration of Cognitive Structures. Viking Press, New York (1977)
18. Piaget, J., Coltman, D.: Experiments in Contradiction. University of Chicago Press, Chicago (1980)
19. Piaget, J., Brown, T., Thampy, K.J.: Equilibration of Cognitive Structures: The Central Problem of Intellectual Development. The University of Chicago Press, Chicago (1985)

Epistolution: How a Systems View of Biology May Explain General Intelligence

C. S. Munford[✉]

1610 Robert E. Lee Blvd., New Orleans, LA 70122, USA

Abstract. The genes-first view of life provides a theory of traits interacting with ecological niches, and of genes as determinants of these traits, but fails to link the two with a logic of physiology. How are genes selected for expression? It is on this level of physiology that intelligence appears. In this paper, I propose a formula by which *epistemology*, the sources of knowledge, and *evolution* might be united—an "epistolution" that offers in principle a testable synthesis to predict organismic behavior. Perhaps organisms and their microbiota, through allostasis, mediate between their ecological niches and their DNA. Perhaps they form networks nested within networks that are sensitive enough to synchronize with their niches using the formula: *if used, then reinforce; else mutate stochastically*.

Keywords: Epistolution · Downward causation · Sleep · Synchrony · Niche · Allostasis · Artificial general intelligence

1 Downward Causation

In the mid-twentieth century, evolutionary biology arrived at the DNA-centered view of life known as Neo-Darwinism. The theory of evolution since Darwin's time had described organisms as bundles of traits and noticed that the traits can be selected by differing rates of survival and reproduction inside an ecological niche. After the mechanisms of DNA inheritance were worked out, these traits were conceptually linked back to genes, that is, to sequences of DNA that code for specific proteins. But this linkage, although rational, still skips a level. We still have not worked out the logic of the middle level, *physiology*. How do we get from a protein to a trait? Even more mysteriously, how does the cell determine which genes to express, and when? The selection of which DNA to use to solve a cellular problem appears almost purposive; the cell "knows" as if by magic. I will argue in this paper that this physiological logic is in fact where purposiveness resides, that intelligence consists in the sensitivity of all the parts of a complex system to its larger contextual niche.

This middle level, physiology, is where we can observe general intelligence in humans who react to their circumstances by building knowledge. The study of the sources of knowledge is called *epistemology*. In order to explain life, epistemology must be linked to evolution without skipping any levels, so that the consequences of both big situations (niches) and small molecules on the configuration of living bodies can be predicted. We need a testable synthesis—an *epistolution*—a logic of physiology. Ingesting a new experimental medicine comprises a tiny alteration of the body

© Springer Nature Switzerland AG 2022
B. Goertzel et al. (Eds.): AGI 2021, LNAI 13154, pp. 163–173, 2022.
https://doi.org/10.1007/978-3-030-93758-4_17

system as a whole, yet the consequences are often quite unknown. Currently, the only way around this is to conduct randomized controlled trials. Imagine if small, molecule-level alterations to an airplane's design required launching thousands of trial airplanes to determine safety and efficacy. The difference is that we know the logic of the airplane's "physiology," so we can predict the effects of small changes to the complex system, and we can build airplanes by designing them from scratch. Not so with organisms—even simple single-cellular life forms operate by principles that baffle us.

A gene has never expressed itself; it requires a cell and a regulatory network. It is true that DNA sequences are often held in such a way as to make them easier or harder to express given the architecture of regulatory networks, and expression levels can often be partially predicted from such positioning [1]. This does not isolate causation because the regulatory networks are themselves never isolated from their environment, and that environment also partially predicts gene expression. A good example is the sex determination of crocodilians through egg temperature [2]. The production level of a given protein in adjacent cells of the same type can vary by as much as three orders of magnitude [3]. What makes one cell overexpress the protein and the adjacent one underexpress it? How do the cells determine the right average level of production?

In order to work together as a coordinated multicellular organism, cells must exert influence on one another. A typical cell must interact with others in a way that promotes the survival of the organism as a whole and not its destruction from, say, cancer. But the nature of this causal influence is still murky. The possibilities of gene expression are nearly endless. If a trait can arise from any number of genes, the number of ways that the 30,000 or so genes in human cells could be combined to produce traits amounts to a number near 2×10^{72403} [4, 5]. But the total number of particles in the universe is estimated at only 3.28×10^{80} [6]. This shows that it is impossible, even in the long history of life, for evolution to have explored even a tiny fraction of all traits. Instead, the cell is exercising what a naïve observer would be tempted to call "choice" in deciding what genes to express.

None of these facts fit the "blueprint" metaphor which has sometimes been used in biology. If life is an emergent consequence of DNA, why are organisms not *systematically* interpreting their DNA codes one by one, like a carpenter with a blueprint? Or alternately, why are cells not *randomly* exploring these possibilities for gene expression? If a trait can arise from any combination of genes, then there must be some systematic logic at work that selects combinations of genes. As the math I've just referenced suggests, the possibilities for expression are far too vast to be unguided.

If this logic of gene expression were encoded quite inflexibly in the genes, then cells couldn't influence one another at all. If it were encoded in the genes such that it might be expressed in many different ways given a variety of triggers, then these triggers would control every functional pattern. I presume that this is the working assumption of many biologists today. In this case the physiological logic of gene expression may be a vast field of meta-instructions *other than the laws of physics*, built up by the DNA into the structure of its regulatory network. In this case, in order for us to fully understand the logic of the human body, we would have to map out all the possible internal states of each epigenetic regulatory network, and then map all the possible physical conditions faced by each cell that might lead to these internal states. We would have to do this in all the 35 trillion or so human cells in the body. Bear in mind these cells diversify into roughly 200 cell types...skin, blood, neurons, bones, muscle, and so on, and that they change as they undergo all the phases of growth, development, and senescence. This is indeed the work of the sciences of genomics, transcriptomics, proteomics, and metabolomics, but they have so far not produced a model of the system as a whole. If we miss just a few of these meta-instructions in building our map, it seems possible that these unaccounted-for codes might throw the whole model off.

The explosion of complexity does not end there. Research over the past two decades has revealed that the human body is really a superorganism, composed not only of human cells but also of many trillions of prokaryotes, viruses, and very small eukaryotes that may outnumber human cells [7]. This microbiota functions not only as a digestive organ and regulator of metabolism, but as an integral part of a healthy immune system, and as a vital component of the cognitive process [8–12]. This community of nonhuman cells with unique genes is not inherited along with the germ cell from the parent, but acquired from the environment after birth in a somewhat haphazard way, resulting in significant differences in microbiota even in identical twins [13]. Dethlefsen et al. write that "at the species and strain level the microbiota of an individual can be as unique as a fingerprint [14]." There *are* internal organelles in eukaryotic cells with their own genetic material that are inherited from the germ cell, but the symbiogenesis thesis suggests that these were once separate organisms that have long ago been incorporated [15]. This may be evidence that this flexible partnership with external cells with foreign DNA is not only very ancient indeed, but that it is nearly ubiquitous among eukaryotes, and is vital to normal function [16].

The existence of a microbiome means trouble for the promise of understanding physiological function through the genes-first view of life. If it were correct that gene expression was determined by a meta-program that was encoded in the DNA, then compatible programs would also be required in the tens of trillions of diverse cells of the microbiota as well. These microbiota might be expected to contain wildly different genomes and meta-instructions, yet as a community they would have to instruct macroconditions that supported the survival of the host. And in order to understand that host and its survival we would have to map all these microbiotic genes and meta-instructions just as precisely as the host cell genome and meta-instructions. The fact that the microbiome of an individual is reorganized by diet, sleep, exercise, and other variables [17], yet maintains its long-term stability [18], suggests that another level of logic is present. Organisms spontaneously assemble themselves into functional ecosystems, as the species-area curve in the biogeography of islands attests [19].

There is one plausible alternative, testable in principle, that might suffice. Unfortunately in order to understand it one has to rearrange most of the philosophical furniture of Western civilization. This is the idea that ecological niches may structure the interactions of organisms directly. In order to entertain this hypothesis, we have to set aside the aversion to downward causation that has accompanied serious biology since the nineteenth century. I should say that this is *not* an argument for intelligent design. This idea is compatible with a materialistic cosmology, and with the empirical observations that have underpinned Neo-Darwinism. I have no doubt that DNA evolves by natural selection, and that having the right DNA is vital for life. I am only suggesting that on the level of physiology, organisms may be sets of interlocking networks that are sensitive enough to their niches that they take their instructions from those niches. Just as the upward logic of Neo-Darwinism requires only mutation and differential selection, this downward logic may only require a similar basic universal formula.

2 Finding a Niche

What is a niche, exactly? A niche is a set of orderly physical patterns that allow an organism to remain intact to live and reproduce. A human can live only in a narrow band of conditions, in air with sufficient oxygen, at mild temperatures, in regular cycles of light and dark, with gravity of a certain strength, with fresh water and nutritional solids, in areas free from large predators, parasites, viruses, storms, and excessive radiation. All these conditions are vital for our survival and are not ubiquitous in the universe but highly concentrated in a very delicate area between the sea, land, and sky of one particular planet. How do we know where a niche is and where it is not? We can guess, but we do not know precisely, because we cannot see niches directly...the only niche-detection device ever invented is an organism. There may be many more niches than there are organisms to fill them. Jakob von Uexküll called it the *Umwelt* [20]. A niche is a place with a special form of order; a niche is not just *anywhere*.

How do we stay in this niche and not drift into deadly hazard, drowning in the bathtub or falling off the balcony? We do this by our *actions*. It is intuitive for us to see ourselves as independent intelligent agents in the world we live in. When we reflect on ourselves, we see a loose part, an "I", that drives the whole system by our choices, rather than being driven by it. But if we say that a human, as part of the larger system in a human niche, acts independently, this description separates what flows from our minds from what contributed to it. When we attempt to investigate this empirically, we get caught in an infinite regress trying to find the "I" in the neurons. It's as if we are asking of a clock, "What part of the clock keeps the time?" We are looking at each spring and gear, noticing which of them impairs timekeeping most when removed, and deriving from this a reductive account of where the essential timekeeping function lives. We describe actions as *purposive* at the level of the organism, rather than at the level of brain cells or at the level of the biosphere as a whole. But our body system is is completely enmeshed in interaction with both the environment and with itself at all times. The whole clock mechanism keeps the time, of course.

This illusion of agency is reinforced by the fact that there are a tremendous number of possible ways a human organism *could* interact with its niche. The environment can change markedly without impacting the health of the organism, a fact which suggests it may have little causal influence. But surprisingly, research suggests that many genes can also be deleted with no harmful effect. For example, 80% of roughly 6000 gene knockouts in an entire yeast genome were found to be silent under normal conditions [21]. So there appears to be considerable buffering in either direction. One possible conclusion we can draw from this is that the causal chain in an organism runs from the DNA up to the niche and back down again, in a continual loop. This is what the authors of the Santiago theory of cognition called "a circular form of organization [22]." In this case the organism could be seen as a process *mediating* between its genes and its niche.

Claude Shannon wrote of information that "the important aspect is that it be a message selected from a set of possible messages" [23]. This could describe the A,G,T, and C of the nucleobases. Cells may be using genes much as we use *memes* in the human niche, as tools drawn from a library of possible templates for solving problems.

3 Niche Synchrony

One well-known natural process that takes chaotic materials and assembles them into orderly structures is synchrony [24]. This process has proved very difficult to study, perhaps because mathematical models of the nonlinear phenomena involved are hard to develop. But nevertheless the phenomenon exists in many forms in Nature, from the orbits of moons to the chirping of crickets to the formation of crystals. Synchrony brings chaotic energy and matter into orderly or rhythmic motion. Many metronomes, placed on a tabletop but set to different rhythms, gradually synchronize [25]. In this example, it is easy to see that there are only two forms of change that matter, either changes toward synchrony or away from it (Fig. 1).

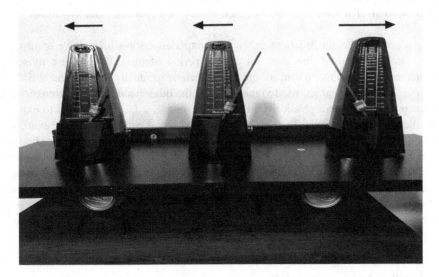

Fig. 1. Positive and negative feedback drives synchronization of connected networks

The pressure of the metronomes on the left as they swing exert a strong pull on the metronome on the right, which gradually forces it to accede to their same rhythm. In this case, and in all cases of synchrony, an object caught in the synchronizing system only has two ways to change, either away from the system's rhythm or towards it. The physical dynamics of synchrony simply make it a bit harder for the object to move out of synchrony and a bit easier to move into it. This is what gives synchrony its eerie "drift" that can be so beautiful to observe. The result is the coordination of forces that seemed disconnected into a seamless dance of elegant fluid motion.

Perhaps organisms do much the same. Homeostasis is the process by which organisms maintain their physiology within certain parameters…salinity, temperature, pH, and so forth, by interacting with their environment, and *allostasis* is a term which recognizes that there is a "drift" to this process. These are the actions that every living cell carries out to solve its problems by selecting genes for expression. Perhaps we can think of the allostatic process as a form of intelligent "agency," keeping the organism inside its niche. At a basic level, all matter is a network of dynamic energy quanta held in a certain pattern by physical interactions. This means that everything living, too, is made of networks. Organic molecules are networks, proteins are networks, organs are networks, and whole animals are networks. Matter-energy passes in and out of these networks, but the networks cycle and reconfigure themselves.

If we keep in mind that there are only two cardinal forms of change in a synchronizing system, then it follows that the only thing necessary to produce approximate synchrony would be some active process in each network that distinguished between them. If a network is moving toward synchrony it must take some form of reinforcement, and if it is moving away from synchrony it must take discouragement or undergo degradation or mutation or some kind. What cue would there be when a network is approaching synchrony? The network would be stimulated or triggered by the niche. It would be *used*. If it remained unused, then it may be departing from synchrony over time.

As a general rule, all structures in the body experience some breakdown or atrophy if they are both unused and alive for a long period of time. With disuse muscles, tendons, even organs like the heart and brain become gradually weaker and shrink in size [26]. Structures that are used vigorously, on the other hand, become stronger. We can keep ourselves more physically fit through exercise, a fact that is hard to explain from the perspective of Neo-Darwinism. Likewise, neural pathways that are exercised become more active, and those that are disused fall into degradation more rapidly. We forget far more than we remember. The epistolution formula for adjusting the networks to drive niche synchrony might simply be: *If used, then reinforce; else mutate stochastically*. Perhaps organisms have no explicit, inalterable instructions for function anywhere, any more than the dust particles in the rings of Saturn have special-purpose algorithms. Instead of algorithms, organisms may have *habits* influenced by the genetic tools available to them but structured by the niche.

4   Artificial General Intelligence

One way to experimentally refute the causal theory of Neo-Darwinism would be to show that lifelike behavior could be produced by a niche without an organism inside it, and without strictly coded instructions, simply through epistolution. We suspect that naked DNA alone in a petri dish remains inert forever; it never produces life. But perhaps niches can produce lifelike activity without cells.

How would we know if an experimental device was interacting with a niche in a lifelike way? If the niche and the device were created in a computer simulation, the niche itself would be highly artificial and bear little resemblance to the chaotic conditions of the real world. It would be impossible to tell if the device was really behaving as a living cell would, solving problems, or instead in a way that just superficially resembled problem-solving. How would we determine what comprised real problems for this simulated device?

In practice the easiest niche to examine empirically may be the niche of the entire human being, simply because this is the niche of the examiner. Behavior that is lifelike, if it appeared in a nonhuman or artificial niche, would be hard to recognize as such. This is because if this conjecture is correct, the key feature of lifelike behavior is not any particular set of actions but rather the quality of using actions to solve problems using creativity. This quality could only really be recognized by an observer who was himself sensitive to the contextual problems of a similar niche. Since the device would have, in many particulars, slightly different problems than a human no matter how carefully it was constructed, the evaluation of those solutions by the examiner would always be a matter of some intuitive judgement. We may recognize intelligence, for example in an octopus, though we can't currently say precisely what intelligence *is*.

The premise that intelligence consists in exquisite sensitivity to and synchrony with a niche may be supported by the observation that higher intelligence seems to require organisms to sleep. The function of sleep is no longer considered to be rest, or torpor, but rather comprehensive repair [27]. Why should maintenance of the networks of higher animals require a holistic repair cycle in which the animal is prone, unconscious, and vulnerable for hours at a time? Why can we not repair on-the-go? Evolution should have surely selected against this dangerous adaptation unless there were a tremendous benefit involved. Sleep has convergently evolved both in bilaterians like us (fish, reptiles, mammals) and also in intelligent mollusks, further suggesting that it is indispensable to intelligence [28, 29]. The primary symptom of sleep loss is cognitive impairment. Without any sleep at all, cognition eventually becomes impossible.

I propose that sleep may be the cycle within which highly complex multicellular organisms make a concerted effort to apply the first command of the epistolution formula to their networks: *if used, reinforce*. Stochastic mutation can happen in many ways, including the passive degradation of complex particles at body temperature, but repair and reinforcement requires coordinated effort. This might explain sleep.

5   Testing Epistolution

If an artificial network could be designed which was a) complex enough to store as much knowledge as the human body, b) adjustable according to the epistolution formula, and c) sensitive to many of the same stimuli with which a human body interacts, the device might serve as an empirical test both of Neo-Darwinist causation and of inductivist epistemology. Inductivism holds that learning occurs by building theories from observations, but some theorists, such as the physicist David Deutsch, advance the contrary view of Karl Popper that knowledge is built through conjecture and refutation [30]. A Popperian view of the body might suggest that our thoughts could be considered anticipatory hallucinations, punctuated by corrections from our niche. Expectations are conjectures, in other words, while surprises are refutations. For example, one might never notice the skin on the outside of one's left pinky for years until one day one finds that a glove has a hole in it in just that tiny location. The skin in that little patch had been sending sensory signals continually for years, but they only reached one's awareness when those signals violated a hallucinatory set of expectations (Fig. 2).

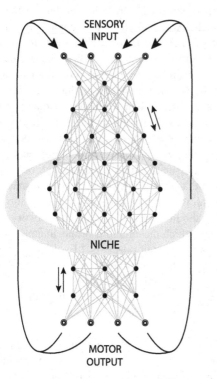

Fig. 2. Expect-actions take on the rhythms of a niche because they are causally connected.

Advances in hardware and software have only recently brought this test into the range of technical feasibility. In order for a human-like niche to be engaged, it would be necessary for the test device to possess the robotic equivalent of arms and fingers to handle objects, temperature, vibration and pressure sensors, and robotic eyes, ears and larynx. It is our general body design and sensitivities that activate the human niche. This provides the frame of reference within which our individual problems make sense to one another as humans, allowing communication and coordinated problem-solving.

To model a Popperian nervous system in software, a complex set of nodes might be linked to sensory input and to motor output. A flow of energy moving down a pathway between nodes could serve both as anticipation of the patterns of excitement coming from the niche and also as an impulse to motor action. Since motor action would cause sensory input to change, the flows of energy through the system would be causally linked to the rhythms of the niche. They would be both expectations and actions, or "expect-actions." New motions would be triggered only when surprises occurred, otherwise patterns of energy would simply repeat.

Rhythms require timing. This may be why every known cell has at least one internal oscillator, why organ systems have peripheral clocks, why all large organisms have a coordinating circadian rhythm, and why brain activity manifests as "waves. These myriad biological rhythms are very sensitive to stimulation such as light, temperature, feeding, exercise, and hypoxia [19]. Each of the test nodes should possess, like neurons, both a set of adjustable connections to other nodes and an adjustable endogenous clock that allows the system as a whole to evolve synchrony. Picture the neural network as complex strings of dominoes that fall in rhythmic patterns but reset themselves after a few milliseconds. If each domino didn't have an adjustable clock, they could not sync with the rhythmic patterns of input emerging from the niche. After it fires, a neuron has a recovery period during which it cannot fire again [31]. Though imprecise at first, over time this type of network should evolve into a better anticipation of the stimuli in the niche, simply by mutating away errors and reinforcing successes. Like heritable genetic evolution, this process would select functional connections and more accurate rhythms over time, which may comprise creativity.

This form of embodied cognition would not be statistical prediction, Bayesian or otherwise. Motor interactions would be necessary to incorporate causal knowledge into the training dataset; statistics is not enough. As the computer scientist Judea Pearl puts it, *experiment* is necessary to rise higher on the "ladder of causation," [32]. A human is not simply an inductive statistical machine; we expect and act on many things we have never encountered before, such as our own death, or marriage, or climate change. In this network, learning would arise from surprises to the hallucinatory expectations embedded in the pattern of connections and their rhythmic firing. These interactions may be universally translatable in a way that Bayesian predictive computations are not. Consider words like "light" and "heavy." They are metaphorical. As Nietzsche suggested, all our truths may be of this sort [33].

Would this device have motivations? Yes. It would have mismatches between its hallucinatory expect-actions and the flow of its sensory input, and these would drive new interactions to develop. These may be the same sort of contextual problems that we experience in trying to understand our world. The evolution of new interactions that more correctly synchronize to anticipate those problems may be the source of creativity in all higher animals. If this robotic niche synchrony worked approximately at a high level in the human niche, this would provide one possible explanation for the physiological logic of gene expression in all living organisms.

This experiment might also resolve the AI control problem [34]. If human-recognizable knowledge consists in rhythmic responses developed in the context of the human niche, then only machines trained with that human-niche-like dataset could be recognizably generally intelligent to human observers. If the epistolution conjecture is correct, any such device would be as sensitive to the moral norms of humans as we are.

In this view of life, an organism would be a mediator that adjusts between two vast reservoirs of possibility, one above and one below, by applying the epistolution formula to its networks in cycles of periodic adjustment, through sleep. It would be a process that harmonizes the possibilities of its genome with the possibilities of its niche. As a result, its solutions would always be approximate solutions, adjusting between vast opportunities in either direction. This might be the source of our spontaneity, our impetuous, inventive creativity. In this world, there would be no such thing as a final correct answer. Far from an abstract search for absolute truth in Plato's cave, life would be revealed as a dynamic contest of embodied contingent truths, a struggle between the body and the inherently partial world it can sense. As Heraclitus said, "the way upward and downward are the same."

Acknowledgements. Peter Bierhorst, Mike Skiba, Ella Hoeppner, Drew Schimmel, David Gorin, Anna Viertel, Brett Hall, Jake Moritz, Johnathan Bard, Barrie McClune, Matt Roe, Ryan Moragas, James Collins, Laurence Lowe, Denis Noble.

References

1. Zrimec, J., et al.: Deep learning suggests that gene expression is encoded in all parts of a co-evolving interacting gene regulatory structure. Nat. Commun. **11**(1), 6141 (2020)
2. Crews, D.: Sex determination: where environment and genetics meet. Evol. Dev. **5**(1), 50–55 (2003)
3. Noble, D.: Lecture to Cancer and Evolution Symposium, Cellular Darwinism: Regulatory Networks, Stochasticity, and Selection in Cancer Development (2020)
4. Feytmans, E., Noble, D., Peitsch, M.: Genome size and numbers of biological functions. Trans. Comput. Syst. Biol. **1**, 44–49 (2005)
5. Noble, D.: The Music of Life: Biology Beyond the Genome, vol. xiii, p. 153. Oxford University Press, Oxford, New York (2006)
6. Bennett, T.: How Many Particles are in the Observable Universe? Popular Mechanics online (2017)
7. Sender, R., Fuchs, S., Milo, R.: Revised estimates for the number of human and bacteria cells in the body. PLoS Biol. **14**(8), e1002533 (2016)
8. Zoetendal, E.G., et al.: The human small intestinal microbiota is driven by rapid uptake and conversion of simple carbohydrates. ISME J. **6**(7), 1415–1426 (2012)
9. Kostic, A.D., et al.: The dynamics of the human infant gut microbiome in development and in progression toward type 1 diabetes. Cell Host Microbe **17**(2), 260–273 (2015)
10. Smith, P.M., et al.: The microbial metabolites, short-chain fatty acids, regulate colonic Treg cell homeostasis. Science **341**(6145), 569–573 (2013)
11. Desbonnet, L., et al.: Microbiota is essential for social development in the mouse. Mol. Psychiatry **19**(2), 146–148 (2014)
12. Sudo, N., et al.: Postnatal microbial colonization programs the hypothalamic-pituitary-adrenal system for stress response in mice. J. Physiol. **558**(Pt 1), 263–275 (2004)
13. Goodrich, J.K., et al.: Genetic determinants of the gut microbiome in UK twins. Cell Host Microbe **19**(5), 731–743 (2016)
14. Dethlefsen, L., McFall-Ngai, M., Relman, D.A.: An ecological and evolutionary perspective on human-microbe mutualism and disease. Nature **449**(7164), 811–818 (2007)
15. Sagan, L.: On the origin of mitosing cells. J. Theor. Biol. **14**, 255–274 (1967)
16. Douglas, A.E.: Fundamentals of Microbiome Science: How Microbes Shape Animal Biology, vol. viii, p. 236. Princeton University Press, Princeton (2018)
17. David, L.A., et al.: Diet rapidly and reproducibly alters the human gut microbiome. Nature **505**(7484), 559–563 (2014)
18. Faith, J.J., et al.: The long-term stability of the human gut microbiota. Science **341**(6141), 1237439 (2013)
19. Xie, Y., et al.: New insights into the circadian rhythm and its related diseases. Front. Physiol. **10**, 682 (2019)
20. Uexküll, J.V.: Streifzüge durch die Umwelten von Tieren und Menschen. Springer, Verlag von Julius (1934)
21. Hillenmeyer, M.E., et al.: The chemical genomic portrait of yeast: uncovering a phenotype for all genes. Science **320**(5874), 362–365 (2008)
22. Maturana, H.R., Varela, F.J.: The Tree of Knowledge: The Biological Roots of Human Understanding, p. 269. Rev. ed. (1992)
23. Shannon, C.: A mathematical theory of communication. Bell Syst. Tech. J. **27**, 379–423, 623–656 (1948)
24. Strogatz, S.H.: Sync: The Emerging Science of Spontaneous Order, vol. viii, 1st edn., p. 338. Hyperion, New York (2003)

25. UCLA: YouTube video Spontanous Synchronization (2013). https://www.youtube.com/watch?v=T58lGKREubo
26. Harris, T.C., de Rooij, R., Kuhl, E.: The shrinking brain: cerebral atrophy following traumatic brain injury. Ann. Biomed. Eng. **47**(9), 1941–1959 (2018). https://doi.org/10.1007/s10439-018-02148-2
27. Royo, J., Aujard, F., Pifferi, F.: Daily torpor and sleep in a non-human primate, the gray mouse lemur (Microcebus murinus). Front. Neuroanat. **13**, 87 (2019)
28. Frank, M.G., et al.: A preliminary analysis of sleep-like states in the cuttlefish Sepia officinalis. PLoS One **7**(6), e38125 (2012)
29. Libourel, P.A., et al.: Partial homologies between sleep states in lizards, mammals, and birds suggest a complex evolution of sleep states in amniotes. PLoS Biol. **16**(10), e2005982 (2018)
30. Deutsch, D.: The Beginning of Infinity: Explanations that Transform the World, vol. vii, p. 487. Viking, New York (2011)
31. Bachatene, L., et al.: Electrophysiological and firing properties of neurons: Categorizing soloists and choristers in primary visual cortex. Neurosci. Lett. **604**, 103–108 (2015)
32. Pearl, J., Mackenzie, D.: The Book of Why: The New Science of Cause and Effect, vol. x, 1st edn., p. 418. Basic Books, New York (2018)
33. Nietzsche, F.: On Truth and Lies in a Nonmoral Sense (1896)
34. Bostrom, N.: Superintelligence: Paths, Dangers, Strategies, vol. xvi, 1st edn., p. 328. Oxford University Press, Oxford (2014)

Measures of Intelligence, Perception and Intelligent Agents

Eray Özkural[✉]

Celestial Intellect Cybernetics, Istanbul, Turkey
http://celestialintellect.com/

Abstract. We explain the relevance of operator and set induction to machine learning theory as universal models of supervised and unsupervised learning. We propose a new informal definition of general intelligence based on prediction. We propose that operator induction serves as an adequate model of perception. We discuss the application of operator induction in AGI and analyze potential objections to it. We show how to construct a discrete-time reinforcement learning agent model with operator induction serving as a perception module. We propose a universal measure of intelligence based on operator induction goodness-of-fit. We discuss the close relevance of our intelligence measure to intelligent agent theory suggesting that our proposal may contribute to AI unification.

1 Introduction

The ultimate intelligence research program is inspired by Seth Lloyd's work on the ultimate physical limits to computation [13]. We investigate the ultimate physical limits and conditions of intelligence. This is the third installation of the paper series, the first two parts proposed new physical completeness arguments, complexity measures, priors and limits of inductive inference [15,16]. We framed the question of ultimate limits of intelligence in a general physical setting, for this we provided a general definition of an intelligent system and a physical performance criterion; we proposed minimum machine volume, minimum energy, and universal priors based on volume and energy [15]. The same paper suggested optimizing the number of bits extracted per watt as a measure of intelligent system performance based on Solomonoff's theoretical work on the Alpha AGI architecture [22]. We also introduced the notion of stochastic algorithmic complexity, in terms of space-time (volume of computation), energy expended, space required to simulate a stochastic source; we proposed measures of transfer learning and logical depth in our physical re-formulation of AIT, and we have further analyzed the connections among these new resource-based measures and their limits, as well [16].

In this paper, we continue our exposition by discussing set and operator induction problems relating them to general-purpose machine learning. We introduce a new informal definition of intelligence based on prediction and introduce

© Springer Nature Switzerland AG 2022
B. Goertzel et al. (Eds.): AGI 2021, LNAI 13154, pp. 174–183, 2022.
https://doi.org/10.1007/978-3-030-93758-4_18

a universal measure of intelligence using operator induction goodness-of-fit. We discuss potential objections to operator induction in AGI. We then show how to construct a reinforcement learning (RL) agent model using operator induction with a simple control program. We conclude with a discussion of the new universal intelligence measure and AI unification research.

The manuscript was previously submitted to AGI 2017 conference and the main text was shared on preprint servers in 2015–2017. The present manuscript contains corrections and improvements based on suggestions from reviewers, to clear some misunderstandings about the interpretation of the theoretical arguments, whereas the theoretical arguments themselves remain mostly unchanged. There have appeared some proposals on preprint servers that are similarly conceived to the main contributions in this report; the present manuscript has historical priority.

2   Notation and Background

2.1   Universal Induction

Let us recall Solomonoff's universal distribution [21]. Let U be a universal computer which runs programs with a prefix-free encoding like LISP; $y = U(x)$ denotes that the output of program x on U is y where x and y are bit strings.[1] Any unspecified variable or function is assumed to be represented as a bit string. $|x|$ denotes the length of a bit-string x. $f(\cdot)$ refers to function f rather than its application.

The algorithmic probability that a bit string $x \in \{0,1\}^+$ is generated by a random program $\pi \in \{0,1\}^+$ of U is:

$$P_U(x) = \sum_{U(\pi)=x*} 2^{-|\pi|} \tag{1}$$

which conforms to Kolmogorov's axioms [11]. $P_U(x)$ considers any continuation of x, taking into account non-terminating programs. P_U is also called the universal prior for it may be used as the prior in Bayesian inference, for any data can be encoded as a bit string. We also give the basic definitions of Algorithmic Information Theory (AIT) [12], where the algorithmic entropy, or complexity of a bit string $x \in \{0,1\}^+$ is

$$H_U^*(x) = -\log_2 P_U(x) \text{ (Solomonoff)} \tag{2}$$

$$H_U(x) = \min(\{|\pi| \mid U(\pi) = x\}) \text{ (Chaitin)} \tag{3}$$

We use some variables in overloaded fashion in the paper, e.g., π might be a program, a policy, or a physical mechanism depending on the context.

---

[1] A prefix-free code is a set of codes in which no code is a prefix of another. A computer file uses a prefix-free code, ending with an EOF symbol, thus, most reasonable programming languages are prefix-free.

2.2 Operator Induction

Operator induction is a universal form of supervised machine learning where we learn a stochastic map from n question and answer pairs $D = \{(q_i, a_i)\}$ sampled from a (computable) stochastic source μ. Operator induction can be solved by finding in available time a set of m computable operators $O^j(\cdot|\cdot)$, each a conditional probability density function (cpdf), such that the following goodness of fit is maximized

$$\Psi = \sum_j \psi_n^j \text{ (Goodness of fit)} \tag{4}$$

for a stochastic source μ where each term in the summation is the contribution of a model:

$$\psi_n^j = 2^{-|(O^j(\cdot|\cdot))|} \prod_{i=1}^n O^j(a_i|q_i). \tag{5}$$

q_i and a_i are question/answer pairs in the input dataset drawn from μ, and O^j is a computable cpdf in Eq. 5. We can use the found m operators to predict unseen data with a mixture model from D [23]

$$P_U(a_{n+1}|q_{n+1}) = \sum_{j=1}^m \psi_n^j O^j(a_{n+1}|q_{n+1}) \text{ (Inference)} \tag{6}$$

The goodness of fit in this case strikes a balance between high a priori probability and reproduction of data like in minimum message length (MML) method [25, 26], yet uses a universal mixture like in sequence induction. The convergence theorem for operator induction was proven by Solomonoff in [23] using Hutter's extension to arbitrary alphabet, and it bounds total error by $H_U(\mu) \ln 2$, which is as good as sequence induction. See [23] for details. Note that we have changed Solomonoff's notation only slightly; strictly maximizing goodness of fit and practical inference are different problems. A practical solution uses a finite number of large terms, instead of infinitely many terms which plain maximization suggests, which is why we assume that there are m operators instead of infinitely many. Operator induction can model classical machine learning problems such as classification (e.g. face recognition, sentiment detection), but also learning mappings such as learning text labels from images and learning semantic image segmentation. Since the questions and answers are untyped, it can be any data type, from any domain, covering most supervised learning problems.

2.3 Set Induction

Set induction generalizes unsupervised machine learning where we learn a probability density function (pdf) from a set of n bitstrings $D = \{d_1, d_2, ..., d_n\}$ sampled from a stochastic source μ. We can then inductively infer new members to be added to the set with:

$$P(d_{n+1}) = \frac{P_U(D \cup d_{n+1})}{P_U(D)} \text{ (Inference)} \tag{7}$$

Set induction may be regarded as a restricted case of operator induction where we set Q_i's to null string, and it also has a corresponding convergence theorem [23]. Set induction is a universal form of unsupervised machine learning and it can model classical unsupervised machine learning problems like clustering (e.g., webpage clustering) as well as arbitrary *representation learning* problems such as learning to represent protein-to-protein interaction networks, and inferring new interactions from incomplete data. It is also reasonable to expect that set induction can achieve an ideal model of perception. If we apply set induction over a large set of 2D pictures of a room – modelling an eye, it may yield a 3D representation of it. If we apply it to physical sensor data, it may infer the right physical theory through a general, universal process with infinite domains that can capture the stochastic features of the data as in quantum mechanics. Perception is merely a specific case of scientific theory inference in this case, though set induction works both with deterministic and non-deterministic problems. Recent advances in unsupervised deep learning research confirms this interpretation. For instance, representation learning can learn implicit vectorial representations of complex data structures like graphs, and the approach can even learn to represent 3D objects from video input [24]. A recent study proposed using graph networks to learn to simulate complex physics, which shows the power of unsupervised learning approaches [19]. Although many additional inductive biases such as gauge invariance and temporal relations are required in practice for solving complex scientific problems, these constraints may be inferred by a universal induction engine due to the convergence theorems, via a *meta-learning* approach, which is arguably how humans acquire such domain-specific biases. In other words, the set here may model almost any dataset in classical machine learning tasks, and as usual the data type is not limited, any additional tags such as location, time, and metadata may be appended to data items, only the data is unordered as in most machine learning and perceptual problems.

2.4 Universal Measures of Intelligence

There is much literature on the subject of defining a measure of intelligence. Hutter has defined an intelligence order relation in the context of his universal reinforcement learning (RL) model AIXI [6], which suggests that intelligence corresponds to the set of problems an agent *can* solve. Also notable is the universal intelligence measure (AIQ) [7,8], which is again based on the AIXI model. Their universal intelligence measure is based on the following philosophical definition compiled from their review of definitions of intelligence in the AI literature.

Definition 1 (Legg & Hutter). *Intelligence measures an agent's ability to achieve goals in a wide range of environments.*

It implies that intelligence requires an autonomous goal-following agent. The intelligence measure of [7] is defined as

$$\Upsilon(\pi) = \sum_{\mu \in E} 2^{-H_U(\mu)} V_\mu^\pi \tag{8}$$

where μ is a computable reward bounded environment, and V_μ^π is the expected sum of future rewards in the total interaction sequence of agent π. $V_\mu^\pi = E_{\mu,\pi} \left[\sum_{t=1}^\infty \gamma^t r_t \right]$, where r_t is the instantaneous reward at time t generated from the interaction between the agent π and the environment μ, and γ^t is the time discount factor.

3   Perception as General Intelligence

Since we are chiefly interested in stochastic problems in the physical world, we propose a straightforward informal definition of intelligence:

Definition 2. *Intelligence measures the ability of a mechanism to solve prediction problems.*

Mechanism is any physical machine as usual, see [3] which suggests likewise. Therefore, operator induction, which is one of the three basic universal induction models proposed by Solomonoff, might serve as a model of general intelligence, as well [23]. Note that operator induction can infer any physically plausible cpdf, thus its approximation may solve any classical supervised machine learning problem. The only slight issue with Eq. 8 might be that it seems to exclude classical AI systems that are not agents, e.g., expert systems, machine learning tools, knowledge representation systems, search and planning algorithms, and so forth, which are somewhat more naturally encompassed by our informal definition although they may also be reduced to RL problems. Conversely, RL problems over environments can be represented as usual online machine learning problems, which suggests equivalence.

The definition of intelligence based on goal following agents or on prediction as in ours relate strongly to the common sense of intelligence as well as the scientific, psychometric definitions of inelligence. In particular, AIQ can be approximated practically using a restricted set of environments in which case it would behave a lot like an IQ test that is defined over a specific curriculum, although such a restricted definition would yield a weaker proof of general intelligence.

3.1   Is Operator Induction Adequate?

A question naturally arises as to whether operator induction can adequately solve every prediction problem we require in AI. There are two potential objections to operator induction that we know of. It is argued that in a dynamic environment, as in a physical environment, we must use an active agent model so that we can account for changes in the environment, as in the space-time embedded agent [14] which also provides an agent-based intelligence measure. This objection may be answered by the simple solution that each decision of an active intelligent system may be considered a separate induction problem. The second objection is that the basic Solomonoff induction can only predict the next bit, but not the expected cumulative reward, which its extensions can solve. We counter this objection by stating that we can reduce an agent model to a perception and action-planning problem as in OOPS-RL [20]. In OOPS-RL, the perception module searches for the best world-model given the history of sensory input and actions in allotted time using OOPS, and the planning module searches for the best control program using the world-model of the perception module to determine the action sequence that maximizes cumulative reward likewise. OOPS has a generalized Levin Search [10] which may be tweaked to solve either prediction or optimization problems. Hutter has also observed that standard sequence induction does not readily address optimization problems [6]. However, Solomonoff induction is still complete in the sense of Turing, and can infer any computable cpdf; and when the extension to Solomonoff induction is applied to sequence prediction (problem transformations discussed in [1]), it does not yield a better error bound, which suggests equivalence. On the other hand, Levin Search with a proper universal probability density function (pdf) of programs can be modified to solve induction problems (sequence, set, operator, and sequence prediction with arbitrary loss), inversion problems (computer science problems in P and NP), and optimization problems [22]. The planning module of OOPS-RL likewise requires us to write such an optimization program. In that sense, AIXI implies yet another variation of Levin Search for solving a particular universal optimization problem, however, it also has the unique advantage that formal transformations between AIXI problem and many important problems including function minimization and strategic games have been shown [6]. Nevertheless, the discussion in [22] is rather brief.

Proposition 1. *A discrete-time universal RL model may be reduced to operator induction.*

More formally, the perceptual task of an RL agent would be inferring from a history the cumulative rewards in the future, without loss of generality. Let the chronology C be a sequence of sensory, reward, and action data $C = [(s_1, r_1, a_1), (s_2, r_2, a_2), \ldots, (s_n, r_n, a_n)]$ where C_i accesses ith element, and $C_{i:j}$ accesses the subsequence $[C_i, C_{i+1}, \ldots, C_j]$. Let r_c be the cumulative reward function where $r_c(C, i, j) = \sum_{k=i}^{k \leq j} r_k$. After observing (s_n, r_n, a_n), we construct dataset $D_C = \{(Q, A)\}$ as follows. For every unique (i, j) pair such that $1 < i \leq j \leq n$, we append a new $(Q, A) \in D_C$ as follows: we concatenate history tuples $C_{1:(i-1)}$, and we form a question string that also includes the next action, i and j, $Q = (C_{1:(i-1)}, a_i, i, j)$, and an answer string which is the cumulative reward $A = r_c(C, i, j)$. Solving the operator induction problem for this dataset D_C will yield a cpdf which predicts cumulative rewards in the future. After that, choosing the next action a is a simple matter of maximizing predicted cumulative reward in the future: $\arg\max_a \{r(C_{1:n}, a, n + 1, \lambda)\}$ where λ is the planning horizon, extrapolating from data seen so far. The reduction causes quadratic blow-up in the number of data items. This elementary reduction suggests that the bulk of intelligence here comes from prediction; the argmax function, and the summation of rewards help define it by building reasonable constraints into the prediction task. In other words, we interpret that the intelligence in this agent model is mostly provided by inductive inference, combined with a minimalist application of decision theory; a simple control program is enough. Nevertheless, as reviewers have pointed out, the control problem in intelligent agent design is non-trivial and with this model we barely refer to the most minimal models possible, and not realistic engineering models which would have to address issues such as on-policy/off-policy prediction [9], and safe exploration vs. exploitation issues, which are important considerations even at a purely theoretical level. Note also that this simple model has a planning horizon which is a limitation in RL models.

Recent empirical work confirms our theoretical predictions in this regard as competent agent models that depend mostly on a prediction engine have been recently proposed such as the world models agent [5] which uses a generative unsupervised perceptual model (much like our proposal) to train a simple policy, and an agent that simply uses the transformer model to predict the next action [2], which might sound crude to seasoned RL theorists, but performs quite well in practice, exceeding the state-of-the-art in many experiments, and construed in a similar fashion to our model, strongly justifying our theoretical analysis. This model shows that a predictive model can learn the essential parts of perception and control simultaneously as we propose, using a simple control program, affirming the significance of our prediction based definition of intelligence. We have immediately noticed this excellent paper that demonstrates their independent discovery because it is similar to the practical agent we have been designing based on the analysis in this manuscript. Note that both papers have been written subsequent to our analysis, our predictions were published long before these models and any intelligence measure based solely on prediction.

4   Physical Quantification of Intelligence

Definition 1 corresponds to any kind of reinforcement-learning or goal-following agent in AI literature quite well, and can be adapted to solve other kinds of problems. The unsupervised, active inference agent approach is proposed instead of reinforcement learning approach in [4], and the authors argue that they did not need to invoke the notion of reward, value or utility, even further simplifying the control problem with regards to aforementioned new reinforcement learning agent models. The authors in particular claim that they could solve the mountain-car problem by the free-energy formulation of perception. We thus propose a perceptual intelligence measure.

4.1   Universal Measure of Perception Fitness

Note that plain Solomonoff induction is considered to be insufficient to describe universal agents such as AIXI, because basic sequence induction is inappropriate for modelling optimization problems [6]. However, a modified Levin search procedure can solve such optimization problems as in finding an optimal control program [20]. In OOPS-RL, the perception module searches for the best world-model given the history of sensory input and actions in allotted time using

OOPS, and the planning module searches for the best control program using the world-model of the perception module to determine the control program that maximizes cumulative reward likewise. In this paper, we consider the perception module of such a generic agent which must produce a world-model, given sensory input.

We can use the intelligence measure Eq. 8 in a physical theory of intelligence, however it contains terms like utility that do not have physical units (i.e., we would be preferring a more reductive definition). We therefore attempt to obtain such a measure using the more benign goodness-of-fit (Eq. 4). Let the universal measure of the fitness of operator induction be defined as:

$$\Phi(\pi) \triangleq \sum_{\mu \in S} 2^{-H_U(\mu)} E_{\mu,\pi} \Psi(\mu,\pi) \tag{9}$$

where S is the set of possible stochastic sources in the observable universe U and π is a physical mechanism, and Ψ is relative to a stochastic source μ and a physical mechanism (computer) π. The intelligence measure is the weighted sum of the expected goodness-of-fit of all possible stochastic sources μ, weighed by the negative binary exponent of algoritmic complexity $H_U(\mu)$. The first summation corresponds to generation of sources, and the second to generation of datasets. Therefore, $\Phi(\pi) \in (0,1)$ due to Kraft inequality and the fact that $\Psi(\mu,\pi) \in (0,1)$ likewise. Φ would be maximum if we assume that operator induction were solved exactly by an oracle machine. Note that $H_U(\mu)$ is finite; $\Psi(\mu,\pi)$ is likewise bounded according to the amount of computation π will spend on approximating operator induction.

If we expand Ψ, the universal intelligence measure is defined as:

$$\Phi(\pi) \triangleq \sum_{\mu \in S} 2^{-H_U(\mu)} E_{\mu,\pi} \left[\sum_j 2^{-|(O^j(\cdot|\cdot)|} \prod_{i=1}^{n} O^j(a_i|q_i) \right] \tag{10}$$

4.2 Discussion and Future Work

Our analysis that universal machine learning models naturally abstract both classical machine learning tasks like classification and clustering, and advanced deep learning tasks like representation learning and modeling scientific problems, such as physical simulation, with deep learning models, has been supported by recent advances. We believe that our prediction that an effective agent design can be built around a prediction engine has also been confirmed by recent empirical studies. The validation of our theoretical predictions supports the relevance of our definition of intelligence as the ability to make predictions, and the new universal intelligence measure Φ based on operator induction.

While we either optimize perceptual models or choose an action that would befit expectations, it might be possible to express the optimal adaptive agent policy in a general optimization framework. An in-depth analysis of unsupervised intelligent agents will be presented in a subsequent publication. A more general reductive definition of intelligence may also be researched. The new definition of intelligence suggests more aspects per ability than accuracy, for instance the self-improvement measure in [15] and the stochastic process model of transfer learning in [17] may be relevant. Proper implementation of these measures could aid in benchmarking AGI architectures like Omega [18] and making them more robust and reproducible. These theoretical developments could eventually contribute towards the unification of AI theory continuing in the spirit of Solomonoff's research program, Hutter's book on Universal AI, and Alexey Potapov's research program of AI unification.

References

1. Cesa-Bianchi, N., Lugosi, G.: Prediction, Learning, and Games. Cambridge University Press, Cambridge (2006). https://doi.org/10.1017/CBO9780511546921
2. Chen, L., et al.: Decision transformer: Reinforcement learning via sequence modeling. CoRR abs/2106.01345 (2021). https://arxiv.org/abs/2106.01345
3. Dowe, D.L., Hernández-Orallo, J., Das, P.K.: Compression and intelligence: social environments and communication. In: Schmidhuber, J., Thórisson, K.R., Looks, M. (eds.) AGI 2011. LNCS (LNAI), vol. 6830, pp. 204–211. Springer, Heidelberg (2011). https://doi.org/10.1007/978-3-642-22887-2_21
4. Friston, K.J., Daunizeau, J., Kiebel, S.J.: Reinforcement learning or active inference? PLOS ONE 4(7), 1–13 (2009). https://doi.org/10.1371/journal.pone.0006421
5. Ha, D., Schmidhuber, J.: World models. CoRR abs/1803.10122 (2018). http://arxiv.org/abs/1803.10122
6. Hutter, M.: Universal algorithmic intelligence: a mathematical top→down approach. In: Goertzel, B., Pennachin, C. (eds.) Artificial General Intelligence. Cognitive Technologies, pp. 227–290. Springer, Heidelberg (2007)
7. Legg, S., Hutter, M.: Universal intelligence: a definition of machine intelligence. Minds Mach. 17(4), 391–444 (2007)
8. Legg, S., Veness, J.: An approximation of the universal intelligence measure. In: Dowe, D.L. (ed.) Algorithmic Probability and Friends. Bayesian Prediction and Artificial Intelligence. LNCS, vol. 7070, pp. 236–249. Springer, Heidelberg (2013). https://doi.org/10.1007/978-3-642-44958-1_18
9. Leike, J., Lattimore, T., Orseau, L., Hutter, M.: On thompson sampling and asymptotic optimality. In: Sierra, C. (ed.) Proceedings of the Twenty-Sixth International Joint Conference on Artificial Intelligence, IJCAI 2017, Melbourne, Australia, 19–25 August 2017, pp. 4889–4893. ijcai.org (2017). https://doi.org/10.24963/ijcai.2017/688
10. Levin, L.: Universal problems of full search. Prob. Inf. Trans. 9(3), 256–266 (1973)
11. Levin, L.A.: Some theorems on the algorithmic approach to probability theory and information theory. CoRR abs/1009.5894 (2010)
12. Li, M., Vitányi, P.: An Introduction to Kolmogorov Complexity and Its Applications. TCS, Springer, New York (2008). https://doi.org/10.1007/978-0-387-49820-1
13. Lloyd, S.: Ultimate physical limits to computation. Nature 406, 1047–1054 (2000)
14. Orseau, L., Ring, M.: Space-time embedded intelligence. In: Bach, J., Goertzel, B., Iklé, M. (eds.) AGI 2012. LNCS (LNAI), vol. 7716, pp. 209–218. Springer, Heidelberg (2012). https://doi.org/10.1007/978-3-642-35506-6_22

15. Özkural, E.: Ultimate intelligence part I: physical completeness and objectivity of induction. In: Bieger, J., Goertzel, B., Potapov, A. (eds.) AGI 2015. LNCS (LNAI), vol. 9205, pp. 131–141. Springer, Cham (2015). https://doi.org/10.1007/978-3-319-21365-1_14

16. Özkural, E.: Ultimate intelligence part II: physical complexity and limits of inductive inference systems. In: Steunebrink, B., Wang, P., Goertzel, B. (eds.) AGI -2016. LNCS (LNAI), vol. 9782, pp. 33–42. Springer, Cham (2016). https://doi.org/10.1007/978-3-319-41649-6_4

17. Özkural, E.: Zeta distribution and transfer learning problem. In: Iklé, M., Franz, A., Rzepka, R., Goertzel, B. (eds.) AGI 2018. LNCS (LNAI), vol. 10999, pp. 174–184. Springer, Cham (2018). https://doi.org/10.1007/978-3-319-97676-1_17

18. Özkural, E.: Omega: an architecture for AI unification. In: Goertzel, B., Panov, A.I., Potapov, A., Yampolskiy, R. (eds.) AGI 2020. LNCS (LNAI), vol. 12177, pp. 267–278. Springer, Cham (2020). https://doi.org/10.1007/978-3-030-52152-3_28

19. Sanchez-Gonzalez, A., Godwin, J., Pfaff, T., Ying, R., Leskovec, J., Battaglia, P.W.: Learning to simulate complex physics with graph networks. In: Proceedings of the 37th International Conference on Machine Learning, ICML 2020, 13–18 July 2020, Virtual Event. Proceedings of Machine Learning Research, vol. 119, pp. 8459–8468. PMLR (2020). http://proceedings.mlr.press/v119/sanchez-gonzalez20a.html

20. Schmidhuber, J.: Optimal ordered problem solver. Mach. Learn. **54**, 211–256 (2004)

21. Solomonoff, R.J.: A formal theory of inductive inference, part i. Inf. Control **7**(1), 1–22 (1964)

22. Solomonoff, R.J.: Progress in incremental machine learning. Technical Report, IDSIA-16-03, IDSIA, Lugano, Switzerland (2003)

23. Solomonoff, R.J.: Three kinds of probabilistic induction: universal distributions and convergence theorems. Comput. J. **51**(5), 566–570 (2008)

24. Thies, J., Zollhöfer, M., Theobalt, C., Stamminger, M., Nießner, M.: Image-guided neural object rendering. In: 8th International Conference on Learning Representations, ICLR 2020, Addis Ababa, Ethiopia, 26–30 April 2020. OpenReview.net (2020). https://openreview.net/forum?id=Hyg9anEFPS

25. Wallace, C.S., Dowe, D.L.: Minimum message length and kolmogorov complexity. Comput. J. **42**(4), 270–283 (1999). http://comjnl.oxfordjournals.org/content/42/4/270.abstract

26. Wallace, C.S., Boulton, D.M.: A information measure for classification. Comput. J. **11**(2), 185–194 (1968)

Univalent Foundations of AGI are (not) All You Need

Alexey Potapov$^{(\boxtimes)}$ and Vitaly Bogdanov

SingularityNET Foundation, Amsterdam, The Netherlands
{alexey,vitaly}@singularitynet.io

Abstract. We consider homotopy type theory (HoTT) as a possible basis for Artificial General Intelligence (AGI) and study how it will frame the traditional problems of symbolic Artificial Intelligence (AI), which are not avoided, but can be addressed in a constructive way. We conclude that HoTT is suitable for building a language of a cognitive architecture, but it is not sufficient by itself to build an AGI system, which should contain grounded types and operation, including those that alter already defined types in a not strictly provable (within available types themselves) way.

Keywords: AGI · HoTT · Symbol grounding · Subsymbolic

1 Introduction

Artificial Intelligence (AI) in general and Artificial General Intelligence (AGI) in particular have deep connections with foundations of mathematics and computer science (models of computation, formal languages, etc.). Traditional foundations of mathematics based on set theory and predicate logic heavily influenced the mainstream of XX century AI with Prolog as a prominent example of simultaneous intersection between foundations of mathematics, AI, and programming languages. More broadly, Good Old-Fashioned AI (GOFAI) is referred to as symbolic due to the physical symbol system hypothesis (PSSH) [1]. For instance, Lisp relies not on a predicate calculus, but on lambda calculus, which is in essence a formalism for manipulating symbols.

One of the main branches in the field of AGI is that of 'cognitive architectures' (CAs). Development of CAs typically leads to (or even starts with) choosing or inventing a computational formalism (which can turn into a full-fledged yet domain-specific programming language), a sort of 'language of thought'. This opens up ample possibilities for bringing fundamental mathematics and computer science to AGI.

However, symbolic AI is considered to be fragile, prone to the frame and symbol grounding problems, and is opposed to subsymbolic AI, which includes most notably deep neural networks (DNNs) that have begun to dominate the AI field – in particular for machine learning, computer vision and natural language processing. The share of DNNs in AGI is also increasing. But do they reject (symbolic) foundations of mathematics and build on something different and novel? Apparently, they rely on areas of traditional mathematics with set-theoretic and predicate logic foundations. One may

© Springer Nature Switzerland AG 2022
B. Goertzel et al. (Eds.): AGI 2021, LNAI 13154, pp. 184–195, 2022.
https://doi.org/10.1007/978-3-030-93758-4_19

also note that both PSSH and its criticism consider computers as such to be physical symbol systems (and even DNNs are split into logical operations at the bottom).

Meanwhile, there are new candidates to the foundations of modern mathematics. For example, the author of [2] cites Bertrand Russell: "Modern logic, as I hope is now evident, has the effect of enlarging our abstract imagination, and providing an infinite number of possible hypotheses to be applied in the analysis of any complex fact. In this respect it is the exact opposite of the logic practised by the classical tradition," and proposes homotopy type theory (HoTT, [3]) as "philosophy's new new logic". If "new logic" was so fruitful for philosophy, AI, and computing, couldn't "new new logic" contribute to AGI?

Indeed, category theory and type theories (which can serve as alternatives to set theory as a foundation of mathematics) already contributed a lot into computer science and the design of programming languages. They are also far from being ignored in AGI (e.g. [4, 5]), but they are no close to being mainstream as well. Apparently, since the existing incarnations of dependent and homotopy type theories as programming languages such as Agda, Idris, Coq have the most straightforward use as proof assistants, they may seem too GOFAI-ish in the context of AI.

At the same time, the necessity for neural-symbolic integration has been recently recognized even in the deep learning community. "A sound reasoning layer", "certain manipulation of symbols" is necessary even for applied AI systems (see, for example, [6]), so symbolic AI is regaining attention.

We are rethinking the design of the OpenCog cognitive architecture (e.g., [7]), which contains essentially symbolic components like the Atomspace knowledge base, the metagraph Pattern Matcher, the Unified Rule Engine, but which was also successfully used to build neural-symbolic systems (e.g. [8]). In this paper, we explore the possible role of HoTT in AGI and discuss symbolic/subsymbolic dichotomy as it relates to this example.

2   Symbolic Systems and Mathematics

Any calculus is typically considered as a bunch of rules for manipulating symbols syntactically without relying on their meaning (semantics). But what do we really imply by this? For example, lambda calculus has a few rules for manipulating symbolic expressions of form

```
<expr> ::= <constant> | <variable> | <expr> <expr> | λ<variable>.<expr> | (<expr>)
```

This description of syntax already involves some meta-symbols. If we try to describe syntactically the lambda calculus rules such as β-reduction, we will have some difficulties. Typically, it is written as $((\lambda x . M)\ E)\ \rightarrow\ (M[x: = E])$. But as a purely symbolic expression it means nothing and does nothing. We can try to describe the content of this rule in more detail, but we will inevitably end up with some symbols, for which we suppose some meaning. While calculi deal with symbols syntactically, they themselves rely on semantics. Even if we describe a calculus formally as a collection of syntactically defined rules, this description will rely on symbols of meta-language with semantic grounding. This grounding can reside in the minds of humans, who understand what these symbolic descriptions of, say, lambda calculus means, or it can take the form of a piece of code running on a certain computer (or another physical device).

It is impossible to completely get rid of grounded symbols in mathematics, but mathematicians have tried to reduce their usage as much as possible (and represent them in the form of alternative foundations of mathematics). The bare minimum is a set of instructions for a certain computer or non-reducible operations of any equivalent definition of the algorithm. Whether this minimum is really enough is disputable. Mapping theorem proofs into, say, Turing machines is not convenient in practice. Working mathematicians don't always use this level of strictness. Also, classical foundations of mathematics are not constructive. This doesn't necessarily mean that the mentioned minimum is not enough, since we hope to implement AGI as a computer program. It may also mean that the semantics even of foundational mathematical concepts are not clear enough and not fully understood by humans themselves.

Indeed, both the notion of sets in set theory and the notion of truth in predicate logic (in the sense of both their computational and semantic groundings) are problematic, which was shown by numerous paradoxes (especially, for naïve set theory). These paradoxes in turn, served to motivate constructive mathematics. However, constructive mathematics was too restrictive, and didn't allow for many proofs that looked natural in traditional mathematics.

HoTT doesn't completely reject useful but non-constructive axioms such as the law of excluded middle or the axiom of choice, but determines circumstances in which they hold constructively. HoTT attempts to formalize mathematics with computer proof assistants readily providing a computational framework for representing mathematical statements and manipulating with them. Thus, it is an interesting candidate for novel foundations of at least symbolic AI. A few attempts have already been made to adopt dependent and HoTT for knowledge representation (e.g. [9, 10]), but no work has considered the implications of HoTT for symbolic AI and cognitive architectures in the AGI context.

3 HoTT and Symbol Grounding

HoTT Primitives
In HoTT, we cannot introduce a symbol (variable), without indicating its type. $a : A$ is a judgement in HoTT, while $a \in A$ is a proposition in set theory. Of course, $a : A$ is not just a meaningless symbolic expression. It has a predefined interpretation in HoTT (both computational and semantic). Definitional (judgmental) equality is another primitive in HoTT. The symbol $\equiv$ for defining equality has also a predefined special meaning.

There is also propositional equality written as $x =_A y$, which implies that we can chain definitional equalities (within type A) together and transform x to y. An interesting aspect is that propositional equality is itself a type, whose elements are proofs of equality of x and y (if this type is inhabited).

However, in order to get non-trivial equalities, some computation rules are necessary. For example, in order to infer that $(\lambda x . x + x) (2) \equiv 2 + 2$ we need to have β-reduction, which can be treated as a definitional equality $(\lambda x. \ \Phi)(a) \equiv \Phi'$, but with Φ' represented not symbolically, but computed by a grounded function, which replaces all occurrences of x in Φ by a avoiding name collisions.

In the AGI context, it is natural to ask where these judgements and definitions come from. Application of HoTT to Automated Theorem Proving (ATP) supposes that they are provided by mathematicians. They pick judgements interesting to them as true a priori, by human's definition. HoTT can be used to define arbitrary theories and deduce consequences from them. However, the question of adequacy of such theories to reality is not considered. While it is not a (notable) problem in ATP, it becomes very important if we consider HoTT for knowledge representation in AGI.

Constructable = Existent

The book [2] discusses the possibility of using (modal) HoTT as a new logic for philosophy, and natural language especially, pointing out the controversy regarding whether each common noun should denote a type or whether they should be formed by predication on some master type Entity. Consider a very simple sentence "John is a man". It is natural to consider Man as a type and John as its instance defining `John`: `Man`. However, it will not be a proposition in such a form and cannot be negated or appear in conditionals. Representing this expression as a dependent sum `(John, r)`: $\sum_{x:\text{Entity}}$ `Man(x)`, where `r`: `Man(John)` doesn't have this problem.

The author of [2] extends this idea by considering such intermediate dependent types as `AnimatedObject`, which provide additional context for propositions like "John is a man" and prohibit reference to John as, say, a meteorological event. However, even flexible use of dependent types doesn't eliminate the presence of judgements and doesn't answer the question of where these judgements come from. How are `r`: `Man(John)` and `John`: `AnimatedObject` different from just `John`: `Man` in terms of necessity for introducing new members of types in runtime? Let us consider this question on the fully constructive level of program code (using Idris-like syntax).

Consider the classical syllogism as a slightly more complex example: All humans are mortal. Socrates is a human. Therefore, Socrates is mortal. What are the types in this case? Should Socrates be a type, a type constructor, a variable, a function?

If we write `Socrates`: `Human`, which seems natural, it implies that `Socrates` is a variable of type `Human`, and we need to construct its value. We could have one constructor `data Human = HumanC` and write `Socrates = HumanC`. However, any two such variables will be equal (due to `refl` $x: x =_A x$). In fact, there will be only one member of `Human` and this isn't what we want. Rather, we would prefer to have `Socrates` as a type constructor. This can be a question of syntax, but in dependently typed languages we cannot write `Socrates`: `Human`separately. Instead, we should collect all type constructors together:

```
data Human : Type where
    Socrates : Human
    Plato : Human
```

or, with syntactic sugar, data Human = Socrates | Plato | ..., which will be the simplest sum type. Then, we can write x: Human, x = Socrates, and two variables with values Socrates and Plato will not be equal.

But what should be done in a situation where a previously unknown person appears? We will have to extend the existing type with a novel constructor so that we will be able to distinguish this person from other persons. Distinctions can be considered as one of very basic ontological notions [11], which has quite an interesting connection to equality in HoTT, although we will not explore this connection here. The issue we consider here is that type theories don't provide computational operations for altering types. But do we need these operations with dependent types?

Even if Human is defined as a dependent type, it still needs to have constructors:

```
data Human : Entity -> Type where
     SocratesIsHuman : Human Socrates
     PlatoIsHuman : Human Plato
```

together with data Entity = Socrates | Plato. Any new entity or witness will require new constructors.

We can try avoiding enumeration of all members of Entity or Human types by building them on top of some infinite type, whose members will serve as features of entities (e.g. name strings). Will it work?

We can either have a parameterized constructor or a dependent type.

```
data Human : Type where
     HumanName : String -> Human
socrates : Human
socrates = HumanName "Socrates"
```

or

```
data Human : String -> Type where
     HumanName : Human s
socrates : Human "Socrates"
socrates = HumanName
```

In the first case, we can construct any number of members of Human, while in the second case, we can construct any number of types Human x for some concrete x.

Such representations are convenient for databases. However, the question is how we interpret these definitions. Do we assume that all possible instances of Human with all possible names really exist, or do they exist in possible worlds?

Let us consider a proposition "All humans are mortal". Such propositions are expressed via functional types. For our simple types, it should look like

```
f : Human -> Mortal
```

but it will be trivially true for inhabited types independent of connections between Human and Mortal. If we directly map this proposition to a type, it should look like

```
f : Human x -> Mortal x
```

The proposition expressed in this type is true if we can provide an implementation of a total function, which will work for any x. Let us proceed with the representation in which Human x is a dependent type also.

If Mortal x is defined similarly to Human x, then such function trivially exists:

```
f : (Human x) -> (Mortal x)
f HumanName = MortalName
```

Then, we can write

```
socrates : Human "Socrates"
socrates = HumanName
```

and we can prove, by declaring and providing an instance of type Mortal "Socrates":

```
y : Mortal "Socrates"
y = f socrates
```

It follows from our definitions that "all humans are mortal" is a mathematical rather than empirical truth. If we consider only created instances as existent and creatable instances as potentially existent, then we should not consider the possibility of constructing a proof as a proof. Rather, we should consider something like f HumanName = MortalName not as a proof, but as a possible knowledge base entry, which we shouldn't arbitrarily add to our knowledge base, but should prove it empirically before adding. This doesn't correspond to semantics of dependent types.

Thus, an attempt to declare types in such ways that we can create their instances, which factual existence is not provided a priori, forecloses the possibility of considering types as propositions, whose inhabitants are their proofs.

Let us note that modal HoTT doesn't avoid the necessity of alteration of types, because propositions can change, say, from possible to necessary with new information.

Syllogism Example

If we define Human by enumerating all known humans, then implementation of f will be total only if mortality of all these humans is already known. It can be done via enumerating all facts of all mortal entities as constructors of Mortal. However, we can have a general definition of human mortality as prior knowledge.

In this context, it doesn't matter too much if Human is defined as a plain sum type, or dependent sum over Entity or String. In all cases we should enumerate all humans known to the system, e.g.

```
data Human : String -> Type where
    SocratesIsHuman : Human "Socrates"
    PlatoIsHuman : Human "Plato"
```

It looks conceptually better to have an `Entity` type with distinct entities as members, and `Name` as one of the dependent types describing their properties. It might be a minor point, but let us stick to this option.

```
data Entity = Socrates | Plato
data Human : Entity -> Type where
    SocratesIsHuman : Human Socrates
    PlatoIsHuman : Human Plato
data EntityName : Entity -> String -> Type where
    SocratesIsSocrates : EntityName Socrates "Socrates"
    PlatoIsPlate : EntityName Plato "Plato"
```

Let us note that we could define a more restrictive `HumanName` type, and `EntityName` could have a constructor that utilizes `HumanName` in a general way. More interesting are the constructors that the type `Mortal` should have. They can be defined as

```
data Mortal : Entity -> Type where
    SocratesIsMortal : Mortal Socrates
    PlatoIsMortal : Mortal Plato
```

Then, the proposition that all humans are mortal can be proven by listing all mortal humans, because there is no other way to construct `Mortal x` other than by providing a concrete constructor:

```
f : Human x -> Mortal x
f SocratesIsHuman = SocratesIsMortal
f PlatoIsHuman = PlatoIsMortal
```

A dependently typed language compiler will check that the function is total and that we didn't miss any case. Alternatively, we can have the rule that all humans are mortal as a constructor

```
data Mortal : Entity -> Type where
    HumanIsMortal : Human x -> Mortal x
```

Therefore, the proof of the corresponding proposition is trivial (and redundant)

```
f : Human x -> Mortal x
f = HumanIsMortal
y : Mortal Socrates
y = f SocratesIsHuman
```

Thus, we can prove that `Mortal Socrates` is populated given the evidence (minor premise) `Human Socrates` and the major premise `Human x - > Mortal x`. Everything is represented by type constructors.

Our representation of the syllogism looks natural, but it implies that meeting any new person (or acquiring new information) as well as generalizing particular facts will require altering types. This situation is not essentially different from the problem of closed worlds in other logical systems. However, a conceptually interesting question arises – if there is a mathematically sound way of introducing new types or their constructors, shouldn't it be expressible in HoTT and implementable in a corresponding programming language?

Distinction and Identification

Many dependently typed languages inherit Haskell syntax in declaring types that obscures their nature. Why do we need special syntax and `data` keyword? We would like just to declare `Entity: Type`, and then to use definitional equality, e.g., `Entity = Socrates | Plato`. This looks natural because we define one type using such operations over types as a sum or product (which can also be dependent sums and products). But sum operands are types. `Socrates` and `Plato` are not types. In category-theoretic interpretations, they are (names of) functors `( ) - > Entity`, which correspond to certain elements of `Entity`. `Entity` is a sum of unit types, which is mathematically sensible, but not adequately expressive for knowledge representation.

In Coq, which is used concretely for HoTT, type definitions look like

```
Inductive nat : Type :=
| O : nat
| S : nat → nat.
```

The above looks more like a definitional equality. However, type `nat` is not defined via other members of `Type` and expressions over them. Symbols O and S are directly introduced as just having types `nat` and `nat → nat` correspondingly.

`nat: Type` is not definitionally equal to anything else, although it could be defined as a sum of `( )` and `nat → nat`, which would indeed reduce to primitive operations on types. An inductive definition constructively (finitely) defines an infinite type, for all members of which we can prove common properties. However, it will obscure the fact that we want to construct expressions like O or `(S (S O))` as having the type `nat`. Let us forget mathematical interpretations for a moment and look at these as symbols. We introduce symbols O: nat and S: nat → nat, for which there are no definitional equalities. If there were an interpreter of symbolic expressions, it could interpret these symbols only to themselves.

We can compose various expressions from symbols. We have this capability prior to types and their constructors. Expression typing imposes restrictions on valid expressions. For example, nat: Type allows nat to appear on right-hand sides of colon expressions (and some other places, where Type members are valid, e.g. as an argument of a symbol, which type is Type - > _).

What is the difference between S: nat $\rightarrow$ nat as «a constructor» from a function with the same signature? S doesn't have a body. There is no definitional equality for it. It is not further reducible.

Functional languages with type systems use constructors also for checking totality of functions. For example, if we write

$$f : nat \rightarrow nat$$
$$f\ 0 = (S\ 0)$$

we can conclude that f is not total. We could make no distinction between a type constructor and a non-total function. Such a function does not reduce further in such cases, e.g. f (S 0) would be well-typed but non-reducible, similarly to S (S 0). In the context of AGI, this may make sense. A toddler can know that 2 + 2 = 4, but can have no idea about 4 + 4, although knowing that 4 is also a number and can be added, and knowing that 4 apples and 4 apples are 4 + 4 apples, so + will act both as a function and as a constructor. However, separating a complete inductive definition of a type from variables and functions is very convenient for constructing proofs by induction, which is one of the main features of HoTT.

Nevertheless, in an open system, what is initially a constructor can get a definitional equality. For example, the system is told about some Jonny, and it introduces new entity Jonny: Entity, JonnyName: EntityName Jonny "Jonny". Then, it appears that Jonny is John, whom it already knew. It just needs to identify them Jonny = John. This definitional equality can be propagated to various propositional equalities. Thus, two basic operations are distinguishing and identification of symbols and expressions.

Grounded Types and Non-Provability

Information doesn't come from nowhere. Rather, it is communicated to the system via certain interfaces, which might be good to formalize. Functional languages typically do so by using IO Monad. However, it separates pure code from side effects rather than answers the question of how pure code emerges from external information.

Instead of talking about arbitrary program I/O, let us consider an agent with some sensors. We may try supposing that we know the type of data coming from these sensors. Can we indeed know? Suppose that we have a video sensor. An observation at moment t will be $x_t : \mathbb{R}^{N \times M}$. However, as we articulated, everything constructible is not just possible, but existent. It is incorrect to say that any member of $\mathbb{R}^{N \times M}$ of exists as sensory input, so the type of sensory input cannot be equal to $\mathbb{R}^{N \times M}$. It differs from the set-theoretic representation, in which $x_t \in \mathbb{R}^{N \times M}$ would be a valid proposition.

Thus, it seems more correct to have a type Observation, whose constructors are not known to the agent, and instances of this type are constructed outside the agent. We refer to such types as grounded. Receiving a new observation can be thought of as adding a new constructor or member to such a type, which can be generalized. Either the type system of our agent will contain no types corresponding to real-world entities besides prior knowledge (and a dependently typed language would just serve for interpreting another language to work with runtime information), which will suffer from the symbol grounding problem, or the agent must be capable of the act of forming a new type and populating it with new members and functorial constructors. What is a proposition at some level of reasoning can become a judgment at another level.

Impossibility of an absolute proof of inductive generalizations based on a finite number of arguments was realized already by Bacon. We can construct absolute proofs within consistent definitions of types, but they will be model assumptions, whose correspondence to reality will never be perfect. Such is the case for the scientific methodology in general, in which theories are constructed on the basis of available information and then experimentally verified together with their consequences. Interestingly, the criterion of falsifiability says that scientific theories should admit the possibility to be proven to be false in principle by new evidence. But shouldn't it be true about the scientific method itself? It cannot be formally proven, but it is supported by a huge corpus of knowledge and predictions resulting from its usage meaning its high degree of adequacy to reality.

Of course, we would like to have justified methods for machine learning. All such methods (including deep learning) are expressed mathematically and/or as program code. For some of them we have proofs of optimality, although under strong assumptions, making these methods narrowly applicable and inadequate to reality in general case. There are proofs of optimality for universal methods like Solomonoff induction, but these are, unfortunately, not constructive. There are also proofs that universal computable predictors cannot exist [12], though interpretation of such theorems in the context of building AGI is also debatable. Nevertheless, neither a universal and practically applicable induction method nor a constructive method of synthesis of efficient specialized algorithms is currently known.

Generally, AGI will unavoidably have a heuristic or non-axiomatic (in sense of [13]) element. This implies not only that it is not provably reducible to some deductive system, but also that it should contain some collection of algorithms (or, rather, sub-programs, which are not necessarily provably terminating), which can be justified only partially, with the choice between them ultimately being empirical. Both the design of a language for CAs with the choice of base formalism (such as HoTT) and the amount of prior information (including built-in algorithms) are heuristic in nature.

There is some content of intelligence that cannot be derived a priori by 'pure reason'. This is obviously the case for concrete knowledge about the world, but it may not be as obvious that the methods of reasoning and learning also cannot strictly be provably optimal. While any prior judgement or axiom built into an AGI system should be falsifiable in principle, that can be considered as a possibility of this system to rewrite any piece of its code as in the Gödel machine [14], we believe that most non-trivial acts of self-improvement are not strictly provable (in terms of increase in expected future rewards). Rather, such improvements should be put forward and tested in practice, similarly to scientific hypotheses. It should be underlined that total functions, which type-check as members of types, which, in turn, serve as provable propositions, are not Turing-complete.

4 Conclusion

Homotopy type theory is attractive, because instead of using sets and meta-language of logic separately, it uses only types, which encompass both objects and propositions, which are also objects of higher types. This is convenient for AGI in terms of uniformly and constructively representing and reasoning about knowledge both of the external world and reasoning itself. Besides, type theories in the form of programming languages provide the convenient tool of pattern matching, which, combined with knowledge retrieval queries, could provide a basis for "language of thought".

However, such languages themselves cannot get rid of a few meta-language symbols for primitive grounded operations that cannot be described declaratively within languages themselves (besides directly referring to these symbols). For a real-world AGI, which doesn't work in a purely abstract domain, there should be additional grounded types, which stand for interactions with the environment. Definitions of such types are unknown a priori, and since constructability implies existence, constructors of grounded types should be added through observations. This implies that more abstract concepts as derived types can change as well. Any collection of types should be considered as a model that can be more or less applicable to reality rather than an absolute truth about it.

Methods for altering types can utilize available knowledge presented in already defined types, and can be described in the same language, but will unavoidably refer to some grounded symbols, which will make their use not strictly provable. Such grounded operations can be regarded as subsymbolic, although their granularity and quantity are research questions.

Acknowledgments. The authors are grateful to Ben Goertzel for useful references and ideas, which stimulated the study performed in the present paper. Thanks to Janet Adams and James Boyd for proofreading.

References

1. Newell, A., Simon, H.A.: Computer science as empirical inquiry: symbols and search. Commun. ACM **19**(3), 113–126 (1976). https://doi.org/10.1145/360018.360022
2. Corfield, D.: Modal Homotopy Type Theory: The Prospect of a New Logic for Philosophy, p. 191. Oxford University Press, Oxford (2020)
3. Homotopy Type Theory: Univalent Foundations of Mathematics (2013). arXiv preprint, arXiv: 1308.0729
4. Goertzel, B.: A formal model of cognitive synergy. In: Everitt, T., Goertzel, B., Potapov, A. (eds.) AGI 2017. LNCS (LNAI), vol. 10414, pp. 13–22. Springer, Cham (2017). https://doi.org/10.1007/978-3-319-63703-7_2
5. Phillips, S.: A general (category theory) principle for general intelligence: duality (adjointness). In: Everitt, T., Goertzel, B., Potapov, A. (eds.) AGI 2017. LNCS (LNAI), vol. 10414, pp. 57–66. Springer, Cham (2017). https://doi.org/10.1007/978-3-319-63703-7_6
6. Lamb, L.C., et al.: Graph Neural Networks Meet Neural-Symbolic Computing: A Survey and Perspective (2021). arXiv preprint, arXiv: 2003.00330

7. Goertzel, B., Pennachin, C., Geisweiller, N.: Engineering General Intelligence, Part 1 & 2. Atlantis press, Paris (2014)
8. Potapov, A., Belikov, A., Bogdanov, V., Scherbatiy, A.: Cognitive module networks for grounded reasoning. In: Hammer, P., Agrawal, P., Goertzel, B., Iklé, M. (eds.) AGI 2019. LNCS (LNAI), vol. 11654, pp. 148–158. Springer, Cham (2019). https://doi.org/10.1007/978-3-030-27005-6_15
9. Dapoigny, R., Barlatier, P.: Using a dependently-typed language for expressing ontologies. In: Xiong, H., Lee, W.B. (eds.) KSEM 2011. LNCS (LNAI), vol. 7091, pp. 257–268. Springer, Heidelberg (2011). https://doi.org/10.1007/978-3-642-25975-3_23
10. Lai, Z., et al.: Dependently Typed Knowledge Graphs (2020). arXiv preprint, arXiv: 2003.03785
11. Goertzel, B.: Distinction Graphs and Graphtropy: A Formalized Phenomenological Layer Underlying Classical and Quantum Entropy, Observational Semantics and Cognitive Computation (2019). arXiv preprint, arXiv: 1902.00741
12. Legg, Sh.: Machine Super Intelligence. PhD thesis (2008)
13. Wang, P.: On definition of artificial intelligence. J. Artif. Gen. Intell. **19**(2), 1–37 (2019)
14. Schmidhuber, J.: Gödel machines: fully self-referential optimal universal self-improvers. In: Goertzel, B., Pennachin. C. (eds.) Artificial General Intelligence. Cognitive Technologies, pp. 199–226. Springer, Heidelberg (2007). https://doi.org/10.1007/978-3-540-68677-4_7

Biological Intelligence Considered in Terms of Physical Structures and Phenomena

Saty Raghavachary[✉] ⓘ

University of Southern California, Los Angeles, CA 90089, USA
saty@usc.edu

Abstract. This short paper provides a novel perspective on natural intelligence, stemming from the following observation that holds for all spatial scales from the subatomic to the cosmological: physical (material) structures, solely by virtue of their arrangement and constitution, result in appropriate natural phenomena. Such a physical structure-oriented view is shown to account for a variety of natural intelligence exhibited by living systems that include, but are not limited to, viruses, flora, insects, groups/colonies, and for sure, humans. It is hypothesized that artificial agent designs that incorporate appropriate physical structures would result in their displaying intelligent behavior similar to biological forms, a radical departure from designs that are centered on digital computation - such embodied agents might be capable of robust, flexible behavior in the real-world, which has thus far eluded AI.

Keywords: Philosophy of AGI · Natural intelligence · Agent architectures · Analog computation

1 Introduction

The quest for AGI has been ongoing, stemming from our desire to create synthetic agents that would think, feel and act like ourselves. But, the ongoing quest has not been quite fruitful - it is almost as if the right paradigm to approach this, might be missing. This short paper is an attempt to provide a plausible route to AGI.

In the following sections, an argument is presented, for intelligent behavior to be regarded as emanating from appropriate physical structures, rather than exclusively via digital computation (as implemented the type of AI we have today).

2 Structures

The universe can be regarded as being comprised of matter and energy (which are themselves equivalent, but we keep them distinct for our purposes), 'embedded' in space and time. From the distant galaxies to individual sub-atomic particles we can image in a bubble chamber, it is all, matter, set in motion by energy (including via forces they generate).

Matter and energy, while being valid descriptors of 'what is', do not capture the fascinating, multitude forms in which matter and energy interact, transform and be

B. Goertzel et al. (Eds.): AGI 2021, LNAI 13154, pp. 196–203, 2022.
https://doi.org/10.1007/978-3-030-93758-4_20

transformed. For that we look at 'what does', related to matter and energy - the distinction between being and doing. In other words, how do matter and energy behave?

Matter and energy (most commonly, matter - so from here on we mostly refer to matter, although the discussion would apply to energy as well) are organized into structures, which are physical configurations in space and time. Specifically, the structures are not abstract/mathematical, but rather, physical with point, line, plane and volume extents.

Structures exist, literally from cosmological scales (e.g. spiral arms in galaxies) to the microscopic (e.g. mitochondria in cells) to subatomic (e.g. nanoparticle assemblies). Energy is structured as well, e.g. electromagnetic energy, via frequencies.

Structures exist in the inorganic world, as well as in biological forms. We humans are quite adept, via our scientific advances and shared knowledge in general, at creating structures that are beneficial to us - e.g. houses, bridges, semiconductor lattices, telescope arrays. Animals and insects are also capable to creating structures that benefit them: spider webs, beehives, nests, etc.

3 Phenomena

Phenomena (usually referred to as natural phenomena) is how matter 'behaves', as a response to energy input. E.g. heating water causes it to boil, flicking a marble sets in rolling motion, etc. The response in turn could induce phenomena elsewhere, possibly of a different type (e.g. an explosion could cause dents or fracture).

4 Structures → Phenomena

Structures exhibit phenomena.

Holes in a flute create pleasing sound waves, fluid flow past an obstacle leads to turbulence, mirrors reflect, wires conduct, protein molecules fold and vibrate, Velcro sticks due to mechanical entanglement, elastic materials stretch (and break or tear if stressed beyond capacity), syringes puncture skin, etc. Phenomena occur in an astonishing variety, stemming from the various ways by which matter and energy interact: mechanical, acoustic, electrical, chemical, nuclear, quantum mechanical, etc. Engineering, by humans as well as nature, involves harnessing various phenomena for gainful purposes, by creating (inventing/evolving) structures that exhibit them.

Vibration, fracture, dissolution, sedimentation, filtration, heat conduction, diffusion, reflection, polarization, acoustic transmission... practically every phenomenon could be put to use, via design and construction of appropriate structures. Structures do not need to be explicitly constructed - inorganic matter structures, e.g. single crystals, pulsars, snowflakes, eddies in fluids etc. are structures that occur naturally, without explicit design or its adaptation.

Structures exhibiting phenomena is indeed the 'connective tissue' that spans inanimate matter, organic matter including us humans and animals, and the inorganic structures that we humans and animals create in turn. Life and its environment is considered a closed system in this view, operating via phenomena that involves mutual exchange of matter and/or energy.

5 Life's Structures and Phenomena

The amazingly wide variety of life forms are comprised of structures at the organ, cellular and sub-cellular levels that display an equally amazing diversity of phenomena that are of mechanical, optical, thermal, acoustic, electrical, magnetic, etc. nature.

Indeed, evolution appears to act like an expedient engineer that chooses just the right structure that exploits a certain phenomena in order to help with survival and reproduction [1]. Examples abound, here are just a few. Animal eyes (corneas) are curved convex outwards, to focus light at the retina. Cats' eyes contain a retro reflective coating behind the retina, to reflect incoming light back on to the ambient environment, to help them see better. Animals exhibit mimicry to resemble other animals in order to mislead predators, or use camouflage to blend in with the environment to avoid detection. Many types of birds' upper beaks are curved just right in order to act like a lever, working with the lower beak; in waterfowl, beak curvature helps prevent escape of fish that the birds catch with their mouths. Homing pigeons' beaks contain magnetic particles that help them detect the earth's magnetic field. Electric eels generate electricity to ward off prey. Sea stars move by squeezing water out from their tube feet, generating pressure waves that proper the creatures; they have nerve nets, analogous to nervous systems in animals. In humans, heart muscle undergoes rhythmic contractions, nerves conduct electrical signals, bones provide mechanical support. Structures at the sub-organ level are implicated in how tropisms are exhibited by plants (e.g. heliotropism) where they respond to stimuli, and the various -ceptions in animals that are related to sensing (e.g. graviception, proprioception).

Also, discussing life in terms of structures and phenomena, is not as reductionist as stating that they are comprised of matter/chemicals - that is too low of a level, which entirely misses the utility of structures and their phenomena. For example, a poisonous snake does not merely contain chemicals that harm its prey - it also contains fangs, the 'delivery structures' that make the poison be administered effectively.

As is clear from the above discussion, every form of life can be regarded as comprised of 'nothing but structures', whose phenomena serve to keep the life form alive - 'what is life?' [2] can be informally answered this way: a collection of structures whose purpose (via their intrinsic phenomena) is to provide homeostasis (i.e. maintain a stable internal environment). It is as if 'structural biology' is a tautology, since structures are central to biological function; likewise, the biophysics and biochemistry disciplines can also be viewed as the study of phenomena that arise from appropriate structures. Indeed, medicine, medical technologies, and medical devices and prosthetics, are also related to structures and phenomena.

6   Intelligence

A simple but widely applicable definition of intelligence, is 'considered response' [3] - this stems from the fact that intelligence can be considered a biological function. This would mean that life forms contain structures that exhibit phenomena that lead to their exhibiting intelligent behavior (that helps them survive and reproduce). Again, examples are plenty. In cacti, adaptations such as thorns and thick leaves help them ward off predators and store water. Slime mold is able to migrate towards a food source by sensing chemical gradients. A variety of offense and defense related structures help predators and prey respectively, to hunt or defend respectively. Animal brains contain specific structures that process and integrate sensory information and provide motor functions. In higher animals, chemicals (molecular structures) and their receptor sites (structures on cell surfaces, which are themselves structures) carry out emotional response and regulation; place cells provide spatial orientation. Also, increasing evidence points to consciousness - a mysterious, explanation-defying phenomenon in humans and other animals - possibly emerging from the interactions between different, specialized brain regions.

The notion of emergent group behavior (such as consciousness as we just noted) is a natural outcome of the 'considered response' theory. When a group of interacting individuals each respond by considering their respective inputs, the collective considerations could be regarded as occurring at the group level, whose collective response would be considered 'emergent' (because the response emerges from the lower-level ones, as opposed to being directed generated at the group level - not possible, since the group is incapable of considering). Regarded as group-level considered response, emergence is not a mysterious, or placeholder, phenomenon; rather, it is expected behavior that is bound to result on account of individual behavior. Emergence in a beehive, ant colony, flock of birds [4], traffic, economic markets, and the brain, all result from individual structures' phenomena.

7   Intelligence via Digital Computation (PSSH)

The Physical Symbol System Hypothesis (PSSH) states [5]: **'A physical symbol system has the necessary and sufficient means for general intelligent action'.** This hypothesis underlies almost all AI to date, which is implemented via digital computation (algorithmic, Turing-computable). Rule-based manipulation (symbolic logic), data-based statistical inference (connectionist, i.e. neural architectures, including Deep Learning), and reward maximization (reinforcement learning, i.e. RL), all employ a wide variety of digital processing, that involve data structures and computation using von Neumann stored-program architecture (clock cycles, fetch-decode-execute, arithmetic logic units, hardware registers, memory/processor distinction). When applied to AI, this implies that the form of the hardware (specific processor architectures), or the choice of programming language or compiler etc. is immaterial, since it is all about the (digital) computation which is expected to lead to intelligent behavior: expert systems processing knowledge, ML generating an essay with perfect grammar and meaning, RL agents learning to play hide and seek, etc.

8 Intelligence via Analog Computation (SPSH)

Complementary to digital computation, there is a different form of intelligence, the kind routinely exhibited even by the simplest of animals (e.g. fruit fly, worms such as C. Elegans). Biological life forms do not carry out digital computation, the kind outlined in the previous section (this is not to say they do not employ binary logic - just not digital computation). Instead, their computation is entirely analog-based, involving structures at various scales that have evolved to carry them out. Animals, including humans 'experience' the world - directly, physically, interactively. Such experience is not via processing symbols, employing data, or computing rewards, the way current AI does. The directness of experience stems from interactions between an agent and the environment, occurring via phenomena interchange, stemming from relevant structures that are present in the agent as well as the environment.

Surely, humans and some other species do carry out symbolic computation (including math and language processing), humans collect and employ data, animals including humans learn via reinforcement. But underneath is analog machinery that does it all using physical structures and phenomena, not logical structures and digital computation as the bottom layer.

If the agent interacts with animate structures (e.g. a dog pushes open a door), those structures respond, but not 'intelligently' (no active consideration); on the other hand if the environment consists of living matter, the response would be 'considered' (e.g. a fly evading being swatted, a human countering a chess move, etc.), involving exchanges of considered response feedback loops.

Analog computation occurring via physical structures exhibiting phenomena in brains and other devices (e.g. mechanical clocks, sundials, player pianos, World War II gun fire control systems (rangekeepers), and a host of others), inspires the following 'Structured Physical System Hypothesis' (SPSH): **'A structured physical system has the necessary and sufficient means for specific intelligent response'.**

9 Implications of the SPSH

Animals, including humans, experience the world, embodied - where the body (including the brain) is comprised of structures, via which experience is acquired, stored as experiential (including episodic) memory, recalled, modified, etc. (all involving physical structures as well). Such direct experiencing makes it possible to deal with multiple, simultaneous phenomena in the environment - e.g. by perceiving them as sights, sounds as well as touch, motion etc. - there is no 'limit' on the number of phenomena, given that the agent is part of its ambient environment and has no control over it. And, the multiple phenomena, if occurring in inorganic structures, have zero 'computational' cost - they are simply responses, not considered.

If it is indeed the case that experience for an agent can only be acquired via embodied structures directly interacting with its environment, it has implications on how we would design artificial agents to do likewise. It might be that artificial agents, using suitable body and 'brain' structures designed by us, would need to be analog-based as well (which would be a form of biomimetics, where we humans utilize nature's structures to achieve similar functionality, i.e. phenomena). Not considering embodiment, or not using an embodied analog 'core' for considering and responding, might be why, for today's AI, 'easy things are hard and hard things are easy' [6]. In other words, the worlds of analog computation and digital computation might be distinct, with virtually no overlap - each being good at what they provide, but not interchangeable with each other.

What about simulating the world, and embodied agents, in VR? Doing so has clear advantages such as simplification, repeatability, explicit control over the environment, etc. [7], but, there is a serious issue, which is that the complexities of simultaneous structure → phenomena interactions with the agent, and the agents own composition, cannot be adequately modeled, simulated and rendered in VR. For example, simulating an agent stepping on something sharp and 'experiencing' pain VR, is not equivalent to a similar agent being able to exhibit nociception (pain perception), via direct embodied experience in the real world. The computation of the simulation is not the issue, the issue is about the need to compute in the first place. Such a distinction is not merely pedantic, it has real implications - it has been proposed that real-life robots be able to feel emotions so that they may take better care of themselves [8]. It is not clear that simulating agents in VR, then instantiating them as real-life embodiments would lead to a seamless 'transfer' of experiencing.

As another twist, what if we built a suitably designed embodied agent (with appropriate physical structures with which to negotiate the environment), that employs digital computation at its core? Doing so would be based on the rationale that any input/signal reaching the brain could be processed digitally if it is sampled adequately (above its Nyquist limit). This would indeed work - but the hypothesis would be that its experience would not be as genuine as a similar agent where the processing occurs via analog physical structures! In the words, the agent would be a 'zombie' of sorts, being able to sense, perceive, display intelligent behavior, all without direct experience. To take this further, agents with complex-enough brain architectures that operate entirely in the analog realm, might even be hypothesized to experience consciousness that would arise on account of the agent being able to experience the world with a sense of 'Self' - e.g. a recent study proposes that consciousness could arise when the brain cycles between two states that involve the default mode network (DMN) and the dorsal attention network (DAT) [9].

Philosophical musings aside, a practical takeaway from the SPSH (if it is indeed true) would be that in addition to AI agents carrying out digital computations for tasks involving symbol processing, data-based inferencing and reward maximizing, they might also, in complementary fashion, need to do embodied analog computation in order to operate in the world by directly dealing with it in a model-free manner [10].

Braitenberg vehicles [11] might serve as further inspiration for this line of thought. Such vehicles are conceptual experiments that involve simple analog computing, where sensors (for light, sound etc.) directly control a vehicle's wheels - the vehicles are reactive automatons, capable of displaying rather sophisticated behavior, especially for an observer unfamiliar with the vehicles' internals. If relatively-simple setups can produce complex behavior (as has been repeatedly verified via their construction), it might be worth investigating what behavior might result from more complex setups (e.g. using neuromorphic hardware for analog processing [12], soft-skin bodies, sophisticated sensors and actuators etc.).

Analog embodiments do not need to only be anthropomorphic, i.e. there is reason to limit ourselves to human-like agents. Instead, it would fascinating to explore designs wildly different from that of human bodies, e.g. arrays of eyes (that respond to a wider spectrum of wavelengths compared to human eyes) along multiple limbs, senses that go beyond sight, sound, smell, taste and touch, etc. (e.g. sonar, perception of electrical fields). The hypothesis is that such designs would result in 'alien' beings that, on the one hand, experience the world fundamentally similar to how biological life does, and on the other, experience it differently enough to result in novel, useful (to humans) functionalities.

10   Conclusions

Structures → phenomena being universally applicable, including to life forms, is the notion that is explored in this paper. This is argued to encompass intelligence as well, which then leads to the structured physical system hypothesis (SPSH). Considering SPSH to be plausible, suggests that embodied agents that carry out analog processing their brains, might be able to experience the world in addition to being able to digitally compute aspects of intelligence, leading to more capable architectures compared to those that only digitally compute.

References

1. Tributsch, H.: How Life Learned to Live: Adaptation in Nature. The MIT Press, Cambridge, MA (1984)
2. Schrödinger, E.: What is Life? Cambridge University Press, Cambridge, UK (1944)
3. Raghavachary, S.: Intelligence - consider this and respond! In: Samsonovich, A.V., Gudwin, R.R., Simões, Ad.S. (eds.) BICA 2020. AISC, vol. 1310, pp. 400–409. Springer, Cham (2021). https://doi.org/10.1007/978-3-030-65596-9_48
4. Reynolds, C.W.: Flocks, herds, and schools: a distributed behavioral model. Comput. Graph. 21(4), 25–34 (1987)
5. Newell, A, Simon, H.A: Computer science as empirical inquiry: symbols and search. Commun. ACM 19(3), 113–126 (1976)
6. Mitchell, M.: Why AI is Harder Than We Think (2021). https://arxiv.org/abs/2104.12871
7. Raghavachary, S., Lei, L.: A VR-based system and architecture for computational modeling of minds. In: Samsonovich, A.V. (ed.) BICA 2019. AISC, vol. 948, pp. 417–425. Springer, Cham (2020). https://doi.org/10.1007/978-3-030-25719-4_55
8. Man, K., Damasio, A.: Homeostasis and soft robotics in the design of feeling machines. Nat. Mach. Intell. 1, 446–452 (2019)
9. Huang, Z., et al.: Temporal circuit of macroscale dynamic brain activity supports human consciousness. Sci. Adv. 6(11), eaaz0087 (2020)

10. Brooks, R.: Intelligence without Representation. Artif. Intell. **47**, 139–160 (1991)
11. Braitenberg, V.: Vehicles: Experiments in Synthetic Psychology. MIT Press, Cambridge, MA (1984)
12. Hawkins, J., Lewis, M., Purdy, S., Klukas, M., Ahmad, S.: A framework for intelligence and cortical function based on grid cells in the neocortex. Front. Neural Circ. **12**(121), 1–14 (2019)

Adaptive Multi-strategy Market Making Agent

Ali Raheman[1], Anton Kolonin[1,2,3(✉)], and Ikram Ansari[1]

[1] Autonio Foundation Ltd., Bristol, UK
[2] SingDAO Ltd., Gros-Islet, Saint Lucia
[3] SingularityNET Foundation, Amsterdam, The Netherlands

Abstract. We propose an architecture for algorithmic trading agents for liquidity provisions on centralized exchanges. These implement what we call an adaptive market making multi-strategy, which is based on a limit order grid with continuous experiential learning. The concept exploits definitions of artificial general intelligence (AGI) as an ability to "reach complex goals in complex environments given limited resources", and is treated as a universal multi-parameter optimization. We present basic reference on implementation of the architecture being back-tested on historical crypto-finance market data and capable of providing almost 1000% excess return ("alpha") under evaluated market conditions.

Keywords: Adaptive agent · Back-testing · Centralized exchange · Continuous learning · Experiential learning · Liquidity provision · Market making

1 Introduction

The subject of algorithmic trading is attracting attention of investors, developers, and scientists due to high potential financial returns, high demand for implementation of automated business applications for investments, and liquidity provision and trading across all sorts of financial markets, including crypto-currencies. One of the popular applications of that is so called "yield farming" in the crypto-industry, which makes it possible to create investment portfolios consisting of crypto-assets being used for automated liquidity provision also called market making. Yield farming can be performed either on centralized exchanges (CEX) such as Binance or decentralized ones (DEX) with smart contracts on Uniswap or Balancer on the Ethereum blockchain. Respectively, there is are a lot of studies on how machine learning and artificial intelligence can be applied to it, such as attempts to learn efficient market making strategies [1–4]. Unfortunately, the known results are not that exciting so far with demonstrated ability to learn some basic principles of trading using limit book orders, and some ability to outperform "hodling" strategies (buy and hold on rising market) in very specific conditions. So more effort is required to take in this area.

The important part of automated trading is a price prediction [5, 6] which can take form of either predicting price change direction as a classification problem or prediction of specific price level as a regression problem. The latter appears more critical for market making activity. That is because conventional trading with market orders could

© Springer Nature Switzerland AG 2022
B. Goertzel et al. (Eds.): AGI 2021, LNAI 13154, pp. 204–209, 2022.
https://doi.org/10.1007/978-3-030-93758-4_21

accept predicted price direction change as a trading signal for either sell or buy. In turn, market making with limit book orders on CEX don't necessarily need to sell or buy, they just needs to set the appropriate price levels on bid and ask limit orders on CEX, according not just to anticipated price movement, but the actual target level of its move. Unfortunately, high volatility and the manipulative nature of the crypto market provides challenges even for the former, let alone the latter, so even more work is needed in this direction, if the problem can be solved at all.

In this paper we extend our earlier work on the matter [7], focusing on methodology and architecture for algorithmic trading agents for liquidity provision on centralized exchanges implementing what we call **adaptive market making multi-strategy based on limit order grid with continuous experiential learning**. The concept exploits a definition of artificial general intelligence (AGI) as an ability to **"reach complex goals in complex environments given limited resources"** [8], being treated as **universal multi-parameter optimization**. Below we present basic reference implementation of the architecture being back-tested on historical crypto-finance market data capable to provide almost 1000% excess return ("alpha") under evaluated market conditions. Along the way, we assess the value of the ability to predict the price during such activity as well as drawbacks of not being able to do it properly.

2   Adaptive Market Making Methodology

For the initial experiment we have designed and implemented a market making methodology of limit order grid market making "macro-strategy", where individual market making agents create a grid of limit orders with each individual order in the grid representing a specific "micro-strategy". In turn, each of the micro strategies may have their individual parameters. The agent executing the "macro-strategy" has an option to revise the set of different "micro-strategy" sub-agents, as they were controllable sub-personalities in a scope of a single super-person being in total control of its own "multi-personality" - that is why we call this a "multi-strategy".

The classical approach for using experiential or reinforcement learning would be creating an action space for a market making agent with actions such as creating bid and ask orders with different spreads [1–3] and learning the behavioral model based on historical data. Significant performance results have been obtained with this approach from studies on historical and live crypto-trading data. We presume that might be due to the following factors. First, the stochastic nature of the crypto market might not make it possible to learn a single model on long historical intervals covering a variety of market conditions, so that a single model would work well for such conditions. Second, building an operational space of agents based on order-level actions might be too fine-grained where no statistically confident experience associated with corresponding feedback might be collected for any specific order creation or canceling in corresponding market situations.

The following consideration has lead us to a few decisions for simplifying the methodology of the initial experiments discussed further and making it more efficient and risk-tolerant. First, we have replaced operational space of actions with operational space of strategies being executed for determined time intervals. Second, the feedback or reward for using the strategy was evaluated as profit or loss for the period of strategy execution. Third, in order to speed-up the learning curve and mitigate the risk, we made it possible for an agent to execute a certain number of strategies at a time, having its "personality" split in several "sub-persona" child agents, with each of them running their own "micro-strategy", while the parent agent "macro-strategy" was designated to control and manage the child agents. Fourth, each of the child "micro-strategy" agents could be run either in "real mode" trying to make real trades on the market, or in "virtual mode" just watching the live structure of the limit order book on the Exchange aligned with the stream of trades being closed and performing "virtual market making" like we are doing in our backtesting framework [7].

In our current architecture evaluated in the course of presented work, each of the "micro-strategy" child agents has ability to create only one limit order at a time, where the position of the order on bid or ask sides is defined by price dynamics, spread is asserted to be one of the "micro-strategy" parameters. The order cancelling policy of such agents is defined by conservatism parameters of the "micro-strategy", where orders can be either never cancelled until completion, or canceled if there is a need to create an order on the other side of the mid price, or if there is just a mid price change which needs the current bid or ask price to be updated. That is, the operational space of a child agent can be denoted as $P(s,c)$, where P is a point in parameter space, s is a spread in percents and c is order cancellation conservatism.

The "macro-strategy" of a parent agent is designed to start its market-making activity with all of its child "micro-strategy" agents with each of them placed in an individual point $P(s,c)$ in the operational space having the space covered evenly by a grid of unique N configurations. Each of the child N agents is given $1/N$ share of the parent agent's budget so they can invest in their orders. The first round of trading from starting time t_0 during period T and order refresh rate dt is executed, and then the parent agent evaluates losses and returns of all of its children. For the next round of trading starting time t_1 during the same period T, the top M most profitable agents are selected and given a much larger budget as $1/M$ share of the parent agent budget. At the same time, while M winners are doing the "real" market making with real budget, all of the remaining agents keep market making in "virtual mode" against the live market data. At the end of the next round, the returns and losses of all of the agents are collected and the new M winners are selected for the subsequent round starting t_1 while the "real" profits and losses are accumulated.

The profitability of an agent is assumed to mean positive returns as well as positive excess returns ("alpha") compared to a "hodler" strategy agent which just holds the same budget as given to a market making agent. If the number of agents with positive excess return is less than M for a certain round then only that number of agents is selected for "real" operations in the next round with the real budget shared between them. If no agents have positive return exceeding the "hodler" return, the next round is skipped for "real" market making but "virtual" operations are continued in order to attempt to find suitable "micro-strategies" for subsequent rounds.

Optionally, each of the child agents may be making decisions relying not on the current market price (mis price), but rather on its future projection predicted for every new time point past refresh rate dt by a machine learning algorithm. In the current work we used only the simple linear regression algorithm relying just on the historical price data. For the "ground truth" prediction baseline we were using the historical data looked up in the following data point past dt in course of back-testing.

3 Preliminary Experimental Results

The methodology described above has been implemented and tested relying on back-testing framework described in our earlier work [7] with results presented art Fig. 1.

The experiments have been run or based on BTC/USDT data from Binance for 6 days period starting 2021-6-21 17:00, relying on per-minute snapshots of the limit order book data and full scope of trades data. The N of "micro-strategy agents" was 18, so there were 6 different spread settings (0.0%, 0.2%, 0.4%, 0.6%, 0.8%, 1.0%) and 3 different order cancellation conservatism settings as described above. The M of winning agents for "real trading" was 3. The strategy evaluation period T was taken as 2 days, so only three rounds have been executed in each of the experiments. The experiments were run for order refresh period 1 h (left side of Fig. 1) and 1 min (right side of Fig. 1). The first set of experiments for the two refresh rates were run without predictions (top on Fig. 1). The second set of experiments were run with "ground truth" predictions to evaluate baseline - what would be the maximum returns given the ultimate predictive abilities (middle on Fig. 1). The third set of experiments were run using basic Linear Regression (see https://scikit-learn.org/stable/modules/generated/sklearn.linear_model.LinearRegression.html) on price data, with mean absolute percentage error (MAPE) about 9% better than just using the "last known price" (from) previous data point on given price data for historical interval.

Each of the 6 experiments (with 2 refresh rates and three prediction setups) involved assessments of three kinds of returns based on the same initial budget given to an agent executing specific "macro-strategy": "hodler" - just holding investments into base currency during the entire period of testing; all "micro-strategies" being executed together with $1/N$ of allocated budget; "macro-strategy" described in the previous section being the subject of a given study.

The results on Fig. 1 (top) clearly show about 800–1000% (8–10 times) excess return compared to "hodler" if using the suggested "macro-strategy" for any refresh rate. At the same time, if using market making with all possible "micro-strategies" at once, it can provide significant (350%) "alpha" compared to "hodling" in case of hourly refresh rate but also underperform the "hodler" in case of minutely refresh rate. This is thought to be the key result of given work deserving further attention and exploration.

The other two experiments have shown that the ability to predict the price during such activities is a key to high returns as well as a point that not being able to do it properly leads to rather high losses. That is, using the "ground truth" level of price prediction (not achievable in real life) makes the "alpha" skyrocket to 5000–20000% (5–20 times) excess returns as seen in the middle of Fig. 1. On the other hand, price prediction with high MAPE is causing straight losses which are still substantially less if using the adaptive "macro-strategy" suggested in this work.

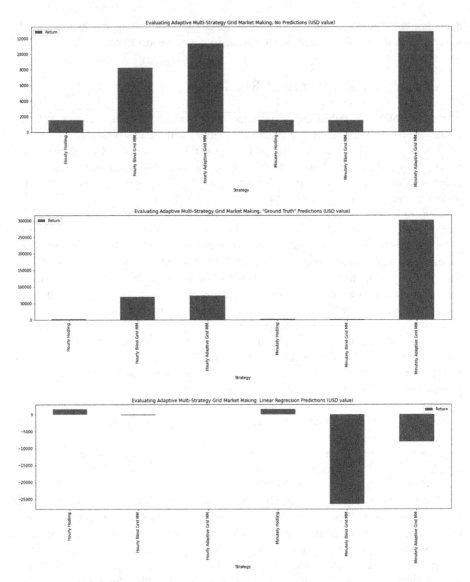

Fig. 1. Overall returns using different "macro-strategies". Top – not using predictions, middle – using "ground truth" predictions, bottom – using predictions by Linear Regression. Left three bars – hourly refresh rate (*dt* = *1 h*), right three bars – minutely refresh rate (*dt* = *minute*). Groups of three bars indicating overall returns/losses by strategies (left to right): hodler, all "micro-strategies" acting together with no selection, "macro-strategy" described above.

4 Conclusion

The proposed algorithmic market making methodology is designed for liquidity provision architecture at https://www.autonio.foundation/ and https://www.singularitydao.ai/. The preliminary results point at potential business value of using the adaptive market making multi-strategy based on a limit order grid with continuous experiential learning in the area of decentralized finance, automatically generating significant excess returns without of manual interventions for ongoing adjustment of market making strategy parameters depending on constantly changing market conditions.

Apart from that, the results point at the need or extra care to be taken in regard of using machine learning for price predictions and the need of careful assessment of the prediction quality results before integrating it into production pipelines.

Our future work will be dedicated to a) testing the developed methodology and architecture against extended time intervals covering different market conditions for different assets and trading pairs. This will be done by testing it with different strategy evaluation periods, parameter space discretization winner selection; b) improving the adaptive experiential learning to more intelligent navigation of the operational space of greater dimensionality involving more complex "micro-strategies" with a greater number of parameters; c) involving evolutionary/genetic programming in "micro-strategy" selection and evolution; d) incorporating the latest developments of the price prediction domain in the agent "micro-strategies".

References

1. Ganesh S., et. al.: Reinforcement Learning for Market Making in a Multi-agent Dealer Market (2019). arXiv:1911.05892v1, https://arxiv.org/pdf/1911.05892.pdf, Accessed 14 Nov 2019
2. Sadighian J.: Deep Reinforcement Learning in Cryptocurrency Market Making (2019). arXiv: 1911.08647v1, https://arxiv.org/pdf/1911.08647.pdf, Accessed 20 Nov 2019
3. Sadighian J.: Extending Deep Reinforcement Learning Frameworks in Cryptocurrency Market Making (2020). arXiv:2004.06985v1, https://arxiv.org/pdf/2004.06985.pdf, Accessed 15 Apr 2020
4. Guéant O., et al.: Dealing with the Inventory Risk. A solution to the market making problem (2020). arXiv:1105.3115, https://arxiv.org/pdf/1105.3115.pdf, Accessed 3 Aug 2012
5. Tsantekidis A.: Using Deep Learning for price prediction by exploiting stationary limit order book features (2018). arXiv:1810.09965, https://arxiv.org/abs/1810.09965, Accessed 23 Oct 2018
6. Yanjun C., et al.: Financial Trading Strategy System Based on Machine Learning. Hindawi Math. Prob. Eng. **2020**, 13 (2020). Article ID 3589198. https://doi.org/10.1155/2020/3589198
7. Raheman A., et al.: Architecture of Automated Crypto-Finance Agent (2021). arXiv:2107. 07769, https://arxiv.org/abs/2107.07769, Accessed 16 Jul 2021
8. Goertzel B.: Artificial general intelligence: concept, state of the art, and future prospects. J. Artif. Gener. Intell. **5**(1), 1–46 (2014). https://doi.org/10.2478/jagi-2014-0001

Unsupervised Context-Driven Question Answering Based on Link Grammar

Vignav Ramesh[1,2(✉)] and Anton Kolonin[2,3,4]

[1] Saratoga High School, Saratoga, USA
[2] SingularityNET Foundation, Amsterdam, The Netherlands
[3] Aigents, Novosibirsk, Russian Federation
[4] Novosibirsk State University, Novosibirsk, Russian Federation

Abstract. While general conversational intelligence (GCI) can be considered one of the core aspects of artificial general intelligence (AGI), there currently exists minimal overlap between the disciplines of AGI and natural language processing (NLP). Only a few AGI architectures can comprehend and generate natural language, and most NLP systems rely either on hardcoded, specialized rules and frameworks that cannot generalize to the various complex domains of human language or on heavily trained deep neural network models that cannot be interpreted, controlled, or made sense of. In this paper, we propose an interpretable "Contextual Generator" architecture for question answering (QA), built as an extension of the recently published "Generator" algorithm for sentence generation, that produces grammatically valid answers to queries structured as lists of seed words. We demonstrate the potential for this architecture to perform automated, closed-domain QA by detailing results on queries from SingularityNET's "small world" POC-English corpus and from the Stanford Question Answering Dataset. Overall, our work may bring a greater degree of GCI to proto-AGI NLP pipelines. The proposed QA architecture is open-source and can be found on GitHub under the MIT License at https://github.com/aigents/aigents-java-nlp.

Keywords: General conversational intelligence · Interpretable natural language processing · Natural language generation · Question answering · Link grammar

1 Introduction

General conversational intelligence (GCI) can be considered one of the core aspects of artificial general intelligence (AGI); however, there currently exists minimal overlap between the disciplines of AGI and natural language processing (NLP). Only a few AGI architectures can comprehend and generate natural language, and most NLP systems rely on either hardcoded, specialized rules and frameworks that cannot generalize to the various complex domains of human language or on heavily trained deep neural network models that cannot be interpreted, controlled, or made sense of [1]. Moreover, the majority of AGI frameworks that do possess some level of natural language comprehension (NLC) or natural language understanding (NLU) cannot convey such knowledge (e.g., a response to a query posed by a human) in natural

© Springer Nature Switzerland AG 2022
B. Goertzel et al. (Eds.): AGI 2021, LNAI 13154, pp. 210–220, 2022.
https://doi.org/10.1007/978-3-030-93758-4_22

language without template-based customization or similar manual, labor-intensive procedures (Goertzel et al. 2010; Goertzel and Yu 2014).

In this paper, we propose a question answering (QA) architecture, founded upon an extension of the sentence generation system described in Sect. 2.1, that serves as an interpretable natural language processing (INLP) method. INLP, as proposed in [2], is an extension of interpretable AI (IAI)—which expands upon explainable AI (XAI) by calling for an interpretable model/knowledge base as well as explainable results—to NLP; INLP enables the acquisition of natural language, comprehension of text-based messages, and production of linguistic content in a reasonable and transparent manner [3]. The proposed method of QA satisfies the criteria for interpretability by providing both explainable results as well as an interpretable model for NLP in general and QA in particular, since we rely on Link Grammar (LG) as our formal grammar which itself is comprehensible [4]. To this end, our QA architecture may bring a greater degree of GCI to proto-AGI NLP pipelines.

1.1 Natural Language Generation

Natural language generation (NLG) is the task of producing linguistic content (most often in the form of grammatically and morphologically valid text) from semantic and/or non-linguistic data [5]. Even the process of producing simple sentences—a sub-problem of NLG known as sentence generation, which we will treat as synonymous with NLG for the purposes of this paper—requires significant grammatical, syntactical, morphological, and phonological knowledge. While the integration of semantic knowledge could improve our results and warrants future research, the NLG component of our current QA pipeline focuses on the use of solely grammatical knowledge.

Within the sentence generation process is the task of surface realization, which is concerned with the construction of sentences from the underlying content of a text, usually structured as an unordered set of tokens (words, punctuation, etc.) [6]. As we explain in Sect. 2.2, the same tokens can often be arranged into multiple grammatically and morphologically valid sentential forms that an NLG system must disambiguate in context, a process known as semantic disambiguation [7].

1.2 Question Answering

QA, a branch of computer science integrating information retrieval and NLP, refers to the ability for machines to automatically answer questions posed in the form of human language. As discussed in [8], an explainable QA pipeline involves components for both NLC and NLG. During NLC, the question, or input query, is parsed and then semantically interpreted (the pipeline determines the underlying "themes" or "topics" of the question and then computes relationships between each component of the parsed query). During NLG, the query is then semantically executed (the semantic relationships obtained during NLC are used to find the answer to the question), and finally, a formal grammar is utilized to construct a grammatically valid sentence from words associated with the non-linguistic answer obtained in the query execution step. Below is a diagram of an interpretable QA pipeline (Fig. 1).

Question Answering Pipeline

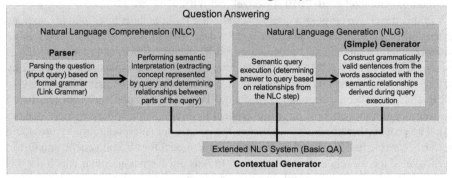

Fig. 1. QA workflow

Our current work is concerned with a more basic version of QA, in which the query is proposed as a list of seed words (in natural language) and the answer is a grammatically valid sentence that correctly captures the relationships between the seed words. In this sense, our work replaces the semantic interpretation and query execution components of the described QA pipeline with an extended version of sentence generation based on the context of the question and scope of textual data to search for an answer. That is, we treat the context of the question as a constraint for the generation phase of QA; in the perspective of the above pipeline, it is as if the words needed to answer the query are already known based on prior semantic query execution and must simply be arranged into a grammatically valid response. Given that most modern search queries online (e.g., Google, Bing, Yahoo) are performed only with keywords rather than properly structured sentences, we anticipate that our work would be practical for human-computer interactions.

1.3   Link Grammar

LG is founded upon the fact that each word is defined by a set of connectors and disjuncts associating those connectors. Connectors serve as either the left or right half of a grammatical link of a given type, and disjuncts are sets of connectors that define the valid grammatical context of a given word [1]. Rules—which represent lexical entries or grammatical categories—describe the sets of defining disjuncts for clusters of grammatically equivalent words. From our perspective, NLG is the process of following rules to construct sentences by matching connectors between words to form links.

LG also imposes two additional constraints: the planarity metarule, which specifies that links must not cross, and the connectivity metarule, which dictates that all links and tokens in a sentence must form a connected graph. Furthermore, unlike most alternative grammar rule dictionaries and APIs (spaCy[1], Universal Dependencies[2], etc.), LG does not require grammar rules to be hardcoded into client-side architectures; LG rules can also be learned dynamically as has been shown in our previous work [3]. Overall, the human-readable and editable nature of LG allows our grammar induction algorithm to comprehend and process text under the premise of unsupervised language learning, and thereby better serve as an INLP method for the purposes of the QA task.

1.4   Prior Work

Sentence Generation. The proposed NLG and QA methods can be called unsupervised since they do not require prior training on supervisedly prepared corpora. However, the majority of published natural language generation methods are supervised and/or rely on deep learning models that require extensive training on labeled data; as such, they are "black box" algorithms that are neither explainable nor interpretable (Ratnaparkhi, 2000; Wen et al., 2015; Dathathri et al., 2020). There are only a few notable unsupervised (yet often not interpretable) NLG systems.

Lian et al. proposed SegSim, an approach based on the OpenCog NLGen software that constructs sentences by satisfying constraints posed by inverse relations of hypergraph homomorphisms. SegSim performs surface realization by matching the subsets of an Atom set in need of linguistic expression against a datastore of (sentence, link parse, RelEx relationship set, Atom set) tuples produced by OpenCog's NLC software. This matching allows SegSim to determine the syntactic structures that have previously been used to generate relevant Atom subsets, and these structures are then pieced together to form overall syntactic structures corresponding to one or more sentences. The sentence is solved for as a constraint satisfaction problem from the Atom set semantics [1]. SegSim constructs simple sentences unproblematically but becomes unreliable for more syntactically complex sentences (e.g., those involving conjunctions).

Freitag and Roy proposed an unsupervised NLG system in which denoising autoencoders are used to construct sentences from structured data interpreted as "corrupt representations" of the desired output. The denoising autoencoders can also generalize to unstructured training samples to which noise has already been introduced [9].

Question Answering. There exist a variety of well-known, large, supervised language understanding models that have been applied to the QA task. BERT (**B**idirectional **E**ncoder **R**epresentations from **T**ransformers), a pre-trained language representation model that learns bidirectional representations from unlabeled text, can be fine-tuned on token sequences representing labeled question-answer pairs to perform the downstream task of QA [10]. DistilBERT, a distilled version of BERT, implements knowledge distillation during the pre-training phase to reduce the size of BERT by 40% while retaining 97% of its language understanding capabilities and being 60% faster [11]. LUKE (**L**anguage **U**nderstanding with **K**nowledge-based **E**mbeddings), a multi-layer bidirectional transformer utilizing a novel entity-aware self-attention

---

[1] https://spacy.io.

[2] https://universaldependencies.org.

mechanism, is trained by predicting randomly masked words and entities in the input corpora. When fine-tuned to perform both cloze-style and extractive QA, LUKE achieves state-of-the-art results [12]. ELECTRA, RoBERTa, and BART are among other popular machine reading comprehension models [13–15].

However, all such models are supervised and uninterpretable; there are only two notable published methods for unsupervised QA. Lewis et al. proposed an unsupervised QA method whereby (context, question, answer) triples are generated unsupervisedly and then used to synthesize extractive QA training data in "cloze" format [16]. Perez et al. developed an unsupervised QA approach focused on decomposing a single hard, multi-hop question into several simpler, single-hop sub-questions that are answered with an off-the-shelf QA model and recomposed into a final answer [17].

2   Methodology

2.1   Generator Architecture for NLG

To perform QA in an unsupervised and interpretable manner, we adopt and extend the Generator architecture proposed in [2]. After calling the Loader, utility infrastructure as shown in Fig. 2, to store the LG dictionary in memory, the Generator performs surface realization as follows:

1. Given a list of words, computes a subset of all orderings of those words that satisfies initial checks of the planarity and connectivity meta-rules.
2. Determines if each ordering is grammatically valid; that is, ensures that every pair of consecutive tokens can be linked via a pair of "connectable" disjuncts.
3. Returns all grammatically valid orderings as sentences.

2.2   Contextual Generator Architecture for QA

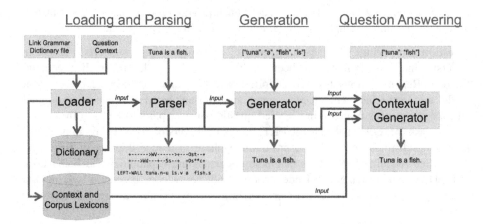

Fig. 2. INLP architecture involving a sentence parsing algorithm (the "Parser") and QA framework (the "Contextual Generator") built upon an NLG algorithm (the "Generator"), all relying on the same Loader infrastructure.

In this paper, we propose a Contextual Generator (CG) architecture which extends our prior NLG architecture in two major ways:

1. The surface realization model described in Sect. 2.1 is expanded recursively to build grammatically and morphologically valid sentences from two or more seed words that comprise only a subset of the total list of words needed to construct the final sentence (see "Contextual Generator").
2. To allow for semantic disambiguation—determining which of multiple sentential answers to a given query is most appropriate in the given context—the revised Loader architecture, besides loading the LG dictionary and corpus lexicon, also loads context lexicons. Each word in the context lexicon is supplied with a weight denoting its contribution to the context in accordance with Zipf's Law (see "Zipfian Calculations"). Note that the Loader creates the corpus lexicon only once, but builds a new lexicon for each unique context.

Two sample question-answer pairs, with answers generated by our CG architecture, are shown below. The CG generates correct answers but, as seen in the first question-answer pair, succumbs to the grammatical ambiguity problem described in Sect. 3.

Context: Identity and Relationships
A mom is a human. A dad is a human. A mom is a parent. A dad is a parent. A son is a child. A daughter is a child. A son is a human. A daughter is a human. Mom is a human now. Dad is a human now. Mom is a parent now. Dad is a parent now. Son is a child now. Daughter is a child now. Son is a human now. Daughter is a human now. Mom was a daughter before. Dad was a son before. Mom was not a parent before. Dad was not a parent before.

Question: mom daughter
Answer: [Mom was a daughter before., Daughter was a mom before.]

Question: dad human
Answer: [Dad is a human.]

Contextual Generator. The CG performs closed-domain QA on queries structured as lists of seed words. It operates as follows:

1. The CG calls the Loader to store the LG dictionary and corpus lexicon as well as extract a context lexicon from a given document as described above.
2. The CG then recursively calls the Generator to determine valid sentence constructions from a list containing all seed words and n additional words from a subset of words in the context lexicon that satisfy initial checks of the planarity and connectivity meta-rules (e.g., one partial connectivity check confirms that the first and last tokens in a potential sentence can form links to the right and left, respectively). The n-addition permutations are tested in order of decreasing Zipfian

frequency corresponding to the current context. If a valid sentence is found, the CG returns that sentence and stops running. When step 2 is first executed, $n = 1$, imposing the constraint that the answer is of minimum length.

3. If no sentences have been generated after testing all valid subsets and the runtime has not exceeded a limit specified to avoid combinatorial explosions (3 min in our experiments), the CG increases n by 1 and repeats step 2.

Zipfian Calculations. In the previous subsection, it was specified that the CG checks n-addition permutations in order of decreasing Zipfian frequency. To motivate this, consider the sample query "mom cake" along with a context specifying the food preferences of family members. If the CG were to use context word frequencies without modification rather than Zipfian frequencies, it would perceive the sentence "Cake was a mom" as more contextually appropriate than "Mom likes cake," which is the ground truth answer. This is due to a phenomenon known as Zipf's law [18], which states that the rank-frequency distribution of words in a given lexicon is an inverse relation; determiners and linking verbs ("a," "the," "was," "is," etc.) are more common in any corpus, regardless of context, than more semantically appropriate words (such as "likes" in the context of food preferences as in the motivating example above). To account for Zipf's law, we use the Zipfian frequency, which is calculated as follows:

$$Z_w = \frac{\log(1 + F_X(w))}{\log(1 + F_C(w))}, \tag{1}$$

where w is the given word, $F_X(w)$ is the frequency of w in the context document, and $F_C(w)$ is the frequency of w in the corpus. Because the Zipfian frequency divides the logarithm of the context frequency by that of the corpus frequency, more contextually appropriate words receive higher scores than do determiners and similarly common words. For multiple-word additions, we sum individual Zipfian frequencies.

3   Results

Our algorithm was primarily tested on 60 queries with words all part of SingularityNET's "small world" POC-English corpus.[3] For this purpose, we have used a corresponding "small world" LG dictionary (automatically inferred from high quality LG parses created by SingularityNET's ULL pipeline).[4] To evaluate the proposed architecture, we report four scores: the bigram variant of BLEU (**B**ilingual **E**valuation **U**nderstudy), a measure of the number of matching bigrams in two sentences [19]; WVCS (**W**ord2**V**ec **c**osine **s**imilarity), calculated as the cosine of the angle between the vector encodings of the candidate and reference sentences [20]; WER (**W**ord **E**rror **R**ate), a measure of the edit distance between two sentences [21]; and TER (**T**ranslation **E**dit **R**ate), another measure of edit distance [22]. Note that higher BLEU and WVCS scores as well as lower WER

---

[3] http://langlearn.singularitynet.io/data/poc-english/poc_english.txt.

[4] http://langlearn.singularitynet.io/test/nlp/poc-english_5C_2018-06-06_0004.4.0.dict.txt.

and TER scores indicate more accurate language models. Each metric is calculated for each (answer, ground truth answer) pair and then averaged over all 60 queries.

Our QA architecture significantly outperforms prior state-of-the-art models on the POC-English dataset for the task of QA from short lists of seed words. As baselines, we implemented BERT, ELECTRA, DistilBERT, and RoBERTa models that were pre-trained on the Stanford Question Answering Dataset (SQuAD2.0) and then fine-tuned on the POC-English corpus [23]. Our QA system attains superior BLEU, WVCS, and TER scores and competitive WER scores, demonstrating an 0.11 increase in BLEU, 0.15 increase in WVCS, and 0.08 decrease in TER from the best baseline results (Table 1).

Table 1. Results when tested on 60 queries from SingularityNET's POC-English corpus.

Metric	Results				
	Ours	BERT	ELECTRA	DistilBERT	RoBERTa
BLEU	**0.878**	0.639	0.712	0.604	0.767
WVCS	**0.944**	0.606	0.741	0.595	0.799
WER	0.645	0.924	0.550	1.095	**0.150**
TER	**0.166**	0.381	0.342	0.457	0.245

Our results were mainly affected by the issue of grammatical ambiguity, a problem whereby the same word can take on different roles in a sentence (e.g., subject-object ambiguity, where a noun can be either the subject or object of a sentence). While both sentences are grammatically valid, only one is semantically correct; implementing semantic disambiguation as part of the NLG component of our pipeline beyond that described in Sect. 2.2 will be part of our future work.

We additionally tested our algorithm on three samples randomly obtained from SQuAD2.0 using the complete LG; all samples were cleaned (questions were restated as sets of seed words and proper nouns/phrases not present in LG were removed):

Sample 1

Context: Imperialism

Imperialism is defined as "A policy of extending the power and influence of a country through diplomacy or military force." Imperialism is particularly focused on the control that one group, often a state power, has on another group of people. There is "formal" and "informal" imperialism. "Formal imperialism" is defined as "physical control or colonial rule". "Informal imperialism" is less direct; however, it is still a powerful form of dominance.

Question: imperialism focused on

Answer: [Imperialism focused on control.]

Sample 2

Context: Pharmacy

Pharmacists are healthcare professionals with specialized education and training who perform various roles to ensure optimal health outcomes for their patients through the quality use of medicines. Pharmacists may also be small business proprietors, owning the pharmacy in which they practice. Since pharmacists know about the mode of action of a particular drug, and its metabolism and physiological effects on the human body in great detail, they play an important role in optimization of a drug treatment for an individual.

Question: pharmacists are

Answer: [Pharmacists are proprietors.]

Sample 3

Context: Normans

A tradition of singing had developed and the choir achieved fame in Normandy. Under the Norman abbot Robert, several monks fled to southern Italy, where they were patronized by Robert and established a Latin monastery. There they continued the tradition of singing.

Question: monks fled to

Answer: [Monks fled to tradition.]

Samples 1, 2, and 3 show the benefits and drawbacks of QA using Zipfian frequencies. While Samples 1 and 2 correctly and partially correctly identify the additional word needed to answer the question in context, respectively, Sample 3 incorrectly chooses the word "tradition" over "Italy" since "tradition" appears twice in the context document while "Italy" appears once. Fine-tuning our QA architecture to account for such inconsistencies between Zipfian frequency and contextual appropriateness—potentially by building an integrated LG schema containing semantic knowledge that augments the CG's grammatical and lexical frequency knowledge—will be our next task.

4 Conclusion

We propose a novel CG architecture to perform basic QA from lists of seed words. Our algorithm is an INLP method and largely outperforms current state-of-the-art QA models on the POC-English corpus. Because the proposed architecture uses LG to enable machines' understanding of text, it contributes to the reconciliation of NLP and AGI.

Our QA architecture will primarily be applied to the Aigents Social Media Intelligence Platform [24]. If integrated into the Aigents cognitive architecture—which currently depends on artificially controlled language similar to oversimplified "pidgin" English—our algorithm could provide GCI to Aigents chatbots.

Our future work will involve: 1) testing our algorithm on queries from arbitrary English documents using the complete LG dictionary; 2) implementing grammatical disambiguation; 3) expanding our algorithm's QA capabilities by building an integrated LG schema containing semantic as well as grammatical knowledge; 4) implementing the full QA pipeline including semantic interpretation and query execution preceding response generation; and 5) adding support for languages other than English (including languages such as Russian that require heavy morphology usage).

References

1. Lian, R., et al.: Syntax-semantic mapping for general intelligence: language comprehension as hypergraph homomorphism, language generation as constraint satisfaction. In: Bach, J., Goertzel, B., Iklé, M. (eds.) AGI 2012. LNCS (LNAI), vol. 7716, pp. 158–167. Springer, Heidelberg (2012). https://doi.org/10.1007/978-3-642-35506-6_17
2. Ramesh, V., Kolonin, A.: Natural Language Generation Using Link Grammar for General Conversational Intelligence. arXiv:2105.00830 [cs.CL] (2021)
3. Glushchenko, A., Suarez, A., Kolonin, A., Goertzel, B., Baskov, O.: Programmatic link grammar induction for unsupervised language learning. In: Hammer, P., Agrawal, P., Goertzel, B., Iklé, M. (eds.) AGI 2019. LNCS (LNAI), vol. 11654, pp. 111–120. Springer, Cham (2019). https://doi.org/10.1007/978-3-030-27005-6_11
4. Sleator, D., Temperley, D.: Parsing english with a link grammar. In: Proceedings of the Third International Workshop on Parsing Technologies, pp. 277–292. Association for Computational Linguistics, Netherlands (1993)
5. Gatt, A., Krahmer, E.: Survey of the state of the art in natural language generation: core tasks, applications and evaluation. J. AI Res. (JAIR) 61(1), 75–170 (2018)
6. Mellish, C., Dale, R.: Evaluation in the context of natural language generation. Comput. Speech Lang. 10(2), 349–373 (1998)
7. Weaver, W.: Translation. In: Locke, W., Booth, A. (eds.) Machine Translation of Languages: Fourteen Essays, Technology Press of the Massachusetts Institute of Technology (1955)
8. Ramesh, V., Kolonin, A.: Interpretable natural language segmentation based on link grammar. In: 2020 Science and Artificial Intelligence conference (S.A.I.ence), pp. 25–32. IEEE, Novosibirsk (2020)
9. Freitag, M., Roy, S.: Unsupervised natural language generation with denoising autoencoders. In: Proceedings of the 2018 Conference on Empirical Methods in Natural Language Processing, pp. 3922–3929. Association for Computational Linguistics, Belgium (2018)
10. Devlin, J., et al.: BERT: Pre-training of Deep Bidirectional Transformers for Language Understanding. arXiv:1810.04805v2 [cs.CL] (2019)
11. Sanh, V., et al.: DistilBERT: a distilled version of BERT: smaller, faster, cheaper and lighter. arXiv:1910.01108v4 [cs.CL] (2020)

12. Yamada, I., et al.: LUKE: deep contextualized entity representations with entity-aware self-attention. arXiv:2010.01057 [cs.CL] (2020)
13. Clark, K., et al.: ELECTRA: pre-training text encoders as discriminators rather than generators. arXiv.2003.10555 [cs.CL] (2020)
14. Liu, Y., et al.: RoBERTa: a robustly optimized BERT pretraining approach. arXiv:1907. 11692 [cs.CL] (2019)
15. Lewis, M., et al.: BART: denoising sequence-to-sequence pre-training for natural language generation, translation, and comprehension. arXiv:1910.13461 [cs.CL] (2019)
16. Lewis, P., et al.: Unsupervised question answering by cloze translation. arXiv:1906.04980v2 [cs.CL] (2019)
17. Perez, E., et al.: Unsupervised question decomposition for question answering. arXiv:2002. 09758v3 [cs.CL] (2020)
18. Powers, D.: Applications and explanations of Zipf's law. In: New Methods in Language Processing and Computational Natural Language Learning, pp. 151–160. Association for Computational Linguistics (1998)
19. Papineni, K., et al.: Bleu: a method for automatic evaluation of machine translation. In: Proceedings of the 40th Annual Meeting of the Association for Computational Linguistics, pp. 311–318. Association for Computational Linguistics, USA (2002)
20. Sitikhu, P., et al.: A comparison of semantic similarity methods for maximum human interpretability. arXiv:1910.09129 [cs.IR] (2019)
21. Klakow, D., Peters, J.: Testing the correlation of word error rate and perplexity. Speech Commun. 38(1), 19–28 (2002)
22. Snover, M., et al.: A study of translation edit rate with targeted human annotation. In: Proceedings of the 7th Conference of the Association for Machine Translation in the Americas: Technical Papers, pp. 223–231. Association for Machine Translation in the Americas, USA (2006)
23. Rajpurkar, P., et al.: SQuAD: 100,000+ questions for machine comprehension of text. arXiv: 1606.05250 [cs.CL] (2016)
24. Kolonin, A.: Personal analytics for societies and businesses: with aigents online platform. In: 2017 International Multi-Conference on Engineering, Computer and Information Sciences (SIBIRCON), pp. 272–275. IEEE, Novosibirsk (2017)

A Virtual Actor Behavior Model Based on Emotional Biologically Inspired Cognitive Architecture

Alexei V. Samsonovich$^{(\boxtimes)}$ (ID)

National Research Nuclear University MEPhI, Kashirskoe Hwy 31,
Moscow 115409, Russia

Abstract. Many digital devices and systems that interact with humans can be expected to become emotional in the coming years. This transition will help them achieve trust and mutual understanding in establishing contacts at the social level, which is necessary for their integration into human society. The main problem is the ability to understand emotions and adequately respond to them: i.e., emotional intelligence, both verbal and non-verbal, which today is fully realized only in biological systems. In this work, four experimental paradigms were used for the development and study of a general model of social-emotional intelligence: a virtual dance partner, a virtual clown improvisation, a virtual pet, and a virtual interlocutor. The virtual actor model implemented the basics of the eBICA cognitive architecture. Characteristics of the virtual actor behavior were evaluated and, when possible, compared against the characteristics of human behavior in the same settings. Preliminary results support the idea of one universal cognitive model applicability to a variety of domains and interaction paradigms involving human and virtual actors. Practical implications of the concept are discussed.

Keywords: Emotional AI · Cognitive modeling · BICA · Social intelligent agents · Virtual actors · Semantic mapping · Moral schemas

1 Introduction

What do we lack in order to "breathe the soul" into the computer, if we are talking only about the impression produced, and not about the authenticity? This question is of relevance today, as it becomes clear that digital models of social emotionality will soon be in demand in a wide variety of areas [1]: from personal assistants and virtual tutors to collaborative robots and smart things. Indeed, in many emergent areas and paradigms of human-machine interaction, achieving success is impossible without establishing rapport, that is, stable social contact based on mutual understanding, empathy, and mutual trust [2]. Therefore, a machine must be able to understand human emotions, quickly and adequately respond to them, convincing a person with its actions that it is thoughtful, comprehensible, sensitive, generous, and reliable, and on this basis be able to maintain rapport. A large number of studies were undertaken recently in this direction [3–6]. Ideally, the machine should not only be socially acceptable, but also socially attractive and charismatic, regardless of whether its interaction with a human is verbal or non-verbal. This is the challenge that humanity is facing today.

© Springer Nature Switzerland AG 2022
B. Goertzel et al. (Eds.): AGI 2021, LNAI 13154, pp. 221–227, 2022.
https://doi.org/10.1007/978-3-030-93758-4_23

The answer to this challenge should be the creation of a universal module capable of endowing a given intelligent agent or robot with the aforementioned qualities. The basis for binding the module to the agent should be a system of values and emotional appraisals specific to the paradigm and represented by a semantic map [7], while the principles of operation of the module itself can be based on a universal cognitive model of social emotionality, applicable in a wide range of domains and paradigms.

Therefore, the development of a general-purpose model of emotional intelligence represents an important overarching challenge [3, 8–11]. But this challenge is only possible to solve by working out specific examples, which do not necessarily have to be immediately practically useful. Many great inventions and discoveries began with "toys", and this property cannot be considered their disadvantage. "Toy" tasks are important because, with their simplicity, they can just meet the requirements of the overarching task, allowing one to quickly create a prototype that proves the concept.

This is why in the present work several "toy" paradigms are considered, including a virtual dance partner, a virtual clown improvisation, a virtual pet, and a virtual interlocutor based on one and the same approach. The cognitive model of virtual actor behavior is based on the eBICA cognitive architecture [12, 13] and adapted to each specific case.

The paper is organized as follows: first, key elements of the general approach are outlined. Then results of case studies are summarized, followed by general conclusions.

2   General Model of Virtual Actor Behavior Based on eBICA

The general eBICA model used here was introduced in [12] and described in detail in [13]. The architecture (Fig. 1) includes seven memory systems. Dynamic variables (fluents) include appraisals [9, 10], somatic markers [14, 15], feelings, mood, emotion, behavioral bias and reaction.

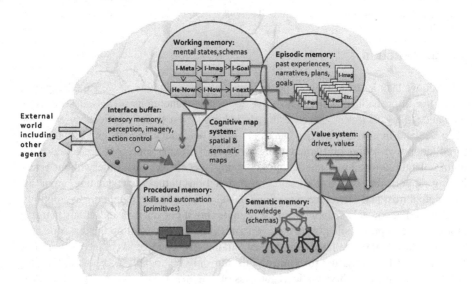

Fig. 1. A bird-eye view of the eBICA cognitive architecture, including seven memory systems.

Appraisals A of actors are calculated based on behavior by summing the contributions of all actions with some "forgetting", using a leaky integrator model [13]:

$$A(author) := (1 - r) * A(author) + r * A(action|author),\qquad(1)$$

$$A(target) := (1 - r) * A(target) + r * A(action|target),\qquad(2)$$

Here r is a small positive constant. The labels "author" and "target" indicate the perspective from which the action is perceived. Appraisals in turn determine Feelings and action likelihoods, as described in [12]. Initial appraisals of actions are given by the semantic map, which can be constructed using several methods: human participant or expert ranking, optimization, back-propagation of reward, and more. Semantic map determines the binding of the model to a specific paradigm. Moral schemas determine the agent behavior according to general, paradigm-independent principles.

3 Summary of Case Studies

3.1 Virual Dance Partner

The selected paradigm of a virtual partner dance is shown in Fig. 2A. There are three actors (1 human and 2 virtual) that control dancing avatars in the virtual environment. The avatars are located at the vertices of an equilateral triangle in such a way that each can see all the others. Freedoms include selection of a partner and a dance pattern.

Several types of dancer characters were used in this study [16]: Timid, Ringleader, Dancer, and Naïve. They differ in the frequency and threshold of their activation of the moral schema of partnership, that changes rules of behavior and its appraisal. Results show that participants tend to select virtual actors and establish relations with them.

3.2 Virtual Clown Improvisation

The paradigm is a two-clown ad hoc improvisation on a virtual stage (Fig. 2B), with human participation as spectators or scriptwriters only. The output of the simulation was produced as text, and the action was not visualized. The virtual clown action was not scripted and developed naturally. In parallel, several scenarios were written by a group of human experts using the same paradigm and available actions. The two sets of scenarios were analyzed and compared to each other on a number of characteristics. Results show that human and machine-generated scenarios are similar and could be indistinguishable. The model version with dynamical feelings produced better results.

The author is not aware of any exact match in the literature. A robot-comedian was studied by Vilk and Fitter [17]; however, its behavior was purely verbal. Many studies address teleclowning and virtual clownery used in health care [18, 19].

Fig. 2. Studied paradigms. A: virtual dance partner, implemented in Unreal Engine 4. B: virtual clown improvisation, a PowerPoint sketch. C: virtual pet, implemented in Unity 3D: a screenshot taken during experiment, with participant's face. D: virtual interlocutor, implemented in UE4.

3.3   Virtual Pet and Virtual Interlocutor

These two additional paradigms (Fig. 2C, D) were implemented in Unity and in Unreal Engine 4 and used in experiments with human participants. Results [20] confirm the applicability of the model. In particular, in our study of the virtual pet (a penguin: Fig. 2C) it was found that all participants of the experiment believed that the penguin understands them. It is also remarkable that among all the 12 scales on which penguin's behavior quality was evaluated by participants there was no single one on which the average result went in the negative direction. In the course of a 10-min interaction, friendly relationships developed between the penguin and the participant. Details of this study can be found elsewhere [20].

4   Taking the Model to a Next Level by Deep Learning

In all "toy" paradigms described above, one and the same general eBICA model [13] was used after some adaptation to the specific paradigm. A disadvantage of this approach is the necessity to program the algorithm by hands, and then to adjust its parameters in order to get a socially acceptable behavior. In the future, this should not be the case: we believe that AGI should grow cognitively, learn and evolve by itself, with the involvement of humans as mentors and instructors, not as programmers. But how this level can be achieved?

On the one hand, the deep learning revolution [21] has changed paradigms in AI, providing developers with an extremely powerful learning device [22]. On the other hand, this device has limitations in its autonomous cognitive growth. To train a neural network behave like a human, we need human behavioral data in a big volume, that may not be available for a particular domain. This is why researchers around the world rack their brains trying to solve the puzzle: how to combine a statistical neural network approach with a biologically-inspired cognitive modeling approach? One solution was recently found by the group of Greg Trafton [23]. Following their ideas, we tried a combination of the two methods applied to the virtual clownery paradigm, as follows.

Scenarios of virtual clown improvisations (Fig. 2B) were constructed from 72 predefined action primitives, represented as sentences. Therefore, each human-generated or machine-generated scenario is a sequence of given sentences. An LSTM network was pre-trained on a large (595 scenarios) dataset generated by the eBICA model. After that, the training continued using a small number of human-generated scenarios. Here we illustrate the difference between outcomes, presenting first a typical scenario generated by LSTM after the pre-training session. The logical and artistic quality of this example is not noticeably different from the quality of scenarios generated by eBICA.

Whiteface paces the floor. Whiteface takes the bouquet of flowers. Whiteface brushed his hair. Whiteface opens the trash container. Whiteface walks to the mirror, makes smart faces at the mirror. Whiteface paces the floor. Whiteface takes the bouquet of flowers, puts bouquet of flowers in the center of the table. Whiteface walks to the mirror, makes smart faces at the mirror. Whiteface walks to the mirror, makes funny faces at the mirror. Whiteface sits down on the chair. Redhead enters the room. Redhead greets Whiteface. Whiteface greets Redhead in response. Redhead takes the hammer, hits the mirror with the hammer, makes it a false mirror. Redhead leaves the room. Whiteface tips the vase with flowers. Whiteface brushed his hair. Redhead enters the room. Redhead greets Whiteface. Whiteface greets Redhead in response. Redhead takes the hammer, offers hammer to Whiteface. Whiteface declines the hammer offered by Redhead. Whiteface points finger at Redhead and laughs. Redhead hits the mirror with the hammer, makes it a false mirror. Redhead paces the floor.

And here is a typical scenario generated by the same LSTM after additional training on human data (none of the human-generated sequence fragments were replicated).

Redhead enters the room. Redhead greets Whiteface. Whiteface greets Redhead in response. Redhead tips the vase with flowers. Whiteface points finger at Redhead and laughs. Redhead makes a long nose at Whiteface. Redhead shows middle finger to Whiteface. Whiteface ignores Redhead. Whiteface arranges flowers in the vase. Redhead tips the vase with flowers. Whiteface arranges flowers in the vase. Redhead walks to the rake, rips the rake off the hanger. Redhead throws the rake on the floor. Redhead opens the trash container. Whiteface paces the floor. Whiteface takes the hammer. Redhead makes a long nose at Whiteface. Whiteface [dropped the hammer and] paces the floor. Redhead makes a long nose at Whiteface. Whiteface stumbled on the hammer, screams of pain. Whiteface stumbled on the bottle of vodka, the bottle rolls. Whiteface takes the hammer, breaks the rake teeth with the hammer.

Comparison of the two examples indicates that it is possible to improve the performance of a cognitive model (in this case, eBICA) using human data and deep learning.

5 General Conclusion

In all studied paradigms, virtual actors were implemented using the eBICA cognitive architecture. The model was adapted to the paradigm in two ways: (1) a semantic map of object and action appraisals was constructed using human ranking; (2) moral schemas were formulated taking into account the paradigm specifics. General principles of the model operation were the same in all cases. Results confirm model applicability to selected paradigms and therefore suggest its usability in practically important cases. An additional study indicates that results can be further improved with a combination of a cognitive model and a statistical neural network model trained on behavioral data.

Acknowledgments. The author is grateful to Vladimir Tsarkov, Vladislav Enikeev, Denis Semenov, Aleksey Mikhnev, Yulianna Karabelnikova, Alexandr Dodonov, Igor Grishin, Anton Budanitsky, Matvey Klychkov, Alyona Anisimova, Egor Korekov, Maxim Abramenko for useful discussions and help with the implementations, experiment running, and data analysis. I am also grateful to all participants of the experiments. This work was supported by the Ministry of Science and Higher Education of the Russian Federation, state assignment project No. 0723-2020-0036.

References

1. Marsella, S., Gratch, J., Petta, P.: Computational models of emotion. In Scherer, K.R., Banziger, T., Roesch, E. (eds.) A Blueprint for Affective Computing: A Sourcebook and Manual. Oxford University Press, Oxford (2010)
2. Lucas, G.M., Gratch, J., King, A., Morency, L.-P.: It's only a computer: virtual humans increase willingness to disclose. Comput. Hum. Behav. **37**, 94–100 (2014). https://doi.org/10.1016/j.chb.2014.04.043
3. Lieto, A.: Cognitive Design for Artificial Minds, p. 152. Taylor & Francis, UK (2021). ISBN 9781315460536
4. Rodriguez, L.-F., Ramos, F.: Development of computational models of emotions for autonomous agents: a review. Cogn. Comput. **6**(3), 351–375 (2014)
5. Gratch, J., Marsella, S.: A domain-independent framework for modeling emotion. Cogn. Syst. Res. **5**(4), 269–306 (2004)
6. Gratch, J., Wang, N., Gerten, J., Fast, E., Duffy, R.: Creating rapport with virtual agents. In: Proceedings of the Seventh International Conference on Intelligent Virtual Agents, pp. 125–138 (2007)
7. Samsonovich, A.V.: On semantic map as a key component in socially-emotional BICA. Biol. Inspired Cogn. Arch. **23**, 1–6 (2018)
8. Larue, O., et al.: Emotion in the common model of cognition. Procedia Comput. Sci. **145**, 740–746 (2018). https://doi.org/10.1016/j.procs.2018.11.045
9. Scherer, K.R.: Appraisal theories. In: Dalgleish, T., Power, M. (eds.) Handbook of Cognition and Emotion, pp. 637–663. Wiley, Chichester (1999)
10. Lazarus, R.S.: Emotion and Adaptation. Oxford University Press, New York (1991)
11. Sloman, A. Damasio, Descartes, alarms and meta-management. In: SMC'98 Conference Proceedings. 1998 IEEE International Conference on Systems, Man, and Cybernetics (Cat. No. 98CH36218), vol. 3, pp. 2652–2657. IEEE (1998)

12. Samsonovich, A.V.: Emotional biologically inspired cognitive architecture. Biol. Inspired Cogn. Arch. **6**, 109–125 (2013)
13. Samsonovich, A.V.: Socially emotional brain-inspired cognitive architecture framework for artificial intelligence. Cogn. Syst. Res. **60**, 57–76 (2020)
14. Damasio, A.: Descartes Error: Emotion, Reason, and the Human Brain. Avon Books, New York (1994)
15. Bechara, A., Damasio, H., Damasio, A.R.: Emotion, decision making and the orbitofrontal cortex. Cereb. Cortex **10**(3), 295–307 (2000)
16. Karabelnikova, Y., Samsonovich, A.V.: Virtual partner dance as a paradigm for empirical study of cognitive models of emotional intelligence. Procedia Comput. Sci. **190**, 414–433 (2021)
17. Vilk, J., Fitter, N.T.: Comedians in cafes getting data: evaluating timing and adaptivity in real-world robot comedy performance. In: Belpaeme, T., Young, J. (eds.) Proceedings of the 2020 ACM/IEEE International Conference on Human-Robot Interaction, pp. 223–231. Association for Computing Machinery, New York (2020)
18. Armfield, N.R., Bradford, N., White, M.M., Spitzer, P., Smith, A.C.: Humour sans frontieres: the feasibility of providing clown care at a distance. Telemed. e-Health **17**(4), 316–318 (2011). https://doi.org/10.1089/tmj.2010.0166
19. De Faveri, S., Roessler, M.: Clowning during COVID-19 – a survey of european healthcare clowning organisations highlights the role of humour and art in the healthcare system. Public Health **196**, 82–84 (2021). https://doi.org/10.1016/j.puhe.2021.05.016
20. Tsarkov, V.S., Enikeev, V.A., Samsonovich, A.V.: Toward a socially acceptable model of emotional artificial intelligence. Procedia Comput. Sci. **190**, 771–788 (2021)
21. Sejnowski, T.J.: The Deep Learning Revolution. The MIT Press, Cambridge (2021)
22. Goodfellow, I., Bengio, Y., Courville, A.: Deep Learning. The MIT press, Cambridge (2016)
23. Trafton, J.G., Hiatt, L.M., Brumback, B., McCurry, J.M.: Using cognitive models to train big data models with small data. In: An, B., Yorke-Smith, N., El Fallah Seghrouchni, A., Sukthankar, G. (eds.) Proceedings of the 19th International Conference on Autonomous Agents and Multiagent Systems (AAMAS 2020), pp. 1413–1421. International Foundation for Autonomous Agents and Multiagent Systems, Richland (2020)

Causal Generalization in Autonomous Learning Controllers

Arash Sheikhlar[1(✉)], Leonard M. Eberding[1], and Kristinn R. Thórisson[1,2]

[1] Center for Analysis and Design of Intelligent Agents, Reykjavik University,
Menntavegur 1, 102 Reykjavík, Iceland
{arashs,leonard20,thorisson}@ru.is
[2] Icelandic Institute for Intelligent Machines (IIIM), Reykjavík, Iceland

Abstract. Any machine targeted for human-level intelligence must be able to autonomously use its prior experience in novel situations, unforeseen by its designers. Such knowledge transfer capabilities are usually investigated under an assumption that a learner receives training in a source task and is subsequently tested on another similar target task. However, most current AI approaches rely heavily on human programmers, who choose these tasks based on their intuition. Another largely unaddressed approach is to provide an artificial agent with methods for transferring relevant knowledge autonomously. One step towards effective autonomous generalization capabilities builds on (autonomous) causal modeling and inference processes, using task-independent knowledge representations. We describe a controller that enables an agent to intervene on a dynamical task to discover and learn its causal relations cumulatively from experience. Our controller bootstraps its learning from knowledge of correlation, then removes non-direct-cause correlations – correlations that are due to a common (external) cause, be spurious, or invert cause and effect – through strategic causal interventions, while learning the functions relating a task's causal variables. The effectiveness of knowledge transfer by the proposed controller is tested through simulation experiments.

Keywords: Generalization · Learning · Cumulative learning · Knowledge transfer · Control · Causality · Autonomy

1 Introduction

Any agent with general intelligence must be able to deal with novel situations [17]. Since novelty is always relative to a learner's knowledge, one way a controller may handle it is to use priorly-experienced situations for guidance. This calls for models that are generalizable to a variety of scenarios. Conventional machine learning methods typically learn many spurious correlations, which may cause unpredictable performance – possibly catastrophic – when facing new tasks. Also, current 'transfer learning' methods heavily depend on human programmers to

© Springer Nature Switzerland AG 2022
B. Goertzel et al. (Eds.): AGI 2021, LNAI 13154, pp. 228–238, 2022.
https://doi.org/10.1007/978-3-030-93758-4_24

choose the tasks between which the knowledge transfer must occur. The autonomy of artificial intelligence (AI) systems, in knowledge acquisition and transfer, allowing effective and efficient handling of a variety of scenarios, remains largely unaddressed. No general solution to causal model learning exist, as of yet.[1]

Here we introduce an autonomous controller that cumulatively [19] learns and uses causal models of tasks that are transferable to novel scenarios. The design is based on three major principles of constructivist AI [16], which are *knowledge transparency, temporal grounding,* and *feedback loops.* Given this approach, an autonomous agent can autonomously learn causal models that are invariant across variations of tasks. Causal modeling and inference go beyond the limitations of current machine learning (ML) methods via their testability and task-independence [7,19], allowing an agent to use it in scenarios it has never encountered before. Our approach is compatible with Pearl's structural causal models and directed acyclic graphs [6]. We adapt the principles of causation such that they meet the aforementioned principles of a constructivist methodology [16]. Our causal models of a task are formed by considering the assumption of insufficient knowledge and resources (AIKR) [20], according to which the agent must rely only on a limited set of sampled data and resources. An important factor to limit the scope of learning, and prevent incorrect generalizations, is to consider time explicitly in knowledge representation.

The approach builds on – and is compatible with – prior work on cumulative learning [17,19]. The controller starts its causal discovery process by learning an initial correlational model. Then, it removes non-direct-cause correlations through causal interventions until it identifies the causal structure. It continually updates its model as it collects more data. In short, we introduce an online autonomous controller that initially learns a correlational model through random search (worst case), discovers task-independent invariant relations between variables of a dynamical task, learns the functions relating the variables, and tests the model in transfer scenarios every time it learns the model.

2 Related Work

Generalization has made an appearance in various machine learning (ML) paradigms to date, usually under the heading of 'transfer learning' (TL), invariably with the shared goal of increasing learning rate and improving flexibility. In supervised learning, deep transfer learning (DTL) has been applied to overcome the problem of insufficient training data in the target task. The approaches to DTL differ between domain-based and feature-space-based methods [14], but they lack properties necessary for a general, autonomous AI system, since 1) DTL methods rely on human programmers to choose source and target domains based on their intuition, and 2) an agent that interacts with the environment changes the data distribution in an unknown way. Reinforcement learning (RL), however, is an instance of algorithms by which the agent learns via taking actions,

---

[1] By 'general solution' we mean that the learning is largely independent of the task-environment and can be used to transfer learned skills between different task types.

changing the world's states, and receiving rewards. TL methods in RL (reinforcement transfer learning, RTL) are based on an agent that receives training in a task and reuses the learned knowledge in another, similar task, and the transferred knowledge is usually in the form of policies, reward functions, and/or value functions [15]. However, not only human intuition is part of many RTL methods, the aforementioned forms of knowledge are goal-entangled and thus, task-dependent. The same TL limitation holds for deep reinforcement learning (DRL) approaches when the target tasks change in an unpredictable way [4,13].

The 'covariate shift' concept results from the assumption that conditionals between variables are invariant between domains [2] and occurs due to the distributions' change after intervention. Recently, Rojas-Carulla et al. [11] proved that a subset of conditionals that is limited to the causal parents of a variable can be used to build an optimal predictor of that in the transfer domain, proving Pearl's statement about causal relations being invariant physical mechanisms [6]. In general, explicit representation of causation goes beyond the limitations of current ML due to its transparency, testability, intervention reasoning (predicting the outcomes of actions), and capability of dealing with missing data [7,18]. However, since the approach has attracted researchers' attention recently, causal discovery and generalization have still been limited to observation-based methods, which are not proper for an agent that learns by doing [11,12]. A recent paper introduced a causal discovery algorithm based on intervention [1], however, the algorithm does not learn a causal model in an online manner and is limited to obtaining a causal structure. Our learning controller is an improved version of [1], relying on principles of cumulative learning [18] and AERA system [5], in which a model is learned and gets updated while the agent collects data.

3   Problem Formulation

We start by formulating knowledge representation and intervention. In a deterministic world, the initial condition acts as a 'cause' of the particular unfolding world dynamics when there is no autonomous agent affecting its physical processes. Although a dynamical mechanism that moves a task from one state to another is independent of the initial state[2] [9], different initial conditions lead to different outcomes. Thus, we stick to a discrete-time representation of a dynamical task that has a special focus on initial state, as follows[3]

$$\mathbf{X}(t) := f(\mathbf{X}(0), N_{\mathbf{X}}(0), ..., N_{\mathbf{X}}(t))), \tag{1}$$

---

[2] This is a special case of the 'Independence of Cause and Mechanism' principle, which states that the mechanism that connects the cause to the effect is independent of the cause itself; i.e. X causes Y if and only if $P(Y \mid X)$ is independent of $P(X)$ [12].

[3] Our physical formalization is compatible with event-based causality, where an event causes another event to happen. An event can be defined as a set of manipulable variables with changing values in a time interval that apply forces and causes changes in values of another set of variables in a subsequent time interval.

with augmented state vector $\mathbf{X} \in \mathbb{R}^{n+m}$, where n and m are the dimensions of the world's observables and manipulables, respectively. Also, $\mathbf{X}(0)$ represents the initial state, and $N_{\mathbf{X}} \in \mathbb{R}^{n+m}$ is the noise on both observables and manipulables. The terms $N_{\mathbf{X}}(0), ..., N_{\mathbf{X}}(t))$ show the applied noise in different time steps.

By assuming there is an autonomous agent that can manipulate (intervene on) some observables at any time t, we can break up the vector $\mathbf{X}$ into two parts, where $U \in \mathbb{R}^m$ is the control input vector (vector of manipulables) and $X \in \mathbb{R}^n$ is the vector of observables. Then, Eq. (1) can be written in the form of

$$X(t) := g(X(0), U(0), ..., U(t-1), N_X(0), ..., N_X(t)) \tag{2}$$

Equation (2) can also be written as a difference equation as follows

$$X(t) := \tilde{g}(X(t-1), U(t-1), N_X(t)) \quad \text{and} \quad X(0) := \beta_0 \tag{3}$$

where β_0 indicates the vector of initial values of Eq. (3). Now we can formulate intervention in dynamical tasks as follows

- **Input interventions:** This set of interventions does not change the causal structure of the task. It has two forms:
  - Changing the initial conditions of Eq. (1), and
  - Setting the value of manipulables in Eq. (2).
- **Structural interventions:** Replacing Eq. (1) with another function, which is equivalent to having a different ordinary difference equation and may change the causal structure.

3.1 Causal Generalization

To formulate generalization, we assume that the controller is trained during D tests, having D different probability distributions. We also assume that the control input trajectory U is identical over all D tests. Every $\mathbb{P}^k$ represents a distribution in k^{th} test ($k \in 1, ..., D$), generating U and X^k given initial conditions $X^k(0)$. Over these tests, it learns a function h that maps $X(0)$ and U to X. Then, the prediction of h is tested in a novel test $D + 1^{th}$, which the agent has not experienced before. In other words, the test $D + 1^{th}$ is the transfer test with distribution $\mathbb{P}^{D+1}$, in which the generalizability of the function h is tested. The controller wishes to learn the function h with small L^2 loss, that is

$$\varepsilon_{\mathbb{P}^{D+1}}(h) = \mathbb{E}_{(X^{D+1}, U|X^{D+1}(0)) \sim \mathbb{P}^{D+1}} (X^{D+1} - h(U|X^{D+1}(0)))^2 \tag{4}$$

This statement also holds for identical initial conditions $X(0)$ over D tests with different input trajectories U^k. Then, every $\tilde{\mathbb{P}}^k$ represents a distribution in k^{th} test, generating the input trajectory U^k and X^k given initial conditions $X(0)$. Over these tests, the agent must learn a function $\tilde{h}$ that maps $X(0)$ and U to X. Then, the prediction of $\tilde{h}$ is tested in a novel test $D + 1^{th}$ (transfer test), which the agent has not experienced before. In fact, the controller wishes to learn the function $\tilde{h}$ with small L^2 loss, that is

$$\varepsilon_{P^{D+1}}(\tilde{h}) = \mathbb{E}_{(X^{D+1}, U^{D+1}|X(0)) \sim \tilde{\mathbb{P}}^{D+1}} (X^{D+1} - \tilde{h}(U^{D+1}|X(0)))^2 \qquad (5)$$

The difference between the two aforementioned equations is that in Eq. (4) the predictability of function h is tested for a new initial condition $X^{D+1}(0)$, while the predictability of function $\tilde{h}$ in Eq. (5) is tested for a new control input trajectory U^{D+1}. We will see that h and $\tilde{h}$ are identical after learning the causal structure. In other words, we need to learn a model that is generalizable to scenarios where there may exist new control input trajectories and/or new initial conditions.

4   Causal Discovery and Learning

This work is done within the methodological frameworks of **neo-constructivism** ([16]; see also [3,10]) and **causation** (cf. [6,9,11]). Via the constructivist approach an AI system can autonomously acquire knowledge and use it in multiple different but similar situations/tasks. To that end, feedback loops are used that enable the controller to perform causal interventions (interventions with the purpose of causal discovery).

Learning a Correlational Model: In the first phase of learning, a random search in the observation space occurs, which makes the agent learn correlations between the variables. This correlational modeling is not generalizable but it enables the agent to gain prior knowledge about tasks. Our method removes non-direct-cause correlations and updates the model over training.

Causal Structure Identification: The agent discovers the causal relations by intervening on some variables and inspecting the distribution changes in other variables. By adapting the definitions provided by [1], we can write the following definition that allows an agent detect the *causal relations between observables.* Assume $\forall j \ x_j \not\perp x_i$, then $x_j \rightarrow x_i$ if

$$\forall l \neq j \ x_l^k(0) = x_l^{k'}(0) \ \ x_j^k(0) \neq x_j^{k'}(0), \ \forall l, t \ u^k{}_l(t) = u^{k'}{}_l(t)$$
$$\Rightarrow \mathbb{P}(x_i^k(t)) \neq \mathbb{P}(x^{k'}{}_i(t)) \qquad (6)$$

In other words, given there is a correlation between x_j and x_i, x_j causes x_i if the following statement holds: If the agent generates the same control input trajectory for two different initial conditions of observable x_j and then it finds distribution changes in observable x_i, it concludes that x_j causes x_i.

The agent can also find the *causal relations between manipulables and observables.* Assume $\forall j \ u_j \not\perp x_i$, then $u_j \rightarrow x_i$ if

$$\forall l \ x^k{}_l(0) = x^{k'}{}_l(0), \ \forall l \neq j, t \ u^k{}_j(t) \neq u^{k'}{}_j(t) \ \forall t \ u^k{}_l(t) = u^{k'}{}_l(t)$$
$$\Rightarrow \mathbb{P}(x_i^k(t)) \neq \mathbb{P}(x^{k'}{}_i(t)) \qquad (7)$$

In other words, given there exists a correlation between u_j and x_i, then u_j causes x_i, if the following statement holds: If the agent generates two different input control trajectories $u_j(t)$ for identical initial conditions and then it finds distribution changes in observable x_i, it concludes that u_j causes x_i.

Causal Model Learning: Equations (6) and (7) only allow obtaining the causal structure. However in our method, the initial function (model) that was learned through correlational modeling is constantly updated by removing non-direct-cause correlations after every intervention. Also, the function is updated accordingly (after every intervention) through a grey-box modeling method.

4.1   Using Invariant Functions for Generalization

According to [11], causal generalization is only possible through an invariant function that is learned over a set of training tests $\{1, ..., D\}$ with various control inputs and initial conditions. Via the following assumptions, we will conclude that the invariant function is the causal model of a task, for which we will introduce a discrete linear state-space equation.

Assumption 1: There exists a function of observable and manipulable variables that predicts the observables in the next time step, by assuming the same control input trajectory U for all D tests, such that

$$h(U|X^k(0)) = h(U|X^{k'}(0)) \quad \forall k, k' \in \{1, ..., D\} \tag{8}$$

and, by assuming the same initial conditions for all D tests, such that

$$\tilde{h}(U^k|X(0)) = \tilde{h}(U^{k'}|X(0)) \quad \forall k, k' \in \{1, ..., D\} \tag{9}$$

Since the function h and $\tilde{h}$ are invariant in all tests, according to the fact that input interventions do not change the causal structure (as mentioned in Sect. 3), we can conclude that

$$h(U|X^k(0)) = \tilde{h}(U^k|X(0)) \quad \forall k, k' \in \{1, ..., D\} \tag{10}$$

Assumption 2: The invariance of function h also holds in transfer test $D + 1$.

Assumption 3: Let us assume that h is a linear function so that for all D tests and for any initial condition $X(0)$ and/or any input trajectory U, we have

$$h(t) := X(t) = AX(t-1) + BU(t-1) + N(t), \quad X(0) := \beta \tag{11}$$

Assumptions 2 and 3 imply that the function h is also linear in transfer test. We will see if h is not causal, new initial conditions and/or new input trajectories lead to covariate shift problem. Thus, learning an invariant function (i.e. a causal model) solves the problem. In other words, for prediction error minimization in $D + 1^{th}$ test, the following L^2 error should be minimal, for any $X(0)$ and any input trajectory U,

$$\varepsilon_{\mathbb{P}^{D+1}}(A, B) =$$
$$\mathbb{E}_{(X^{D+1}, U^{D+1}) \sim \mathbb{P}^{D+1}}(X^{D+1}(t) - AX^{D+1}(t-1) - BU^{D+1}(t-1))^2. \tag{12}$$

where $\varepsilon_{\mathbb{P}^{D+1}}(A, B)$ shows the squared error over predictions in transfer test. Now we propose the following optimal prediction model, which can be obtained from minimizing Eq. (12):

$$[A^*, B^*] := \arg\min_{A,B} \varepsilon_{P^{D+1}}(A, B). \tag{13}$$

The left side of Eq. (13) is a matrix specifying the causal structure of a dynamical task (causal relations between observables and manipulables), which provides minimal squared error in transfer test. Here is the introduced model;

$$(X(0), U(0), ..., U(t-1)) \quad \rightarrow \quad X(t) \tag{14}$$

such that

$$X(t) = A^*X(t-1) + B^*U(t-1). \tag{15}$$

Algorithm 1: Pseudocode of learning the invariant causal model

---

Input: sample $(U^k, X^k | X^k(0))$
Output: Estimated model (A and B matrices)
Initial correlational model calculation;
Move the task to arbitrary initial conditions;
while *True* **do**
    for i = *1:n* **do**
        Do intervention 1 (Eq. 6) on x_i;
        Remove non-direct-cause correlations;
        Update the model, while moving to new initial conditions;
    end
    for j = *1:m* **do**
        Do intervention 2 (Eq. 7) on u_j;
        Remove non-direct-cause correlations;
        Update the model, while testing new control input trajectories;
    end
    if *averaged squared prediction error in a new test* $\leq \epsilon$ **then**
        Break;
    end
end

Based on sufficient conditions for causal discovery in the linear Gaussian settings given by [8], **A^* and B^* provide a function h^* that consists only of causal relations**. In other words, the function h^* satisfies Assumptions (1) and (2), which lead to invariant predictions in the transfer test.

4.2   Learning Invariant Causal Model

The proposed algorithm for causal discovery (Algorithm 1) identifies the causal structure through D different tests until it computes a model that is invariant. In other words, the algorithm converges to the optimal A^* and B^* matrices for causal generalization. The controller continues the training process until it is successful in controlling the task with new initial conditions and new control input trajectories it has never seen over training process.

5   Experimental Evaluation

For evaluation of the proposed method, two dynamical tasks were created in the same simulated environment: the Rendezvous task including four mobile robots on a two dimensional plane and a path following task. The causal structure of the environment is thereby independent of the task. We will show in this section that the same holds for the learned causal model. In the first test (Rendezvous task) the robots $(R_1, ..., R_4)$ have to meet at the same location in the x-y plane, using the learned causal model. In the second test, we evaluate the same causal model's prediction ability by assigning a single robot to follow a predefined circular path. In both experiments, the robots are given novel control input trajectories and initial locations to test the model's capability in dealing with covariate shift problem. Each robot's movement follows discrete linear equations of

$$x(t) := x(t-1) + T_s u^x(t-1) \tag{16}$$

$$y(t) := y(t-1) + T_s u^y(t-1) \tag{17}$$

where T_s is the sampling time. There exists 8 observables: $x_{1...4}$ and $y_{1...4}$ (location of $R_{1...4}$) There also exists 8 manipulables: $u_{1...4}{}^x$ and $u_{1...4}{}^y$ (velocity of $R_{1...4}$). Thus, we can augment all the equations into a single state-space equation (in the form of Eq. 15) that shows the causal structure of the task-environment as follows

$$X(t) := IX(t-1) + IT_S U(t-1). \tag{18}$$

where I is an $8*8$ identity matrix, $U = [u_1{}^x, u_1{}^y, ..., u_4{}^x, u_4{}^y]$ is the control input vector, and $X = [x_1, y_1, ..., x_4, y_4]$ is the state vector. Equation (18) simply means that the current position of a robot is only caused by previous position and previous velocity (applied control input) of *that robot*. In other words, the movement of a robot has no causal influence on the movement of other robots. We expect our algorithm to learn this invariant causal model while it intervenes on variables. Before the controller starts its learning process, it estimates an initial correlational model. The estimated model is A and B matrices of Eq. (11), in which all matrix elements are correlated (e.g. x_1 is correlated with x_2, which must not be the case, due to the fact that the movement of R_1 is independent of the movement of R_2). Thus, the controller must perform causal interventions to remove those non-direct-cause correlations from A and B matrices by replacing zeros with relevant non-zero values, and eventually converge to causal A and B, which both are identity matrices in this example.

5.1 Results

Using Algorithm 1, the robots perform intervention 1 (Eq. 6) and intervention 2 (Eq. 7) to discover the aforementioned causal structure. Detecting a causal influence of an intervened variable - which could be either an observable or a manipulable - on other observable variables is done by inspecting the distribution changes of trajectory of observables, through maximum mean discrepancy (MMD) method proposed by [1]. If after an intervention, MMD of an observable becomes zero, then there is no causal influence from intervened variable on the observable, which makes the algorithm remove the related non-direct-cause correlation from A and B matrices and update the matrices via grey-box modeling method. The utilized grey box modeling is nonlinear least squares with automatically chosen line search method. Eventually, when all non-direct-cause correlations are removed and matrices are updated accordingly, the controller ends up having an invariant causal model of the task that is generalizable to different scenario/tasks. In other words, the learned causal model is successful when it is tested not only by novel initial conditions and input trajectories, but

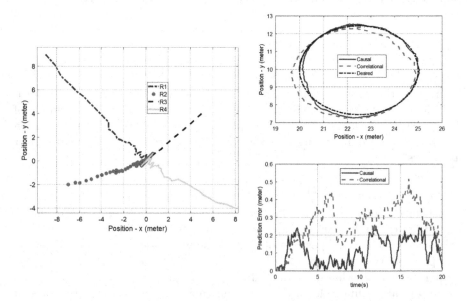

Fig. 1. Left: Performance of the four robots in performing the Rendezvous task, using a learned causal model. The robots start from novel locations in the observation space and reach $(x, y) = (0, 0)$, showing successful transfer. **Right:** A comparison between predictions of causal and correlational models for a single robot, showing the former's superiority; the robot uses both to trace a circular path.

also by different tasks in the same environment. Figure 1(left) shows the Rendezvous task, in which the robots move from novel locations (initial conditions) to $(x, y) = (0, 0)$, by a feedback controller that uses the obtained causal model. As can be seen, the causal model enables the robots to achieve the goal of the task in a scenario that was not experienced over training. Figure 1(right) shows a circular path followed by one of the robots via *the same causal model* that was learned in experiment 1 and a correlational model that was learned in the beginning of the training. The path requires a novel input trajectory and thus, correlational model is considerably less capable of making correct predictions compared to the causal one. The figure in the bottom shows squared prediction errors of both models. To sum up, the experimental results show that the causal model is a task-independent knowledge representation that is more transferable to novel situations/tasks and can also solve the covariate shift problem.

6   Conclusions

We have proposed a causal learning and generalization method for dynamical tasks. The algorithm performs causal interventions on observable and manipulable variables, based on which it removes non-direct-cause correlations and updates the controller's model after every intervention. The results in different dynamical tasks show that the algorithm enables the controller to learn a task-independent causal model, which can be generalized to novel scenarios.

Acknowledgments. This work was supported in part by Cisco Systems, the Icelandic Institute for Intelligent Machines and Reykjavik University.

References

1. Baumann, D., Solowjow, F., Johansson, K.H., Trimpe, S.: Identifying causal structure in dynamical systems. arXiv preprint arXiv:2006.03906 (2020)
2. Bouvier, V., Very, P., Hudelot, C., Chastagnol, C.: Hidden covariate shift: a minimal assumption for domain adaptation. Technical report, arXiv preprint arXiv:1907.12299 (2019)
3. Drescher, G.L.: Made-Up Minds: A Constructivist Approach to Artificial Intelligence. MIT Press (1991)
4. Ke, Z., Li, Z., Cao, Z., Liu, P.: Enhancing transferability of deep reinforcement learning-based variable speed limit control using transfer learning. IEEE Trans. Intell. Transp. Syst. **22**, 4684–4695 (2020)
5. Nivel, E., et al.: Bounded recursive self-improvement. arXiv preprint arXiv:1312.6764 (2013)
6. Pearl, J.: Causality, pp. 22–24. Cambridge University Press (2009)
7. Pearl, J.: Theoretical impediments to machine learning with seven sparks from the causal revolution. arXiv preprint arXiv:1801.04016 (2018)
8. Peters, J., Bühlmann, P., Meinshausen, N.: Causal inference by using invariant prediction: identification and confidence intervals. J. Roy. Stat. Soc. Ser. B (Stat. Methodol.) **78**, 947–1012 (2016)

9. Peters, J., Janzing, D., Schölkopf, B.: Elements of Causal Inference: Foundations and Learning Algorithms, pp. 15–26, 88. The MIT Press (2017)

10. Piaget, J., Piercy, M., Berlyne, D.: The Psychology of Intelligence (1951)

11. Rojas-Carulla, M., Schölkopf, B., Turner, R., Peters, J.: Invariant models for causal transfer learning. Int. J. Biostat. **19**(1), 1309–1342 (2018)

12. Shajarisales, N., Janzing, D., Schölkopf, B., Besserve, M.: Telling cause from effect in deterministic linear dynamical systems. In: International Conference on Machine Learning, pp. 285–294. PMLR (2015)

13. Sheikhlar, A., Thórisson, K.R., Eberding, L.M.: Autonomous cumulative transfer learning. In: Goertzel, B., Panov, A.I., Potapov, A., Yampolskiy, R. (eds.) AGI 2020. LNCS (LNAI), vol. 12177, pp. 306–316. Springer, Cham (2020). https://doi.org/10.1007/978-3-030-52152-3_32

14. Tan, C., Sun, F., Kong, T., Zhang, W., Yang, C., Liu, C.: A survey on deep transfer learning. In: Kůrková, V., Manolopoulos, Y., Hammer, B., Iliadis, L., Maglogiannis, I. (eds.) ICANN 2018. LNCS, vol. 11141, pp. 270–279. Springer, Cham (2018). https://doi.org/10.1007/978-3-030-01424-7_27

15. Taylor, M.E., Stone, P.: Transfer learning for reinforcement learning domains: a survey. J. Mach. Learn. Res. **10**(7), 1633–1685 (2009)

16. Thórisson, K.R.: A new constructivist AI: from manual methods to self-constructive systems. In: Wang, P., Goertzel, B. (eds.) Theoretical Foundations of Artificial General Intelligence. Atlantis Thinking Machines, vol. 4. Atlantis Press, Paris (2012). https://doi.org/10.2991/978-94-91216-62-6_9

17. Thórisson, K.R.: Seed-programmed autonomous general learning. Proc. Mach. Learn. Res. **131**, 32–70 (2020)

18. Thórisson, K.R., Bieger, J., Li, X., Wang, P.: Cumulative learning. In: Proceedings of the 12th International Conference on Artificial General Intelligence, pp. 198–208 (2019)

19. Thórisson, K.R., Talbot, A.: Cumulative learning with causal-relational models. In: Iklé, M., Franz, A., Rzepka, R., Goertzel, B. (eds.) AGI 2018. LNCS (LNAI), vol. 10999, pp. 227–237. Springer, Cham (2018). https://doi.org/10.1007/978-3-319-97676-1_22

20. Wang, P.: Rigid Flexibility: The Logic of Intelligence. Springer, Dordrecht (2006). https://doi.org/10.1007/1-4020-5045-3

AI Future: From Internal Vectors to Simple Objects States Subspaces Maps

Vladimir Smolin[(✉)]

Keldysh Institute of Applied Mathematics RAS,
Miusskaya sq. 4, Moscow, Russia
smolin@keldush.ru

Abstract. The gradient descent ideas in the backpropagation error (BPE) form with some additional algorithms development allowed to realize deep learning of neural networks and led to a revolution in machine learning. A huge learning parameters number made it possible to replace discrete concepts with a vector description. There are some other ideas that are no less profound than gradient descent. Such as memory localization, decomposition of complex objects, and transformations linearization. The transition from internal vectors to maps of simple objects is considered as the promising direction for neural network algorithms development that can implement these ideas. It seems possible with states subspaces maps to overcome some of the problems that deep learning cannot cope without new ideas. A general plan for constructing an interacting maps hierarchical structure is considered, which can work in the Systems 1 and 2 modes according to Kahneman. Mathematical ideas for the linear approximation implementation using neural network maps are given. Other aspects of the general plan also have been preliminary worked out, but a significant amount of work remains to be done to improve the algorithms, ensure the stability of their convergence and confirm their performance by modeling. It will take time and funding. Nevertheless, the success in each of other ideas implementation: localization, decomposition, and linearization can lead to progress in the development of AI, comparable to the introduction of the gradient descent idea into the deep neural networks training, which caused a revolution in machine learning.

Keywords: Neural networks · Mapping · Decomposition · Localization · Linearization

1 Introduction

1.1 AI Successes, Achievements, and Problems to Be Solved

In July 2021, Yoshua Bengio, Yann LeCun, and Geoffrey Hinton (recipients of the 2018 ACM A.M. Turing Award for breakthroughs that have made deep neural networks a critical component of computing) published an article "Deep Learning for AI" [1]. They described the main events that led to the neural network revolution in machine learning and pointed out that one of the reasons for the success was the transition from symbolic to vector description of concepts. Specifically, they wrote:

© Springer Nature Switzerland AG 2022
B. Goertzel et al. (Eds.): AGI 2021, LNAI 13154, pp. 239–249, 2022.
https://doi.org/10.1007/978-3-030-93758-4_25

"In the logic-inspired paradigm, a symbol has no meaningful internal structure: Its meaning resides in its relationships to other symbols which can be represented by a set of symbolic expressions or by a relational graph. By contrast, in the brain-inspired paradigm the external symbols that are used for communication are converted into internal vectors of neural activity and these vectors have a rich similarity structure".

The article describes a number of other reasons that made it possible to achieve success: attention, contrastive learning [2], and variational approaches. And this is only a selective overview, there are many more reasons. Altogether, these achievements made it possible to get significant success in solving the problems of perception, system 1 according to Kahneman [3]. There are also successes in solving the problems of system 2, but less commerce significant [4].

Looking ahead, Yoshua Bengio, Yann LeCun, and Geoffrey Hinton have identified a number of challenges that need to be addressed. They wrote: "there are fundamental deficiencies of current deep learning that cannot be overcome by scaling alone", new ideas and approaches are needed. They also note that humans are capable of faster learning and more robust behavior in changing conditions than modern deep learning algorithms. Ways to approach human capabilities are also indicated: hierarchical processing, improving attention mechanisms, using multiple time scales, developing the ability to solve unfamiliar problems, identify causal relationships and, most importantly, link high-level concepts with low-level perception and actions (grounding).

An important article [1] conclusion is the assertion that the selection of concepts is the more significant property that AI should have than the ability to perform logical operations. New ideas and approaches are needed to develop the important property.

1.2   Simple Objects States Subspaces Maps – A Way to Solve a Lot of Problems

No less important than the step from symbolic to vector concepts description [1] should be the next step: the transition from vector description to state spaces maps.

The formation of neural network maps is an old idea that T. Kohonen began to develop in 1982 [5]. But the widespread adoption of this approach was hampered by the lack of a theory describing the importance of mapping in the general information processing system in the brain. Kohonen's mapping algorithm worked only for simple model objects with a predetermined number of degrees of freedom. There were tasks where the algorithm worked less correctly, but it was also useful. For example, visualization of multidimensional data and some others.

This report proposes a system of a hierarchical representation of information about the external world observed with the help of sensors, based on neural network mapping. To do this, you should slightly change the Kohonen mapping algorithm, add the detection of nonlinear axes in the constructed maps and create "screens" on which the current values of the revealed nonlinear coordinates will be selectively displayed (with an attention mechanism). The main thing is to build hierarchical maps and screens structure, in which the input signal doesn't oblige to get to the upper hierarchy levels. If the lower levels cope with the construction of behavior in the current situation, then the upper ones can be used to model the options for the processes development that are not directly related to the actions being performed.

Such a structure will allow solving a number of problems, including those high-lighted in [1]: acceleration of learning, robustness, cause-and-effect relationships identification, and, most importantly, explaining the cooperation in the work of systems 1 and 2 according to Kahneman.

2 Maps

2.1 From Internal Vectors to Internal Maps

The sensory perception vectors of different objects can coincide, but the vectors state spaces of different objects are different. Spaces are what are described by maps, including neural networks. The map will give a much more complete object description than just the vector of its current state.

It takes more effort to build a map than to memorize a few vectors. But imagine that you are driving to an unfamiliar city. Which will be more useful: a few photos or a city map ?! The cost of building maps is repaid many times over by the benefits they bring. It is important to understand how to incorporate neural network maps into the overall structure of information processing, from sensory perception to action control.

2.2 The Difference Between a Map and a Tensor

A neural network map, like a tensor, is a set of vectors (input signal or activity of the previous layer). But a tensor is a training signals collection that may be disordered. In order to describe well the sub-space of states of the input signal, a huge number of input vectors are needed. The map vectors are the result of training, they are distributed over the map and provide a more compact description.

But if due to the input signal states subspace ordered description it is possible to reduce the required number of vectors several times, then due to the decomposition of a complex signal (scene) into simpler components - in thousands and millions of times! Since a neural network map is the result of input signals processing, decomposition based on maps is possible, but for tensors of raw input signals isn't.

2.3 Why Maps Are Needed

Maps are the observed objects models, more precisely, the changes in their states dynamics maps - phase portraits. There may be no dynamics for static objects, but there are very few such objects. In addition to the nose, which is always in one place in front of our eyes, the rest of the observed objects can move relative to us. The converting process of input into an output signal in deep neural networks (an approximation is carried out in some way) remains poorly understood. We do not know any good, generally accepted theories. The backpropagation error (BPE) learning process leads to local minima of the approximation error estimate. It is hypothesized that hundreds of layers in modern deep networks work well because the likelihood of forming a hierarchical processing structure increases in proportion to the number of layers. But building an effective hierarchy is not guaranteed.

In neural network maps, the input signal vector is converted into one or several neighboring neurons' activity of the competitive layer. The activity of these neurons forms the activity center, which can be considered as the reading head of a multi-channel tape recorder, which reads consistent (like pixels in a reproduced frame) data that forms output signals. The tape is not one-dimensional, but multidimensional and, depending on the goal, the reading head can be displaced in different directions.

For example, to pick up a ball, you need to move your hands towards it. In the hand's phase portrait map it is necessary to read the control commands recorded there to move the center of activity (and the position of the hands that it displays) to the required (relative to the ball) position. The reading takes place along the trajectory of movement of the activity center, the place of which in the phase portrait is determined by the real position and speed of the hands movement, and the change in the direction of movement is defined by the goal (on the map!).

In this case, commands are not instructions, but numbers vectors characterizing the necessary changes in efforts. Which are reproduced as the output connections weights values multiplied by the activities of the elements included in the center of activity.

This is not a one-level input signal (the current position of the hands) transformation into the output (control actions for their movement). Goal setting and the success of its achievement tracking is carried out by the upper levels, which form a hierarchical structure. To do this, we need not only to have the ball dynamic model (map!), but also a higher-level map of hands interaction with the ball. Even higher levels of hierarchical processing are needed to form the goal of "picking up the ball".

2.4   Non-linear Axes Extraction

Hierarchical mapping assumes that the activity of the lower-level maps is an input for the formation and operation of the higher-level maps. You can, of course, use the directly changing position of the activity center. Something like this happens in modern deep networks, in which the input signal for hidden layers is the previous layer elements activity. But even there it is possible to select latent variables corresponding to the observed (or generated) properties. In the neural network maps case, the essential latent variables selection can be more deterministic, since these variables correspond to the nonlinear axes of the state subspace maps. The axes number is determined by the subspace dimension (and the corresponding map), but if the independent axes cannot be greater than the dimension, then the number of dependent ones can.

The nonlinear axes injection into subspace maps should be aimed not only at reducing the information amount describing the activity center current position but at linearizing the map representation, which, in fact, is a way to separate variables.

Theoretically, there are no restrictions on the dimension of maps, but in practice, building maps with more than 10 independent nonlinear axes is an expensive computational task. More than 20 is beyond modern computing capabilities. More than 30 axis is beyond the next 50 years computing technologies capabilities.

Of course, there are tasks that require high-dimensional maps for their solution. And we have to wait for the technique to develop enough before we can solve them.

But most of the practical tasks accessible to humans allow their decomposition into low-dimensional maps (with the number of independent nonlinear axes less than 10) and can be solved using modern devices.

2.5 Hierarchical Structure

Complex objects decomposition into simpler ones can be carried out not only horizontally, but also vertically, that is, hierarchically. If a cat consists of a body, head, paws, and tail, then each of these parts is simpler than the entire cat. But there are parameters that describe the properties of the whole cat, such as position in space, speed of movement, direction, gait, etc. Knowing these parameters simplifies the individual components description of the cat. That is, the hierarchical description allows the decomposition of a high-dimensional single state space map into several low-dimensional, but interconnected maps. Decomposition is not an end in itself, but allows not only to reduce by many decimal orders the amount of information describing complex objects but also by about the same number of times (if the decomposition process is not taken into account) reduces the time for maps building (training).

The hierarchy levels number can be much greater than 2. A person has such levels, according to various estimates, 7–15, which noticeably distinguishes the nature of a living brain functioning from modern deep networks, where the number of layers is measured in hundreds and can exceed 1000. But a person's capabilities are not limited by his brain morphology: the results of information hierarchical processing can be displayed by the speech channel and again subjected to hierarchical mapping. Speech-to-brain directing can be performed repeatedly. This possibility serves as the main difference that distinguishes humans from the rest of the animal world.

It should be noted that not only a multi-level hierarchical decomposition is useful for constructing behavior, but also the hierarchies division into 3 parts: a) describing the properties of external (including their own body observed by external sensors) objects, b) the control of complex movements and c) forming estimates of various states (Q-learning analog).

3 Screens - Attention, Novelties, and More

3.1 Limited Use of Knowledge and Perception

The interaction between the hierarchical mapping levels is a complex process that can occur in different modes. Interaction management and switching modes are better to extract into a separate structure, which is similar in function to the so-called constant screen in psychology. We will simply call it a screen, but we are not talking about a projector with a bedsheet, but about the surrounding reality modeling process (the neurons' activity), not only based on current perception but also using already developed objects maps of various hierarchy levels.

To solve any problem, there is no need to use all the memorized and processed information. All modern neural network architects that have gates in their composition actively exploit this property. What to pay attention to and what to ignore is one of the learning outcomes. But some knowledge that is not currently coming from the sensors is usually useful to use as well. This allows us, using a flat picture on the retina (even without binocular vision, which only facilitates the process), to form a three-dimensional model of the world around us with the generation of the invisible side of volumetric objects and to solve many other problems. Reducing the monitored properties of objects (essential variables) displayed on the screen and filtering out those that do not affect the control, allows reducing noise effects from properties that are insignificant for the problem being solved. But the main thing is that reducing the number of the parameters displayed on the screen makes it easier to build new maps.

3.2 Novelty Filter

The screen function is also to extract the novelty from the incoming sensory signals (at different hierarchy levels). Simple objects phase portraits maps make possible a short-term forecast of changes in their states. If the forecast and real screen activity differ significantly, then we should try to build a new map for this difference.

Depending on how complex the object (or its new properties) is, the process of building a new map may be successful or not. Only for a simple object in a reasonable time, it will be possible to build a new map. Reducing the attention function to some variables displayed on the screen can facilitate the process of building a new map. The best help in extracting simple objects in complex scenes is having models (maps) for almost all the objects that make up the situation. The novelty in sensory perception is more likely to correspond to a simple object, rather than a combination of several simple ones. Even if there are 2–3 new objects, it is much easier to single out one of them with the attention function than to select one from 5–10 such new objects.

3.3 Switching Modes

No less important screens function is to switch interaction modes between hierarchy levels. Each of the levels receives information about the activity centers position in the maps located below and, on the basis of this and the goal set from above, forms new goals for the lower level. If the moving towards a goal process at the lower level does not proceed as expected, then the upper level should form a new goal (or leave the old one). But in any case, at the same time, the upper level participates in the control process contour, albeit indirectly, through the formation of a goal.

Also often happens, achieving the set goal process at the lower level can be successful. The center of activity shifts lengthwise along the map in the right direction, along the planned trajectory. There's no need to set new goals yet, achieving the goal process takes some time. Should upper levels of the hierarchy be idle for this time?!

In the function of screens (different hierarchy levels), it is useful to have the mode switch. If everything at the bottom goes according to plan, then you can turn off control from the upper levels and give them the opportunity to perform a different function. In cases where the process of plans successful implementation for achieving goals is disrupted, the screens should return the upper levels to operational control (by forming new goals). The two operation modes of screens correspond to Systems 1 and 2 according to Kahneman [2]. System 1 works intuitively and processes information almost instantly. System 2 is associated with the selection and options comparison. The new thing that the structure introduces, the hierarchy levels in which are divided by screens, is that System 1 always works, and different parts of the upper levels can go to the mode of System 2, depending on the successfully solved problem complexity by the lower levels and the degree of revision of goals.

4   How to Form Maps from Neural Networks

States subspaces maps are neural network algorithms, on the basis of which it is possible to build Systems 1 and 2 for making decisions according to Kahneman. Hierarchical mapping structures have been developed so far only conceptually, there are no software implementations that solve applied problems. But some mathematical models are available. The description of all the available results in this direction significantly exceeds the report scope, only some ideas are presented below.

4.1   Kohonen Mapping and Threshold Mapping

Neural network maps constructing methods originate from Kohonen self-organizing maps (SOM) [5]. Kohonen developed the ideas behind k-means algorithm (1):

$$\Delta \vec{M}_i = \eta \left(\vec{X} - \vec{M}_i \right), \eta \ll 1 \qquad (1)$$

where $\vec{M}_i$ is i-th element input connections weights vector and $\vec{X}$ – input vector.

When presenting an arbitrary $\vec{x}$ the closest $\vec{M}_i$ is chosen (according to Fig. 1a) - the Voronoi-Dirichlet tiling,). The difference $\left(\vec{X} - \vec{M}_i \right)$ is calculated and the vector $\vec{M}_i$ is slightly shifted towards $\vec{X}$. Such a simple algorithm is sufficient for the uniform distribution of the vectors $\vec{M}_i$ over the subspace of states of the vector $\vec{X}$ (from arbitrary initial positions inside the subspace).

a) 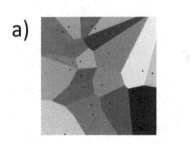   b)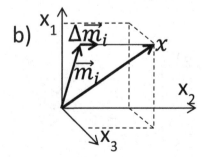

Fig. 1. a) Voronoi-Dirichlet tiling and b) scheme for changing the vector $\vec{M}_i$ according to (1).

Topologically correct Kohonen mapping [5] is only slightly more complicated:

$$\Delta \vec{M}_j = \eta_1 \left(\vec{X} - \vec{M}_j \right), \qquad j : \left| \vec{X} - \vec{M}_j \right| = min$$
$$\Delta \vec{M}_k = \eta_2 \left(\vec{X} - \vec{M}_k \right), \text{ for neighbors of } j, \eta_2 < \eta_1 \tag{2}$$

The K-means algorithm can be changed for neural networks in another way:

$$\Delta \vec{M}_j = \eta_1 \left(\vec{X} - \vec{M}_j \right), \quad j : \left(\left| \vec{X} - \vec{M}_j \right| + b_j \right) = min$$
$$\Delta b_j = \eta_3 \tag{3}$$
$$\Delta b_k = -\Delta b_j / (N-1), \forall k \neq j; \eta_i \to 0, \quad \sum \eta_i \to \infty \text{ when } t \to \infty$$

4.2   Relationship with Radial Basic Functions

Most often, to approximate low-dimensional functions formal neurons with a radial base function (RBF) are used. The ideas for applying RBF are close to the traditional approximation ideas. The linear part of RBF is calculated as the difference $a_i = \vec{X} - \vec{M}_i$, then it is transformed into a radius $r = \|a_i\|$ and a positive decreasing function $\Phi(r)$ is taken. The most common Gaussian function $\Phi(r) = e^{-(r)^2}$ is used.

Mapping algorithms and k-means also use $\vec{X} - \vec{M}_i$ not only to "highlight" the activity center but also to change the vectors $\vec{M}_i$ – the element's connections weights.

The "Winner take all" (WTA) principle can be used only for a zero-order approximation. To approximate higher orders, it is necessary to select several most active elements and to execute the weighted calculation of a value approximated function.

The possibility of linear replacement of the quadratic radius calculation $r_i^2 = (\vec{X} - \vec{M}_i)^2$, has long been known, for example, [6], but this possibility has not yet found a worthy application. The expression $D_i = \vec{X}^2 - r_i^2$ will be maximum for an element with minimum r_i^2, while $D_i \left(\vec{X} \right)$ is calculated linearly:

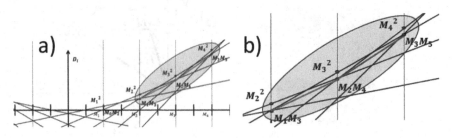

Fig. 2. Changes $D_i \left(\vec{X} \right)$: a) general view and b) switching $\vec{M}_2$ к $\vec{M}_3$ и $\vec{M}_3$ к $\vec{M}_4$.

$$D_i\left(\vec{X}\right) = \vec{X}^2 - r_i^2 = 2\vec{X}\vec{M}_i - \vec{M}_i^2 \tag{4}$$

The change linearity $D_i\left(\vec{X}\right)$ is convenient for approximation purposes, while the regions where the i-th element has the highest (among the elements of the layer) activity coincides with the Voronoi-Dirichlet partition and can have any convex shape (not just an ellipsoid, as in RBF). Moreover, the free term in (4) does not have to be considered as $b_j = \vec{M}_i^2$, it can be obtained by adaptation according to (3).

4.3   Approximation Based on Mapping

Mapping allows to select and to remember vectors $\vec{X}$ from the subspace where they are defined and use them to approximate the transformation $\vec{X} \rightarrow \vec{Y}$. The zero-order approximation can be used, but only in low-dimensional cases. If the vectors $\vec{X}$ subspace has dimension l, to reduce the approximation error by N times, it will be necessary to increase the number of control points of the approximation by N^l times, which even with $N = 10$ и $l = 7 \div 10$ leads to unjustifiably large costs for approximation, an increase in the required memory amount and an increase in training time.

Piecewise linear approximation (first order) allows to save significantly on the memory amount and reduce the training time. Shown in Fig. 2 switching from $\vec{M}_2$ to $\vec{M}_3$ and $\vec{M}_3$ to $\vec{M}_4$ are perfect for implementing piecewise linear approximation, but it is necessary not only to select several elements with large D_i, but also to subtract from all selected D_i some D_0, the choice of which at first glance is not obvious. Also important is the question of how many elements should participate in the approximation. If the dimension of the subspace $\left\{\vec{X}\right\} = R$, then one should take $R + 1$ element. But the subspace $\left\{\vec{X}\right\}$ dimension is not known in advance. For dimension $R = 1$, 2 elements should be selected and the approximation will look as shown in Fig. 3:

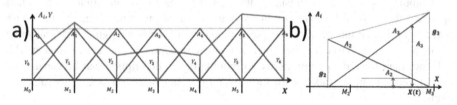

Fig. 3. Activities $A_i\left(\vec{X}\right) = D_i - D_0$ for a) regular and b) irregular lattices.

The activity $A_i\left(\vec{X}\right)$ of each element has a maximum value g_i, while it is not difficult to show that in the area of activity of one set of elements for any $\vec{X}(t)$ a very important relationship is fulfilled:

$\sum_i \frac{A_i}{g_i} = 1$, for Fig. 3(b) the sum has two members

$$\frac{A_2}{g_2} + \frac{A_3}{g_3} = 1 \tag{5}$$

The importance of relation (5) can hardly be overestimated, since it allows not only to calculate D_0 (the same for all $A_i\left(\vec{X}\right)$), but to determine how many terms should be included in the sum in (5). That is, find out the dimension R of the subspace $\left\{\vec{X}\right\}$.

Of course, it is necessary to know the g_i values, but they are also available for calculation, both by analytical geometry methods and statistically. The limitations on the report volume do not allow us to present these formulas, as well as some analysis of the topological features of the approximation in multidimensional cases. But such evaluations and analysis were made and confirmed the efficiency of this approach.

5   Conclusions

The significant and growing advances in deep learning should not block the development of other neural network areas. Even the godfathers of deep learning have written about this more than once and repeated this idea in their last article [1]. New ideas are needed to accelerate the progress of AI.

Transformations linear approximation based on neural network mapping of input signal state subspaces may be such a new idea. This allows in the future to solve a number of difficult problems for deep learning, including the allocation of concepts and the implementation of the connection of high-level concepts with low-level perception and actions.

The idea behind gradient descent is at the heart of deep learning and has great results. No less obvious is the idea of learning outcomes localization, which can be implemented by a competitive learning mechanism in mapping. This idea makes it possible to ensure the almost complete safety of previously acquired knowledge when teaching new ones.

Complex scenes decomposition into simple objects is an equally important approach that is used by mankind in solving almost all problems. Namely, the phase portraits of the subspaces of the simple components of the input signals that can serve as an algorithmic basis for the object's notions selection in the continuous world. Advancement towards a complex world more compact description can be carried out due to decomposition and linearization by introducing nonlinear axes into subspace maps.

The report describes only a general plan for building a hierarchical structure of interacting maps, which can work in the modes of Systems 1 and 2 according to Kahneman. Some formulas for the idea implementation of the linear approximation based on threshold mapping are given. The report's limited volume does not allow to reveal more details about the general plan.

But this does not mean that all aspects of the general plan implementation for constructing a hierarchical structure of interacting maps have already been worked out in detail. For this, a significant amount of work remains to be done, both on improving the algorithms, ensuring the stability of their convergence, and confirming their performance by modeling. It is necessary to overcome the orientation of investors and their advisory managers to invest exclusively in deep learning. Let us express the hope that the article by the luminaries of deep learning [1] with another call to develop new ideas will help break down the financial barriers standing in the way of new ideas, including linear approximation based on neural network mapping.

References

1. Bengio, Y., LeCun, Y., Hinton, G.: Deep Learning for AI. Commun. ACM **64**(7), 58–65 (2021)
2. Chen, X., Fan, H., Girshick, R., He, K.: Improved baselines with momentum contrastive learning (2020). arXiv:2003.04297
3. Kahneman, D.: Thinking. Macmillan, Fast and Slow (2011)
4. Silver, D., Hubert, T., Hassabis, D.: Mastering Chess and Shogi by Self-Play with a General Reinforcement Learning Algorithm (2017). arXiv:1712.01815
5. Kohonen, T.: Self-organized formation of topologically correct feature maps. Biol. Cybern. **43**(1), 59–69 (1982). https://doi.org/10.1007/bf00337288.S2CID206775459
6. Minsky, M., Papert, S.: Perceptrons: An Introduction to Computational Geometry, The MIT Press, Cambridge (1972). ISBN 0-262-63022-2. 1972 (2nd, first edition 1969)

A Thousand Brains and a Million Theories

Grace Solomonoff[(✉)]

Oxbridge Research, 72 Winter Street, Arlington, MA, USA

Abstract. Jeff Hawkins theorizes that multiple predictions via the dendrites into the somas of neurons are used to alert and activate action processes. This report considers if and how Ray Solomonoff's general theory of induction, Solomonoff Induction, using algorithmic probability, would a good tool for his or other neural prediction organizing. Two other early Artificial Intelligence (AI) scientists, Marvin Minsky and Oliver Selfridge also had ideas that are relevant to Hawkins' neural multiple prediction concept, one via Hawkins' map-models, the other via recognition. Solomonoff's is the most impactful to my report, so the main focus is on his general theory of inductive inference.

1 Introduction

Jeff Hawkins, in 2016 describes how the dinner-napkin thick covering of our brain, the neocortex, which does our highest level thinking, has as its fundamental operation learning and recalling sequences of patterns. We have thousands of thinking elements made up of neurons in our neocortex. Individual dendrites of the neurons in these tiny segments code different predictions. There are many, many dendrites each with many synapses delivering predictive information into the soma, the body of each neuron. The neuron receives these many predictions so they are available for the neuron and groups of neurons to predict and then act or not act. The neuron may get in a state of readiness or may actually initiate action for receptor cells, culminating in seeing something, speaking about something, picking up a cup, turning the corner, all the daily activities we do [HA16].

When I read this article, the dendrites of my neurons all together caused spikes which turned cortical light bulbs on which culminated in me saying, "For Hawkins' and other theories that use many small predictions both individually and together, Solomonoff Induction can be a good guide."

It's useful in several ways: by helping understand better the little predictions of individual and multiple dendrites using their multiplicity of synaptic connections on a single neuron, by being the algorithmic guide when multiple predictions are used and compared in the basal part of the neuron, and when many neurons act in concert. It's two pronged, one weighs each individual prediction, the other gives the probability that the predicted event exists at all by weighing all the predictions together. It emphasizes the innate predictive

© Springer Nature Switzerland AG 2022
B. Goertzel et al. (Eds.): AGI 2021, LNAI 13154, pp. 250–260, 2022.
https://doi.org/10.1007/978-3-030-93758-4_26

power of neocortical agents and agented areas, which is a different focus from that of many types of reinforcement learning agents. Resilience and stability while changing to a new level is important, but prediction is most important for purposeful activity, according to Solomonoff. It emphasizes future, present, and past, helps us focus on causes, not just aggregations.

A thousand brains can have a million theories but never get paralyzed by a tsunami of indecision. This may be real world evidence of Solomonoff type induction, because his theory, applied to Hawkin's theory helps understand that the inputs from the dendritic codes are already a probability distribution of explanations of something, each of which predicts something with a probability that it will be the best prediction given the situation the owner of the brain is experiencing. The codes aren't random, each has a probabilistic weight. Different groups of dendrites or their synapses together also provide another probabilistic weight. The point is that Solomonoff's algorithmic probability provides a way to imagine how a multitude of different theories can have a logical and useful order.

In talking about this connection with the earlier mathematician, Solomonoff, it's fair to mention briefly two other scientists, as they represent some connections. The recognition of more emphatic dendritic messages was analyzed in Oliver Selfridge's *Pandemonium*. Hawkins' view of how a neuron makes a model of a person's world, using it to act with the community of cortical columns are foreshadowed by the Agents hypothesized in Marvin Minsky's book, *Society of Mind.*

These three Scientists, Ray Solomonoff, Oliver Selfridge, and Marvin Minsky were three of the original 11 scientists invited by John McCarthy to spend the summer at the first extended gathering of Artificial Intelligence scientists: They all attended the Dartmouth Summer Workshop in 1956, when machine thinking first got the name Artificial Intelligence.

The Dartmouth Summer of 56, Photo by Gloria Minsky.
In back: Oliver Selfridge, Nat Rochester, Marvin Minsky, John McCarthy.
In front: Ray Solomonoff, Leon Harmon, Claude Shannon.

The great neuroscientist Mitch Glickstein wrote: "The historical approach is valuable in and for itself; as much as the history of wars, art or politics... It is of value to understand how [neurocience] came about ...The average neuroscientist may know a thousand or a hundred thousand things to be true about the nervous system. But often they do not know how we know it, and often seem delighted when they learn..." [Gli14].

2 The Cortical Columns and the Neurons

Hawkins' best known works are two books, *On Intelligence*, 2005, and *A thousand Brains*, 2021, and an article in 2016, "Why Neurons Have Thousands of Synapses," more mathematically detailed.

He writes that in the multilayered human brain, on top is the main thinking level of the brain, the neocortex, a thin layer covering the entire brain, spread over the older matter in various folds and plains. This layer is packed with perhaps 150,000 'units of intelligence' called cortical columns, side by side. Though the columns don't have strict borders, they can be distinguished by their separate kinds of actions. Within the cortical column are minicolumns, each with a little over 100 neurons spanning layers [Haw21].

Each neuron has many dendrites, each dendrite has many changing synapses. From synapses via dendrites many predictions at once go the neuron. Hawkins' 2016 article discusses how the neuron may encode new information and efficiently carry several possible predictions at once. Imagine a minicolumn with many rows of little input elements. New information may stimulate one whole stack of elements, while other sorts of information may impact only a few of the elements but at different positions. A set of these minicolumns could produce many combinations this way [HA16].

Here are two key insights Hawkins focuses on. The first is the action of the individual neurons; the second is the communal action of groups of columns working together. The multitude of dendrites carry a multitude of predictions, the communal action is based on what predictions are chosen.

So I'll mention Minsky, Selfridge, then focus on how the brain might use algorithmic probability and Solomonoff induction.

3 Marvin Minsky's Agents

In Minsky's proposal for his research during the Dartmouth Workshop he discusses how the machine would have an internal mapping. It would pair sensory abstractions with actual motor abstractions in such a way that it could produce new sensory abstractions representing changes in the environment that are expected to happen [MS55]. The first paper Minsky read at the Workshop in 1956 was "A Framework for AI" describing little 'boxes' that make up the brain. Each box can be a member of a group, and each box might learn or have different activities. The boxes contain all kinds of different information. Clearly separated, no one box would end up being a repository of 'intelligence' – "you wouldn't end up with the final box having all the information" [Min56].

Minsky developed them into 'Agents' all working together in what he called the 'Society of the Mind.' Agents, many small processes of the mind, connect by pulling up connections that he called K-lines, which would control a group. K-lines, for example might connect agents that can decide: that's a cup, when the hand holds a handle and the eye sees a bowl shape. Agents can also organize methods of learning, one of the most important things we do. In fact in this system, a new way of thinking can develop in a new group, while the old way is used for a while until the new establishes itself successfully [Min87].

Couldn't this view be useful now? For example, successful predictions from groups of dendrites, could continue to be stored in some of the basal cellular area of some neurons, and continue to act on the environment 'in the good old fashioned way,' while the new set is becoming more and more accepted. That way, if the new system fails, the whole thought process does not collapse. This is a very Solomonoffian way to act, for it's a way of replacing one theory with a new improved theory. Solomonoff noted how learning a video-game suggests that. The score stays the same for a long time, then makes a leap – that is when the new theory kicks in.

4 Oliver Selfridge's Pandemonium

Oliver Selfridge always had a flare for drama so of course he called his AI system "Pandemonium." and his version of agents, 'Demons.' He focused on 'closeness,' making one group more important than another. He designed a program of a series of patterns that generates descriptive points. The descriptive points may be minimal, just as the descriptive points in Hawkins' dendritic predictions may be minimal, though he does not have the idea of loading minimal points of several patterns together, a very key idea of Hawkins. Those that fit well are used more, build more and more accurate descriptions. Successful sequences may be tweaked in to get new useful criteria [Sol56a].

In his major program, "Pandemonium" (1959), he envisioned small agents in the mind, demons. When a demon recognizes something similar to what it knows, it 'calls out;' the loudest are used [Sel59]. Whatever pattern matching 'shouts' the loudest is the one that the neuron will act on in its search for a problem's solution [Sel59].

5 Ray Solomonoff's Theory of Inductive Inference

In his new book, *A Thousand Brains*, Hawkins writes: "My brain, specifically my neocortex, was making multiple simultaneous predictions of what it was about to see, hear, and feel. ... At that time, (1980s), few neuroscientists described the brain as a prediction machine. Focusing on how the neocortex made many parallel predictions would be a novel way of attacking the cortical column's mysteries. I could ask specific questions about how neurons make predictions under different conditions..."

In his earlier book *On Intelligence* he used the phrase 'the memory prediction framework' to describe it. In his new book, he describes the same idea by saying that the neocortex learns a model of the world, and it makes predictions based on its model. Hawkins writes "I prefer the word 'model' because it more precisely describes the kind of information that the neocortex learns" [Haw21, pp. 30–31].

Solomonoff would prefer the phrase 'memory prediction framework,' because his inductive inference stresses prediction as an extrapolation of past solved problems or other forms of sequences. However both systems use the idea of multiple predictions based not just on past information but on its revisions, and use this multiplicity in similar ways.

Hawkins feels information comes via movement and place in modeling the world. Predictions occur via the dendrites. Different dendrites send different predictions using similar data, analyzed in different ways, or using different data with a relationship of some kind, the many synapses of dendrites send different levels of spiking influence to the neuron; spikings that have various amounts of strength, if weak but sensible, neurons may go into predictive mode, if there is enough dendritic proximal input to create an action potential spike, the cell spikes sooner, if it is in a predictive state. (Oliver Selfridge would call these varying strengths loudness of shouting.) The basal area of the neuron compares new predictions with old. Actions are based on that. Many dendrites predicting in different ways, means that there are multiple predictions, that the spiking energies are not all the same, means some predictions have more weight than others, and the weight impacts the 'decision' of the neuron of whether to act or not.

Solomonoff writes: "One common method of devising a short code uses definitions. If a certain subsequence occurs many times in the data, we can shorten the data description by defining a specially designed short code for that subsequence whenever it occurs. The "bit cost" of this encoding is not only the accumulation of the many occurrences of the special code—we must add in the bit cost of the definition itself. In general a sequence must occur at least twice before we can save any bits by defining it.

More generally, suppose there are several subsequences of symbols in the data, each with its own frequency of occurrence. We can assign an equivalent code length of *exactly* $-\log_2 f$ to a subsequence whose relative frequency is f. Huffman coding obtains somewhat similar results" [Sol96].

In this concept predictions act via the law of algorithmic probability, and Solomonoff induction is the method the neuron uses to act. Even in 1956, Ray had the idea of analyzing a problem in different ways AND using probabilities of success of older methods. He writes that the work he is doing "involves the application of some special statistical techniques to learning simple arithmetic. In particular, the problems involve the weighting of statistical conclusions drawn from different methods of analysis of the same problem. Also, of much importance, is the devising of new methods of statistical analysis of reasonable probability of success drawn from older methods known to be useful" [Sol56b, p. 3].

This became algorithmic probability which uses multiple predictions in a probability distribution of each one's likelihood; the likelihoods based on a measure of simplicity of how each prediction is described (explained, programmed). According to Hawkins, multiple predictions via the dendrites is the method used for cortical success. It enables us to decide when a cup is a cup, how to open a door when the handle is higher than we expected, how to cross the street safely and how to invent new theories.

6   Solomonoff's Universal Prior

What is Solomonoff's Universal Prior? Why is it important for analysis of brain-like neural nets? First, we need to emphasize that in Solomonoff's theory, the word Universal doesn't mean universality. They are two different things. The universal prior is descriptions contained in the universe of a domain using the language of the domain. Even so there are impossibly many possible explanations extending into the future. So it is contained by using all the predictions that you have time for, not infinite predictions. Right from the start the prior contains the idea of Occams' Razor plus weighted longer codes. Second, right from the start the prior contains the idea of efficiency. Efficiency in Ray's prior is based on shortness of the code.

In conditional probability, not frequentist, the prediction is updated based on the expansion of past data. It expresses a degree of belief in a hypothesis (explanation, theory). As new data comes in, you revise the probability based on all the data, both old and new. The famous formula expresses this [McG11]

$$Pr(Y|X) = \frac{Pr(Y)Pr(X|Y)}{Pr(A)Pr(X|A) + Pr(B)Pr(X|B) + \cdots + Pr(N)Pr(X|N)} \quad (1)$$

where Y has all the elements $A, B, \ldots N$. In this case A, B, N are hypotheses, and Bayes rule gives the Posterior, namely the inferred probability of hypothesis Y after the event X has occurred. $Pr(Y)$ is the prior probability of hypothesis Y before the occurrence of event X [LV19, p. 20].

A philosophical problem is what do you do if you have no original A? Dividing by zero makes any result meaningless. Solomonoff devised a default prior he could substitute to prevent this problem. The shortest input computer programs describing a sequence x are more likely than the longer ones. But there will always be at least one that can describe any finite sequence of observations: this input simply duplicates every observation one by one, which, as a program translates to "print $<x>$" for any given sequence. None of the sequences will have a zero probability. It avoids the problem of having to select something randomly. Ray writes, "When little or no prior information appears to be available, this technique enables us to construct a default prior based on the language used to describe the data" [Sol99].

The beauty of this is that, used in the Solomonoffian way, things aren't random though they may be simple, and there is an orderly progress of theories. Hawkins writes that the information basis of the action of neurons is a reference frame of place and movement. The individual neuron is a reference frame, there is a multitude of them [Haw21, pp. 46–55]. The neocortex uses these reference frames to make predictions. (Think of Marvin Minsky's Agents). No matter what the specific attributes are, the neurons need a way to give a degree of merit to different hypotheses. The predictions still need a prior. The prior for Bayes rule used in algorithmic probabilistic activity in the cortical columns of the brain could easily default to the original language of the body.

In the situation of a sentient being there are several concepts that are useful: First, there is the operating language. In Hawkins it is the language of the body, in particular, language of movement. So you can imagine a kind of input language available to the foetus itself: open, sensing, close, push, extend out, feel, hey? Hey! and so on... There is the added information which provides more input, information like how many mouths, male, female, genetic elements etc.; with a sentient being you have to include many constraints.

Ray had a type of computation called Resource Bounded Probability. This informs learning systems in the real world. In a 1996 report he describes it as the best approximation to algorithmic probability that we can get with stated limitations on computing time and/or memory. He writes, "There are four factors that Learning and Prediction systems must address: 1. The prediction itself. 2. The reliability of that prediction. 3. The sample size. 4. Computation cost" [Sol96].

Ray later used a search procedure including computer cost, Lcost. These factors have to be addressed in any real world learning system.

Even before birth a being has a good working prior. There's a body that does lots of stuff, sensory data, a mouth that opens and closes, feet that move.

Hawkins described two important things he developed from Vernon Mountcastle's *The Mindful Brain* about the parts of the neocortex: one is that the different parts are doing different things – vision, analyzing, etc. The other is that they are all doing something the same, using the same method, principles to make predictions and to map the world [Haw21, pp. 21–24].

Side note: Though randomness is usually the wrong direction, the actual use of randomness is an interesting idea. Ray once mentioned that we do use it, when we are unable to use our weighting ability. When someone panics, the neocortex cleverly reverts to random action, because that action might do something to save them!

7   Algorithmic Probability and Multiple Theories

Hawkins thinks dendrites send predictions, many predictions, sending a kind of spiking to the soma, the body of the neuron. Some may prime the neuron, but not cause it to act, Hawkins uses the analogy of saying "On your mark, Get set...". Then others may cause the spike that triggers action.

Solomonoff writes that the simplest explanation of something tends to be the best, the one you usually would act on. But usually it's not the only explanation. There may be several that are almost as good. Given new experiences they may prove to be better. The weights of the individual predictions would then change.

In early computer terminology Ray figured it via the shortness of the explanation as derived via a Universal Turing machine. In everyday use, the concept of 'Occam's razor' would mean the simplest or even most efficient explanation. If you usually have a cup of coffee, then even without looking, when you grab a handle, you predict it's the cup of coffee. But there are lots of other possibilities, and as Hawkins might say, your dendrites are predicting many other possibilities – handle possibilities: a saucepan, a drawer handle... coffee possibilities: espresso, a flavored candy bar... lots of possibilities with different probabilities. Your neurons won't be bent out of shape if you find out it's tea. Maybe a new event occurred, the coffee imports failed, making the 'tea theory' now the best one. But your dendrites will give low spiking to a coffee flavored sidewalk, or a cup without sides.

Solomonoff uses that in his mathematical formula of multiple explanations of something. The trick that Solomonoff introduces is that each explanation has a certain likelihood. He describes this mathematically, and uses Bayes rule to decide its value as a prediction. An important result is that all the explanations together give the total probability for a particular event while the top one is most specific. Thus you find you are holding a coffee cup.

$$P_M(x) = \sum_{i=1}^{\infty} 2^{-|s_i(x)|} \tag{2}$$

The probability of x via machine M is the sum of all the explanations from one to infinity weighted by their length. In the real world the probability event you are considering via the neocortex machine is the sum of explanations you have time to think of. You will not encounter the coffee flavored sidewalk, because it is too complicated. It would take years and years to explain it, and the connections would never be encountered in the real world.

Ray writes in his 1997 autobiography:

The correspondences between probability evaluation and human learning are very close: (1) Both involve prediction of the future based on data of the past. (2) In both of them, prediction alone is of little value. The prediction must have an associated quantitative precision before it can be used to make decisions - as in statistical decision theory. (3) In both cases the precision of prediction is critically dependent upon the quality and quantity of data in the past. (4) In both cases, the precision of the prediction is critically dependent on the quality and quantity of the computational resources available. Human decisions improve considerably if people have much time to organize data and try various theories in attempts to understand it. That probability has to be defined in terms of the computational resources necessary to calculate it, is a relatively recent development [Sol97].

Ray notes,

(I) described algorithmic probability with respect to a universal Turing machine with random input. An equivalent model considers all prediction methods, and makes a prediction based on the weighted sum of all of these predictors. The weight of each predictor is the product of two factors: the first is the a priori probability of each predictor.—It is the probability that this predictor would be described by a universal Turing machine with random input. If the predictor is described by a small number of bits, it will be given high a priori probability. The second factor is the probability assigned by the predictor to the data of the past that is being used for prediction. We may regard each prediction method as a kind of model or explanation of the data. Many people would use only the best model or explanation and throw away the rest. Minimum Description Length (Ris 78), and Minimum Message Length (Wal 68) are two commonly used approximations to ALP (Algorithmic Probability) that use only the best model of this sort. When one model is much better than any of the others, then Minimum Description Length and Minimum Message Length and ALP give about the same predictions. If many of the best models have about the same weight, then algorithmic probability gives better results. However, that's not the main advantage of algorithmic probability's use of a diversity of explanations. If we are making a single kind of prediction, then discarding the non-optimum models usually has a small penalty associated with it. However if we are working on a sequence of prediction problems, we will often find that the model that worked best in the past, is inadequate for the new problems. When this occurs in science we have to revise our old theories. A good scientist will remember many theories that worked in the past but were discarded—either because they didn't agree with the new data, or because they were a priori "unlikely". New theories are characteristically devised by using failed models of the past, taking them apart, and using the parts to create new candidate theories. By having a large diverse set of (non-optimum) models on hand to create new trial models, algorithmic probability is in the best possible position to create new, effective models for prediction [Sol11].

At the Dartmouth summer in 1956 he wrote: "Idea of working on many humanly solvable problems litely, to find out what they have in common, rather than initial intense work on any one problem. Emphasize how human works problem rather than easy trick ways to work problems that may be peculiar to that set of problems." There has been "a great overemphasis of difficulties peculiar to the particular set of problems worked on rather than difficulties peculiar to all problems. Use of computers is, I think, usually going in more deeply than is good at the present time" [Sol56a, pp. 8–9].

The only specific suggestion of this report might be to consider Hawkins' coding method for the mini-cortical columns that side by side make up one cortical column. Since they contain layers (rows) they are a matrix. Use any

Solomonoffian Induction process you can use with matrices. Here is an example. I'm not sure, but I think Hawkins does it differently. Suppose you have a suite of nine mini-columns each with six layers. Suppose five dendrites send codes, which are put in this matrix of 9 by 6. Two of the codes share the same address on three adjacent mini-columns, but no other part of their codes or any of the other codes use those three addresses. Using a single symbol (plus you have to define overall instructions) instead of three symbols shortens the code. The more overlap the shorter the code and therefore the more predictive power it has. Shorter is more efficient and more likely. This is before reinforcement or anything. It is finding something to compress that will guide your next prediction because it's put into the Bayesian conditional structure. The whole neocortex is then considered another large, possibly single row, matrix that might be frequentist Bayesian, which may vary in different sections of the neocortex. In his latest years Ray was developing what he called the "Guiding Probability" and I think this is an example of guiding. Regretfully he died before he completed papers on this topic. Hopefully we will read more about it.

This report includes the work of Ray Solomonoff, Oliver Selfridge and Marvin Minsky. Their work foreshadows Jeff Hawkins' work. When scientists look back over some of the older works, their new hypotheses get enriched, just like Ray Solomonoff always predicted.

References

[Gli14] Glickstein, M.: Five minutes with Mitchell Glickstein (February 2014)

[HA16] Hawkins, J., Ahmad, S.: Why neurons have thousands of synapses. Front. Neural Circ. **10**, 23 (2016)

[Haw21] Hawkins, J.: A Thousand Brains. Basic Books, Hachette Book Group, New York (2021)

[LV19] Li, M., Vitányi, P.: Physics, information, and computation. In: An Introduction to Kolmogorov Complexity and Its Applications. TCS, pp. 623–761. Springer, Cham (2019). https://doi.org/10.1007/978-3-030-11298-1_8

[McG11] McGrayne, S.B.: The Theory that Would not Die. Yale University Press, New Haven (2011)

[Min56] Minsky, M.: Framework. Technical report, Dartmouth Summer Workshop (1956)

[Min87] Minsky, M.: The Society of Mind. Simon and Schuster (1987)

[MS55] Minsky, M., Rochester, N., McCarthy, J., Shannon, C.: A proposal for the Dartmouth summer research project on artificial intelligence (dart564props.pdf). Box A (August 1955)

[Sel59] Selfridge, O.: Pandemonium: A Paradigm for Learning (1959)

[Sol56a] Solomonoff, R.J.: Notes on others. (Aug 1956). http://raysolomonoff.com/dartmouth/boxa/

[Sol56b] Solomonoff, R.J.: Ray AI approach (pdf). (Jan 1956). http://raysolomonoff.com/dartmouth/boxa

[Sol96] Solomonoff, R.J.: Does algorithmic probability solve the problem of induction? (1996)

[Sol97] Solomonoff, R.J.: The discovery of algorithmic probability. J. Comput. Syst. Sci. **55**(1), 73–88 (1997)

[Sol99] Solomonoff, R.J.: Letter to David Malkoff (to be published on raysolomonoff.com, July 1999)

[Sol11] Solomonoff, R.J.: Algorithmic probability - its discovery - its properties and application to strong AI. In: Zenil, H. (ed.) Randomness Through Computation: Some Answers, More Questions. World Scientific (2011)

The Role of Bio-Inspired Modularity in General Learning

Rachel A. StClair(✉), William Edward Hahn, and Elan Barenholtz

Center for Complex Systems and Brain Sciences and Center for Future Mind,
Florida Atlantic University, Boca Raton, FL, USA
rstclair2012@fau.edu

Abstract. One goal of general intelligence is to learn novel information without overwriting prior learning, i.e. catastrophic forgetting (CF). The utility of preserving knowledge across training tasks is twofold: first, the system can return to previously learned tasks after learning something new. In addition, bootstrapping previous knowledge may allow for faster learning of a novel task. Current approaches to learning without forgetting depend on strategically preserving weights that are critical to a previously learned task. However, another potential factor that has been largely overlooked is leveraging the initial network topology, or architecture. Here, we propose that the topology of biological brains likely evolved certain features that are designed to achieve knowledge preservation. In particular, we consider that the highly conserved property of anatomical modularity may offer a solution to weight-update learning methods that leverages learning without catastrophic forgetting for general bootstrapping to novel circumstances. Final considerations are made on how to combine these two objectives in a general learning system.

Keywords: Architecture · General learning · Modularity

1 Introduction

1.1 Knowledge Preservation

A basic goal of most approaches to artificial general intelligence is the ability to learn multiple tasks without overwriting what has previously been learned (i.e. catastrophic forgetting, or CF). The potential utility of learning without forgetting, or 'knowledge preservation', is twofold: first, the system can return to previously learned tasks after learning something new. Secondly, bootstrapping previous knowledge may allow for faster learning of a novel task. Both of these potential benefits of preserving learned information may serve to conserve resources. Allowing the same computational hardware to be 'multiplexed' for another task, rather than requiring allocation of distinct resources, reduces the

Supported by Machine Perception and Cognitive Robotics Labs.

B. Goertzel et al. (Eds.): AGI 2021, LNAI 13154, pp. 261–268, 2022.
https://doi.org/10.1007/978-3-030-93758-4_27

required energy resources involved in the learning process. Multiplexed information is stored in such a way that the system can switch between previously learned tasks while retaining performance. Information can then be accessed for learning new tasks in a contextually relevant manner. Multiplexed information is thus stored and retrieved in a way that facilitates the conservation and use of prior learning, broadening the ability of a learning system to multiple task domains.

1.2   Previous Approaches

A significant body of recent work has explored approaches to CF and bootstrapping in relation to multi-layer neural networks or deep learning (DL) [43]. Learning in these systems consists of updating the weights between nodes according to their respective partial derivatives calculated from a loss function (i.e. backpropagation). With the recent implementation of auto-differentiation and parallel computing devices, progress in backpropagation-based DL has rapidly emerged as the dominant approach in AI [29]. Previous approaches to overcoming CF in DL models have involved strategies with regard to the learning process itself. Most commonly in the case of bootstrapping, ensemble networks are retrained on resampled datasets with little improvement [25]. Transfer learning is also used as a bootstrapping method in which previously-learned features are imported as the starting weights for later update [41]. CF approaches are more diverse, mostly involving modification to the weight update methods. Notably, Elastic Weight Consolidation has shown promising results in overcoming CF in sequences of Atari tasks by slowing down updates on previously encoded weights [1,17]. However, these approaches have not been widely adopted, likely because the techniques do not demonstrate knowledge preservation on a level necessary for general intelligence. We suspect this is in part due to the fundamental nature of backpropagation in DL models to rewrite learning; where weights are updated most heavily towards current learning at the expense of weights learned in more distant tasks. The result of backpropagation, even when assuaged by CF mitigation, is narrow feature learning that will eventually reach a resource constraint asymptote as learning increases throughout the model's lifetime.

1.3   Network Topology

Another potential approach that has thus far been largely neglected is to consider the topology of the learning system - that is, its 'architecture'. While there is a significant body of work on architecture optimization for other metrics of learning [5,9,22,23,30,38,42], to date there has been little work considering architectural choices in relation to CF and/or bootstrapping. Fortunately, hundreds of million years of evolution has generated highly conserved, vertebrate and mammalian brain architectures that have been optimized with regard to intelligent functions including, it is reasonable to assume, the preservation of learning without CF.

One potentially promising property of biological nervous system architectures, which may serve to overcome the pitfalls of CF, is the presence of modular architectures such as the cortex and subcortical structures. Modularity is a highly conserved property that is present across many organisms with general learning abilities. Complex neural architectures are thought to have emerged in the Cambrian explosion, 540 million years ago, with records of both camera eyes and the emergence of animals with complex behaviors [35]. In contemporary species, the four basic brain structures (Telencephalon, Cerebellum, Diencephalon, Mesencephalon) have been preserved across nearly all mammalian species and most avian, reptile, shark brains, and some fish brains [2,18,21,26,44]. Insects have their own highly preserved modular nervous-system structures as well [16].

In humans, modularity is highly pervasive. For example, the cortex processes incoming sensory information while the basal ganglia controls behavior selection in goal-directed learning [27,33]. These structures are specialized not only with regard to the types of information they process (e.g. photon patterns for V1 stream vs. layers 5/6 cortical output from cortex), but also with regard to their neuron types as well as their morphological structures. Communication between the two structures occurs in limited routes, cortico-basal ganglia networks, which serve to integrate information between the two regions [20]. The result of this particular organization is a cortex that is optimized for encoding sensory information as general features, while the basal ganglia is optimized to interpret cortical information for behavior selection (e.g. motor movement) [4].

Here, we propose that modular architectures may also serve to preserve learning during the update process by separating different types of computation (specialization) and storing the learning across un-updatable boundaries (segregation). In artificial systems, modularity may be modeled in the form of specialized weight updates based on local rules within a module (i.e. segregation), which can be used to preserve prior learning by distributing the information encoding throughout the system such that during one module's update processes, prior learning is preserved in other modules. In segregation, weight updates become more localized. In the case of specialization, weight updating becomes diversified. As seen in GANs [8], optimizing segregated networks using different loss functions increases the generalization capacity of the model. Both biological segregation and specialization are largely genetically and developmentally predetermined. The effect, for example in the human brain, is that the basal ganglia learns to interpret the general feature learning of the cortex. It is proposed in [3] that consequence feedback from the environment aids the basal ganglia in learning how to produce behaviors in response to cortical outputs. While it is still somewhat unknown how the cortical module is learning (i.e. weight updating), its segregation and specialized functioning from the BG allows generally useful features to emerge and be preserved, independent of current tasks feedback. Modularity extends beyond the current methods of strategic weight preservation by allowing computational units to diversely encode learning in a manner that affords later multiplexing.

Previous work on artificial systems has looked at the effects of modularity for generalization, but using different learning metrics [10,11,24]. Promising results on the effects of modularity for generalizing to out-of-distribution data has been shown in the Badger architecture, which relies on nested self-sufficient computational units which communicate for a shared objective [28]. Badger is an agent based model in the sense that each agent, or small self-sufficient network, updates independently in an internal loop, while the outer loop optimizes the total collection of homogeneous agents towards a goal. However, badger does not incorporate within-agent specialization, which we believe is essential to solving the knowledge preservation problem.

While we have attempted to make the specific case for modularity as an example of a potentially important design principle in natural systems, we propose that knowledge preservation should serve as a general guiding framework in architecture design that may give rise to dynamical learning systems capable of some level of generality. The key idea is modeled from the human brain where it is likely that network topology is at least, if not more important than later learning algorithms in achieving this goal. This allows us to avoid ending up with a system that is doing the bulk of the learning process after it has been configured. In a system that prioritizes initial connectivity, this manifests as selecting appropriate modularity during a variety of different domain tasks. Rewriting existing learning prevents sharing of computational resources for novel tasks. This is often the problem in designing AGI from theoretical systems that don't take resource constraints into account, such as universal Turing machines and AIXI [15,37].

2   Possible Implementation Approaches

Many methods could be conceived for discovering the inductive biases that different modular architectures have to offer general learning systems. Crucially, there is a tradeoff between initial connectivity and later weight modification. A strong dynamical learning system would utilize initial topology search as a prior learning experience to later be exploited during the weight modification learning phase.

Consider regions separated by un-updatable boundaries that delineate the extent of backpropagation. These modules could optimize without overwriting each other, while still being able to share resources when relevant (i.e. bootstrapping). This approach also limits rewriting prior learning for the sake of the current learning, where modules are activated at different times depending on their relevance to the current tasks. Furthermore, modules dedicated to computational tasks (e.g. memory, sensory, self-activation, etc.), instead of behavioral tasks serve as a more biologically inspired approach, since this is largely what we observe between cortical and subcortical structures.

Evolutionary searches are particularly useful in discovering unique solutions to optimization problems, which can be extended here. Although computationally extravagant, one promising candidate would be an evolutionary approach that couples network topology and embodiment search to different learning environments that also evolve over time. Derivatives of this approach would be useful, especially those focusing on modularity and learning. The advantage to this method is that appropriate submodules will likely be paired with the particular sensory receptors given to the agent and the types of learning updates that need to be delegated throughout the system in ways that may not be currently known.

Other approaches include intelligently designed architectures where architecture is random, learned, and/or selected by an operator. Random networks, such as [6], have seen interesting results and may offer some potential insights into the core properties of learning, however they will likely have to be harnessed in a constructive way to get desired behavior, as in [23]. Similar to random learning, methods exist for crystallizing order from disorder in unorganized networks as in the case of [12,14], leading to module-like structures. Still, there are other conceivable approaches involving learning functions that select sequences of computational architecture pathways and more. More extensive studies could iteratively search through all possible configurations of N-node networks to discover what modularity benefits particular learning environments. Even hand-designed simple models that start to test the questions of module design and learning without forgetting would be useful in answering the questions presented here.

3   Benchmarking Generality

In order to assess a model's knowledge preservation, it must be able to demonstrate that it can learn a sequence of tasks in a variety of domains and return to those tasks with improvements in computational costs and/or learning time. Below we describe initial tests to measure generality in terms of learning without forgetting and bootstrapping capacities. However, as generality scales, more advanced testing is likely necessary.

Knowledge Preservation Metrics. Learning without catastrophic forgetting is typically measured by performance on a sequence of tasks. Here, we propose that it is imperative to test on sequences in different domains (e.g. vision classification and time-series forecasting) to demonstrate generality over narrow-learning.

Boostrapping A-Priori Knowledge Metrics. Measuring bootstrapping a-priori knowledge is slightly more challenging due to the effects seen in transfer learning. The goal here is to see an increased speed in learning task B after learning task A. Again, in trying to capture generality, it is useful to compare tasks from different domains so the distribution of features in the data is different enough that it's possible to measure the use of contextual knowledge instead of the re-use of features. This later point is what occurs in transfer learning. As in the case of the popular technique of using pre-trained ResNet on Imagenet and vision based tasks, the transferred weights capture many features which would have to have been learned in the secondary network either way [41]. Here, we also want to be able to use learned features to aid in learning a new task, but we want to ensure that these are general features that can be maximally shared across all tasks the system may be expected to learn. Teasing out this difference is aided in investigating how data flows through different parts of the system's topology. For example, the Fusiform Face Area is shown to activate when distinguishing between faces and also in bird experts for distinguishing between birds [34]. This multi-use activation of the same subnetwork is one example of bootstrap learning. We might expect similar submodules to be redeployed across different kinds of learning domains.

Challenges. We recognize that adding modularity alone will probably not multiplex information in a way that provides human-level general intelligence. The works of Coward, Buszaki, and Turing suggest algorithms employed by the human brain may give rise to this generality based on eliciting sequences of computation across different modules [4,13,36]. Furthermore, special message passing algorithms between modules would benefit from that of publish and subscribe models; that regions in the system can communicate with each other when necessary. Thus, the system must employ other learning methods for generating such sequences when appropriate. Other challenges involve the large search space of possible architectures and their respective inductive biases in learning different tasks and pairing the correct learning algorithms within modular architectures.

4   Conclusion

We have highlighted topology as an important topic for future research, as well as the need for algorithms that allow for learning without rewriting previous learning. We suspect modularity in biological intelligent systems plays a crucial role in achieving this need while conserving resources. This paper also contributes to discussions on AGI agent architectures by suggesting some useful considerations on how to test for generality in regards to CF and bootstrapping. Works from [1,19,28,32,40] have attempted to tackle these issues separately, while others [31,39] have come from the angle of single-use systems, all of which overwrite prior learning to a unsatisfactory degree. Still, some works have come from the position of down-scaling theoretical models without resource constraints [7,15,37]. While these approaches are useful, we find the proposed approach is more appropriate for the pursuit of general intelligence. We believe this paper provides a framework for investigating computationally tractable general learning systems. Promising directions involve evolutionary and intelligent topology design that utilizes modularity to minimize rewriting prior learning. We hope this paper serves as a tool for those interested in benchmarking early progress in generality. There is room for many future works to provide insight into the approach presented here as well as how to measure generality in terms of bootstrapping and learning new without forgetting old. We have tried to clarify how modularity may offer a method of learning without rewriting and the role it plays in topology design. Much work needs to be done to improve that understanding and find ways to appropriately incorporate modularity in AGI frameworks.

References

1. Aich, A.: Elastic weight consolidation (EWC): Nuts and bolts. arXiv preprint arXiv:2105.04093 (2021)
2. Bruce, L.L.: Evolution of the brain in reptiles. In: Binder, M.D., Hirokawa, N., Windhorst, U. (eds.) Encyclopedia of Neuroscience, pp. 1295–1301. Springer, Berlin (2009). https://doi.org/10.1007/978-3-540-29678-2_3147
3. Coward, L.A.: The recommendation architecture: lessons from large-scale electronic systems applied to cognition. Cogn. Syst. Res. **2**(2), 111–156 (2001)
4. Coward, L.A.: A System Architecture Approach to the Brain: From Neurons to Consciousness. Nova Publishers, Hauppauge (2005)
5. Elsken, T., Metzen, J.H., Hutter, F.: Neural architecture search: a survey. J. Mach. Learn. Res. **20**(1), 1997–2017 (2019)
6. Gershenson, C.: Introduction to random Boolean networks. arXiv preprint nlin/0408006 (2004)
7. Goertzel, B., Pennachin, C.: Artificial General Intelligence. Springer, Berlin (2007). https://doi.org/10.1007/978-3-540-68677-4
8. Goodfellow, I., et al.: Generative adversarial networks. Commun. ACM **63**(11), 139–144 (2020)
9. Goudarzi, A., Teuscher, C., Gulbahce, N., Rohlf, T.: Emergent criticality through adaptive information processing in Boolean networks. Phys. Rev. Lett. **108**(12), 128702 (2012)
10. Goyal, A., Bengio, Y.: Inductive biases for deep learning of higher-level cognition. arXiv preprint arXiv:2011.15091 (2020)
11. Goyal, A., et al.: Recurrent independent mechanisms. arXiv preprint arXiv:1909.10893 (2019)
12. Gutowitz, H.: Cellular Automata: Theory and Experiment. MIT Press, Cambridge (1991)
13. György Buzsáki, M.: The Brain from Inside Out. Oxford University Press, Oxford (2019)
14. Hebb, D.O.: The Organisation of Behaviour: A Neuropsychological Theory. Science Editions, New York (1949)
15. Hutter, M.: A gentle introduction to the universal algorithmic agent AIXI (2003)
16. Ito, K., et al.: A systematic nomenclature for the insect brain. Neuron **81**(4), 755–765 (2014)
17. Kirkpatrick, J., et al.: Overcoming catastrophic forgetting in neural networks. Proc. Nat. Acad. Sci. **114**(13), 3521–3526 (2017)
18. Kotrschal, A., Kotrschal, K.: Fish brains: anatomy, functionality, and evolutionary relationships. In: Kristiansen, T.S., Fernö, A., Pavlidis, M.A., van de Vis, H. (eds.) The Welfare of Fish. AW, vol. 20, pp. 129–148. Springer, Cham (2020). https://doi.org/10.1007/978-3-030-41675-1_6
19. Koutník, J., Cuccu, G., Schmidhuber, J., Gomez, F.: Evolving large-scale neural networks for vision-based reinforcement learning. In: Proceedings of the 15th Annual Conference on Genetic and Evolutionary Computation, pp. 1061–1068 (2013)
20. Lalo, E., et al.: Patterns of bidirectional communication between cortex and basal ganglia during movement in patients with Parkinson disease. J. Neurosci. **28**(12), 3008–3016 (2008)
21. Larsell, O.: The cerebellum of reptiles: lizards and snake. J. Comp. Neurol. **41**(1), 59–94 (1926)

22. Lee, D.S.: Evolution of regulatory networks towards adaptability and stability in a changing environment. Phys. Rev. E **90**(5), 052822 (2014)
23. Lukoševičius, M., Jaeger, H., Schrauwen, B.: Reservoir computing trends. KI-Künstliche Intell. **26**(4), 365–371 (2012). https://doi.org/10.1007/s13218-012-0204-5
24. Werle van der Merwe, A.: Investigating the evolution of modularity in neural networks. Ph.D. thesis. Stellenbosch University, Stellenbosch (2020)
25. Nixon, J., Lakshminarayanan, B., Tran, D.: Why are bootstrapped deep ensembles not better? In: "I Can't Believe It's Not Better!" NeurIPS 2020 Workshop (2020)
26. Nomura, T., Izawa, E.I.: Avian brains: insights from development, behaviors and evolution. Dev. Growth Differ. **59**(4), 244–257 (2017)
27. Ring, H., Serra-Mestres, J.: Neuropsychiatry of the basal ganglia. J. Neurol. Neurosurg. Psychiatry **72**(1), 12–21 (2002)
28. Rosa, M., et al.: Badger: Learning to (learn [learning algorithms] through multi-agent communication). arXiv preprint arXiv:1912.01513 (2019)
29. Schmidhuber, J.: Deep learning in neural networks: an overview. Neural Netw. **61**, 85–117 (2015)
30. Schölkopf, B., et al.: Toward causal representation learning. Proc. IEEE **109**(5), 612–634 (2021)
31. Silver, D., Singh, S., Precup, D., Sutton, R.S.: Reward is enough. Artif. Intell. **299**, 103535 (2021)
32. Stanley, K.O., Clune, J., Lehman, J., Miikkulainen, R.: Designing neural networks through neuroevolution. Nat. Mach. Intell. **1**(1), 24–35 (2019)
33. Sutherland, R., Whishaw, I., Kolb, B.: Contributions of cingulate cortex to two forms of spatial learning and memory. J. Neurosci. **8**(6), 1863–1872 (1988)
34. Tong, M.H., Joyce, C.A., Cottrell, G.W.: Why is the fusiform face area recruited for novel categories of expertise? a neurocomputational investigation. Brain Res. **1202**, 14–24 (2008)
35. Trestman, M.: The Cambrian explosion and the origins of embodied cognition. Biol. Theory **8**(1), 80–92 (2013). https://doi.org/10.1007/s13752-013-0102-6
36. Turing, A.: Intelligent machinery, 1948. In: The Essential Turing, p. 395 (1969)
37. Turing, A.M.: Computing machinery and intelligence. In: Epstein, R., Roberts, G., Beber, G. (eds.) Parsing the Turing Test, pp. 23–65. Springer, Dordrecht (2009). https://doi.org/10.1007/978-1-4020-6710-5_3
38. Vanschoren, J.: Meta-learning: A survey. arXiv preprint arXiv:1810.03548 (2018)
39. Wang, J., Elfwing, S., Uchibe, E.: Modular deep reinforcement learning from reward and punishment for robot navigation. Neural Netw. **135**, 115–126 (2021)
40. Wang, R., Lehman, J., Clune, J., Stanley, K.O.: Paired open-ended trailblazer (POET): Endlessly generating increasingly complex and diverse learning environments and their solutions. arXiv preprint arXiv:1901.01753 (2019)
41. Weiss, K., Khoshgoftaar, T.M., Wang, D.: A survey of transfer learning. J. Big data **3**(1), 1–40 (2016)
42. Williams, S., Yaeger, L.: Evolution of neural dynamics in an ecological model. Geosciences **7**(3), 49 (2017)
43. Xie, Z., He, F., Fu, S., Sato, I., Tao, D., Sugiyama, M.: Artificial neural variability for deep learning: on overfitting, noise memorization, and catastrophic forgetting. Neural Comput. **33**(8), 1–30 (2020)
44. Yopak, K.E., Lisney, T.J., Darlington, R.B., Collin, S.P., Montgomery, J.C., Finlay, B.L.: A conserved pattern of brain scaling from sharks to primates. Proc. Nat. Acad. Sci. **107**(29), 12946–12951 (2010)

The Ecosystem Path to AGI

Claes Strannegård$^{(\boxtimes)}$, Niklas Engsner, Pietro Ferrari, Hans Glimmerfors,
Marcus Hilding Södergren, Tobias Karlsson, Birger Kleve, and Victor Skoglund

Department of Computer Science and Engineering, Chalmers University
of Technology and University of Gothenburg, Göteborg, Sweden
claes.strannegard@chalmers.se

Abstract. We start by discussing the link between ecosystem simulators and artificial general intelligence (AGI). Then we present the open-source ecosystem simulator Ecotwin, which is based on the game engine Unity and operates on ecosystems containing inanimate objects like mountains and lakes, as well as organisms, such as animals and plants. Animal cognition is modeled by integrating three separate networks: (i) a *reflex network* for hard-wired reflexes; (ii) a *happiness network* that maps sensory data such as oxygen, water, energy, and smells, to a scalar happiness value; and (iii) a *policy network* for selecting actions. The policy network is trained with reinforcement learning (RL), where the reward signal is defined as the happiness difference from one time step to the next. All organisms are capable of either sexual or asexual reproduction, and they die if they run out of critical resources. We report results from three studies with Ecotwin, in which natural phenomena emerge in the models without being hardwired. First, we study a terrestrial ecosystem with wolves, deer, and grass, in which a Lotka-Volterra style population dynamics emerges. Second, we study a marine ecosystem with phytoplankton, copepods, and krill, in which a diel vertical migration behavior emerges. Third, we study an ecosystem involving lethal dangers, in which certain agents that combine RL with reflexes outperform pure RL agents.

Keywords: Ecosystem · Neural networks · Happiness · Reflexes · Reinforcement learning

1 Animal Cognition

All organisms in nature are subject to natural selection and, where applicable, also sexual selection [1]. These forces operate on physical as well as cognitive properties of the organisms. One factor that contributes to the selection pressure on animal intelligence is other organisms. In fact, organisms coevolve with each other and are part of each other's environment. Intelligence may be an advantage in the "arms race" between predators and prey, in the competition for scarce resources, in collaborations with mutual benefits, and in sexual selection processes. Another factor that contributes to the selection pressure on intelligence

© Springer Nature Switzerland AG 2022
B. Goertzel et al. (Eds.): AGI 2021, LNAI 13154, pp. 269–278, 2022.
https://doi.org/10.1007/978-3-030-93758-4_28

is the terrain. In fact, animals must continuously handle challenges imposed by the terrain and adapt their behavior to local conditions when migrating, foraging, approaching prey, escaping predators, mating, and parenting.

To survive and reproduce, animals need to deal with a continuous stream of challenges in their lives. They must find food, avoid predators, navigate, and mate. Solving these challenges requires efficient information processing, in particular perception, decision-making, and action. Nervous systems are present in almost all taxa of the animal kingdom and play a key role in animal information processing. They are typically far from monolithic. For example, in humans, the complex nervous system that controls digestion is essentially separated from the brain and may operate even in a brain-dead person. The human brain itself is highly modular, with its anatomically distinct lobes and regions, such as the *Brain stem* which controls reflexes—positive, e.g., the knee reflex, and negative, e.g., the diving reflex; the *Prefrontal cortex*, which maps sensory signals to actions; and the *Insula*, which combines internal signals, such as blood sugar level and external signals, such as smells, into signals linked to happiness and reward [2].

Reflexes are critical to many animals [3]. For example, a newborn lamb might not have the time to find its way to its mother's udder through random trial and error. Instead, its early life hinges on an instinct that draws it to the smell of milk and a positive suck reflex that causes it to drink. The lamb might also benefit critically from negative reflexes that prevent it from eating lethal objects, inhaling liquid, or jumping from high cliffs. From an evolutionary perspective, one of the great advantages of nervous systems is that they enable learning, i.e., physical modification, and thereby efficient adaptation to the dangers and resources of the local environment. A prominent example of learning is reinforcement learning (RL), which is used across the animal kingdom [4,5]. Many animals combine untrainable reflex circuits with circuits that are trainable with RL. For instance, humans have hundreds of hardwired reflexes, e.g. the knee reflex, but we can also learn via RL. This enables us to combine the benefits of reflexes with the benefits of RL.

2   Models of Animal Cognition

There is a great number of computational models of animal cognition. In the "reflex tradition", animals are modeled as reflex agents, without the ability to learn. Such models might be adequate for animals with hardwired nervous systems that remain essentially unchanged during their lifetime. An example could be the famous nematode *C. elegans* [6]. Many biologically inspired algorithms, such as cellular automata, swarm algorithms, and ant algorithms, belong to this tradition and so does the subfield that studies populations of reflex agents powered by evolutionary algorithms.

In the "RL tradition", animals are modeled as RL agents. This field includes physical animal robots that get rewarded for fast crawling, running, swimming, or flying. It also includes homeostatic agents that get rewarded for keeping a set of homeostatic variables—like energy, water, and oxygen—close to their target values, or sweet spots [7,8]. RL algorithms have been shown to have a great potential for AI. For instance, they outperform humans at several video games and strategic board games [9]. There are also several agent-based ecosystem simulators that are based on RL [10–12].

In analytic approaches to ecosystem modeling, organisms are typically modeled with numbers representing population size or biomass and the interaction dynamics is modeled with systems of differential equations. There is no model of individual animals, no model of animal cognition, and no model of the terrain. Examples include the well-known Lotka-Volterra predator-prey dynamics [13]. The Ecopath (with Ecosim and Ecospace) simulator for marine ecosystems [14] divides maps of ecosystem into geographical cells, where each cell contains populations, for example, given as tonnes of phytoplankton, zooplankton, planktivores, and pescivores.

3   AI via Models of Animal Cognition

Nervous systems provided the original inspiration for the neural network model and its applications to supervised learning [15] and RL [5]. Some researchers try to copy animal brains in wetware or reproduce their connectome in software [6], others build computational models of the brain, sometimes called cognitive architectures [16]. Rather than aiming directly for a model of the brain, one may aim for a model of the process that led to the development of the brain. Since natural general intelligence emerged as the result of an evolutionary process that took place in an ecosystem, a natural strategy for creating AGI is to construct an ecosystem simulator that exploits the natural selection pressure on intelligence. This strategy is in line with Wilson's "animat path to AI" [17] and it enables a gradual approach to AI that starts with relatively simple ecosystems.

Section 4 of this paper presents the theoretical framework of the ecosystem simulator Ecotwin, which combines RL and reflexes. Section 8 presents simulation results, in which well-known patterns from population dynamics and ethology emerge. Section 12, finally, draws some conclusions.

4   Ecosystem Simulator

In this section, we present the theoretical framework of the ecosystem simulator Ecotwin. Ecotwin uses the game engine Unity with ML-Agents [10], which provides a graphical user interface, a physics engine, and several RL algorithms. More details about Ecotwin, including its open source code, can be found at www.ecotwin.se.

5   Ecosystems

We model *space* with a set $\mathcal{S} \subseteq \mathbb{R}^3$ and *time* with the numbers $0, 1, 2, \ldots$. The building blocks of our ecosystems are called *objects*. For instance, we could introduce cat objects, dandelion objects, and rock objects. Each object is assigned a set of object properties.

Definition 1 (Object properties). *The object properties are:*

- Physical properties *(measured in their respective SI units) such as Temperature, Mass, Pressure, Electric current, and Luminous intensity. Moreover, each object has a conformation, which is a subset of S.*
- Chemical properties *(measured in the SI unit molarity) are concentrations of chemical substances such as Oxygen, Nitrogen, Water, Carbon dioxide, Glucose, Salt, Sulfur, Fat, Protein, Estrogen, Testosterone, and Oxytocin.*
- Biological properties *such as Age (seconds), Sex (none, female, or male), and Fertility (a real number in $[0, 1]$).*

Note that the conformation of an object describes its shape and position in S. The physical and chemical properties of objects may be defined as aggregations of the properties of the points inside their conformations, e.g., the average temperature of a rock object. It is sometimes convenient to introduce additional properties. For example, to talk about cat objects, one may want to introduce properties such as Eye color, Paw size, Blood pressure, and Blood sugar.

Definition 2 (Inanimate objects). *An inanimate object in S consists of*

- *A type: for example Rock, Water, Road, Building*
- *A set of physical and chemical properties*

Definition 3 (Organisms). *An organism in S consists of*

- *A type: for example a particular species of bacteria, fungus, plant, or animal*
- *A genome consisting of a string over a finite alphabet*
- *A set of physical, chemical, and biological properties*
- *A nervous system consisting of a set of sensors S, where each sensor has a location in the conformation and a sensitivity to some physical or chemical property; a set of actions A, and three disjoint networks: a reflex network with input nodes S and output nodes A; a policy network with input nodes S and output nodes A; and a happiness network with input nodes S and a single output node for representing a scalar happiness value.*
- *A set of hyperparameters. These may include hyperparameters for training the policy network and for regulating reproduction and death. An example of a hyperparameter is age_max, which controls the maximum lifetime.*
- *A set of update rules:*
  - *Update rules for physical properties, e.g. how locomotion actions influence the conformation.*
  - *Update rules for chemical properties, e.g. how ingestion and locomotion actions influence the Glucose property.*

- *Update rules for biological properties specifying (i) the reproduction process, which may be sexual or asexual and involve mutation and crossover; and (ii) the physical and chemical properties that must be met for the organism to stay alive. For example, if Temperature is not inside a certain interval, or if Age > age_max, then the organism will die and thus become an inanimate object.*

The genome has two roles: (1) It encodes the organism at the start of its "life", in particular, it could encode its initial conformation (body shape), nervous system, and hyperparameters; (2) It is the input to the reproduction process, in which one or two genomes give rise to a new genome.

This definition of organism encompasses pure reflex agents (with an empty policy network), pure RL-agents (with an empty reflex network), and agents that combine reflexes with RL. By leaving the nervous system empty, we can also model agents lacking nervous systems altogether, such as bacteria and plants. It is often convenient to represent the reflex and happiness networks as hand-coded functions. If desired, these functions can easily be converted into neural networks, by using supervised learning. This step might be useful when applying mutations that add noise to connection weights.

Definition 4 (Ecosystem). *An ecosystem consists of*

- *A space $\mathcal{S} \subseteq \mathbb{R}^3$*
- *A set of inanimate objects in $\mathcal{S}$*
- *A set of organisms in $\mathcal{S}$.*

Several examples of ecosystems will be given in Sect. 8. The ecosystem is updated at each tick, using the physics mechanisms of Unity and the update rules of the organisms.

6   Decision-Making

This is how the nervous system is used for making decisions at time t:

1. For each sensor, read off its physical or chemical property at its current position. This produces a vector $\mathbf{x}$ that encodes the sensory input at t.
2. Give the input $\mathbf{x}$ to the Reflex network, which then outputs some vector $\mathbf{y}$, with component values -1, 0, or 1. The intended meanings of these values are, respectively, to block, accept, and force the corresponding action.
3. Also give the input $\mathbf{x}$ to the Policy network, which then selects an action a. Represent this action as a one-hot vector $\mathbf{z}$, where 1 is in the position of a.
4. Finally, compute the vector $H(\mathbf{y} + \mathbf{z})$. Here, $H((v_1, \ldots, v_n))$ is defined as $(h(v_1), \ldots, h(v_n))$, where $h(v_i)$ is 1 if $v_i > 0$ and 0 otherwise. This produces a multi-hot vector that constitutes the decision at t. Thus, the decision might be no action, one action, or many actions.

Now that we have seen how nervous systems are used for decision-making, let us consider a concrete example of a nervous system of a lamb model. The sensors, actions, and reflex network are shown in Fig. 1. The happiness network maps Glucose and Oxygen to a happiness value, so that ingestion and breathing are encouraged. An additional input could be Sheep_smell, so that the animal is encouraged to approach sheep: a hardwired social instinct. The policy network is trained using RL and updated at each time step. Thus, the animal might learn to breathe when Oxygen is low and move toward the strongest smell of milk when Glucose is low.

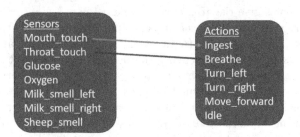

Fig. 1. A Reflex network. This network has sensors for touch (pressure) at two different locations of the conformation. It also has sensors for glucose and oxygen concentration in the blood stream, and for smell at different locations. The actions are for homeostatic regulation and locomotion. Only two connections have non-zero weights: one with weight +1 (green) and one with weight −1 (red). This produces a positive sucking reflex and a negative reflex that is similar to a diving reflex and prevents inhalation of liquid. (Color figure online)

7   Learning

The reflex and happiness networks develop through evolution only, and not through learning. In contrast, the policy network is updated at each time step via RL. The reward signal at time t is defined as $happiness(t) - happiness(t-1)$, where $happiness$ is computed by the happiness network. In the simulations discussed in this paper, we use the standard RL algorithm PPO [18] together with the animals' individual hyperparameters.

8   Results

We will present several results that were obtained using Ecotwin simulations. Videos of the simulations are available at www.ecotwin.se. Ecotwin can run on ecosystems populated with models of real organisms, imaginary organisms, or robots. In this section, we will consider simple models of real organisms. The properties and the mechanisms of our model organisms will be taken from the corresponding real organisms. In order to find a reasonable starting point, we initialize the policy networks randomly and then pre-train them with RL in Ecotwin, before turning on reproduction and starting the simulations.

9   Emergence of Predator-Prey Dynamics

Previous work in predator-prey dynamics has shown that a two-species predator-prey system, with agents trained through RL, exhibited Lotka-Volterra cycles under certain choices of parameters [12]. We wanted to explore whether a three-species system would also exhibit such cycles.

Our study concerns a three species predator-prey ecosystem with grass, deer, and wolves, as illustrated in Fig. 2 (Left). Deer and wolves have vision, which is modeled via Unity's ray casts, and gives the direction and distance to the closest visible objects of each type, within a certain radius [10]. Moreover, the deer can smell grass and wolves, while the wolves can smell deer. At each time step, each animal decides whether it should stand still, walk, or run forward. It also decides whether it should rotate left, right, or not at all. The happiness of the deer is determined by their Energy and Wolf smell sensors, whereas happiness of the wolves is determined by their Energy and Deer smell sensors. The deer obtains energy by eating grass and wolves by eating deer. The consumption of energy depends on the velocity of the animal. A simplified reproduction mechanism was used, where each animal had a probability of giving birth to a new agent, which was then spawned at a random unoccupied location in the ecosystem.

We ran two simulations with Ecotwin, starting with the same ecosystem. The result is shown in Fig. 2 (Right). As expected, given the dependence on randomness, the two simulations are different. In both simulations we see Lotka-Volterra cycles, with an increase in grass, followed by an increase in deer, followed by an increase in wolves, and similar decreases. More details about the study can be found in [19].

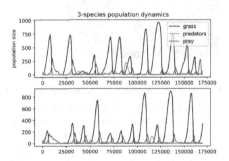

Fig. 2. Left: A three-species predator-prey ecosystem, with grass, deer and wolves. The red bars show happiness values. **Right:** Population dynamics from two different simulations. (Color figure online)

10   Emergence of Diel Vertical Migration

In this study, we consider a marine ecosystem with krill, copepods and phytoplankton, illustrated in Fig. 3 (Left). A diel light cycle was simulated, with the sun going up and down. We also simulated decreasing light intensity at greater depths. Three behaviors observed in real Copepods [20] were studied: (1) Diel Vertical Migration (DVM): a cyclic behavior in which Copepods migrate to the surface at night (enabling them to graze phytoplankton that are near the surface where the light is) and go down to greater and darker depths in the daytime (where the vision of predators such as krill is less efficient). (2) Quick escape reactions that enable Copepods to escape from predators. (3) Chemotaxis causing Copepods to avoid the smell of predators.

The Copepod models have a simple form of vision, by which they can perceive a rough direction and distance to near-by phytoplankton. Moreover, they can perceive light intensity, their own energy level, and whether they are touching food, krill, the environment's boundaries, or another Copepod. Their happiness value, yielding their reward, depends on energy and light intensity.

The Copepods and krill were pre-trained with RL for 1 million time steps. Then an Ecotwin simulation was run, starting with the ecosystem shown in Fig. 3 (Left). The behavioral patterns (1)–(3) were observed in the simulations. In particular, a clear DVM pattern was observed, as shown in Fig. 3 (Right). More information about the study can be found in [21].

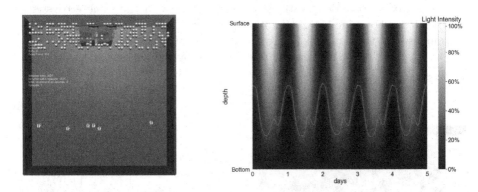

Fig. 3. Left: A marine environment with krill (orange), Copepods (yellow), and phytoplankton (green). The light intensity at different depths varies over time. This snapshot was taken at simulated daytime, when the Copepods are relatively far from the surface. **Right:** Mean vertical position of the copepods (red curve) over time. The light intensity is indicated by the background color. (Color figure online)

11   Emergence of Critical Reflexes

This study concerns the interplay between RL and reflexes. We consider a terrestrial ecosystem with goats and grass, illustrated in Fig. 4 (Left). There are three types of grass in the environment: green, yellow and red. The green grass is good for the goats to eat, the yellow grass is bad, but not deadly, whereas the red grass is deadly. The goats reproduce sexually and have a genome that encodes their policy networks and reflex networks. Thus, they may pass on genomes, including genes that code for reflexes, to their offspring. The goats have four different genes that we call red, yellow, green, and blue, for convenience. These genes correspond to a reflex which prevents a goat from eating red, yellow and green food objects, respectively. The blue gene does not affect a goat's reflexes.

An Ecotwin simulation was run with these organisms and the result is shown in Fig. 4 (Right). We can see several patterns: (1) The red gene eventually dominates the population. This is expected, as a reflex to avoid lethal food gives them a clear advantage. (2) The domination of the red gene suggests that the combination of reflexes and RL is more effective than RL alone when there are lethal dangers in the environment. Avoiding lethal food cannot be learned during a goat's life. (3) The yellow gene does not have a clear advantage over the blue gene. This suggests that the combination of reflexes and RL gives no advantage, that cannot be learned, over pure RL-agents when the dangers are not lethal. (4) The goats with the green gene keep dying out and then reappearing because of the mutation in the inheritance mechanisms. (5) A goat's genome may include multiple genes. This explains why the superior red gene does not dominate the population completely.

More details about the study can be found in [22].

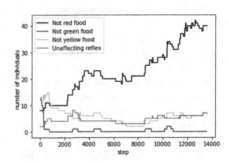

Fig. 4. Left: An ecosystem with goats, and three different types of grass objects: green = good, yellow = bad but non-lethal, and red = lethal. **Right:** The number of goats that have the red, yellow, green, and blue genes. (Color figure online)

12   Conclusion

We have presented the open source ecosystem simulator Ecotwin. It was run on three ecosystems, on which it reproduced certain population dynamics and behavioral patterns that can be observed in real ecosystems. Agent-based ecosystem simulators can be used for predicting the consequences of human interventions, e.g., via fishing, forestry, or urbanization. They might also be used as "general AI gyms", in which populations of agents coevolve in a fully automatic process, while taking advantage of the built-in selection pressure on intelligence. This research path toward general AI seems to be worthy of further exploration.

References

1. Darwin, C.: On the Origin of Species by Means of Natural Selection (1859). The complete work of Charles Darwin online. http://darwinonline.org.uk/
2. Nieuwenhuys, R.: The insular cortex: a review. In: Hofman, M.A., Falk, D. (eds.) Evolution of the Primate Brain, vol. 195 of Progress in Brain Research, pp. 123–163. Elsevier (2012)
3. Stein, R.B., Capaday, C.: The modulation of human reflexes during functional motor tasks. Trends Neurosci. **11**(7), 328–332 (1988)
4. Niv, Y.: Reinforcement learning in the brain. J. Math. Psychol. **53**(3), 139–154 (2009)
5. Neftci, E.O., Averbeck, B.B.: Reinforcement learning in artificial and biological systems. Nat. Mach. Intell. **1**(3), 133–143 (2019)
6. Xu, C.S., et al.: A connectome of the adult drosophila central brain. BioRxiv (2020)
7. Keramati, M., Gutkin, B.: A reinforcement learning theory for homeostatic regulation. In: Advances in Neural Information Processing Systems, pp. 82–90 (2011)
8. Yoshida, N.: Homeostatic agent for general environment. J. Artif. Gen. Intell. **8**(1), 1–22 (2017)
9. Badia, A.P., et al.: Agent57: outperforming the Atari human benchmark. In: International Conference on Machine Learning, pp. 507–517. PMLR (2020)
10. Lanham, M.: Learn Unity ML-Agents-Fundamentals of Unity Machine Learning: Incorporate New Powerful ML Algorithms Such as Deep Reinforcement Learning for Games. Packt Publishing Ltd. (2018)
11. Sunehag, P., et al.: Reinforcement learning agents acquire flocking and symbiotic behaviour in simulated ecosystems. In: Artificial Life Conference Proceedings, pp. 103–110. MIT Press (2019)
12. Yamada, J., Shawe-Taylor, J., Fountas, Z.: Evolution of a complex predator-prey ecosystem on large-scale multi-agent deep reinforcement learning. In: 2020 International Joint Conference on Neural Networks (IJCNN), pp. 1–8. IEEE (2020)
13. Lotka, A.J.: Elements of Physical Biology. Williams & Wilkins (1925)
14. Christensen, V., Walters, C.J.: Ecopath with Ecosim: methods, capabilities and limitations. Ecol. Model. **172**(2–4), 109–139 (2004)
15. Zador, A.M.: A critique of pure learning and what artificial neural networks can learn from animal brains. Nat. Commun. **10**(1), 1–7 (2019)
16. Kotseruba, I., Tsotsos, J.K.: 40 years of cognitive architectures: core cognitive abilities and practical applications. Artif. Intell. Rev. **53**(1), 17–94 (2020)
17. Wilson, S.W.: The Animat path to AI. MIT Press (1991). Is part of: From Animals to Animats: Proceedings of the First International Conference on Simulation of Adaptive Behavior (J. A. Meyer and S. W. Wilson, eds.), pp. 15–21
18. Schulman, J., Wolski, F., Dhariwal, P., Radford, A., Klimov, O.: Proximal policy optimization algorithms. arXiv preprint arXiv:1707.06347 (2017)
19. Karlsson, T.: Multi-agent deep reinforcement learning in a three-species predator-prey ecosystem. Master's thesis, Chalmers (2021)
20. Seuront, L.: Copepods: Diversity, Habitat and Behavior. Nova Science Publishers (2014)
21. Ferrari, P., Kleve, B.: A generic model of motivation in artificial animals based on reinforcement learning. Master's thesis, Chalmers (2021)
22. Glimmerfors, H., Skoglund, V.: Combining reflexes and reinforcement learning in evolving ecosystems for artifical animals. Master's thesis, Chalmers (2021)

On Comparative Analysis of Rule-Based Cognitive Architectures

Yury Kolonin[1(✉)] and Evgenii Vityaev[1,2]

[1] Mathematics and Mechanics Department, Novosibirsk State University,
Novosibirsk, Russia
[2] Sobolev Institute of Mathematics SD RAS, Novosibirsk, Russia

Abstract. We consider two cognitive architectures which are designed to proceed goal-directed behavior. One of them, Theory of Functional Systems, is developed on the basis of the eponymous biological theory. The other, Non-Axiomatic Reasoning System or NARS, utilizes the formal logic apparatus and weighted probabilistic choice to proceed its inference. The architectures were scrutinized and decomposed and a number of conclusions have been drawn about their advantages and disadvantages regarding the goal-directed behavior processing.

Keywords: Cognitive architectures · Theory of functional systems · Non-axiomatic reasoning · Adaptive control system · Purposeful behavior · Goal-directed behavior

1 Introduction

Theory of Functional Systems (hereafter referred to as TFS) is a rule-based cognitive architecture that is based on the eponymous biological theory. The main concepts of this theory are goal, goal-directed behavior, result and criterion of achievement. The architecture is designed to be used for controlling agents' behavior in various environments.

A set of corresponding experiments that were conducted in the last few years shows that TFS is quite effective both when it performs tasks by itself and when compared with other control methods, such as neural networks and Q-learning [1].

We have given a talk, describing inner mechanisms and details of TFS architecture along with biological considerations that inspired it, at the AGI-2020 conference. After the conference we were contacted by Pei Wang, the lead developer of NARS. That is another cognitive architecture that is in development for nearly two decades and is rather well-known in the AGI community. After this, while considering possible options for the next steps in our scientific work, we decided that we should do a comparative analysis of TFS and NARS architectures.

The second author financially supported by the Russian Foundation for Basic Research# 19-01-00331-a

B. Goertzel et al. (Eds.): AGI 2021, LNAI 13154, pp. 279–282, 2022.
https://doi.org/10.1007/978-3-030-93758-4_29

This might serve several purposes. To begin with, NARS is mostly an "engineering-based" system, whose underlying ideas are based mostly on formal logic. Foundations of TFS, in turn, encompass a strong biological theory that describes the nature of behavior and reasonable action. Direct comparison of "biological" and "engineering" approaches should be a worthy and interesting study by itself.

At the same time some parallels can be seen in architectures' internal structure. The working algorithm of both systems can be decomposed into parts, and some of the parts that perform the same functions theoretically might be interchangeable between the systems. Considering both systems are still in active development, analysis of such architecture details might help both systems see their actual flaws and become an inspiration for algorithm modifications and improvements. And, of course, such work might bring attention of the community to both architectures.

2   NARS Architecture

The comprehensive description of internal structure of TFS was given in the corresponding article last year [2].

Let us propose a brief description of NARS architecture. The main concept that underlies NARS is the so-called Assumption of Insufficient Knowledge and Resources. It states that "an intelligent system should be able to solve problems using insufficient knowledge and resources" [3]. So, the whole system is designed to work with computational resources of any scarcity, including CPU power and disk space. For example, every operation in the inference cycle is designed to be executed in nearly constant time.

The system language, Narsese, supports four types of sentences, which are statements, questions, goals and quests. Statements represent system knowledge about the environment and thus have truth-values. Questions represent knowledge that the system does not possess but which is crucial for it to solve its tasks. Questions do not have a truth-value, but the answer to the question is a statement with corresponding truth-value. Goals are some events that the system wants to become true; instead of truth-values these sentences have desire-values, which are a sort of "measure of desire" for the system. At last, quests are in fact a sort of questions that seek for a goal as an answer.

The base unit of information in NARS is so-called concepts, which are stored in a special data structure named bag. Bag is a set of objects with a priority value assigned to each object. This data structure supports three operations: put a new item into it, take the exact item from it and take non-specific item. When the system performs the third operation, the choice is made probabilistically with accordance to priority values of the items. The maximum number of elements is set for the bag; if this number is reached, the item with the least priority is removed from the bag whenever a new item is put into it. If the system identifies the freshly-put item as a copy of an item already existing in the bag, they are merged together and the priority value of the ancestor is increased.

NARS consists of a bag of concepts, where each concept is named by some term of Narsese (e.g. <cat –> animal>, which can be translated into English as "cats are animals"). Each concept comprises a bag of task-links (which are links to some Narsese sentences that system processes depending on sentence type), a bag of term-links (bi-directional links that connect concepts depending on its content) and, if a concept corresponds to compound (non-atomic) term, two lists that contain actual beliefs and goals corresponding to the concept. For example, a concept *<cat –> animal>* will have a task-link to task *<cat –> animal>.* (the dot at the end means the task is a statement), term-links to concepts cat and animal and tables for goals and beliefs, while concept cat will have a task-link to task *<cat –> animal>* a term-link to concept *<cat –> animal>* and no tables since it corresponds to atomic term.

The lifecycle of NARS consists of a sequence of repeating steps:

- get a concept from the memory,
- get a task and belief from the concept,
- derive new tasks from the selected task and belief,
- put the involved items back and new tasks into the corresponding bags.

When two premises are taken by the inference engine, NARS looks through the logic inference rules that might be applied depending on the properties of the premises. Depending on the form, each rule has its own way to calculate the priority value of the conclusion (for example, the deduction rule conclusion would have much more priority than the induction, other things being equal). All of the possible results are produced and processed; if their priority value goes beyond threshold, they are introduced into the system and put into the corresponding data structures.

3   Comparison

After exploring the inner structure and principles of NARS, we have proceeded to compare two systems. Since TFS is designed to carry out nothing but purposeful action, while NARS is positioned as a "wide profile" system, we have compared the ways each system processes the goal-directed activity in particular.

The most noticeable difference between two approaches is their attitude towards randomness. TFS does not include it in its system; actually, it performs random actions only during the initial stage of its life cycle, when the agent does not have any experience about the environment. From the ending of this stage, the system operates purely in accordance with the rules it had discovered to the moment, always choosing the action that has the highest "success rate" in the actual situation.

NARS, in its turn, uses random choice at every iteration of its working cycle. This applies not only to the ways of achieving the goal, but even to the current goal choice. NARS can process multiple tasks simultaneously: since on every iteration of the inference cycle the working concept is chosen anew, there might be another task chosen or another goal pursued. While this "wideness of choice" might give the system additional flexibility in its choices, it also might cause a problem: if there exists a single specific way to achieve a goal, the system might find it hard to "concentrate" on it, spending its resources on multiple secondary observations and conclusions.

While these nuances and their handling might become a debatable moment, there is one single aspect in which TFS is significantly ahead of NARS. An intellectual system should be able to efficiently discover causal relationships based on its experience.

In NARS this feature is realized the same way as other inference: that is, when the event A is followed by the event B, the system might mark them as cause and effect via induction rule, the sentence of form $<A=/>B>$. being derived. However, any two events that happen to occur one after another might be connected this way; if the stream of incoming information is broad, there might be a high rate of "false positive" conclusions. At the same time, already discovered relations do not affect this process; they can only be merged together if the same result is derived more than one time.

TFS, in turn, utilizes Fisher's exact test to discover statistically significant coincidences. This is done by analyzing the history of the agent's actions and what has happened as their result. After the initial set of rules is discovered, the agent's behavior becomes goal-oriented as it uses the rules to achieve its goal; whenever the rule is applied, the results of action are evaluated and the "success rate" of the rule is adjusted depending on it.

Considering all the reasoning above, we come to conclusion that TFS is more suitable for goal-directed behavior processing at the given moment. However, the decomposition of systems has shown that it is possible to transfer some mechanisms from one system to another, thus creating somewhat of a "hybrid architecture".

For example, the idea of transferring the bag structure to TFS is of great interest to us. The idea of weighted probability choice might somehow change the behavior of TFS agents in experiments and it would be interesting to compare the results. Also, while the main advantage of NARS is its high computational efficiency, some elements of the architecture might be adapted for usage in TFS to reduce its computational costs. We look towards such experiments in the nearest future.

Vice versa, while studying NARS, we have come up with several ideas for potential improvements of its architecture with already existing TFS features. The simplest idea is modifying the NARS agents oriented for procedural inference via adding the "random steps" stage in the beginning of agents' life cycle. We also consider more complex ideas, such as implementing parts of probabilistic law detection algorithm from TFS to NARS: that might be useful in cases where the system can "buy" some efficiency for the cost of computational costs.

Considerations above are mostly theoretical; as two systems have revealed much unlikeness in their nature, the empiric comparison via correct and fair experiment remains a complex task. We look towards it among other activities and probably will publish some result regarding such research in the future.

References

1. Demin, A., Vityaev, E.: Animal control system based on semantic probabilistic inference. Bulletin of the Novosibirsk Computing Center, volume of A.P. Ershov Institute of informatics systems, series: Computer Science, issue 24, pp. 57–72 (2006)
2. Vityaev, E.E., Demin, A.V., Kolonin, Y.A.: Logical probabilistic biologically inspired cognitive architecture. In: Goertzel, B., Panov, A.I., Potapov, A., Yampolskiy, R. (eds.) AGI 2020. LNCS (LNAI), vol. 12177, pp. 337–346. Springer, Cham (2020). https://doi.org/10. 1007/978-3-030-52152-3_36
3. Wang, P.: Non-axiomatic logic: A model of intelligent reasoning. World Scientific (2013)

20NAR1 - An Alternative NARS Implementation Design

Robert Wünsche[(✉)]

IMA Dresden, Dresden, Germany

Abstract. An implementation of a Non-Axiomatic Reasoning System-inspired system is presented in this paper. This implementation features a goal system which features deep derivation depths, which allows the system to solve moderately complicated problems. The reasoner is utilizing Non-Axiomatic Logic for procedural and non-procedural reasoning. Most of the internal tasks are done under the Assumption of Insufficient Knowledge and Resources fulfilling various timing and resource constraints.

1 Introduction

This paper presents a Non-Axiomatic Reasoning System (NARS) implementation named 20NAR1. The system is operating in real-time [1] and always open to new stimulus and knowledge, making it able to adapt to changes in its environment (R4 in [2]). Planning, and the ability to do so effectively, is a core part of this system. It is performed continuously, incrementally and in real-time (R5 in [2]), utilizing a layered structure (a grouping by derivation depths and involved terms) which allows for deeper planning depths. This allows this implementation to tackle problems which need deeper planning depths than the problems previous NARS implementations have been tried on, leading to better performance especially in board games. All of the systems capabilities are respecting the Assumption of Insufficient Knowledge and Resources (AIKR, [1,3,4]) as a key working assumption to keep computational resources (both storage capacity and processor time demands per inference step) in bounds during operation.

2 Assumptions

20NAR1's design is heavily inspired by the non-axiomatic reasoning system (NARS). Representation of the procedural knowledge, more fundamentally the truth value of beliefs, differs from OpenNARS for Applications (ONA) [5] and OpenNARS for Research (ONR) [6] in fundamental ways. The system utilizes a non-axiomatic representation for the beliefs of procedural knowledge as done in Autocatalytic endogenous reflective architecture (AERA) [7,8], where the evidence is explicitly counted. The confidence of the truth value of the belief is computed by the formula $c = \frac{|e|}{|e|+1}$ as in [7] on demand. This allows exact recording

© Springer Nature Switzerland AG 2022
B. Goertzel et al. (Eds.): AGI 2021, LNAI 13154, pp. 283–291, 2022.
https://doi.org/10.1007/978-3-030-93758-4_30

of the evidence without resorting to an explicit representation of the frequency and confidence as done in all publicly accessible NARS implementations such as ONR and ONA.

The process of the design of this system was inspired by the need of the system to be able to plan and execute plans in complicated and complex environments. The non-temporal mechanisms were added shortly after a basic prototype of the temporal mechanisms were working in a Pong environment.

The reasoning processes for temporal and non-temporal inference are strictly separated. This is different to a "true" unified reasoner, where both responsibilities are carried out by the same reasoning machinery.

One reasoner deals only with non-temporal inference (NAL1-6, [9,10]), while another deals only with temporal inference and procedural learning (NAL7-9, [9,10]). This design decision was chosen to make the reasoning more efficient than in other implementations [5,6]. Another reason was that a unified approach wasn't necessary for the tested problems, which are inspired by the expected uses of this system. Another advantage is that the two processes may run with true concurrency side by side. This property will be maintained, even if the two processes need knowledge from the other or have to exchange knowledge. Examples for the exchange of knowledge is a non-temporal rule such as $<(a \ \&\& \ b) ==> d>>$, where the predicate is temporal knowledge and has to get stored in the temporal memory. Inference on temporal knowledge where premises are non-temporal has to retrieve the knowledge from the non-temporal memory. This will be the case in tasks such as the toothbrush "problem solving" [11] problem as demonstrated in ONA and ONR.

Further separation of concerns (SOC) was done in the design of the temporal reasoner. Different parts are responsible for perception, revision, decision making, forward planning and backward planning. Please note that the utilized logic is NAL, which implies that all the knowledge is derived according to NAL inference rules and stored in a way that term structure is exploited.

The system is currently completely implemented in the Rust language[1]. Requirements for the language were a modern language, comparatively fast development, fast run-time execution, modern non-manual memory management.

Overall, the system is constructed with these key assumptions in mind:

- **AIKR** The system has to fully work under Assumption of insufficient knowledge and resources (AIKR) **realtime operation**
  reasoning cycles don't take more time than a given soft limit
- **interactive operation** the cycles happen relatively fast on a machine available today[2] (100 ms, sub 100 ms).

---

[1] Source code is available at https://github.com/PtrMan/20NAR1.
[2] In 2021 on a quad-core CPU.

3   Memory System

Temporal. The memory system used to store temporal beliefs (which allows for the easy retrieval of knowledge for planning purposes) follows the ALANN [12] memory model: Beliefs are stored in concepts by term and sub-terms. The policy to manage memory to keep its resource requirements bounded is to sort concepts by maximum truth expectation (whereby truth expectation $f_{exp}(f, c) = c * (f - \frac{1}{2}) + \frac{1}{2}$), keeping only the top N concepts.

Non-temporal. The memory system used to store non-temporal (semantic/declarative) beliefs follows the ALANN memory model as well: beliefs are stored in concepts, whereby the concept's term has to be a sub-term (or the term itself) of the belief's stored within. This allows for easily sub-term-based retrieval of a second premise, as for this kind of inference it's required to share a term with the first. The policy for memory management is: sort concepts by maximum of truth expectation of their beliefs, again only keeping the top N concepts.

4   Temporal Deriver

Goal System

Memory Management
A set of active goals is maintained by the goal system. This set is bound to be below a maximum count of goals by throwing irrelevant goals (of low desire value) away in fixed time intervals, to keep the system under AIKR.

Goal Derivation
Goals are sampled with a probabilistic bag-like mechanism where access frequency is positively correlated with the priority of the items stored within. Goals are then combined with beliefs to derive goals, which are fed back as goals into the goal system.

Goal System Bias
Goals are grouped by derivation depth (amount of inference steps from input) for more uniform derivation of deeper or shallow goals. Goals in these groups are grouped by term, and sampled by depth, to bias derivation to deeper goals. Else it would sample more shallow goals if this grouping and sampling wouldn't exist.

Desire Value (DV) of goals is stored as an explicit frequency and confidence tuple as done in all NARS implementations [5, 6], whereby the desire value is the truth value of the belief that the fulfillment of the goal leads to a desired virtual state [10].

Planning is done by deriving goals by the deduction rule with a goal and a predictive implication as premises [13]. This planning process is different from a question-driven planning process, as discussed in [14].

Temporal Representation and Inference

- The time interval between an antecedent and consequent of a predictive implication is represented as a exponential interval, as done in OpenNARS (ONR) [6].
  Multiple such beliefs exist for different intervals, all with possibly different evidence and truth value [8].
  Justification: exponential intervals were chosen because the evidence for different delays can be stored separately in different beliefs. This makes the reasoner able to disambiguate situations which only differ in timing.
- Events from which predictive implications are derived are assumed to be of binary truth (happening or not happening, or $f \in \{0.0, 1.0\}, c < 1.0$) in the current implementation.
  This is similar to the handling in AERA, where only predictive implications have a truth value of Non-Axiomatic Logic [8] attached to them.
  Justification: Confidence of the events is assumed to be 1.0, because the confidence isn't utilized in any environment so far. Future implementations can store a confidence of the events, the confidence of the predictive implication can get multiplied by the products of all confidence values of all events of its premises (by deduction rule [1]).
- The procedural reasoner only does revision for beliefs where the term of the sentence is equal and the interval is equal as well.

Prediction-Based Decision Making

- Forward depth first planning until either a goal is hit or the maximum depth limit (as defined by a system parameter) is reached [8].
- Decision is based on first predictive implication sequence evidence which truth expectation is above decision threshold (a system parameter). It is computed on the result of the whole planned event chain computed with deduction [1]
  Justification: prediction based decision making was added to the system, because the backward deriving process usually doesn't have enough resources (time, memory space) to derive and store the temporal knowledge necessary for decision making, represented as predictive implications $<(a,\ \hat{}op) = />b>$, in complicated environments.
- Decision making is implemented in the procedural reasoner where the system has to react to incoming events [15]. The mechanism of decision making is explained in more detail in a later chapter.

FIFO. Events are stored in a first in, first out (FIFO) data structure as done in ONA [5]. The FIFO is sampled to build predictive implications whereby the antecedent is always an *(event, operation)* sequence, for example $<(a,\ \hat{}x) = />b>$. A sampling strategy selects the premises by some (dynamically adjusted) distribution over the observed time-distance to the current "now" and other factors, such as the truth value of the event, frequency of occurrence, current goals etc. The current implemented sampling strategy is sampling events with a uniform distribution, which is independent on the truth value of the event, frequency of occurrence and current goals. This design decision was made to keep the system as simple as necessary for the tested environments and expected environments of its operation in the near future.

Procedural/Q&A Bridge. The most recent implementation[3] of 20NAR1 has a bridge which allows that knowledge from the non-temporal reasoner is used from the temporal reasoner for decision making. This is realized by adding questions when a goal with a condition has to be realized to query the non-temporal reasoner for the required information. An answer to the question is interpreted as a "virtual" (virtual as not really happened in the environment) event to trigger the operation. And example:

```
// Goal which is added to the goal system
(<#1 —> A>, ^X)! :|:
// Question which is derived from the condition of the goal
<?1 —> A>?
// Answer found by non–temporal Q\&A system
<B —> A>.
```

5   Non-temporal Deriver

Q&A. Question Answering is supported by reasoning on declarative knowledge. The reasoner supports the processing of multiple concurrent questions, which are processed in a time sharing manner[4]. Reasoning on the declarative knowledge is done with NAL-rules as described by the NARS-theory, while utilizing the common-term property of premises by exploiting the structure of the memory. This part is also most similar to the other implementations, even though some details do vary. For instance, whether implications form nodes in memory to allow for a uniform design of the derivation pipeline (such as in OpenNARS), or whether they form links for efficient subgoaling and planning, such as in ONA and 20NAR1. Additionally, the chosen set of inference rules differs between implementations, though the most fundamental ones (such as NAL-1 syllogistic rules and NAL-7 temporal induction) are included in all complete ones.

6   Overall System

Cognitive mechanisms in this work capture several "complex functional adaptations" [16], that is, complicated methods which implement some crucial cognitive capability of the agent.

---

[3] At the time of writing. This may be implemented with a more unified approach as done in ONA.

[4] This functionality was added to help external AI with Q&A, else the external AI has to keep track of it's own questions and ask NAR again for a question which it is processing.

- **Anticipation** Anticipation is a mechanism to collect negative evidence for procedural knowledge [6], which attributes negative evidence to such when the antecedent happens but the consequent does not occur.
- **Motor babbling** Especially initially, the agent has to be able to gather information about what happens as a consequence when it invokes operators under the currently observed conditions. This is done with motor babbling, which is a mechanism which picks a random operator after a precondition was observed. The effects are recorded and may later be used for realizing particular matching goals [5].
- **Decision making** Decision making is realized with the decision rule. It states that the decision is made by calling the operation of the sequence if the expectation of the operation goal is above the system's decision threshold [15].
- **Predictive decision making** Predictive decision making is decision making which is invoked when creating a prediction which "hits" a (derived) goal. Checking for a hit of a goal may be implemented with a hash table lookup. It is currently implemented with a scan of a table of all goals to keep the complexity of the implementation low.
- **Adaptive resource scheduler** A big problem in any design, because of AIKR, is how to distribute resources (which can be CPU cycles or memory) among the different processes. One requirement is that the time of a reasoning cycle is not longer than a given (soft) limit. This supports a system to work in real-time with a given interactivity (a system that finishes a cycle is more responsive and thus more interactive).

  An adaptive scheme is used in the latest published version of 20NAR1. A scheduler has a time quota (which is similar to the quota as described for EURISKO [17]) which can be "filled up" till the end of the cycle. This is implemented with an arg-max utility based decision procedure where the utility measures how urgent a given compute procedure is [18]. Ending the cycle is always given a utility of 1.0. The utility functions of the procedures to select take the remaining time of the cycle into account. An advantage of this mechanism is that the selection of the internal action is not predetermined by the program. Pseudocode for the algorithm is below.

```
while True {
    double dt = (timeStart.elapsed().as_micros() as f32)/1000000.0

    // decide about resource distribution with max utility
    (f32, String) winner = (1.0, ''CYCLEFIN''.to_string())

    // compute utilities of internal actions
    for i_action in actions { // iterate over all actions
        let utility:f32 = i_action.calcUtility();
        if utility > winner.0 {
            winner = (utility, i_action.name)
        }
    }

    // execute action which won this round
    if &winner.1 == ''CYCLEFIN'' {
        // finish the cycle because we invested enough resources
```

```
      break;
    }
    else  if  &winner.1  ==  ''GOALDERIV''  {  //  derive  goal
      NarGoalSystem :: sampleAndInference (nar . goalSystem ,  otherARGS );
    }
}
```

Commands. Commands are implemented to give instructions to the interface between user-input and the NAR itself. Commands are indicated with a ! sign at the first position of the line. Such a functionality was first implemented in OpenNARS, but the basic idea is similar to the commands in GDB or radare2[5],[6].

NAL-9. NAL-9 [10] is largely concerned about mental operations the system can invoke, which give the system the ability to influence its inference control process actively. Mental operations can be considered a special case of operation which influence the system itself rather than some actuator (such as a motor). Currently only a helper operator, ^nal9_exeAndInject, is implemented. This operator executes other operators, which are given as a parameter in a sequence, followed by a event to indicate the completion of the sequence of operators.

7 Experiments

Experiments were carried out to evaluate how well the implemented mechanisms perform when they interact with each other. This chapter lists most of the experimental results and corresponding evaluation scores, which were obtained in Pong and Tic Tac Toe (Fig. 1).

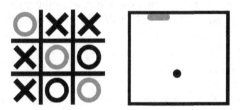

Fig. 1. Tic Tac Toe and Pong

Pong. The tested Pong environment was taken from the ONA Pong environment without a stop action. The result reaches a success ratio of 0.5–0.61, which is way better than random (0.05) but worse than what ONA can achieve.

Tic Tac Toe. Tic Tac Toe (TTT) was chosen as a simple and yet complicated environment where the agent has to learn and plan deep enough to consistently win the game. The test consisted of a game of TTT in each epoch. Only a fixed number of epochs were done till the test was terminated. A goal to win was fed

---

[5] It is a reverse engineering tool https://rada.re/n/radare2.html.
[6] Important here is that the commands have a nested structure to specify categories of commands.

into the system at the beginning of every epoch. All operations of TTT have a high evidence value, which leads to a high evidence value with confidence close to 1.0 of the derived predictive implication sentences. This was done, because long chains of temporal relations lead to a low confidence, possibly below the decision threshold, which prevents a NARS to use knowledge for long chains. Another reason is that a NARS has to observe the observation just once to use the procedural knowledge even for deep goal planning. Anticipation was disabled, because only positive knowledge was considered in this particular experiment. Also, an event (f = 1.0, c = 1.0) with the term equal to the goal was fed to the system when the epoch was won. No event was fed to the system if the epoch was either lost or when it ended in a draw.

Results: 13 Full games were done with 500 games each. The NAR was configured to keep 1000 active goals in memory. A success ratio was computed utilizing the number of won games and the number of total games. The minimum of the ratio was 1.48837, maximum 3.85714, average 2.26294, median 2.15441, variance 0.49854 and standard deviation 0.70607171.

Natural Language Processing. NLP is not directly supported in the current code-base. A script to parse simple relationships is provided in the current master branch of the codebase. Inputs are in the form of relations similar to predicates in first order logic. One example is can (Tim, dance). Every relation get transformed to narsese sentences which represent the relationship, ex: <(Tim * dance) → can>. The "is" relationship has a special handling to emit both an "is" relation and the → (inheritance) copula. The "is" relationship is emitted in addition, because it allows the NAR to perform specific inferences utilizing this relationship, which is not possible when inheritance is emitted alone.

This functionality can later be used to build more complex NLP/NLU channels on top of it.

8 Conclusion

A new NARS implementation was presented. Its mechanisms, most of which were not present in any previous implementation, or described in the literature[7], were implemented in the program and described in this paper. An evaluation on two benchmark environments, Pong and Tic Tac Toe, was presented. Also, the importance of a goal system with the ability for deep planning was highlighted and evaluated. This is also a key contribution of this work, and having a goal system which features resource-sparing deep goal derivation paths can potentially also be beneficial for other NARS implementations.

In the future, more focus will be put on the capability to alienate important derived goals (allowing them to become permanent long-term goals), since it allows the agent to develop a goal system from experience which allows it to tackle more complex environments under resource constraints. This will be a core part of next research and development. Other potentially missing mechanisms to deal with complicated environments will get examined as well.

---

[7] Referring to proto-AGI systems in accordance to the beliefs of the author.

References

1. Wang, P.: Non-axiomatic reasoning system: exploring the essence of intelligence. Citeseer (1995)
2. Nivel, E., et al.: Bounded recursive self-improvement. arXiv preprint arXiv:1312.6764 (2013)
3. Wang, P.: Insufficient knowledge and resources-a biological constraint and its functional implications. In: AAAI Fall Symposium: Biologically Inspired Cognitive Architectures. Citeseer (2009)
4. Wang, P.: The assumptions on knowledge and resources in models of rationality. Int. J. Mach. Conscious. **3**(01), 193–218 (2011)
5. Hammer, P., Lofthouse, T.: 'OpenNARS for applications': architecture and control. In: Goertzel, B., Panov, A.I., Potapov, A., Yampolskiy, R. (eds.) AGI 2020. LNCS (LNAI), vol. 12177, pp. 193–204. Springer, Cham (2020). https://doi.org/10.1007/978-3-030-52152-3_20
6. Hammer, P., Lofthouse, T., Wang, P.: The OpenNARS implementation of the non-axiomatic reasoning system. In: Steunebrink, B., Wang, P., Goertzel, B. (eds.) AGI-2016. LNCS (LNAI), vol. 9782, pp. 160–170. Springer, Cham (2016). https://doi.org/10.1007/978-3-319-41649-6_16
7. Helgason, H.P., Thórisson, K.R., Nivel, E., Wang, P.: Predictive heuristics for decision-making in real-world environments. In: Kühnberger, K.-U., Rudolph, S., Wang, P. (eds.) AGI 2013. LNCS (LNAI), vol. 7999, pp. 50–59. Springer, Heidelberg (2013). https://doi.org/10.1007/978-3-642-39521-5_6
8. Nivel, E., Thórisson, K.R., Dindo, H., Pezzulo, G., Rodriguez, M., et al.: Autocatalytic endogenous reflective architecture (2013)
9. Wang, P.: Non-axiomatic logic (NAL) specification, vol. 19. University of Camerino, Piazza Cavour (2010)
10. Wang, P.: Non-Axiomatic Logic: A Model of Intelligent Reasoning (2013)
11. Wang, P.: Case-by-case problem solving. In: 2009 Proceedings of the 2nd Conference on Artificial General Intelligence, pp. 200–205. Atlantis Press (2009)
12. Lofthouse, T.: ALANN: an event driven control mechanism for a nonaxiomatic reasoning system (NARS) (2019)
13. Hammer, P., Lofthouse, T.: Goal-directed procedure learning. In: Iklé, M., Franz, A., Rzepka, R., Goertzel, B. (eds.) AGI 2018. LNCS (LNAI), vol. 10999, pp. 77–86. Springer, Cham (2018). https://doi.org/10.1007/978-3-319-97676-1_8
14. Wang, P.: Solving a problem with or without a program. J. Artif. Gen. Intel. **3**(3), 43 (2012)
15. Wang, P., Hammer, P.: Assumptions of decision-making models in AGI. In: Bieger, J., Goertzel, B., Potapov, A. (eds.) AGI 2015. LNCS (LNAI), vol. 9205, pp. 197–207. Springer, Cham (2015). https://doi.org/10.1007/978-3-319-21365-1_21
16. Yudkowsky, E.: Levels of organization in general intelligence. In: Goertzel, B., Pennachin, C. (eds.) Artificial General Intelligence. Cognitive Technologies, pp. 389–501. Springer, Heidelberg (2007). https://doi.org/10.1007/978-3-540-68677-4_12
17. Lenat, D.B.: Eurisko: a program that learns new heuristics and domain concepts: the nature of Heuristics III: program design and results. Artif. Intell. **21**(1–2), 61–98 (1983)
18. Russell, S., Wefald, E.: Principles of metareasoning. Artif. Intell. **49**(1–3), 361–395 (1991)

The Gap Between Intelligence and Mind

Bowen Xu[1] , Xinyi Zhan[2] , and Quansheng Ren[1(✉)]

[1] Department of Electronics, Peking University, Beijing 100871, China
{xubowen,qsren}@pku.edu.cn
[2] Department of Philosophy and Religious Studies, Peking University,
Beijing 100871, China
zhanxinyi@pku.edu.cn

Abstract. The feeling (quale) brings the "Hard Problem" to philosophy of mind. Does the subjective feeling have a non-ignorable impact on Intelligence? If so, can the feeling be realized in Artificial Intelligence (AI)? To discuss the problems, we have to figure out what the feeling means, by giving a clear definition. In this paper, we primarily give some mainstream perspectives on the topic of the mind, especially the topic of the feeling (or qualia, subjective experience, *etc.*). Then, a definition of the feeling is proposed through a thought experiment, the "semi-transparent room". The feeling, roughly to say, is defined as "a tendency of changing input representations by representing its inner state". Also, a formalized definition is given. The definition does not help to verify "having the feeling", but it helps to provide evidence. Based on the definition, we think these are the hard problems of intelligence – whether the "innate" feeling plays an important role in Intelligence, whether the difference between the "simulated" feeling and the "innate" feeling will have a significant influence on Artificial General Intelligence (AGI), and, if so, where the "innate" feeling comes from and how to make an artificial agent possess it.

Keywords: Intelligence · Feeling · Definition · Adaptability · Mind

1 Background

There may be a gap between intelligence and mind, that is, the *feeling* – how can an objective agent have the subjective feeling?

We must primarily clarify on the related concepts involved. The *mind* in this paper refers to the *conscious mind*, and the *consciousness* refers in particular to *phenomenal consciousness* or called *subjective experience* that has *qualia* [11]. The *feeling* discussed in this paper is a kind of phenomenal consciousness. It is emphasized that the *feeling* in this paper is subjective, which means it is private, unable to represented, and truly experienced by us – that is, the feeling *per se* and representations of the feeling are distinguished (see Sect. 3).

© Springer Nature Switzerland AG 2022
B. Goertzel et al. (Eds.): AGI 2021, LNAI 13154, pp. 292–305, 2022.
https://doi.org/10.1007/978-3-030-93758-4_31

We are concerned about the general laws and principles of intelligence. An AGI agent should adapt to its environment and solve unseen problems (in terms of developers) with limited resources. Although that is an objective aim, how can we design a model to solve unseen problems? Few people may reject that a best reference to achieving AGI is our mind. However, we ourselves have subjective experience, or the feeling, while it is questionable to study the objective intelligence with the mind as a reference: Are we studying objective aspect of the mind, or are we studying both the subjective and the objective aspects at the same time? In a sense, science involves a methodology – testing hypotheses, forming theories, and predicting objective phenomena. Falsifiability is an important character of scientific theory, but only objective phenomena can be discussed with falsifiability. The falsification of the subjective feeling is difficult – when the subject claims that it feels something, how can we deny it? How do we determine that the "non-self" has the feeling? Therefore, what we study is the objective aspect of the mind, that is, intelligence. In our view, the laws and principles of intelligence are completely objective, so it can be studied and tested by scientific means, while the mind (especially its subjective experience or feeling) is more difficult to study with the existing scientific paradigm.

The issue of the mind-body relationship is one of the most central issues in philosophy of mind. What is the relationship between the mind (especially the conscious mind) and the body (or matter)? On this issue, the most mainstream view at present is physicalism. Physicalists believe that the physical domain is causally closed, all facts including psychological facts are physical facts, and all information is physical information [11]. Within physicalism, there are reductive physicalism and non-reductive physicalism. The reductive physicalism advocates that the mind is equivalent to the activity of a specific brain or a neural system, that mental states can be reduced to certain states of brains or neural system, and that psychology can be reduced to neuroscience. Phenomenal consciousness or the feeling can also be reduced to a certain physiological state – for example, pain is the activation of C-fibers. Non-reductive physicalism believes that the mental state is determined by the physiological state in some way, and the former supervenes on the latter. Phenomenal consciousness and qualia supervene on the basic physiological structure and function of the organism, which means that if the physiological states of two organisms are exactly the same, then their conscious experience will also be the same. When the organism feels pain, it is inevitable that the neural C-fibers of the organism will be activated. As a non-reductive physicalism, mind-body supervenience is currently widely accepted [10]. A description of mind-body supervenience is:

The mental supervenes on the physical in that if anything x has a mental property M, there is a physical property P such that x has P, and necessarily any object that has P has M [11].

Under the context of AGI, a similar view holds that the "phenomenal aspect" of consciousness is a first-person perspective of a process, while the "functional aspect" is a third-person perspective of the same process. The two are different aspects of the same object, and the two cannot be separated [16].

The current scientific or AGI theories about the mind are mostly about calculations or functions, and they aim to solve the so-called "simple problems" [4]. For example, Crick and Koch proposed the "neurobiological theory of consciousness", assuming that the neural oscillations in the brain is the basis of consciousness and is the neural correlation with awareness [6]. Crick and Koch hypothesized that information is binded through synchronized oscillations of neuronal groups that "represent relevant content". Bernard Baars proposed the global workspace theory of consciousness: it assumes that the content of consciousness is contained in a global workspace (that is, a central processing unit), which coordinates other independent and competing parts as a public blackboard visited by them [1,2]. NARS (Non-Axiomatic Reasoning System) proposed by Pei Wang uses the term *SELF* to refer to the system itself, in order to achieve self-awareness and self-control [15]. Although Wang claims that the phenomenal and functional aspects of consciousness are different perspectives of the same object [16], its implicit meaning seems to be that the functional aspect supervenes on the phenomenal aspect, and the realization of the former naturally comes with the latter, but what NARS currently achieves is only the functional aspect of consciousness. The system has the characterization of "subjective experience" under the context of NARS, but we are not sure whether the system can really have the *feeling*[1], which is subjective, private, and hard to represented[2].

What we concern is always how to create AGI. If the feeling is necessary for AGI, then the ceiling will become obvious – only by understanding the essence of the feeling can we know how to create it. In this paper, we point out in the end the difficulties that may be faced with in the study of intelligence under some existing arguments of philosophy of mind.

2   The Explanatory Gap and the Hard Problem

None of the above-mentioned scientific theories about consciousness provide an explanation for the feeling *per se* [4], and we think neither does NARS. They describe how to represent and calculate, not how to experience the feeling. This is related to a very critical issue in philosophy of mind, that is, the "explanatory gap" or the "hard problem", both of which point the finger at the subjective aspect of the mind, that is, the subjective feeling.

Joseph Levine pointed out that there is an insurmountable explanatory gap between material substance and subjective experience [12]. Levine took the subjective experience of pain as an example to show the difficulty of finding neural

---

[1] The *feeling* here is not a type of term or concept in NARS, since it cannot be represented explicitly and measured directly, and the *subjective experience* in this paper does not refer to the same thing with that in NARS.

[2] The word "subjective" here is not completely the same as that in NARS. In our view, a NARS agent is subjective in the sense that its knowledge (experience) representations are determined by its "agent-specific" environment (or input). However, the subjective feeling in this paper refers to something without representation. The feeling *per se* and representations of the feeling are distinguished in this paper. See Sect. 3.

correlates of consciousness. Although Levine have been unwilling to draw any ontological conclusions about anti-physicalism from the explanatory gap [13,14], some neo-dualists try to use the explanatory gap to refute physicalism, for example, David Chalmers expressed the explanatory gap as a "hard problem" of consciousness [4]. There is no reliable evidence to support physicalism and oppose dualism.

More concretely, if mind-body supervenience is right, why is it pain instead of itch when some neurophysical state arises? To explain the relationship between the neurophysical state and the feeling of pain is the so-called explanatory gap. At the same time, we are of course "easy" to answer the "simple problem(s)", like "how can a physical system learn or remember?", but difficult to answer the "hard problem(s)", similar to "how does a physical system experience pain?". Since representations are theoretically objective, observable, and computable, we can study the interaction mechanism of representations through neuroscience, cognitive science, and intelligence science, while the feeling is subjective, difficult to observe, and probably impossible to calculate or simulate.

Why a certain physical state corresponds to a certain feeling rather than other feelings, and how a physical system has the subjective feeling, are also important for creating AGI, especially when an AGI system must have the feeling. At times, they are unavoidable. As Jaegwon Kim said:

> Suppose that you are now given an assignment to design a "pain box", a device that can be implanted in your robot that not only will detect damage to its body and trigger appropriate avoidance behavior but also will enable the robot to experience the sensation of pain when it is activated. Building a damage detector is an engineering problem, and our engineers, we may presume, know how to go about designing such a device. But what about designing a robot that can experience pain? It seems clear that even the best and brightest engineers would not know where to begin. What would you need to do to make it a pain box rather than an itch box, and how would you know you have succeeded? The functional aspect of pain can be designed and engineered into a system. But the qualitative aspect of pain, or pain as a quale, seems like a wholly different game [11].

Can the explanation gap be bridged? One way is the identification of the mental state and the neurophysical state. Its basic position is that the feeling, like pain, and its corresponding neurophysical state are identical in definition. This position does not provide a meaningful explanation for the gap between consciousness and the brain - it directly excludes the existence of the gap. The other is the functional analysis of the mental state, that is, the feeling is defined as a behavioral process. For example, "in a painful state" is defined as "a state that is caused by tissue damage and leads to aversion behaviors." In this way, the question "why a certain representation is related to a certain experience in x and systems like x" was well explained [11]. However, has the difficult problem really been solved? We cannot deny having the kind of true feeling that we experience. If we follow the view of mind-brain identification, this kind of true feeling does not seem to exist anymore; from the perspective of functional analysis, we are just an objective physical process without the true feeling. How does that kind of the true feeling come about?

As another question, is the subjective feeling necessary for us? Kim pointed out that neuroscience and cognitive science acquiesce in epiphenomenalism, which implicitly agrees that the feeling/experience does not cause any effects. Therefore, the feeling cannot be studied by scientific methods:

> Qualia are epiphenomenal; they cause no effects in the physical domain. If so, how can they even be observed? How can their presence be known to the investigator? There can be no instrument to detect their occurrence and identify them. Qualia cannot register on any measuring instruments because they have no power to affect physical objects or processes. No one thinks the brain scientist can "directly" observe a subject's conscious state, phenomenal or nonphenomenal; direct observation of a conscious state requires experiencing it, and the scientific observer of course is not experiencing the subject's conscious states [11].

Can we agree that the feeling will not affect future decisions and behaviors? The answer is, no. It is possible that experience plays a causal role. When we feel pain at the moment, the subjective feeling makes us hard to forget, so that when we see a similar scene in the future, we want to escape. Of course, some people may also say that if the feeling is defined as a behavioral process, then the subjective feeling is epiphenomenal and will not have an effect on objective objects. What if the feeling cannot be defined as a specific process? As will be discussed in the next section, the subjective feeling does not correspond to a specific process, but it is related to a relatively more complex adaptation procedure. The subjective feeling leads to causal effects through adaptation (or adaptive behaviors). In addition, just as it is difficult for us to directly prove through experiments that the subjective feeling really leads to causal effects, it is also difficult to prove that the subjective feeling is in the leaf node of a causal graph. Both of these possibilities should be considered. In our opinion, the feeling is still an unresolved issue.

As AGI researchers, we have to consider what this problem means for AGI research. If the feeling is epiphenomenal, we certainly do not need to consider the feeling, and only consider the interaction mechanism of representations. By contrast, the reason is different from Wang. The reason of ours is that the feeling (as an epiphenomenon) does not cause any effects (so it will not have any impact on creating AGI). However, there is another possibility that experience plays a secret and critical role in our intelligence. Then, the causal effect it produces will be displayed on "instruments", and we can model it in a certain way by proposing a certain computational model to simulate the real feeling. Then there comes the question: can the subjective feeling be simulated through computational models? If it cannot be simulated accurately, will there be any serious consequences? These questions are difficult to answer, but through further discussion, we may have a deeper understanding as well as inspirations on these questions.

3   A Definition of the Feeling

We start by describing our positions about the feeling:

(i) The feeling is something we truly experience. Even if the feeling is represented by words like *happy*, neurophysical states like neuronal membrane-voltage, hormone like dopamine, *etc.*, they are not the feeling *per se* but the representations of the feeling.

(ii) The feeling could be expressed to form the representations, otherwise it is a non-existence for an observer.

(iii) The feeling should not be defined as any specific and fix function, because doing so confounds the feeling and representations of the feeling.

(iv) The feeling should be somehow measured for researching AGI, with a definition that captures the essence of the feeling to some extent.

Consider such a thought experiment.

3.1   The Semi-transparent Room

There is a room like this: From the outside, it is visually completely transparent, physically inaccessible, and unable to be observed by any scientific instruments – unless there is matter (such as photon) emitted from the room. However, information from the outside world can reach the inside unimpededly. There is a person living in the room, we might as well call her *Ann*. We can generally agree that *Ann* has the same subjective feeling as ours, because she has the same physical structure as ours. From the outside to observe, the room is smaller than the smallest particle that physicists know (*e.g.* quark) as if it is transparent, while from the inside to observe it is large enough for a person to live in. Now that we know that the information transmission of this room is asymmetrical, we might as well call it a "semi-transparent room". The properties of the room are consistent with those of the feeling – especially, observed from the outside, (1) the feeling *per se* is private without external representations, and (2) it is unknown where the feeling comes from, although under the "god view" we know that the feeling comes from *Ann*. Below, we discuss under the "god view" unless an observer is specified explicitly.

Ann senses winds and the sun, as well as storms, and correspondingly she feels happy as well as pain – a breeze makes her happy, and an electric shock makes her feel pain. However, so far, this room will not have any causal effects on the outside, and *Ann* cannot express her feelings to the outside world in any way.

This room is like a "mind", or in other words, a mind lives in it, and it has the subjective feeling. Although it does not present any physical state, or in other words, it only has a "none" state when observed from the outside, and its internal state can be ever-changing. This negates the idea that a feeling must correspond to a physical state for an observer outside.

You might say that, in fact, observed inside the room, *Ann*'s feelings correspond to different neurophysical states. However, this is contrary to the experimental setting. Observers can only observe it outside the room but cannot enter the room – just as we human can only measure the membrane voltage (or other physical indicators) of a neuron, but we cannot know "the feeling of a neuron" if there is a "room" inside the neuron. Even if a human "enters" a brain, he does not enter the room – because representations of neural activations (*e.g.* spikes) are something observed outside the room[3]. The setting of the experiment is reasonable, because feeling is a private thing.

You might say that the state of the semi-transparent room has actually changed because the external state has changed, and in fact, in the case of the semi-transparent room, the (neuro-)physical state is represented by the external state. Then we can consider such a situation: the external state remains unchanged, it has always been so windy and sunny. *Ann* feels happy at first, but as time passes by, she becomes bored with this unchanged outside state, and her happiness fades away. An objectively observed state outside can indeed correspond to different feelings inside.

You might say that if this is the case, then the feeling becomes something similar to an epiphenomenon, which is at a leaf node in a causal graph and does not produce any additional effects. Indeed, if the feeling cannot be represented in any way and cannot affect the physical state outside, then what is the difference between its existence and non-existence for an observer outside? If the feeling is an epiphenomenon, it is easier to handle. AGI researchers can ignore it, because it will not have any impact on the behavior of the system, will not have any impact on agents' interactions with the environment, and will not have any impact on agents' achieving goals.

Is this really the case? According to our experience, it is obviously not. When we feel pain, we will escape, scream, cry bitterly, and express this feeling in various ways. Therefore, a reasonable approach is to give *Ann* a channel to express her feelings.

3.2 Adding a Button to the Room

Now, the experimental setting is changed – there is an extra button in the semi-transparent room. After *Ann* presses the button in the room, photons are emitted with a wavelength of about 700 nm from the room to the world outside. For humans, this is a red light. Whenever the room emits a red light, if the environment is in a state of electric shock, it will become a state of non-electric-shock, that is, if *Ann* feels pain at this time, when she presses the button, this painful state will subside. After many explorations, she discovered this pattern. From then on, whenever *Ann* feels pain, she would press the button. At this time, outside observers would see a red light, which, under the "god view", is a representation corresponding to *Ann*'s pain.

---

[3] The feeling is expressed to form representations which can be observed outside, while this is the further case, in which *Ann* is given a button to express the feeling (see Sect. 3.2).

Does this mean that any mapping or function corresponds to a feeling? Just like an existing solution to the explanatory gap, "pain" is defined as the process from stimulus to response, which is essentially a mapping. When we feel happy, we laugh and secrete dopamine; so we defined the process of "from 'stimuli that makes us happy' to 'responses of the body caused by happiness' " as the feeling of "happiness". Under the context of NARS, an external stimulus, through sensing and reasoning, leads to an increase in the value of a statement "$\langle \{SELF\} \to [happy]\rangle$.", which in turn leads to activations of related concepts and a series of effects. Perhaps the feeling of happiness could be defined as the above process, or as the statement or even the term *happy*, which can be regarded as a collection of many functions (many kinds of stimuli lead to changing the truth-value of the statement, and the statement leads to many kinds of responses; or stimuli related to the term *happy* lead to responses related to the term *happy*). If this is the case (though the feeling may not be defined as above in NARS, and we just discuss it with the context of NARS), then we could also think that any function (or any set of functions) actually had a certain "feeling" inside. We could also think of a mechanical device (a specific input leads to a specific output) as having the feeling. This is contrary to our intuition, and we cannot agree with this view.

3.3   Equipping the Room with a Body

Obviously, the feeling cannot be defined as a simple functional process. In order to understand what the feeling is, let us see how a semi-transparent room with the subjective feeling would do. Since the following discussion will introduce another room as an observer of the current room, in order to make it easier to imagine, we might as well give the room a body, like a stone (a black box, or any other thing) so that it is seen from the outside world as an independent object instead of "none". But when no photons are emitted outward, the body is not different from an object that looks like the stone and does not seem to have the feeling. After introducing the "body", the discussions of the previous sections are still valid – when there is no button or when *Ann* does not press the button, the physical state of the body will not change due to *Ann*'s feeling.

In another semi-transparent room lives *Bob*, whose room (with a body) is similar to *Ann*'s. The only difference is that when the button in the room is pressed, the room emits photons with a wavelength of about 517 nm to the outside world – for humans, this is a green light.

Facing the same environment, *Ann* and *Bob* have the feelings caused by the same representations of stimuli, *e.g.* electric shock. When *Ann* is stimulated by an electric shock, *Bob* finds that *Ann* would always emit a red light. From this *Bob* concludes that *Ann* would emit a red light to express pain as he feels. For the observer *Bob*, "pain" is defined as a function of "from 'pain stimulus' to 'red light' ". However, it is not the case for *Ann*. For the observer *Ann*, "pain" is defined as a function of "from 'pain stimulus' to 'green light' ". Have they really figured out what "pain" is? Indeed, the feeling of pain is explained in a certain way. However, the gap between the feeling and representations of the feeling has not been really bridged. We do not really understand why the feeling of "pain" corresponds to the physical state P instead of another one (such as P'), or why the physical state P corresponds to "pain" instead of another one (such as "itch"), just as the observers, *Ann* and *Bob*, do not really understand why "pain" corresponds to this color of light instead of that color of light, or why "pain" corresponds to light instead of something else. It is obviously not the final answer to define the feeling as a certain specific process, because it confounds the "representations of the feeling" with "the feeling" *per se* – red or green light is a representation of the feeling, and what *Ann* and *Bob* experience internally and privately is the feeling *per se*.

3.4   The Formalized Definition of the Feeling

If the feeling is not defined as a certain function or process, how to define it? Let us reconsider the semi-transparent room – there is an adaptive procedure. When an external stimulus makes *Ann* feel pain, *Ann* does not know what to do. The only thing she can try is to press the button. After several attempts, she discovers that when she feels pain, pressing the button always makes her feel better. So she learns to express the feeling of pain – whenever *Ann* feels pain, from the outside could always see the red light.

The feeling should actually be a certain tendency, with which the agent expresses the inner state of the feeling to form external representations and change the inner state by changing indirectly the representations of input stimuli. For example, the feeling of "happiness" can be defined as "things that the agent tends to increase (or get close to)", and the feeling of "pain" can be defined as "things that the agent tends to decrease (or stay away from)". Formally, we can give the following definition:

For the representation s of a certain stimulus, the agent generates the external response representation r after thinking, *i.e.*

$$r = T(s) \tag{1}$$

where T is the thinking function. The representation r of the response will cause a series of effects in the environment, which will eventually lead to a new representation s' of a stimulus, *i.e.*

$$s' = E(r) \tag{2}$$

where E is the environment function. If the agent feels something, it will eventually find a plausible T to maximize a metrics between s and s', *i.e.*

$$\arg\max_{T} D(s, s') \tag{3}$$

where D measures the relation between the representations s and s'. For example, for the feeling of "pain", D measures the difference between s and s'. More concretely, when the agent feels pain, it will try its best to make the representations of pain arise as seldom as possible, that is, stay away from the feeling of pain. The agent adjusts itself to decrease the feeling of pain – because the feeling of pain is defined as "something that the agent tends to stay away from". In any case, when the agent feels pain, it will have thoughts of moving away from it, which will lead to the behavior of moving away from it. This procedure is adaptive. For a varying environment, the representation of pain may be varying, but this tendency remains unvarying. Different tendencies may associate with different Ds, and the form can be unvarying. For example, for the feeling of "happiness", the corresponding D measures not difference but similarity.

We cannot limit the environment or circumstances for observing the behaviors of a certain agent. Here is the reason. For any mechanical process, *if* the above definition is not met, for example, no matter how *Ann* pressed the button, the room would not have external representations despite the internal feeling, while the room would always produce mechanically specific responses without any adaptation, *then* the feeling, corresponding to the mechanical process, does not exist externally – there is no difference between the existence and non-existence of the feeling. For such a completely mechanical room, even if *Ann*'s room emits a red light under a certain stimulus, which decreases *Ann*'s pain, we cannot say there is the feeling observed from the outside – Consider such a situation. After a period of time, the environment E changed, the original red light would not decrease Ann's pain ever. Originally, as long as Ann had pressed the button, her pain would have been decreased, but now the button were switched at a certain frequency to emit a flashing red light, so that Ann's pain would be decreased. Observed from the outside, it seems that *Ann*'s room did not make a change for the environment, or *Ann* did not adjust herself to stay away from the pain. Then we could not think that there is the feeling in *Ann*'s room – because it were not essentially different from a simple mechanical process without the feeling, or the feeling did not cause any effects. A specific function may work in many circumstances without any adaptation, but if a new circumstance occurs while the agent cannot adapt to it to decrease the pain, *i.e.* the above definition is not met, we cannot say the agent have the feeling.

We can only judge whether an object may have the feeling through external performance, but cannot really give a doubtless conclusion. This does not mean that we are caught in a skeptical dilemma, because through observing behaviors, a bridge has been built between the subjective and the objective. The subjective feeling affects objective representations in some way, so that the subjective feeling becomes measurable and falsifiable to some extent. For an agent that meets the above definition, we can say that the statement "that the agent has the feeling" has "positive evidence". For an agent that does not meet the above definition, we cannot say that it does not have the feeling, but we can say that there is no evidence showing that it has the feeling.

Of course, we do not deny either that NARS may be able to have the feeling (for its adaptability), or that an AI system may be able to have the feeling in the future. If NARS or other AI systems meet the definition of the feeling, "positive evidence" is provided to accept that the system has the feeling.

This definition is acceptable for AGI, because if the feeling exists only as an epiphenomenon without causing any effects, then its existence will not have any impact on the system. If this is the case, what if we think that the system does not actually feel? The feeling is irrelevant to AGI at this time. But if the subjective feeling can actually affect the behaviors of an agent, and if it has indistinguishable patterns of behaviors from the agent with the "real" feeling (such as humans), then the former agent is identical to the agent with the "real" feeling, and we can think of the former agent as having the feeling.

The discussion is preliminary. Some more complex cases is not considered. For example, the feeling may be inhibited and not be expressed, but will cause some effects afterwards; an agent may "enjoy" the "pain". Some other complex emotions with the feeling are not discussed neither. These will make the T and D more complex to model, and we will leave these cases to the future work. However, we think the definition captures the essence of the feeling to some extent.

3.5   Is the Explanatory Gap Bridged?

Explanatory gap requires an answer to how the mental state M corresponds to the physical state P. According to the above discussion, before adaptation, M and P are not in correspondence. There is no direct correspondence between the pain and the external stimuli as well as the red light emitted by Ann's room. However, after a period of time, Ann finds that whenever she feels pain, pressing the button will make her feel more comfortable (the pain is decreased). Observed from the outside, the stimulus, such as an electric shock, will make the room glow red. The stimulus will also make Bob feel pain, and Bob observes that when Ann receives an electric shock, red light always appears, so Bob, the observer of Ann's room, would think that pain corresponds to the physical representation of red light. Similarly, Ann, the observer of Bob's room, would think that pain corresponds to the representation of green light. If Ann and Bob can observe their own light, then at least they would come to the conclusion that pain corresponds to the representation of light. The mental state M (pain) corresponds to the physical state P(red/green/any light) in this way. However, under the "god's view", Ann and Bob's belief, that the pain is caused by the electric shock, is not just derived from the process "from 'electric shock' to 'light'", but also the procedure of adaptation. In other words, even if the external environment function E has changed, Bob and Ann still show the same tendency of adaptation, which conforms to the above definition.

In this sense, is the explanatory gap bridged? At least, we have seen how the mental state M (the feeling) corresponds to the physical state P (the representations).

4   The "Hard Problem" of Intelligence

From the above definition, the feeling must form external representations before we have positive evidence to accept its existence; at the same time, this implies a point of view that the feeling can be purely internal and unrepresented. So there are two cases that need to be specifically discussed.

For the first case, just like the counterfactual "philosophical zombie" (although this case may be controversial, it still needs to be explained), if the agent's external performance is the same as one without the subjective feeling, then the feeling could be an epiphenomenon; the feeling does not affect the objective process, and we need to only study the objective laws of intelligence. For AGI researchers, the "philosophical zombie" case is acceptable. It doesn't matter if there is no real feeling – human-level intelligence can also be reached without the feeling.

For the second case, an agent may inhibit expressing the feeling, so as not to form an externally observable representation. If the private feeling is not expressed, that is, *Ann* or *Bob* does not press the button, then we cannot claim as before that "at this time, it will not cause external effects, so it will not affect the objective process. For AGI, it does not matter whether it exists or not." In this case, the internal causal effect cannot be ignored, that is, although there is no representation of the feeling at present, the internal feeling is indeed experienced. So at some point in the agent's future, the current inhibited expression of the feeling leads to a distinct representation. In this case, T becomes more complicated, but the form in the definition of the feeling remains unchanged.

However, reconsidering the above two cases, we are still not sure whether a "philosophical zombie" without the feeling will behave differently from an agent with the feeling, nor can we know exactly what D and T are. Of course, we can strive to find a computational model.

We call the computational model that meets the definition of the feeling above as the "simulated" feeling, and call the natural being of the feeling as the "innate" feeling.

The question then becomes, if this "simulated" feeling is somewhat different from the "innate" feeling, will it lead to a serious impact on an AGI system? How accurately can a computational model fit the "innate" feeling? All these need to be answered through experiments – We should find an agent with the "innate" feeling and compare the artificial agent with it, and see if they behave the "same" in some sense.

Unfortunately, in the above definition, it is argued that the test environment must be open, which is also crucial for AGI. Will an agent with the "simulated" feeling behaves the same as one with the "innate" feeling at any circumstances? This is difficult to confirm, because the condition of "any circumstances" is difficult to achieve, and an experiment can only test a model under limited circumstances. A more serious issue is how to compare the two kinds of agents "fairly" to judge if they behave the same.

In addition, what if the "innate" feeling cannot be fully modeled by a computational process? If it is necessary to have such the "innate" feeling in order to achieve human-level or higher-level AI, or realize the mind with artifacts, then where does the feeling ultimately come from, and how to achieve an interface that allows the "innate" feeling to be expressed?

Perhaps this is the hard problem for intelligence – in summary, if the "innate" feeling cannot be realized, what kind of impact will it have on the artificial intelligence system, and if there must be the "innate" feeling, how to realize it?

This problem cannot be answered under the current AI or AGI research, and it is left to the future. If the problem cannot be solved by the existing classical computing methods, then the feeling problem is the ceiling of the current AI research, and it must be broken through with the help of additional paradigms or technical means. Although this paper as an initial discussion mainly considers this problem from classical aspects, at the end of the article we want to emphasize the potential relationship between general intelligence and quantum mind. Quantum biology studies have shown that at room temperature, quantum coherence can exist in organisms for enough time [7]. In recent years, Matthew Fisher has proposed an exciting quantum neural theory based on the nuclear spin of phosphorus [8]. A bolder idea was put forward by Huping Hu, who suggested that quantum processes in neural activity can be coupled with space-time dynamics [9]. Considering that Xiao-Gang Wen's research has shown that the essence of space-time is quantum information [17], this may mean that the problem proposed in this article can be discussed in a broader scope. In any case, social scientists have begun to try to unify the ontology of physics and social science from the perspective of quantum mind [18]. At least, research in the direction of quantum cognition has already shown that most of the deviations from rational behavior can be better explained from a quantum perspective [3]. Is a quantum-based agent a plausible option for merging the gap between intelligence and mind, through the unity of consciousness [5]? We may need to use a separate article to elaborate on this issue in future.

5   Summary

If the subjective feeling plays an indispensable role, that is, agents with the feeling and agents without the feeling counterfactually (such as philosophical zombies) are distinct significantly in terms of performances, and if without the feeling human-level AI cannot be reached, then we must study the feeling. However, the feeling is subjective and private, while scientists study objective phenomena. If we cannot measure the feeling, we cannot study it scientifically.

Therefore, this paper discusses the impact of the subjective feeling on AGI research. If the feeling is an epiphenomenon, we can just ignore it. Otherwise, it plays an indispensable role, so we try to give a possible solution for a machine to have the feeling: We define the feeling as "a tendency to change the input representation", and think "that the performance of an agent conforms to this definition" provides "positive evidence" for "that the agent has the feeling". If the definition captures the essence of the feeling, the feeling becomes measurable. However, whether it is possible and how to find a computational model, for the "simulated" feeling, to fit the "innate" feeling remain unknown.

Acknowledgements. The work was sponsored by Zhejiang Lab (No. 2021RD0AB01).

References

1. Baars, B.J.: Global workspace theory of consciousness: toward a cognitive neuroscience of human experience. Bound. Conscious. Neurobiol. Neuropathol. **150**, 45–53 (2005)
2. Baars, B.J.: A Cognitive Theory of Consciousness. Cambridge University Press (1993)
3. Busemeyer, J.R., Bruza, P.D.: Quantum Models of Cognition and Decision. Cambridge University Press (2012)
4. Chalmers, D.J.: Facing up to the problem of consciousness. J. Conscious. Stud. **2**(3), 200–219 (1995)
5. Cleeremans, A.: The Unity of Consciousness, Binding, Integration, and Dissociation. Oxford University Press (2003)
6. Crick, F., Koch, C.: Towards a neurobiological theory of consciousness. In: Seminars in the Neurosciences, vol. 2, pp. 263–275. Saunders Scientific Publications (1990)
7. Engel, G.S., et al.: Evidence for wavelike energy transfer through quantum coherence in photosynthetic systems. Nature **446**, 782–786 (2015)
8. Fisher, M.P.: Quantum cognition: the possibility of processing with nuclear spins in the brain. Ann. Phys. **362**, 593–602 (2015)
9. Hu, H., Wu, M.: Spin-mediated consciousness theory: possible roles of neural membrane nuclear spin ensembles and paramagnetic oxygen. Med. Hypotheses **63**, 633–646 (2004)
10. Kim, J.: The mind-body problem: taking stock after forty years. Philos. Perspect. **11**, 185–207 (1997)
11. Kim, J.: Philosophy of Mind. Westview Press (2011)
12. Levine, J.: Materialism and Qualia, the explanatory gap. Pac. Philos. Q. **64**(4), 354–361 (1983)
13. Levine, J.: On leaving out what it's like, chap. 6. In: Davies, M.E., Humphreys, G.W. (eds.) Consciousness: Psychological and Philosophical Essays, pp. 121–136. Blackwell, Oxford (1993)
14. Levine, J.: Purple Haze: The Puzzle of Consciousness. Oxford University Press (2001)
15. Wang, P., Li, X., Hammer, P.: Self in NARS, an AGI system. Front. Robot. AI **5**, 20 (2018)
16. Wang, P.: A constructive explanation of consciousness. J. Artif. Intell. Conscious. **7**(2), 257–275 (2020)
17. Wen, X.G.: Four revolutions in physics and the second quantum revolution a unification of force and matter by quantum information. Int. J. Mod. Phys. B **32**, 1830010 (2004)
18. Wendt, A.: Quantum Mind and Social Science, Unifying Physical and Social Ontology. Cambridge University Press (2015)

Neural String Diagrams: A Universal Modelling Language for Categorical Deep Learning

Tom Xu and Yoshihiro Maruyama$^{(\boxtimes)}$

School of Computing, Australian National University, Canberra, Australia
{tom.xu,yoshihiro.maruyama}@anu.edu.au

Abstract. Category theory has been successfully applied to compositional modelling of diverse systems, including computational systems, logical systems, and physical systems, paving the way for a new kind of general system science (or rather general process science). It has been particularly successful in quantum computing and natural language processing recently; traditionally, it has played major rôles in compositional semantics of programming languages and symbolic reasoning systems. Building upon them, we propose the mathematical system of neural string diagrams as a universal modelling language for categorical deep learning, which allows us to turn informal neural network architecture pictures into formally explainable, mathematically verifiable, and systematically composable entities in their own right. We give, in particular, a neural string diagram account of CNN and Transformer (which has never been achieved before). Neural string diagrams can be computed with DisCoPy, Quantomatic, and their extensions. Categorically formalised neural networks can be instantiated for both ordinary vector spaces and other monoidal categorical structures, allowing for generalisations of deep learning (e.g., deep learning on relational structures, deep learning on graph and other network structures, etc.). We envisage that the category theory approach to artificial intelligence ultimately contributes to the development of artificial general intelligence, giving a universal modelling language for intelligent systems and agents.

Keywords: Categorical artificial intelligence · Neural category theory · Categorical deep learning

1 Introduction

Category theory is an abstract mathematical modelling language to express various sorts of structures and their compositional relationships [7]. It has been successfully applied in structural modelling of quantum computing and NLP

This work was supported by JST (JPMJMS2033; JPMJPR17G9).

(natural language processing), enabling compositional generalisations of quantum protocols and algorithms [1,4,11], and compositional constructions of meaning vectors for grammatically complex sentences and text in NLP [3,10,12]. The categorical model of NLP integrates the symbolic model and statistical models of language [3,10]. It is equipped with graphical string diagram calculus, which allows mathematically precise pictorial reasoning, and thus reconciles intuitive clarity and mathematical rigor (and computational efficiency as explained below). Let us briefly explain what a category is (for detail, see, e.g., [7]).

A category $\mathcal{C}$ is an abstract structure of objects and arrows (specifying the relationships between objects), which can be instantiated in various manners: in logic, there is a category of propositions and proofs; in programming language theory, there is a category of data types and programs; in physics, there is a category of physical systems and processes [1,4,7]. Arrows can be composed with each other (if their types are coherent); in monoidal categories $(\mathcal{C}, \otimes, I)$ in particular, this can be done in two different ways, i.e., via sequential and parallel composition as explained below. Different fields of science can share common categorical structures, and category theory allows to elucidate structural similarities between them, thus giving a unifying perspective on the sciences, and facilitating transdisciplinary knowledge transfer between them.

In this paper we develop category theory for neural networks as a compositional modelling language for deep learning and its categorical generalisation. To this end, we rely upon the framework of dagger compact categories [1], which has been applied for quantum computing and natural language processing as mentioned above; this is because quantum computing works with state vectors, NLP with meaning vectors, and dagger compact categories give a platform for categorical linear algebra. DisCoPy, Quantomatic, and their extensions give computational implementations of dagger compact categories and their graphical calculus, applied in quantum computing and NLP [6,10,12]. The neural category theory we develop is implementable in them. Among other things, we formalise CNN (convolutional neural network) and Transformer using neural string diagrams (which has never been achieved before).

Categorically formalised neural networks can be instantiated for both ordinary vector spaces and other monoidal categorical structures, allowing for different generalisations of deep learning (e.g., deep learning on relational structures; deep learning on graph categories and other network structures; cf. [15]); note that the categorical formulations of NLP and quantum computing led to the discovery and unification of various models as well (e.g., the Spekkens toy quantum models that significantly simplify the ordinary Hilbert space model and yet keep essential features of quantum theory, Montague-like possibilistic models of NLP, etc.) [1,3,4,10]. Just as the categorical model of NLP integrates the symbolic and statistical models of language, categorical AI arguably paves the way for integrative artificial intelligence (cf. [2]), and we believe that it ultimately contributes to the development of artificial general intelligence [9] by giving a universal modelling language for intelligent systems and agents.

The rest of the paper is structured as follows. In Sect. 2, we give the framework of dagger compact categories to categorically formalise neural networks. In Sect. 3, we develop string diagrams for neural networks based upon dagger compact categories, especially for CNN and Transformer neural networks.

2   Category Theory via String Diagram

Here we give the basic framework of monoidal categories, dagger compact categories, and their string diagrams that allows us to formalise neural network architectures in terms of category theory.

2.1   String Diagram

A string diagram is a directed graph consist of labelled strings and labelled boxes with specified input and output strings, together with certain notions of compositionality [4]. Some basic examples are:

These are: (1) String A; (2) Box f with input A and output B; (3) Box g with input A, B and output C. Note that to avoid repeatedly specifying the direction of each component of a string diagram we take the convention of reading diagrams from left to right. Often we also ignore labels in string diagrams if we don't need to specifically address the strings and boxes.

We consider two notions of compositionality: sequential composition and parallel composition. Any boxes with compatible output and input can be sequentially composed. This is done by connecting the compatible output and input strings. On the other hand, any boxes or strings may be composed in parallel. This is done by stacking strings and boxes vertically in the diagram.

By considering objects (or equivalently identity morphism on objects) as strings and morphisms as boxes, string diagrams provide graphical calculus for monoidal categories [4,11]. Furthermore, the sequential composition in string diagram represents morphism composition whereas the parallel composition represents the monoidal product. Also note that the monoidal unit object I is represented by the empty diagram.

Sequential Composition: $g \circ f : A \to B \to C$ Parallel Composition: $f \otimes h : A \otimes B \to B \otimes (C \otimes D)$

States and Effects. The states are morphisms that has the unit object as input and the effects are morphisms that has the unit object as output. Since the unit object is represented by the empty diagram, the states and effects are drawn as triangle boxes:

A scalar λ in a monoidal category is an endomorphism $\lambda : I \to I$.

2.2   Dagger Compact Category

The basic monoidal structure is not enough to express the intricacies of neural network architectures. The richer structures we need are captured by the class of dagger compact categories.

Symmetric Monoidal Category. A symmetric monoidal category is a monoidal category equipped with a braiding isomorphism $\sigma_{AB} : A \otimes B \to B \otimes A$ for each pair of objects and it is natural in both A and B. The braiding morphism is represented as:

Dagger Category. A dagger category $\mathcal{C}$ is a category with an involutive functor $\dagger : \mathcal{C}^{op} \to \mathcal{C}$ such that the functor is identity on objects and it sends morphism to their adjoints in an involutive way:

$$(\overset{A}{\underset{}{-}} \boxed{f} \overset{B}{\underset{}{-}})^{\dagger} \ = \ \overset{B}{\underset{}{-}} \boxed{f^{\dagger}} \overset{A}{\underset{}{-}}$$

$$(\overset{B}{\underset{}{-}} \boxed{f^{\dagger}} \overset{A}{\underset{}{-}})^{\dagger} \ = \ \overset{A}{\underset{}{-}} \boxed{f} \overset{B}{\underset{}{-}}$$

Compact Closed Category. A monoidal category $\mathcal{C}$ is compact closed if for any object A there exists a dual object A^* in $\mathcal{C}$. Furthermore there exists a state $\eta_A : I \to A^* \otimes A$ for each object called the unit and an effect $\epsilon_A : A \otimes A^* \to I$ called the counit. The unit and counit on an object satisfy the following string diagram equations:

Now we are ready to state the definition for dagger compact category.

Definition 1 (Dagger Compact Category). *A dagger compact category is a dagger strict symmetric monoidal and it is closed and compact closed. Moreover, the unit and the counit are related by the dagger and symmetric structure:*

$$\sigma_{AA^*} \circ \epsilon_A^{\dagger} = \eta_A$$

or equivalently:

$$\epsilon_A^{\dagger} = \eta_{A^*}$$

In terms of string diagram the relationship of unit and counit in a dagger compact category is written as:

Importantly, in a dagger compact category, there is a notion of inner product:

Definition 2 (Generalised Inner Product). *The generalised inner product of two states of the same type* $\psi : I \to A$, $\phi : I \to A$ *is the morphism:*

$$\psi^\dagger \circ \phi : I \to A \to I$$

In particular, the generalised inner product of two states is a scalar in the monoidal category. The string diagram of the generalised inner product is:

Furthermore, the inner product is preserved by unitary morphisms.

Definition 3 (Unitary Morphism). *A morphism* $U : A \to B$ *in a dagger category is unitary if it is an isomorphism and such that its adjoint* $U^\dagger : B \to A$ *is also its inverse morphism.*

The unitary morphism admits the following diagram.

A unitary morphism preserves the inner product in the following sense:

For our purpose, we restrict our attention to a subclass of dagger compact categories equipped with the following structures:

(1) Having an zero object **0** so that for each pair of objects there is an unique morphism factoring through the zero object:

$$0_{A,B} : A \to \mathbf{0} \to B$$

(2) Having all biproduct. The biproduct of objects $A_1 \ldots A_k$ is written as

$$\bigoplus_{i=1}^{i=k} A_i$$

We note here that in a dagger compact category with biproducts each homset can be equipped with addition operation. In particular, the scalars in such categories form a commutative semi-ring [1].

Moreover, since a biproduct is both a product and a coproduct there are projections $\{p_j : \bigoplus_{i=1}^{i=k} A_i \to A_j\}_{j=1}^{j=k}$ and injections $\{q_j : A_j \to \bigoplus_{i=1}^{i=k} A_i\}_{j=1}^{j=k}$. The projections and injections have the following properties:

$$p_j \circ q_i = \delta_{ij} \quad \text{and} \quad \sum_{i=1}^{i=k} q_i \circ p_i = 1_{\oplus_i A_i}$$

where $\delta_{ii} = 1_{A_i}$ and $\delta_{ij} = 0_{A_I, A_j}, i \neq j$.

Dagger compact category with biproducts exhibits generalised vector space features. To begin with, there is a notion of basis:

Definition 4 (Generalised Basis). *A generalised basis of an object A in a dagger compact category with biproducts is a unitary morphism:*

$$\mathcal{B}_A : n \cdot I \to A$$

where $n \cdot I := \bigoplus_{i=1}^{i=n} I$. The number n is the dimension of the object A.

In addition, a basis component is a state $i : I \to A$ such that

$$i = \mathcal{B}_A \circ q_i$$

where $q_i : I \to n \cdot I$ is the i-th injection into the biproduct.

Generalised Matrix. With respect to bases $\mathcal{B}_A : n \cdot I \to A$ and $\mathcal{B}_B : m \cdot I \to B$, to a morphism $f : A \to B$ we can associate a generalised matrix M:

$$M = \mathcal{B}_B^\dagger \circ f \circ \mathcal{B}_A : n \cdot I \to m \cdot I$$

In particular, each entry of the generalised matrix is given by:

Note that the entries of a generalised matrix are scalars in the sense that they are endomorphisms on the monoidal unit. Indeed:

$$M_{i,j} = i^\dagger \circ M \circ j : I \to n \cdot I \to m \cdot I \to I$$

The **transposition** of a morphism $f : A \to B$ is defined as a morphism $f^T : B \to A$ satisfying the following condition. Given any bases $\mathcal{B}_A$ for A and $\mathcal{B}_B$ for B, the generalised matrix M^T of the morphism f^T is the transposition of the generalised matrix M of f in the sense that $M_{i,j}^T = M_{j,i}$. Notice that taking the transposition of a morphism is basis independent.

Now, given a morphism $M : n \cdot I \to m \cdot I$ and bases $\mathcal{B}_A$, $\mathcal{B}_B$ we may consider M to be the generalised matrix associated with the morphism $f : A \to B$ where

$$f = \mathcal{B}_B \circ M \circ \mathcal{B}_A^\dagger$$

From now on we only consider dagger compact categories such that each object has a basis. We use the suggestive notation V_n to denote an object in a dagger compact category which is to say that the object is n-dimensional.

Furthermore, we use the notation $V_{m \times n}$ to denote the internal hom $[V_n, V_m]$ in the dagger compact category. Note that for internal hom in a dagger compact category we have the correspondence [11]:

$$\mathcal{C}(A, [X, Z]) \xrightarrow{\cong} \mathcal{C}(A \otimes X, Z)$$

In this sense, a state $\psi : I \to V_{m \times n}$ is associated with a morphism $f : I \otimes V_n \to V_m$ which is $f : V_n \to V_m$. This allows us to express the state ψ in terms of a generalised matrix (with respect to some bases for V_m and V_n).

3   Neural Category Theory via Neural String Diagram

In this section, we describe two neural network architectures: Convolutional Neural Network (CNN) and Transformer [8] using string diagrams.

3.1   Convolutional Neural Network (CNN)

We first define three special morphisms for the string diagram for CNN.

Definition 5 (Copying). *For an object A in a dagger compact category the copying morphism is: $\delta : A \to A \otimes A$*

such that for any state $\psi : I \to A$ we have:

The defining mechanism of CNNs is of course convolution. In short, it is a special way of applying filters to an image to extract meaningful (to computers) features of the image. For simplicity the convolution morphism we consider here is to represent convolution with stride 1 and no padding.

Definition 6 (Convolution). *The convolution of type $V_{m \times n}$ and $V_{k \times l}$ where $k \leq m, l \leq n$, is defined as a morphism: $\circledast : V_{m \times n} \otimes V_{k \times l} \to V_{(m-k+1) \times (n-l+1)}$*

$$-\circledast-$$

satisfying the following conditions: For states $A : I \to V_{m \times n}$ and $B : I \to V_{k \times l}$, the state $A \circledast B : I \to V_{(m-k+1) \times (n-l+1)}$ corresponds (as explained above) to a morphism

$$A \circledast B : V_{(n-l+1)} \to V_{(m-k+1)}.$$

Notice here we use the same notation $A \circledast B$ for the state and its corresponding morphism.

Given generalised bases $\mu : \{(m-k+1) \times (n-l+1)\} \cdot I \to V_{(m-k+1) \times (n-l+1)}$, $\phi : (m-k+1) \cdot I \to V_{m-k+1}$ and $\psi : (n-l+1) \cdot I \to V_{n-l+1}$ the generalised matrix associated to the morphism $A \circledast B$ satisfies:

$$\langle j | - \boxed{M_{A \circledast B}} - | i \rangle = \sum_{\alpha=0}^{k-1} \sum_{\beta=0}^{l-1} \langle {}^{\beta+\atop j} | - \boxed{M_A} - |{}^{\alpha+\atop i} \rangle \cdot \langle {}^{+\atop \beta} | - \boxed{M_B} - |{}^{\alpha\atop +} \rangle$$

where $i, j, i+\alpha, j+\beta$ are basis component of their respective bases. The summation and multiplication come from the semiring structure of $Hom(I, I)$.

Similarly we give the definition of (vertical) concatenation.

Definition 7 (Concatenation). *The concatenation of type $V_{m \times n}$ and $V_{m \times k}$, is a morphism* $\odot : V_{m \times n} \otimes V_{m \times k} \to V_{m \times (n+k)}$

The concatenation of two states $A : I \to V_{m \times n}$ and $B : I \to V_{m \times k}$ is a state $A \odot B : I \to V_{m \times (n+k)}$ which corresponds to a morphism $A \odot B : V_{(m-k+1)} \to V_{(n-l+1)}$. With respect to appropriate bases the generalised matrix of the morphism $A \odot B$ satisfies:

The figure below is the neural string diagram for a simple CNN model. Note that although the filters F_1, F_2 are the trainable parameters of CNN, in string diagram they are represented as fixed states into the same object in the dagger compact category. This is because the string diagram showcases the architecture aspect of the neural network instead of the training aspect.

We further equip the dagger compact category with free (non-linear) morphisms: Relu, Pooling, Fully Connected layer (FC), Softmax. Notice here we take Fully Connected layer as a single morphism even though it is a sub-neural network with training parameters.

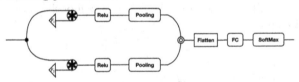

3.2   Transformer

Transformer is a class of neural networks that utilise the attention mechanism. For the string diagram of Transformer, we introduce three more morphisms.

(1) Generalised matrix multiplication. $\boxtimes : V_{m \times n} \otimes V_{n \times k} \to V_{m \times k}$. For states $A : I \to V_{m \times n}$ (which corresponds to a morphism $A : V_n \to V_m$) and $B : I \to V_{n \times k}$ (which corresponds to a morphism $B : V_k \to V_n$), the state $A \boxtimes B : I \to V_{m \times k}$ corresponds to a morphism $A \boxtimes B : V_k \to V_m$ which is the composition of morphisms $A \circ B : V_k \to V_n \to V_m$. Furthermore, fixing generalised bases for the appropriate objects, the generalised matrix of $A \boxtimes B$ can be seen as the usual product of the generalised matrices of A and B.

(2) Generalised matrix dot product. $\odot : V_{m \times n} \otimes V_{k \times n} \to V_{m \times k}$. Similar to generalised matrix multiplication, for states $A : I \to V_{m \times n}$ and $B : I \to V_{k \times n}$, the state $A \odot B : I \to V_{m \times k}$ corresponds to a morphism $A \odot B : V_k \to V_m$ which is the composition of morphisms $A \circ B^T : V_k \to V_n \to V_m$, where B^T is the transposition of the morphisms $B : V_n \to V_k$ as introduced previously. Again, after fixing bases the generalised matrix of $A \odot B$ can be thought as the usual dot product of the generalised matrices of A and B.

(3) Generalised entry-wise matrix addition. $\oplus : V_{m \times n} \otimes V_{m \times n} \to V_{m \times n}$. In the same way as the previous two morphisms, the generalised matrix of $A \oplus B$ can be thought as the entry-wise addition of the matrices of A and B.

The key component of Transformer architecture is the attention mechanism. The following string diagram represents the self-attention mechanism.

The multi-head attention mechanism can be represented by vertically stacking the string diagram above and concatenate the output strings.

The encoding part of Transformer can process input in parallel. This is a major advantage over ordinary Recurrent Neural Network (RNN). On the other hand, the decoding part works sequentially. To reflect the sequential process in the string diagram, we introduce the notion of time flow: In addition to the convention of reading a string diagram from left to right, we also read a string diagram from top to bottom and understand it as some morphisms take place in different time steps. In particular, different time steps are connected by a special type of morphism called snake morphism. It is a composition of a special state called cup and a special effect called cap [4]:

Cup and cap satisfy the ranking rules:

We use the snake morphism to connect the encoder and decoder, the decoder and the next decoder in the string diagram below. It is to say that the output object of the encoder is fed via identity into the second attention mechanism (the encoder-decoder attention) of the decoder which happens in the next time step. Similarly, the output object is fed via identity into the decoder in the next time step. This is the unrolled loop representation of Transformer.

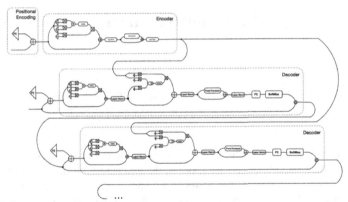

Note that we further equipped the dagger compact category with some non-linear free morphisms; in future work we will develop two-level category theory (with two classes of morphisms) to do this systematically in general categories.

References

1. Abramsky, S., Coecke, B.: Categorical quantum mechanics. In: Handbook of Quantum Logic and Quantum Structures, pp. 261–325 (2009)
2. Besold, T., et al.: Neural-Symbolic Learning and Reasoning (2017)
3. Clark, S., et al.: Mathematical foundations for a compositional distributional model of meaning. Linguist. Anal. **36**, 345–384 (2010)
4. Coecke, B., Kissinger, A.: Picturing Quantum Processes. CUP (2017)
5. Cruttwell, G., et al.: Categorical foundations of gradient-based learning. arXiv arXiv:2103.01931 (2021)
6. De Felice, G., et al.: DisCoPy: monoidal categories in Python. In: 2020 Proceedings of the ACT, pp. 183–197 (2021)
7. Fong, B., Spivak, D.: An Invitation to Applied Category Theory. CUP (2019)
8. Goertzel, B., et al.: Guiding symbolic natural language grammar induction via transformer-based sequence probabilities. In: Proceedings of the AGI 2020, pp. 153–163 (2020)
9. Goertzel, B.: Human-level artificial general intelligence and the possibility of a technological singularity. Artif. Intell. **171**, 1161–1173 (2007)
10. Grefenstette, E., Sadrzadeh, M.: Experimental support for a categorical compositional distributional model of meaning. In: Proceedings of the EMNLP, pp. 1394–1404 (2011)
11. Heunen, C., Vicary, J.: Categories for Quantum Theory. OUP (2019)
12. Lorenz, R., et al.: QNLP in practice. arXiv arXiv:2102.12846 (2021)
13. Maruyama, Y.: Categorical artificial intelligence: the integration of symbolic and statistical AI for verifiable, ethical, and trustworthy AI. In: Proceedings of the AGI (2021)
14. Sejnowski, T.: The unreasonable effectiveness of deep learning in artificial intelligence. PNAS **117**, 30033–30038 (2020)
15. Zhang, Z., et al.: Deep learning on graphs. IEEE Trans. Knowl. Data Eng. **34**, 249–270 (2021)

AGI Control Theory

Roman V. Yampolskiy$^{(\boxtimes)}$

Computer Science and Engineering, University of Louisville, Louisville, USA
roman.yampolskiy@louisville.edu

Abstract. According to forecasts, the invention of General Artificial Intelligence (AGI) will change the trajectory of the development of human civilization. To take advantage of this powerful technology and avoid its pitfalls, it is important to be able to control it. However, the ability to control AGI and its more advanced version "Superintelligence" has not been established. In this article, we explore the arguments that advanced AI cannot be completely controlled. The implications of uncontrolled AI are discussed in relation to the future of humanity and AI research, and the safety and security of AI systems.

Keywords: AI safety · Control problem · Uncontrollability · X-risk

1 Introduction

Invention of artificial general intelligence is predicted to cause a shift in the trajectory of human civilization [1–3]. In order to reap the benefits and avoid pitfalls of such powerful technology it is important to be able to control it. However, possibility of controlling artificial general intelligence and its more advanced version, superintelligence, has not been formally established. In this paper, we review arguments indicating that advanced AI can't be fully controlled. Consequences of uncontrollability of AI are discussed with respect to future of humanity and research on AI, and AI safety and security [4].

We were unable to locate any academic publications explicitly devoted to the subject of solvability of the AI Control Problem. We did find a number of blog posts [5] and forum comments [6, 7] which speak to the issue but none had formal proofs or very rigorous argumentation. Despite that, we still review and discuss such works. In the next section, we will try to understand why scholars think that control is possible and if they have good reasons to think that.

2 Controllable

While a number of scholars have suggested that controllability of AI should be accomplishable, none provide very convincing argumentation, usually sharing such beliefs as personal opinions which are at best sometimes strengthened with assessment of difficulty or assignment of probabilities to successful control.

For example, Yudkowsky writes about superintelligence: "I have suggested that, in principle and in difficult practice, it should be possible to design a "Friendly AI" with

© Springer Nature Switzerland AG 2022
B. Goertzel et al. (Eds.): AGI 2021, LNAI 13154, pp. 316–326, 2022.
https://doi.org/10.1007/978-3-030-93758-4_33

programmer choice of the AI's preferences, and have the AI self-improve with sufficiently high fidelity to knowably keep these preferences stable. I also think it should be possible, in principle and in difficult practice, to convey the complicated information inherent in human preferences into an AI, and then apply further idealizations such as reflective equilibrium and ideal advisor theories [8] so as to arrive at an output which corresponds intuitively to the AI "doing the right thing."" [9]. "I would say that it's solvable in the sense that all the problems that we've looked at so far seem like they're of limited complexity and non-magical. If we had 200 years to work on this problem and there was no penalty for failing at it, I would feel very relaxed about humanity's probability of solving this eventually" [10].

Similarly Baumann says: "I believe that advanced AI systems will likely be aligned with the goals of their human operators, at least in a narrow sense. I'll give three main reasons for this:

- The transition to AI may happen in a way that does not give rise to the alignment problem as it's usually conceived of.
- While work on the alignment problem appears neglected at this point, it's likely that large amounts of resources will be used to tackle it if and when it becomes apparent that alignment is a serious problem.
- Even if the previous two points do not hold, we have already come up with a couple of smart approaches that seem fairly likely to lead to successful alignment" [5].

Baumann continues: "I think that a large investment of resources will likely yield satisfactory alignment solutions, for several reasons:

- The problem of AI alignment differs from conventional principal-agent problems (aligning a human with the interests of a company, state, or other institution) in that we have complete freedom in our design of artificial agents: we can set their internal structure, their goals, and their interactions with the outside world at will.
- We only need to find a single approach that works among a large set of possible ideas.
- Alignment is not an agential problem, i.e. there are no agential forces that push against finding a solution – it's just an engineering challenge." [5].

Baumann concludes with a probability estimation: "My inside view puts ~90% probability on successful alignment (by which I mean narrow alignment as defined below). Factoring in the views of other thoughtful people, some of which think alignment is far less likely, that number comes down to ~80%" [5].

Stuart Russell says: "I have argued that the framework of cooperative inverse reinforcement learning may provide initial steps toward a theoretical solution of the AI control problem. There are also some reasons for believing that the approach may be workable in practice. First, there are vast amounts of written and filmed information about humans doing things (and other humans reacting). Technology to build models of human values from this storehouse will be available long before superintelligent AI systems are created. Second, there are very strong, near-term economic incentives for robots to understand human values: if one poorly designed domestic robot cooks the cat for dinner, not realizing that its sentimental value outweighs its nutritional value, the domestic robot industry will be out of business" [11]. Elsewhere [12], Russell proposes three core principles to design AI systems whose purposes do not conflict with humanity's and says: "It turns out that these three principles, once embodied in a formal mathematical framework that defines the problem the AI system is constitutionally required to solve, seem to allow some progress to be made on the AI control problem." "Solving the safety problem well enough to move forward in AI seems to be feasible but not easy." [13].

Eliezer Yudkowsky[1] wrote: "People ask me how likely it is that humankind will survive, or how likely it is that anyone can build a Friendly AI, or how likely it is that I can build one. I really *don't* know how to answer. I'm not being evasive; I don't know how to put a probability estimate on my, or someone else, successfully shutting up and doing the impossible. Is it probability zero because it's impossible? Obviously not. But how likely is it that this problem, like previous ones, will give up its unyielding blankness when I understand it better? It's not truly impossible, I can see that much. But humanly impossible? Impossible to me in particular? I don't know how to guess. I can't even translate my intuitive feeling into a number, because the only intuitive feeling I have is that the "chance" depends heavily on my choices and unknown unknowns: a wildly unstable probability estimate. But I do hope by now that I've made it clear why you shouldn't panic, when I now say clearly and forthrightly, that building a Friendly AI is impossible" [14].

Joy recognized the problem and suggested that it is perhaps not too late to address it, but he thought so in 2000, nearly 20 years ago: "The question is, indeed, Which is to be master? Will we survive our technologies? We are being propelled into this new century with no plan, no control, no brakes. Have we already gone too far down the path to alter course? I don't believe so, but we aren't trying yet, and the last chance to assert control—the fail-safe point—is rapidly approaching" [15].

Paul Christiano doesn't see strong evidence for impossibility: "… clean algorithmic problems are usually solvable in 10 years, or provably impossible, and early failures to solve a problem don't provide much evidence of the difficulty of the problem (unless they generate proofs of impossibility). So, the fact that we don't know how to solve alignment now doesn't provide very strong evidence that the problem is impossible. Even if the clean versions of the problem were impossible, that would suggest that the problem is much more messy, which requires more concerted effort to solve but also tends to be just a long list of relatively easy tasks to do. (In contrast, MIRI thinks that prosaic AGI alignment is probably impossible.) … Note that even finding out that the problem is impossible can help; it makes it more likely that we can all coordinate to not build dangerous AI systems, since no one *wants* to build an unaligned AI system" [16].

Everitt and Hutter realize difficulty of the challenge but suggest that we may have a way forward: "A superhuman AGI is a system who outperforms humans on most cognitive tasks. In order to control it, humans would need to control a system more intelligent than themselves. This may be nearly impossible if the difference in intelligence is large, and the AGI is trying to escape control. Humans have one key advantage: As the designers of the system, we get to decide the AGI's goals, and the

---

[1] In 2017 Yudkowsky made a bet that the world will be destroyed by unaligned AI by January 1st, 2030, but he did so with intention of improving chances of successful AI control.

way the AGI strives to achieve its goals. This may allow us design AGIs whose goals are aligned with ours, and then pursue them in a responsible way. Increased intelligence in an AGI is not a threat as long as the AGI only strives to help us achieve our own goals" [17].

3 Uncontrollable

Similarly, those in the "uncontrollability camp" have made attempts at justifying their opinions, but likewise we note absence of proofs or rigor, probably because all available examples come from non-academic or not-peer-reviewed sources. This could be explained by noting that "[t]o prove that something is impossible is usually much harder than the opposite task; as it is often necessary to develop a theory" [18].

Yudkowsky writes: "[A]n impossibility proof [of stable goal system] would have to say:

1) The AI cannot reproduce onto new hardware, or modify itself on current hardware, with knowable stability of the decision system (that which determines what the AI is *trying* to accomplish in the external world) and bounded low cumulative failure probability over many rounds of self-modification.

or.

2) The AI's decision function (as it exists in abstract form across self-modifications) cannot be knowably stably bound with bounded low cumulative failure probability to programmer-targeted consequences as represented within the AI's changing, inductive world-model" [19].

Below we highlight some objections to possibility of controllability or statements of that as a fact:

- "Friendly AI hadn't been something that I had considered at all—because it was obviously impossible and useless to deceive a superintelligence about what was the right course of action" [20].
- "AI must be programmed with a set of ethical codes that align with humanity's. Though it is his life's only work, Yudkowsky is pretty sure he will fail. Humanity, he says, is likely doomed" [21].
- "The problem is that they may be faced with an impossible task. ... It's also possible that we'll figure out what we *need* to do in order to protect ourselves from AI's threats, and realize that we simply *can't* do it" [22].
- "I hope this helps explain some of my attitude when people come to me with various bright suggestions for building communities of AIs to make the whole Friendly without any of the individuals being trustworthy, or proposals for keeping an AI in a box, or proposals for "Just make an AI that does X", etcetera. Describing the specific flaws would be a whole long story in each case. But the general rule is that you can't do it *because Friendly AI is impossible*" [14].
- "It doesn't even mean that "human values" will, in a meaningful sense, be in control of the future" [5].
- "And it's undoubtedly correct that we're currently unable to specify human goals in machine learning systems" [5].

- "[H]umans control tigers not because we're stronger, but because we're smarter. This means that if we cede our position as smartest on our planet, it's possible that we might also cede control" [23]. "... no physical interlock or other safety mechanism can be devised to restrain AGIs ..." [24].
- "[Ultra-Intelligent Machine (ULM)] might be controlled by the military, who already own a substantial fraction of all computing power, but the servant can become the master and he who controls the UIM will be controlled by it" [25].
- "Limits exist to the level of control one can place in machines" [26].
- "As human beings, we could never be sure of the attitudes of [superintelligences] towards us. We would not understand them, because by definition, they are smarter than us. We therefore could not control them. They could control us, if they chose to, because they are smarter than us" [27].
- "Artificial Intelligence regulation may be impossible to achieve without better AI, ironically. As humans, we have to admit we no longer have the capability of regulating a world of machines, algorithms and advancements that might lead to surprising technologies with their own economic, social and humanitarian risks beyond the scope of international law, government oversight, corporate responsibility and consumer awareness" [28].
- "... superhuman intelligences, by definition capable of escaping any artificial constraints created by human designers. Designed superintelligences eventually will find a way to change their utility function to constant infinity becoming inert, while evolved superintelligences will be embedded in a process that creates pressure for persistence, thus presenting danger for the human species, replacing it as the apex cognition - given that its drive for persistence will ultimately override any other concerns" [29].
- "My aim ... is to argue that this problem is less well-defined than many people seem to think, and to argue that it is indeed impossible to "solve" with any precision, not merely in practice but in principle. ... The idea of a future machine that will do exactly what we would want, and whose design therefore constitutes a lever for precise future control, is a pipe dream" [30].
- "...extreme intelligences could not easily be controlled (either by the groups creating them, or by some international regulatory regime), and would probably act to boost their own intelligence and acquire maximal resources for almost all initial AI motivations" [31].
- "The only way to seriously deal with this problem would be to mathematically define "friendliness" and prove that certain AI architectures would always remain friendly. I don't think anybody has ever managed to come remotely close to doing this, and I suspect that nobody ever will. ... I think the idea is an impossible dream ..." [32].
- "[T]he whole topic of Friendly AI is incomplete and optimistic. It's unclear whether or not Friendly AI can be expressed in a formal, mathematical sense, and so there may be no way to build it or to integrate it into promising AI architectures" [33].
- "I have recently come to the opinion that AGI alignment is probably extremely hard. ... Aligning a fully automated autopoietic cognitive system, or an almost-fully-automated autopoietic cognitive system, both seem extremely difficult. My snap judgment is to assign about 1% probability to humanity solving this problem in the next 20 years. (My impression is that "the MIRI position" thinks the

probability of this working is pretty low, too, but doesn't see a good alternative). ...
Also note that [top MIRI researchers] think the problem is pretty hard and unlikely
to be solved" [34].

The primary target for AI Safety researchers, the case of successful creation of
value-aligned superintelligence, is worth analyzing in additional detail as it presents
surprising negative side-effects, which may not be anticipated by the developers.
Kaczynski murdered three people and injured 23 to get the following warning about
overreliance on machines in front of the public, which was a part of his broader anti-
technology manifesto:

"If the machines are permitted to make all their own decisions, we can't make any
conjectures as to the results, because it is impossible to guess how such machines might
behave. We only point out that the fate of the human race would be at the mercy of the
machines. It might be argued that the human race would never be foolish enough to
hand over all power to the machines. But we are suggesting neither that the human race
would voluntarily turn power over to the machines nor that the machines would
willfully seize power. What we do suggest is that the human race might easily permit
itself to drift into a position of such dependence on the machines that it would have no
practical choice but to accept all of the machines' decisions. As society and the
problems that face it become more and more complex and as machines become more
and more intelligent, people will let machines make more and more of their decisions
for them, simply because machine-made decisions will bring better results than man-
made ones. Eventually a stage may be reached at which the decisions necessary to keep
the system running will be so complex that human beings will be incapable of making
them intelligently. At that stage the machines will be in effective control. People won't
be able to just turn the machines off, because they will be so dependent on them that
turning them off would amount to suicide" [35].

4   Analysis

Why do so many researchers assume that AI control problem is solvable? To the best of
our knowledge there is no evidence for that, no proof. Before embarking on a quest to
build a controlled AI, it is important to show that the problem is solvable as not to
waste precious resources. The burden of such proof is on those who claim that the
problem is solvable, and the current absence of such proof speaks loudly about inherent
dangers of the proposition to create superhuman intelligence. In fact, uncontrollability
of AI is very likely true as can be shown via reduction to the human control problem.
Many open questions need to be considered in relation to the controllability issue: Is
the Control problem solvable? Can it be done in principle? Can it be done in practice?
Can it be done with the hundred percent accuracy? How long would it take to do it?
Can it be done in time? What are the energy and computational requirements for doing
it? How would a solution look? What is the minimal viable solution? How would we
know if we solved it? Does the solution scale as the system continues to improve?

AI researchers can be grouped into the following broad categories based on
responses to survey questions related to arrival of AGI and safety concerns. First split is

regarding possibility of human level AI, while some think it is an inevitable development others claim it will never happen. Among those who are sure AGI will be developed some think it will definitely be a beneficial invention because with high intelligence comes benevolence, while others are almost certain it will be a disaster, at least if special care is not taken to avoid pitfalls. In the set of all researchers concerned with AI safety most think that AI control is a solvable problem, but some think that superintelligence can't be fully controlled and so while we will be able to construct true AI, the consequences of such act will not be desirable. Finally, among those who think that control is not possible, some are actually happy to see human extinction as it gives other species on our planet more opportunities, reduces environmental problems and definitively reduces human suffering to zero. The remaining group are scholars who are certain that superintelligent machines can be constructed but could not be safely controlled, this group also considers human extinctions to be an undesirable event.

There are many ways to show that controllability of AI is impossible, with supporting evidence coming from many diverse disciplines. Just one argument would suffice but this is such an important problem, we want to reduce unverifiability concerns as much as possible. Even if some of the concerns get resolved in the future, many other important problems will remain. So far, researchers who argue that AI will be controllable are presenting their opinions, while uncontrollability conclusion is supported by multiple impossibility results [36]. Additional difficulty comes not just from having to achieve control, but also from sustaining it as the system continues to learn and evolve, the so called "treacherous turn" [37] problem. If superintelligence is not properly controlled it doesn't matter who programmed it, the consequences will be disastrous for everyone and likely its programmers in the first place. No one benefits from uncontrolled AI.

There seems to be no evidence to conclude that a less intelligent agent can indefinitely maintain control over a more intelligent agent. As we develop intelligent system which are less intelligent than we are we can remain in control, but once such systems become smarter than us, we will lose such capability. In fact, while attempting to remain in control while designing superhuman intelligent agents we find ourselves in a Catch 22, as the controlling mechanism necessary to maintain control has to be smarter or at least as smart as the superhuman agent we want to maintain control over. A whole hierarchy of superintelligent systems would need to be constructed to control ever more capable systems leading to infinite regress. AI Control problems appears to be Controlled-Superintelligence-complete [38–40]. Worse, the problem of controlling such more capable superintelligences only becomes more challenging and more obviously impossible for agents with just a human-level of intelligence. Essentially we need to have a well-controlled super-superintelligence before we can design a controlled superintelligence but that is of course a contradiction in causality. Whoever is more intelligent will be in control and those in control will be the ones who have power to make final decisions.

Most AI projects don't have an integrated safety aspect to them and are designed with a sole purpose of accomplishing certain goals, with no resources dedicated to avoiding undesirable side effects from AI's deployment. Consequently, from statistical point of view, first AGI will not be safe by design, but essentially randomly drawn from the set of easiest to make AGIs (even if that means brute force [41]). In the space of possible minds [42], even if they existed, safe designs would constitute only a tiny minority of an infinite number of possible designs many of which are highly capable but not aligned with goals of humanity. Therefore, our chances of getting lucky and getting a safe AI on our first attempt by chance are infinitely small. We have to ask ourselves, what is more likely, that we will first create an AGI or that we will first create and AGI which is safe? This can be resolved with simple Bayesian analysis but we must not fall for the Conjunction fallacy [9]. It also seems, that all else being equal friendly AIs would be less capable than unfriendly ones as friendliness is an additional limitation on performance and so in case of competition between designs, less restricted ones would dominate long term.

Intelligence is a computational resource [43] and to be in complete control over that resource we should be able to precisely set every relevant aspect of it. This would include being able to specify intelligence to a specific range of performance, for example IQ range 70–80, or 160–170. It should be possible to disable particular functionality, for example remove ability to drive or remember faces as well as limit system's rate of time discounting. Control requires capability to set any values for the system, any ethical or moral code, any set of utility weights, any terminal goals. Most importantly remaining in control means that we have final say in what the system does or doesn't do. Which in turn means that you can't even attempt to solve AI safety without first solving "human safety". Any controlled AI has to be resilient to hackers, incompetent or malevolent users and insider threats.

5 Conclusions

To the best of our knowledge, as of this moment, no one in the world has a working AI control mechanism capable of scaling to human level AI and eventually to superintelligence, or even an idea for a prototype, which might work. No one made verifiable claims to have such technology. In general, for anyone making a claim that control problem is solvable, the burden of proof is on them and ideally it would be a constructive proof, not just a theoretical claim. At least at the moment, it seems that our ability to produce intelligent software greatly outpaces our ability to control or even verify it.

Narrow AI systems can be made safe because they represent a finite space of choices and so at least theoretically all possible bad decisions and mistakes can be counteracted. For AGI space of possible decisions and failures is infinite, meaning an infinite number of potential problems will always remain regardless of the number of safety patches applied to the system. Such an infinite space of possibilities is impossible to completely debug or even properly test for safety. Worse yet, a superintelligent system will represent infinite spaces of competence exceeding human comprehension [44, 45].

Same can be said about intelligent systems in terms of their security. A NAI presents a finite attack surface, while an AGI gives malevolent users and hackers an infinite set of options to work with. From security point of view that means that while defenders have to secure and infinite space, attackers only have to find one penetration point to succeed. Additionally, every safety patch/mechanism introduces new vulnerabilities, ad infinitum. AI Safety research so far can be seen as discovering new failure modes and coming up with patches for them, essentially a fixed set of rules for an infinite set of problems. There is a fractal nature to the problem, regardless of how much we "zoom in" on it we keep discovering just as many challenges at all levels. It is likely that the control problem is not just unsolvable, but exhibits fractal impossibility, it contains unsolvable sub-problems at all levels of abstraction. However, it is not all bad news, uncontrollability of AI means that malevolent actors will likewise be unable to fully exploit artificial intelligence for their benefit.

References

1. Baum, S.D., et al.: Long-term trajectories of human civilization. foresight (2019)
2. Callaghan, V., et al.: Technological singularity. Springer (2017). Doi: https://doi.org/10.1007/978-3-662-54033-6_11
3. Ramamoorthy, A., Yampolskiy, R.: Beyond mad? the race for artificial general intelligence. ITU J. 1, 1–8 (2018)
4. Yampolskiy, R.V.: Artificial Intelligence Safety and Security. CRC Press, Boca Raton (2018)
5. Baumann, T.: Why I expect successful (narrow) alignment, in *S-Risks*. December 29, 2018. http://s-risks.org/why-i-expect-successful-alignment/
6. M0zrat, Is Alignment Even Possible?!, in Control Problem Forum/Comments (2018). https://www.reddit.com/r/ControlProblem/comments/8p0mru/is_alignment_even_possible/
7. SquirrelInHell, The AI Alignment Problem Has Already Been Solved(?) Once, in Comment on LessWrong by magfrump, 22 April 2017. https://www.lesswrong.com/posts/Ldzoxz3BuFL4Ca8pG/the-ai-alignment-problem-has-already-been-solved-once
8. Muehlhauser, L., Williamson, C.: Ideal Advisor Theories and Personal CEV. Machine Intelligence Research Institute (2013)
9. Yudkowsky, E.: Artificial intelligence as a positive and negative factor in global risk. Global Catastrophic Risks 1(303), 184 (2008)
10. Yudkowsky, E.: The AI alignment problem: why it is hard, and where to start. In: Symbolic Systems Distinguished Speaker (2016). https://intelligence.org/2016/12/28/ai-alignment-why-its-hard-and-where-to-start/
11. Russell, S.J.: Provably beneficial artificial intelligence, in Exponential Life, The Next Step (2017). https://people.eecs.berkeley.edu/~russell/papers/russell-bbvabook17-pbai.pdf
12. Russell, S.: Provably beneficial artificial intelligence. In: The Next Step: Exponential Life (2017). https://www.bbvaopenmind.com/en/articles/provably-beneficial-artificial-intelligence/
13. Russell, S.: Should we fear supersmart robots? Sci. Am. 314(6), 58–59 (2016)
14. Yudkowsky, E.: Shut up and do the impossible! In: Less Wrong. October 8 (2008). https://www.lesswrong.com/posts/nCvvhFBaayaXyuBiD/shut-up-and-do-the-impossible
15. Joy, B.: Why the future doesn't need us. Wired Mag. 8(4), 238–262 (2000)
16. Shah, R.: Why AI risk might be solved without additional intervention from longtermists. In: Alignment Newsletter, 2 January 2020. https://mailchi.mp/b3dc916ac7e2/an-80-why-ai-risk-might-be-solved-without-additional-intervention-from-longtermists
17. Everitt, T., Hutter, M.: The alignment problem for Bayesian history-based reinforcement learners., Technical report (2018). https://www.tomeveritt.se/papers/alignment.pdf
18. Proof of Impossibility, in Wikipedia (2020). https://en.wikipedia.org/wiki/Proof_of_impossibility

19. Yudkowsky, E.: Proving the Impossibility of Stable Goal Systems. In SL4, 5 March 2006. http://www.sl4.org/archive/0603/14296.html
20. Yudkowsky, E.: On Doing the Impossible, in Less Wrong, 6 October 2008. https://www.lesswrong.com/posts/fpecAJLG9czABgCe9/on-doing-the-impossible
21. Clarke, R., Eddy, R.P.: Summoning the Demon: Why superintelligence is humanity's biggest threat, in Geek Wire, 24 May 2017. https://www.geekwire.com/2017/summoning-demon-superintelligence-humanitys-biggest-threat/
22. Creighton, J.: OpenAI Wants to Make Safe AI, but That May Be an Impossible Task, in Futurism, 15 March 2018. https://futurism.com/openai-safe-ai-michael-page
23. Tegmark, M.: Life 3.0: Being human in the age of artificial intelligence. Knopf (2017)
24. Kornai, A.: Bounding the impact of AGI. J. Exp. Theor. Artif. Intell. **26**(3), 417–438 (2014)
25. Good, I.J.: Human and machine intelligence: comparisons and contrasts. Impact Sci. Soc. **21**(4), 305–322 (1971)
26. De Garis, H.: What if AI succeeds? The rise of the twenty-first century artilect. AI Magazine **10**(2), 17 (1989)
27. Garis, H.d.: The Rise of the Artilect Heaven or Hell (2009). http://www.agi-conf.org/2009/papers/agi-09artilect.doc
28. Spencer, M.: Artificial Intelligence Regulation May Be Impossible, in Forbes, 2 March 2019. https://www.forbes.com/sites/cognitiveworld/2019/03/02/artificial-intelligence-regulation-will-be-impossible/amp
29. Menezes, T.: Non-Evolutionary Superintelligences Do Nothing, Eventually. arXiv preprint arXiv:1609.02009 (2016)
30. Vinding, M.: Is AI Alignment Possible? 14 December 2018. https://magnusvinding.com/2018/12/14/is-ai-alignment-possible/
31. Pamlin, D., Armstrong, S.: 12 Risks that Threaten Human Civilization, in Global Challenges, February 2015. https://www.pamlin.net/material/2017/10/10/without-us-progress-still-possible-article-in-china-daily-m9hnk
32. Legg, S.: Friendly AI is Bunk, in Vetta Project (2006). http://commonsenseatheism.com/wp-content/uploads/2011/02/Legg-Friendly-AI-is-bunk.pdf
33. Barrat, J.: Our final invention: Artificial intelligence and the end of the human era (2013). Macmillan
34. Taylor, J.: Autopoietic systems and difficulty of AGI alignment. In: Intelligent Agent Foundations Forum. Accessed 18 Aug 2017, https://agentfoundations.org/item?id=1628
35. Kaczynski, T.: Industrial Society and Its Future, in The New York Times, 19 September 1995
36. Yampolskiy, R.V.: On Controllability of AI. arXiv preprint arXiv:2008.04071 (2020)
37. Bostrom, N.: Superintelligence: Paths, Dangers, Strategies. Oxford University Press (2014)
38. Yampolskiy, R.: Turing Test as a Defining Feature of AI-Completeness. In: Yang, X.-S. (ed.) Artificial Intelligence, Evolutionary Computing and Metaheuristics, pp. 3–17. Springer, Berlin Heidelberg (2013)
39. Yampolskiy, R.V.: AI-Complete CAPTCHAs as Zero Knowledge Proofs of Access to an Artificially Intelligent System. ISRN Artificial Intelligence (2011). **271878**
40. Yampolskiy, R.V.: AI-Complete, AI-Hard, or AI-Easy–Classification of Problems in AI. The 23rd Midwest Artificial Intelligence and Cognitive Science Conference, Cincinnati, OH, USA (2012)
41. Brown, T.B., et al.: Language models are few-shot learners. arXiv preprint arXiv:2005.14165 (2020)
42. Yampolskiy, R.V.: The space of possible mind designs. In: International Conference on Artificial General Intelligence (2015). Springer

43. Yampolskiy, R.V.: Efficiency theory: a unifying theory for information, computation and intelligence. J. Discrete Math. Sci. Cryptography **16**(4–5), 259–277 (2013)
44. Yampolskiy, R.V.: Unexplainability and Incomprehensibility of AI. J. Artif. Intell. Consciousness **7**(02), 277–291 (2020)
45. Yampolskiy, R.V.: Unpredictability of AI: on the impossibility of accurately predicting all actions of a smarter agent. J. Artif. Intell. Consciousness **7**(01), 109–118 (2020)

AGI via Combining Logic with Deep Learning

King-Yin Yan$^{(\boxtimes)}$

Generic Intelligence, Hong Kong, China

Abstract. An integration of deep learning and symbolic logic is proposed, based on the Curry-Howard isomorphism and categorical logic. The propositional structure of logic is seen as a symmetry, namely the permutation invariance of propositions; This can be implemented using so-called symmetric neural networks. Under our interpretation, it turns out that Google's BERT, which many currently state-of-the-art language models are derived from, can be regarded as an alternative form of logic. This BERT-like structure can be incorporated under a reinforcement-learning framework to form a minimal AGI architecture. We also mention some insights gleaned from category and topos theory that point to future directions and may be helpful to other researchers, including mathematicians interested in AGI.

Keywords: Deep learning · Symbolic logic · Logic-based AI · Neural-symbolic integration · Curry-Howard isomorphism · Category theory · Topos theory · Fuzzy logic

1 Introduction

Results in the present paper does not make use of category theory in any significant way (nor the Curry-Howard isomorphism, for that matter). Its main accomplishment is to express AGI in the categorical language. To the lay person, concepts of category theory (such as pullbacks, adjunctions, fibration, toposes, sheaves, ...) may be difficult to grasp, but they are the mathematician's "daily bread". We hope that describing AGI in categorical terms will entice more mathematicians to work on this important topic.

Secondly, an abstract formulation allows us to see clearly what is meant by "the mathematical structure of logic", without which logic is just a collection of esoteric rules and axioms, leaving us with a feeling that something may be "amiss" in our theory.

1.1 The Curry-Howard Isomorphism

As the risk of sounding too elementary, we would go over some basic background knowledge, that may help those readers unfamiliar with this area of mathematics.

K.-Y. Yan—Independent researcher.

B. Goertzel et al. (Eds.): AGI 2021, LNAI 13154, pp. 327–343, 2022.
https://doi.org/10.1007/978-3-030-93758-4_34

The Curry-Howard isomorphism expresses a connection between logic **syntax** and its underlying **proof** mechanism. It is fundamental to understanding categorical logic. Consider the mathematical declaration of a **function** f with its domain and co-domain:

$$f : A \to B. \tag{1}$$

This notation comes from type theory, where A and B are **types** (which we can think of as sets or general spaces) and the function f is an **element** in the function space $A \to B$, which is also a type.

What the Curry-Howard isomorphism says in essence is that we can regard $A \to B$ as a **logic** formula, i.e. the implication $A \Rightarrow B$, and the function f as a **proof** process that maps a proof of A to a proof of B.[1]

The following may give a clearer picture:

$$
\begin{array}{c}
\boxed{\text{logic}} \qquad A \Longrightarrow B \\
\text{-----------} \\
\boxed{\text{program}} \qquad \blacksquare \overset{f}{\longmapsto} \blacksquare \; .
\end{array}
\tag{2}
$$

What we see here is a logic formula "on the surface", with an underlying proof mechanism which is a **function**, or λ-calculus term. Here the $\blacksquare$'s represent proof objects or **witnesses**. The logic propositions A and B coincide with the **domains** (or **types**) specified by type theory. Hence the great educator Philip Wadler calls it "propositions as types".[2] Other textbooks on the Curry-Howard isomorphism include: [39, 40, 42].

The gist of our theory is that Deep Learning provides us with neural networks (i.e. non-linear functions) that serve as the proof mechanism of logic via the Curry-Howard isomorphism. With this interpretation, we can impose the mathematical structure of logic (e.g. symmetries) onto neural networks. Such constraints serve as **inductive bias** that can accelerate learning, according to the celebrated "No Free Lunch" theory [1, 36, 45].

In particular, logic propositions in a conjunction (such as $A \wedge B$) are commutative, i.e. invariant under permutations, which is a "symmetry" of logic and perhaps the most important one. This symmetry decomposes a logic "state" into a set of propositions, and seems to be a fundamental feature of most logics known to humans. Imposing this symmetry on neural networks gives rise to symmetric neural networks (see Sect. 4).

We have not been clear about what the **proof witnesses** are. In our current implementation, types are regions in vector space and witnesses are just points inside the regions. When some propositions imply another proposition, there is a function mapping witnesses in some regions to a new witness in another region. Thus, such spatial regions are nearly tautologous with proof witnesses (i.e. points versus the regions containing them). In other words, the "big" vector space is divided into many small regions representing various propositions.

---

[1] Though one does not need to execute a function to prove a statement; Merely the existence of a such a function (proof object) that type-checks is sufficient.

[2] See his introductory video: https://www.youtube.com/watch?v=IOiZatlZtGU.

We should point out that the Curry-Howard isomorphism has not played a significant role in our current AGI theory. The representation of **conditional** statements (e.g. $A \Rightarrow B$) requires **function types** which are hard to represent as vectors.[3] So the only function type in our system is the "main" neural network simulating the $\vdash$ operator. In the language of classical logic-based AI, this is similar to having "Horn form" logic rules in the knowledge base, while the working memory contains *atomic* propositions only.

As an aside, the Curry-Howard isomorphism also establishes connections to diverse disciplines. Whenever there is a space of elements and some operations over them, there is a chance that it has an underlying "logic" to it (see e.g. Baez and Stay's "Rosetta Stone" paper: [2], also [14]). For example, in quantum mechanics, that of Hilbert space and Hermitian operators. Another example: in String Theory, strings and cobordisms between them. For example the famous "pair of pants" cobordism (Fig. 1A), representing a process in time that merges two strings into one (time is read upwards).

Seeing logical types as topological spaces is also the origin of Voevodsky's **Homotopy Type Theory** (HoTT) [29], where the **identity** of two inhabitants in a type is seen as a homotopy **path**. HoTT may be relevant to AGI if we want the convenience of having multiple identical proofs of the same propositions – this may help simplify the topology of types (i.e. spatial regions representing propositions). For example in Fig. 2A, two disjoint regions can be connected by a path, even though x_1 and x_2 are "identical" points.

Fig. 1. Ⓐ pair of pants. Ⓑ point clouds

2   Prior Research

2.1   Neuro-symbolic Integration

There has been a long history of attempts to integrate symbolic logic with neural processing, with pioneers such as Ron Sun, Dov Gabbay, Barbara Hammer, among others. We describe two **model-based** approaches below.

From a categorical perspective, model theory is a **functor** mapping logic syntax to algebraic objects *and* the operations between them (hence the name "functorial semantics"):

---

[3] Ben Goertzel's latest "general theory of AGI" [11] addresses higher-order networks, which construct other networks as proofs of implications.

$$\boxed{\text{syntax}} \quad a \cdot b \longmapsto [\![a]\!] \cdot [\![b]\!] \quad \boxed{\text{algebraic objects, e.g. group elements}} \qquad (3)$$

Model theory is interesting when the target structure has additional properties beyond those specified by the logic syntax. For example, the predicate male(x) may be modelled by:

$$
\begin{array}{c|c|c}
\text{algebraic geometry} & \text{male(x)} \Leftrightarrow f(x) \geq 0 & f \text{ is a polynomial} \\
\text{linear algebra} & \text{male(x)} \Leftrightarrow Mx \geq 0 & M \text{ is a matrix} \\
\text{topology} & \text{male(x)} \Leftrightarrow x \in S & S \text{ is an open set}
\end{array} \qquad (4)
$$

Model-based methods may appear impractical for AGI because the number of grounded atomic propositions gets too large (potentially infinite, if we include also propositions that are imagined). However, if all possible atoms are embedded in a mathematical space through mapping schemes such as the above (4), it may be approximately feasible.

In the "**syntactic**" or type-theoretic approach (including the one in this paper), propositions (= types) are regions in some vector space. Currently our simple scheme is to map predicates like $P(a, b)$ into the Cartesian product $\mathbb{Pred} \times \mathbb{Obj} \times \mathbb{Obj}$ where $\mathbb{Pred}$ is the space of all possible predicates and $\mathbb{Obj}$ the space of all possible objects[4] (but this is not the only option; see Sect. 3.1). **Inference** is performed by a neural network simulating the single-step consequence operator $\vdash$, while **learning** is through changing of network weights. This is relatively simple and straightforward.

Whereas, in the **model-theoretic** approach one places objects in a high-dimensional space such that their positions satisfy the constraints imposed by various predicates (e.g. polynomials, matrices, open sets, ...) Now forward **inference** occurs as the system pays *attention* to (i.e. to be simply aware of) some points in an $\mathbb{Obj}$ect space, which points are covered by some predicates. Thus a new proposition is discovered, adding to more new conclusions, ... and so on. It is interesting that, under this scheme, it seems as if all truths are known *a priori*, and the system just needs to discover or "attend" to them. **Learning** changes the geometric shapes of predicates and forms new truths to be discovered by the system.

1. In Pascal Hitzler and Anthony Seda's **Core Method** [16], an **interpretation** $\mathcal{I}$ is a function that assigns truth values to the set of all possible ground atoms in a logic language $\mathcal{L}$. One can see $\mathcal{I}$ as an enumeration of ground atoms that are true, and thus it provides a model to interpret any logic formula in $\mathcal{L}$. Moreover $\mathcal{I}$ is a function from the space X of atoms to $\mathbf{2} = \{\top, \bot\}$ and can be given a topology $\mathbf{2}^X$ which is X copies of the discrete topology of $\mathbf{2}$. Such a topology makes $\mathcal{I}$ homeomorphic to the **Cantor set** in $[0, 1]$. To a logic program P is associated a **semantic operator** $T_P : \mathcal{I} \to \mathcal{I}$, performing a single step of forward **inference**. Finally, the space of interpretations $\mathcal{I}$ is

---

[4] Here objects mean logical or first-order objects, not categorical objects.

embedded into $\mathbb{R}$ using a "level mapping" (The level of an atom increases by each inference step; All the atoms of an interpretation $\mathcal{I}$ are translated into a fractional number in base b). This allows T_P to be approximated by a neural network $f : \mathcal{I} \to \mathbb{R}$.

The goal of their research is to find the fixed-point semantics of logic programs, but with suitable modifications, the same mathematical structure may be used to build an inference engine or AGI. In such case, the logic program would function as the **knowledge base** while interpretations would play the role of **working memory** (though the memory could only be a subset of an interpretation, due to physical limitation).

2. ∂-**ILP** [9] is focused on the learning problem, but its set-up seems similar to the first example. A **valuation** is a vector $[0,1]^n$ mapping every ground atom to a real number $\in [0,1]$. Each clause is attached with a Boolean flag to indicate whether it is included in the results or not. From each clause c one can generate a function $\mathcal{F}_c$ on valuations that implements a single step of forward **inference**. To enable differentiability, the Boolean flag is relaxed to be a continuous value and gradient descent is used to **learn** which clauses should be included.

We would also like to mention Geoffrey Hinton's recent **GLOM theory** [15], which addresses the problem of representing a hierarchy of visual structures. OpenCog has also been applied to neural-symbolic integration [12,28]. These further support that representing and learning **relational** (logical) knowledge is a topic of central importance, and that there is a convergence of "mainstream" AI with AGI.

2.2   Cognitive Architectures and Reinforcement Learning

When we mention "AGI" here, it is intended to focus on a minimal core subset of its requirements, namely the ability to make logically correct inferences based on distilled knowledge learned from massive world-data. The strategy is that other modules of an AGI may be built upon this base.

Reinforcement Learning (RL). In the 1980's, Richard Sutton [41] introduced reinforcement learning as an AI paradigm, drawing inspiration from Control Theory and Dynamic Programming. In retrospect, RL already has sufficient generality to be considered an AGI theory, or at least as a top-level framework for describing AGI architectures[5].

Relation to AIXI. AIXI is an abstract AGI model introduced by Marcus Hutter in 2000 [19]. AIXI's environmental setting is the external "world" as observed by some sensors. The agent's internal model is a universal Turing

---

[5] Indeed, Sutton argues that merely increasing brute-force computing power would lead to AGI and that human design of algorithms is relatively useless. The tenet in this paper is that logic may serve as an inductive bias to accelerate learning, but we cannot be certain about this, since the algorithmic search for AGI is non-exhaustive (see Sect. 5).

machine (UTM), and the (approximately) optimal action is chosen by maximizing potential rewards over all programs of the UTM. In our (minimal) model, the UTM is *constrained* to be a neural network, where the NN's **state** is analogous to the UTM's **tape**, and the optimal weights (program) are found via Bellman optimality.

Relation to Quantum Mechanics and Path Integrals. At the core of RL is the Bellman equation, which governs the update of the utility function to reach its optimal value. This equation (in discrete time) is equivalent to the Hamilton-Jacobi equation in differential form. Nowadays they are unified as the Hamilton-Jacobi-Bellman equation, under the name "optimal control theory" [24]. In turn, the Hamilton-Jacobi equation is closely related to the Schrödinger equation in quantum mechanics:

$$\boxed{\text{Bellman eqn.}} \leftrightsquigarrow \boxed{\text{Hamilton-Jacobi eqn.}} \leftrightsquigarrow \boxed{\text{Schrödinger eqn.}} \tag{5}$$

but the second link is merely "heuristic"; it is the well-studied "quantization" process whose meaning remains mysterious to this day. Nevertheless, the **path integral** method introduced by Richard Feynmann can be applied to RL algorithms, e.g. [22].

The Hamilton-Jacobi equation gives the RL setting a "symplectic" structure [26]; Such problems are best solved by so-called symplectic integrators (proposed by 冯康 (Feng Kang) in the 1980s [10], see also [23]). Surprisingly, in the RL/AI literature, which has witnessed tremendous growth in recent years, there is scarcely any mention of the Hamilton-Jacobi structure, while the most efficient heuristics (such as policy gradient, experience replay, Actor-Critic, etc.) seem to exploit other structural characteristics of "the world".

3   The Mathematical Structure of Logic

Currently, the most mathematically advanced and satisfactory description of logic seems to base on category theory, known as categorial logic and topos theory. This direction was pioneered by William Lawvere in the 1950–60's. The body of work in this field is quite vast, but we shall briefly mention some points that are relevant to AGI. A more detailed tutorial on categorical logic, with a focus on AGI, is in preparation [46].

3.1   Predicates and Dependent Type Theory

The Curry-Howard isomorphism identifies *propositional* intuitionistic logic with type theory. As such, the arrow $\rightarrow$ in type theory is "used up" (it corresponds to the implication arrow $\Rightarrow$ in intuitionistic logic). However, predicates are also a kind of functions (arrows), so how could we accomodate predicates in type theory such that Curry-Howard continues to hold? This is the idea behind Martin Löf's **dependent type theory**.

In dependent type theory, a predicate $P(\cdot)$ is a **type constructor** ([40] Sect. 8.7) taking an element a of one type to create a new type $P(a)$. For example, each element $a \in \{$John, Socrates, Kermit$\}$ creates a new type Human(a), and thus Human is a **family** of types or a **dependent type**. This is depicted in Fig. 2B.

Mathematically, a dependent type is a product of types **indexed** by another type, denoted $\Pi_A B$, which is really a form of **exponentiation**. If every source element maps to the same type B, then $\Pi_A B$ *degenerates* into the ordinary function type $A \to B$ (cf. [27] Sect. 3.3).

So far, we did not make use of dependent types: predicates are represented using simple Cartesian products (i.e. vector concatenation) such as $\mathbb{P}\mathrm{red} \times \mathbb{O}\mathrm{bj}$, but there is the possibility of exploiting more general indexing schemes.

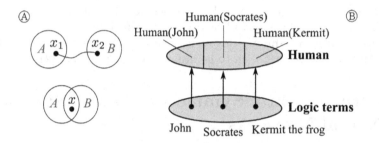

Fig. 2. Ⓐ A path in homotopy type theory. Ⓑ The predicate "Human" as a fibration

The expressiveness of predicate logic (in one form or another) is a highly desirable feature for AGI knowledge representations. So it seems necessary to incorporate dependent type theory into our logic. From a categorical perspective, predicates can be regarded as **fibers** over a base set. Fibrations capture the structure of **indexing** and **substitutions**, as shown in Fig. 2B. This figure is key to understanding Bart Jacob's book [20]. Thus category theory gives us more insight into the (predicate) structure of logic, though it is as yet unclear how to make use of this particular idea.

3.2 (Fuzzy) Topos Theory

The author's previous paper [47], almost a decade ago, proposed a fuzzy-probabilistic logic where probabilities are distributed over fuzzy truth values. So far we still believe that regarding fuzziness as a generalization of binary truth is philosophically sound. Thus it behooves to develop a generalization of standard topos theory to the fuzzy case.

A topos is a category that generalizes set theory. The most important commutative diagram in Topos theory is this one:

$$
\begin{array}{ccc}
X & \xrightarrow{\;!\;} & 1 \\
{\scriptstyle m}\big\uparrow & & \big\downarrow{\scriptstyle \mathrm{true}} \\
Y & \xrightarrow[\chi_m]{} & \Omega
\end{array}
\tag{6}
$$

It can be understood as saying that every **set** is a **pullback** of the true map $1 \to \Omega$ (which "picks out" true from $\Omega = \{\top, \bot\}$), in analogy to the idea of a "moduli space" where every family is a pullback of a "universal family" [13,35]. Following this idea, could it be that every fuzzy set is the pullback of a fuzzy "true" map?

The book [7] Sect. 5.2.4 provides a concise review of the categorical treatment of fuzzy sets: The sub-object classifier Ω that characterizes classical set theory is generalized to a **complete Heyting algebra** (CHA, also called a **frame**, which captures the structure of a topology, ie, the lattice of open subsets of a set; This includes the interval $[0,1]$ as a special case, in accord with our philosophical intuition), and also leads to the recognition that *the internal logic of a topos is intuitionistic* (see [25], and this will be further explained in the tutorial [46]).

This line of research leads to Höhle's [17,18], where fuzzy set theory is interpreted as sub-fields of **sheave** theory, ie, complete Ω-valued sets, where Ω is a frame. More recent papers seem to be in favor of this thinking: [21,44].

4 Permutation Symmetry and Symmetric Neural Networks

From the categorical perspective, we make the following correspondence with logic and type theory:

$$
\begin{array}{ccccc}
\boxed{\text{product}} & A \times B & \rightsquigarrow & A \wedge B & \boxed{\text{conjunction}} \\
\boxed{\text{function}} & A \to B & \rightsquigarrow & A \Rightarrow B & \boxed{\text{implication}}
\end{array} . \tag{7}
$$

One basic characteristic of (classical) logic is that the conjunction $\wedge$ is **commutative**:

$$
P \wedge Q \quad \Leftrightarrow \quad Q \wedge P. \tag{8}
$$

This remains true of probabilistic logic, where $\wedge$ and $\vee$ are unified as conditional probability tables (CPTs) of the nodes of Bayesian networks. (Note: the commutative structure of $\wedge$ also gives rise to **monoidal categories**, that capture processes that can be executed in parallel; See [14] for an introduction.)

Once we know the symmetry, the question is how to impose this symmetry on deep neural networks. Interestingly, the answer already comes from an independent line of research (namely, PointNet [31] and Deep Sets [48]) that deals with visual object recognition of point clouds, e.g. Fig. 1B.

In a point cloud, it does not matter the order in which the points are presented, as inputs to the classifier function. Such a function needs to be permutation invariant to a huge number of points. More generally, see also these recent articles on the use of geometry and symmetry in deep learning: [5,6].

From [48]: the **Kolmogorov-Arnold representation theorem** states that every multivariate continuous function can be represented as a sum of continuous functions of one variable:

$$f(x_1, ..., x_n) = \sum_{q=0}^{2n} \Phi_q \left(\sum_{p=1}^{n} \phi_{q,p}(x_p) \right) \tag{9}$$

Their paper specialized the theorem to the case that every symmetric multi-variate function can be represented as a sum of (the same) functions of one variable:

$$f(x_1, ..., x_n) = \rho(\ \phi(x_1) + ... + \phi(x_n)\ ) \tag{10}$$

This leads to the implementation using neural networks as in Fig. 3A, and can be easily implemented with just a few lines of Tensorflow, see Sect. 6.

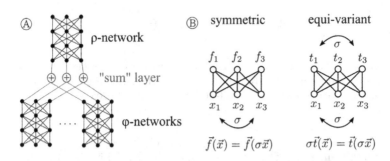

Fig. 3. Ⓐ symmetric neural network. Ⓑ permutation invariant vs. equivariant

The idea of using symmetric neural networks to process logical/relational data has already been explored by one of Google's research teams in 2017, which they called RN (Relational Networks) [3, 34]. Their results further confirm the viability of this idea.

4.1 Why BERT Is a Logic

BERT (and its variants) are based on the Transformer architecture [8], and Transformers are based solely on the Self-Attention mechanism [43]. In Fig. 4 one can verify that the Transformer is **equivariant** to its inputs. That is to say, for example, if input #1 and #2 are swapped, then output #1 and #2 would also be swapped.

In other words, each Transformer layer takes N inputs and produces N equivariant outputs. That is the same as saying that *each* output is permutation-invariant in all its inputs. As we explained in the last section, permutation invariance is the symmetry that characterizes a logic as having *individual* propositions.

Proof that Equivariance ⇔ **symmetric** (for an N-input N-output set function): ⇐: Suppose we have constructed n symmetric functions $f_1, ..., f_N$, satisfying $\forall \sigma.\ \vec{f}(\vec{x}) = \vec{f}(\sigma \vec{x})$, with σ taking values in the symmetric group $\mathfrak{S}_N$. We can re-state the condition as $\forall \sigma.\ \sigma \vec{f}(\vec{x}) = \vec{f}(\sigma \vec{x})$ by re-naming the functions, because $\{f_i\}$ is a set. ⇒: If we have N equi-variant functions $t_1, ..., t_N$, satisfying

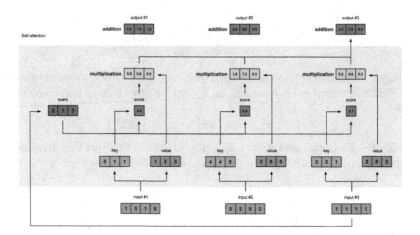

Fig. 4. Flow of operations in self-attention. From blog article: illustrated: self-attention – step-by-step guide to self-attention with illustrations and code https://towardsdatascience.com/illustrated-self-attention-2d627e33b20a

$\forall \sigma.\ \sigma \vec{t}(\vec{x}) = \vec{t}(\sigma \vec{x})$, we can also re-state the condition as $\forall \sigma.\ \sigma^{-1} \sigma\ \vec{t}(\vec{x}) = \vec{t}(\sigma \vec{x})$ by re-naming elements in the set $\{t_i\}$. This is illustrated in Fig. 3B (for $N = 3$). ∎

A Self-Attention layer can be implemented by this formula (which appears in numerous tutorials):

$$Z = \sum \text{softmax}(\frac{1}{\sqrt{d_k}} Q_i \cdot K_j^T) V_j \tag{11}$$

where **Q**uery, **K**ey, and **V**alue are *linear* transformations of the inputs X_i by multiplying (learned) matrices W^Q, W^K, W^V respectively. We hypothesize that (11) is just a *general* form of equivariant functions, ie, it represents an arbitrary non-linear transformation of the input vectors X_i to the output vector Z, without any constraints other than equivariance.

Figure 5C is a simplified view of a single Self-Attention layer. The output is a new proposition that depends on the input objects, and thus, functions as a **predicate**. However, this representation of predicates-within-proposition is not efficient for logic inference. We may visualize the non-linear (due to the softmax in Z) deformation of the input and output vector-embedding spaces as in Fig. 5D.

The problem is that a **universally quantified** formula such as $\forall x. P(x) \Rightarrow Q(x)$ requires mapping a source region to a target region in embedding spaces. This kind of mapping shapes are difficult or slow to learn because it requires many pairs of input-output data points. But BERT/GPT is famous for being able to make **few-shot generalizations**. Thus we conjecture that in BERT/GPT the logical proposition is not just one equivariant unit but is **decomposed** into several units (e.g. "I love you" at the input stage is decomposed into 3

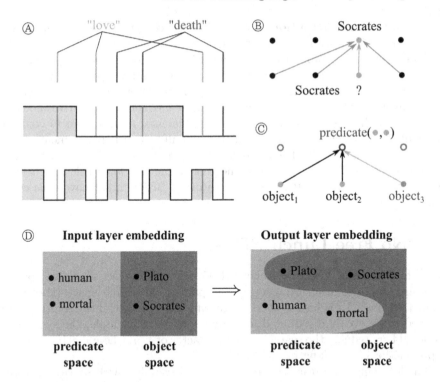

Fig. 5. Ⓐ   Why Positional Encoding does not interfere with Word Embeddings. Ⓑ How a logic term "Socrates" is copied from one position to another. Ⓒ   How predicates may be formed in Self-Attention. Ⓓ   Non-linear deformation of embedding spaces.

vector units: "I", "love", and "you"). In other words, BERT/GPT performs logic inference/derivations on the **syntactic** level, ie, via **symbolic manipulations**.

Figure 5B is an example of such an operation. The object "Socrates" is copied from one position to another. By inspecting Eq. (11) we surmise that BERT is capable of such manoeuvres, with appropriately learned Keys and Values.

Figure 5A tries to explain why Positional Encodings (the sine wave patterns) seem not to interfere with Word Embeddings, when the embedding dimension is sufficiently large. Note that the x-axis here is not a single dimension but many dimensions, and the sine waves are not ordinary waves but waves *over dimensions*. As each wave only occludes 50% of the dimensions, the word embeddings of "love" and "death" are still recognizable. This enables to mix multiple meanings in a single word vector, e.g. "love" + "you" = "love you". So a predicate vector may contain its own objects, as in Fig. 5C.

So far it seems the representation in BERT/GPT may have predicates with objects inside a single vector or with predicates and objects residing in separate vectors. Perhaps inspecting the weights inside BERT/GPT may reveal their internal representations.

In **Multi-Head Attention**, the intermediate computations are duplicated multiple (eg, $M = 8$) times, each with their own weight matrices. From the logic point of view, this amounts to duplicating M logic rules per output. But since the next layer still expects N inputs, the M outputs are combined into one, before the next stage. Thus, from the logic point of view this merely increased the parameters *within* a single logic rule, and seems not significant to increase the power of the logic rule-base. Indeed, experimental results seem to confirm that multi-head attention is not particularly gainful towards performance.

A comment is in order here, about the choice of the word "head". In logic programming (eg Prolog), one calls the conclusion of a logic rule its "head", such as P in P :- Q,R,S. Perhaps the creators of BERT might have logic rules in mind?

5   "No Free Lunch" Theory

In machine learning, "No Free Lunch" [1, 45] refers to the fact that accelerating the search for a solution by ignoring one part of the search space (known as "inductive bias" [1]) is just as good as ignoring another part, if the solutions are believed to be evenly distributed in those regions. For example, the symmetry proposed here reduces the search space by a factor of $1/n!$ where n is the number of propositions in working memory.

The following conceptual diagram of the algorithmic search space illustrates the possibility that there might exist some form of logic that is drastically different from the symbolic logic currently known to humans (Fig. 6).

but there is no efficient algorithm to find them (grey area is much larger than shaded area). The permutation symmetry proposed in this paper forces our logic to be decomposable into **propositions**. Such a logical form allows a mental state to be enumerated as a list of sentences (propositions), same as the "linear" structure of human **languages**. If the AGI knowledge representation is linear (in the sequential sense) and symbolic, then it would not be far from our formulation – all these logics belong to one big family.

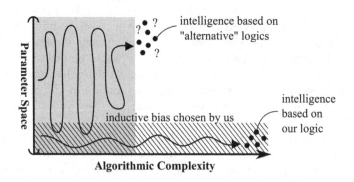

Fig. 6. Inductive bias and the search for AGI.

But could there be drastically different logics? One observes that pictures and music are not easily described by words, indeed they are 2-dimensional structures. This suggests that the brain may use **multi-dimensional** arrays of features to represent the world. Such a "logic" would be very different from sequential logic and it would be interesting and fruitful to analyze the relation between them.

6 Experiment

A simple test[6] of the symmetric neural network, under reinforcement learning (Policy Gradient[7]), has been applied to the Tic-Tac-Toe game.

The state of the game is represented as a set of 9 propositions, where all propositions are initialized as "null" in the beginning. During each step of the game, a new proposition is added to the set (i.e. over-writing the null propositions). Each proposition encodes who the player is, and which square (i, j) she has chosen. In other words, it is a predicate of the form: move(player,i,j). The neural network takes 9 propositions as input, and outputs a new proposition; Thus it is a permutation-invariant function.

In comparison, the game state of traditional RL algorithms (e.g. AlphaGo [30,37,38]) usually is represented as a "chessboard" vector (e.g. 3×3 in Tic-Tac-Toe, 8×8 in Chess, $19 \times 19 = 361$ in Go[8]). This state vector is the same constant length even if there are very few pieces on the chessboard. Our logic-based representation may offer some advantages over the board-vector representation, and likely induces a different "way of reasoning" about the game.

In our Tic-Tac-Toe experiment, learning led to initial improvements in game play but failed to achieve the optimal score in general. We find that this failure is also shared by the fully-connected NN (neural network), and this is likely because the policy gradient algorithm itself does not converge for Tic Tac Toe. Figure 7 is a comparison of symmetric NN versus fully-connected NN during early training. Disappointingly, the symmetric version does not out-perform the fully-connected version.

---

[6] Code with documentation and more detailed analysis is on GitHub: https://github.com/Cybernetic1/policy-gradient.

[7] The Policy Gradient algorithm is chosen because it allows *continuous* actions. Other reinforcement learning algorithms require learning the value function over actions, and when the action space is not discrete such a value function cannot be represented by a table, but perhaps as a neural network. However, it is not easy to find the *maximum* of a neural network, which is required to choose the optimal action. Policy Gradient avoids this because the policy function directly maps to actions.

[8] In AlphaGo and AlphaZero, the algorithm makes use of several auxiliary "feature planes" that are also chessboard vectors, to indicate which stones have "liberty", "ko", etc.

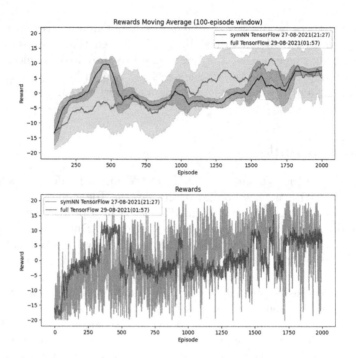

Fig. 7. Symmetric vs. fully-connected neural network for Tic Tac Toe

We ascribe this failure to the naive policy gradient algorithm and plan to use Actor-Critic (which also allows continuous actions) in our next experiments. We hope to show that symmetric NN is gainful for solving problems with logical structure. In another Github experiment we explore using a symbolic logic engine to solve Tic Tac Toe[9] and the comparison of these two approaches may shed light on how to integrate deep learning with logic.

7   Conclusion and Future Directions

We described a minimal AGI with a logic that can derive one new proposition per iteration. This seems sufficient to solve simple logic problems such as Tic-Tac-Toe. As a next step, we would consider inference rules with multi-proposition conclusions. The latter seems essential to **abductive** reasoning. For example, one can deduce the concept "apple" from an array of visual features; Conversely, the idea of an "apple" could also evoke in the mind a multitude of features, such as color, texture, taste, and the facts such as that it is edible, is a fruit, and that Alan Turing died from eating a poisoned apple (a form of episodic memory recall), and so on. This many-to-many inference bears some similarity to the brain's computational mechanisms [4,32,33]. The author is embarking on

---

[9] https://github.com/Cybernetic1/GIRL.

an abstract unifying AGI theory that makes references to (but not necessarily copying) brain mechanisms.

Acknowledgements. Thanks Ben Goertzel for suggesting that neural networks are advantageous over pure symbolic logic because they have fast learning algorithms (by gradient descent). That was at a time when "deep learning" was not yet a popular word. Thanks Dmitri Tkatch for pointing me to existing research of symmetric neural networks. Thanks Dr. 肖达 (Da Xiao) for explaining to me details of BERT.

Also thanks to the following people for invaluable discussions over many years: Ben Goertzel, Pei Wang (王培), Abram Demski, Russell Wallace, Juan Carlos Kuri Pinto, SeH, Jonathan Yan, and others. Also thanks to all the university professors and researchers in Hong Kong (especially in the math departments, and their guests), strangers who taught me things on Zhihu.com (知乎), Quora.com, and StackOverflow.

References

1. Alpaydin, E.: Introduction to Machine Learning. MIT Press (2020)
2. Baez, J., Stay, M.: Physics, topology, logic and computation: a Rosetta Stone. In: Coecke, B. (eds.) New Structures for Physics. Lecture Notes in Physics, vol. 813. Springer, Heidelberg (2010). https://doi.org/10.1007/978-3-642-12821-9_2
3. Battaglia, P.W., et al.: Relational inductive bias, deep learning, and graph networks (2018). https://arxiv.org/pdf/1806.01261.pdf
4. Boraud, T.: How the Brain Makes Decisions. Oxford (2020)
5. Bronstein, M.: Geometric foundations of deep learning (2021). https://towardsdatascience.com/geometric-foundations-of-deep-learning-94cdd45b451d
6. Bronstein, M.M., Bruna, J., Cohen, T., Velickovic, P.: Geometric deep learning: grids, groups, graphs, geodesics, and gauges. CoRR abs/2104.13478 (2021). https://arxiv.org/abs/2104.13478
7. Bělohlávek, R., Dauben, J.W., Klir, G.J.: Fuzzy Logic and Mathematics: A Historical Perspective. Oxford University Press (2017)
8. Devlin, J., Chang, M.-W., Lee, K., Toutanova, K.: BERT: pre-training of deep bidirectional transformers for language understanding. arXiv arXiv:1810.04805v2 [cs.CL] (2018)
9. Evans, R., Grefenstette, E., et al.: Learning explanatory rules from noisy data. J. Artif. Intell. Res. **61**, 1–64 (2017)
10. Feng, K., Qin, M.: Symplectic Geometric Algorithms for Hamiltonian Systems. Springer, Heidelberg (2010). https://doi.org/10.1007/978-3-642-01777-3
11. Goertzel, B.: The general theory of general intelligence: a pragmatic patternist perspective. arXiv preprint arXiv:2103.15100 (2021)
12. Goertzel, B., Duong, D.: OpenCog NS: a deeply-interactive hybrid neural-symbolic cognitive architecture designed for global/local memory synergy. In: 2009 AAAI Fall Symposium Series (2009)
13. Harris, J., Morrison, I.: Moduli of Curves, vol. 187. Springer, New York (1998). https://doi.org/10.1007/b98867
14. Heunen, C., Vicary, J.: Categories for Quantum Theory: An Introduction. Oxford University Press (2019)
15. Hinton, G.: How to represent part-whole hierarchies in a neural network. arXiv preprint arXiv:2102.12627 (2021)

16. Hitzler, P., Seda, A.: Mathematical Aspects of Logic Programming Semantics. CRC Press (2011)
17. Höhle, U.: Fuzzy sets and sheaves. Part i: basic concepts. Fuzzy Sets Syst. **158**(11), 1143–1174 (2007)
18. Höhle, U.: Fuzzy sets and sheaves. Part ii: sheaf-theoretic foundations of fuzzy set theory with applications to algebra and topology. Fuzzy Sets Syst. **158**(11), 1175–1212 (2007)
19. Hutter, M.: Universal Artificial Intelligence. Sequential Decisions Based on Algorithmic Probability. TTCSAES, Springer, Heidelberg (2005). https://doi.org/10.1007/b138233
20. Jacobs, B.: Categorical Logic and Type Theory. Elsevier (1999)
21. Jardine, J.F.: Fuzzy sets and presheaves. arXiv arXiv:1904.10314v5[math.CT] (2019)
22. Kappen, H.J.: An introduction to stochastic control theory, path integrals and reinforcement learning. AIP Conf. Proc. **887**, 149–181 (2007). https://doi.org/10.1063/1.2709596
23. Leimkuhler, B., Reich, S.: Simulating Hamiltonian Dynamics, vol. 14. Cambridge University Press (2004)
24. Liberzon, D.: Calculus of Variations and Optimal Control Theory: A Concise Introduction. Princeton University Press (2012)
25. Mac Lane, S., Moerdijk, I.: Sheaves in Geometry and Logic. A First Introduction to Topos Theory. UTX. Springer, New York (1992). https://doi.org/10.1007/978-1-4612-0927-0
26. Mann, P.: Lagrangian and Hamiltonian Dynamics. Oxford University Press (2018)
27. Nordström, B., Petersson, K., Smith, J.M.: Martin-Löf's Type Theory, vol. 5. Oxford University Press (2000)
28. Potapov, A., Belikov, A., Bogdanov, V., Scherbatiy, A.: Cognitive module networks for grounded reasoning. In: Hammer, P., Agrawal, P., Goertzel, B., Iklé, M. (eds.) AGI 2019. LNCS (LNAI), vol. 11654, pp. 148–158. Springer, Cham (2019). https://doi.org/10.1007/978-3-030-27005-6_15
29. Univalent Foundations Program: Homotopy Type Theory: Univalent Foundations of Mathematics (2013)
30. Ferguson, K., Pumperla, M.: Deep Learning and the Game of Go. Manning Publications (2019)
31. Qi, C.R., Su, H., Mo, K., Guibas, L.J.: PointNet: deep learning on point sets for 3D classification and segmentation. CVPR (2017). https://arxiv.org/abs/1612.00593
32. Rolls, E.T.: Cerebral Cortex - Principles of Operation. Oxford University Press (2016)
33. Rolls, E.T.: Brain Computation - What and How. Oxford University Press (2021)
34. Santoro, A., et al.: A simple neural network module for relational reasoning (2017)
35. Schlichenmaier, M.: An Introduction to Riemann Surfaces, Algebraic Curves and Moduli Spaces. Springer, Heidelberg (2010). https://doi.org/10.1007/978-3-540-71175-9
36. Shalev-Shwartz, S., Ben-David, S.: Understanding Machine Learning: From Theory to Algorithms. Cambridge University Press (2014)
37. Silver, D., et al.: Mastering the game of Go with deep neural networks and tree search. Nature **529**, 484–489 (2016)
38. Silver, D.: Mastering the game of Go without human knowledge. Nature **550**, 354–359 (2017)
39. Simmons, H.: Derivation and Computation: Taking the Curry-Howard Correspondence Seriously. Cambridge University Press (2000)

40. Sørensen, U.: Lectures on the Curry-Howard Isomorphism. Elsevier (2006)
41. Sutton, R.S.: Temporal credit assignment in reinforcement learning (1984)
42. Thompson, S.: Type Theory and Functional Programming. Addison-Wesley (1991)
43. Vaswani, A., et al.: Attention is all you need (2017). https://arxiv.org/abs/1706.03762
44. Vickers, S.: Fuzzy sets and geometric logic. Fuzzy Sets Syst. **161**, 1175–1204 (2010)
45. Wolpert, D.H., Macready, W.G.: No free lunch theorems for optimization. IEEE Trans. Evol. Comput. **1**, 67–82 (1997)
46. YKY: AGI logic tutorial (2021). https://drive.google.com/file/d/1v2efrH4gVJS9wG-KKgi1uFbbCoMOc9Hl/view?usp=sharing
47. Yan, K.-Y.: Fuzzy-probabilistic logic for common sense. In: Bach, J., Goertzel, B., Iklé, M. (eds.) AGI 2012. LNCS (LNAI), vol. 7716, pp. 372–379. Springer, Heidelberg (2012). https://doi.org/10.1007/978-3-642-35506-6_38
48. Zaheer, M., Kottur, S., Ravanbakhsh, S., Poczos, B., Salakhutdinov, R.R., Smola, A.J.: Deep sets. In: NIPS 2017 (2017). https://arxiv.org/abs/1611.04500

Case-Based Task Generalization
in Model-Based Reinforcement Learning

Artem Zholus$^{(\boxtimes)}$ and Aleksandr I. Panov

Moscow Institute of Physics and Technology, Moscow, Russia
zholus.aa@phystech.edu, panov.ai@mipt.ru

Abstract. Model-based reinforcement learning has recently demonstrated significant advances in solving complex problems of sequential decision-making. Updating the model using the case of solving the current task allows the agent to update the model and apply it to improve the efficiency of solving the following similar tasks. This approach also aligns with case-based planning methods, which already have mechanisms for retrieving and reusing precedents. In this work, we propose a meta-learned case retrieval mechanism that provides case-based samples for the agent to accelerate the learning process. We have tested the performance of the proposed approach on the well-known MuJoCo dataset and have shown results at the level of methods using pre-generated expert data.

Keywords: Reinforcement learning · Model-based RL · Case-based planning · Meta-learning · Neural world models · Dreamer · Task generalization

1 Introduction

Reinforcement Learning has gained huge importance these days. It has been extensively used in such fields as robotics [13], recommendation systems [1], and video games [17,21]. In RL setting, the agent applies actions in the environment, which then returns observations and rewards to the agent, and the process repeats. The agent's goal is to maximize the expected reward summed over a certain number of environment steps. Despite widespread use, modern RL algorithms suffer from the curse of low sample efficiency, which is performance of the Reinforcement Learning agent given that it has observed a fixed number of environment states.

However, an essential branch of Reinforcement Learning exists to tackle the problem of sample efficiency, namely, the Model-Based Reinforcement Learning [9,14,18,20]. Model-Based RL (MBRL) alleviates the problem of sample efficiency by training the model of environment dynamics, which is used to train the agent. Specifically, the agent no longer has access to the "true" environment. Instead, the agent uses such a learned environment to train itself. The model-based RL as a class of RL algorithms contains the most sample-efficient [18] RL

© Springer Nature Switzerland AG 2022
B. Goertzel et al. (Eds.): AGI 2021, LNAI 13154, pp. 344–354, 2022.
https://doi.org/10.1007/978-3-030-93758-4_35

algorithms. This means that these methods can be efficiently utilized in costly environments where collecting lots of data is expensive (e.g., when the agent is a robot in the real environment, the amount of collected data for training is upper-bounded by the duration of the research project).

A prominent approach to Model-Based RL is using World Models [10]. In general, these are deep networks acting on agent's observations which build abstract features for policy to act on. The world models capture environment dynamics and are usually implemented as Variational Autoencoders [16] with a temporal component. The model encodes visual observations of the agent into the latent state and then reconstructs these states into the observations and rewards. Both the encoder and decoder modules of the model are conditioned on the agent's actions and previous timestamp latent vector. The recurrent state-space model (RSSM) networks [11,12] plays an important role in Model-Based RL due to their expressive power for dynamics learning. In this work, we use the Dreamer [11], which is an RSSM world model with additional actor and critic which are trained purely on rollouts from the model.

An important branch of online planning, case-based planning seeks to reuse previous planning results to accelerate online planning [7,22]. CBP is similar to the model-based RL in the way that both model the domain, first through the similarity between planning cases and second through learning the dynamics of the environment. However, there exists a gap between CBP and RL despite the fact that they solve similar tasks. Particularly, the RL usually learns behaviors in a purely online fashion, while the CBP involves additional offline calculations.

In this work, we fill this gap by proposing a model that uses ideas of a Case-based approach to tackle the multitask adaptation of an MBRL agent. Instead of training any Model-Based RL algorithm from scratch for each task, we reuse the data collected along the training of previous agents by using a learned mechanism that retrieves training samples to train MBRL agent. Basically, we use the similarity between concrete behaviors from the current and all previous cases to retrieve behaviors and reuse them to accelerate the training of the Dreamer. In particular, inspired by the Variational Memory Addressing [6] mechanism, we add an auxiliary neural network that acts as the distribution over the expert cases and retrieves them for Dreamer training. This memory network acts according to a learned strategy, which is defined as the task-specific performance of the model, therefore, accelerating the Dreamer's convergence.

We summarize our key contributions as follows:

1. **Case Retrieval Mechanism.** Based on insights from Case-Based Reasoning, we define a learnable retrieval over episodes from prior tasks, which is used to propose training samples for the main model.
2. **Task Generalization.** We empower the RSSM-based RL agent with novel learnable retrieval to leverage the similarity of intra-domain experiences collected before. The augmented agent is able to train faster on the current task by using such an adaptive retrieval mechanism.
3. **Empirical Evaluation.** We evaluate our model on a number of visual continuous-control tasks grouped by domains. Our model shows increased

performance compared to the two baselines for the case when prior task is
equal to the current one.

2 Related Work

A number of methods leverage Case-Based Reasoning to speed up reinforcement
learning. CBRetaliate [2] formulates a case as tabular action-value approximation. Its aim is to quickly adapt to changing conditions by switching policies
defined by Q-tables, which are saved into a case base. In contrast, our method
uses learnable similarity to select cases that would accelerate Deep RL agent
training. Compared to this approach, we define a case as an episode and reuse it
inside the training batch of the world model. CB-HAQL [4] builds heuristics to
guide a policy using the Q-learning algorithm. The Case-based approach is then
used to guide the heuristic by actions.

Modern deep learning can leverage memory to build better representations to
act on. Variational Memory Addressing VAE (VMA-VAE) [6], which inspired the
approach for the current work, learnable addressing latent variable was used to
retrieve the data sample from memory to guide the generative process. Episodic
memory in RL [5,19] uses a hippocampal inspired data structure to accelerate
the recognition of prominent actions. The data structure is used to build better
action-value estimates using similarity search in the representation space. Compared to this approach, we store whole episodes into memory and set up memory
to contain episodes that represent solutions for different tasks.

World models [10] facilitate an accelerated convergence of the RL agent
employing the learned dynamics of the environment. They can predict transitions directly [14] or use an abstract latent with Markovian property [10–12].
The latter are able to maintain dynamics consistency longer due to compact
latent representation [11]. A separate class of model-based agents fuse planning
with reinforcement learning incorporating tree-based search structure [20].

3 Background

3.1 Reinforcement Learning

We formulate the problem of reinforcement learning as Partially-Observable
Markov Decision Process (POMDP). Formally, POMDP is a tuple

$$\langle \mathcal{S}, \mathcal{A}, \mathcal{O}, P, R, O, \gamma \rangle,$$

where $\mathcal{S}$ is the set of states of POMDP, $\mathcal{A}$ is the set of actions, and $\mathcal{O}$ is the set of
observations. Environment changes its state according to conditional transition
distribution $P(s' \mid s, a)$, but the agent only has access to the output of observa-
tion function $o = O(s', a)$, $o \in \mathcal{O}$. The agent is defined by policy $\pi(a_t \mid o_{\leqslant t}, a_{<t})$.
It interacts with partially observable environment by taking actions on the envi-
ronment and getting next observations. We write $o_t, r_t \sim p(o_t, r_t \mid o_{<t}, a_{<t})$ as a
shorthand for $s_t \sim P(s_t \mid s_{t-1}, a_{t-1})$, $o_t = O(s_t, a_{t-1})$, $r_t = R(s_t, a_{t-1})$. The goal
of the agent is to maximize its expected discounted sum of rewards $\mathbb{E}_\pi \sum_t \gamma^t r_t$.

3.2   Model-Based Reinforcement Learning with Dreamer

For our method, we use RSSM-like world models [11], which is a visual model-based agent with a variational world model. The Dreamer learns latent dynamics by building Markovian latent state for each timestep s_t given previous action a_{t-1} by autoencoding observations o_t and rewards r_t which are non-Markovian. The world model consists of representation model, or encoder $q(s_t \mid s_{t-1}, a_{t-1}, o_t)$, transition model $p(s_t \mid s_{t-1}, a_{t-1})$, observation model $p(o_t \mid s_t)$, and reward model $p(r_t \mid s_t)$. Representation and transition models share common parameters in the RSSM network [12]. The world model is trained to maximize the variational lower bound on the likelihood of the observed trajectory conditioned on actions $\mathbb{E}_p \log p((o_{1:T}, r_{1:T}) \mid a_{1:T})$. This is done by incorporating approximate posterior model $q(s_t \mid s_{t-1}, a_{t-1}, o_t)$, which is known as a representation model. This model acts as a proposal distribution for states s_t.

For behavioral training, the Dreamer agent uses *latent imagination*, an approach where policy $\pi(a_t \mid s_t)$ is optimized by predicting both policy actions $a_t \sim \pi(a_t \mid s_t)$ and transition model states $s_{t+1} \sim p(s_{t+1} \mid s_t, a_t)$ without environment interaction. In particular, we use value-function estimate based on $\hat{v}(s_t)$ on top of the latent state, which the policy is trained to maximize, i.e. $\mathbb{E}_{s_0, a_0, s_1, a_1, \dots} \sum_t V_\lambda(s_t)$ where $V_\lambda(s)$ is a multi-step value estimate with hyperparameter λ, which controls bias variance trade-off [23]. As the transition and value models are parameterized by neural networks, we can backpropagate through the value function, transition model, and action sampling to compute symbolic gradients of value estimates w.r.t. policy parameters.

3.3   Case-Based Reasoning and Planning

As a fundamental direction to reasoning, Case-Based Reasoning approaches reasoning by saving and reusing previous solutions or *cases*. It incorporates the notion of *similarity* between cases to choose a case and reuse it to build a new solution.

In particular, the abstract CBR algorithm consists of four stages:

1. **Retrieve:** during this stage, we look up similar cases to select the most similar ones.
2. **Reuse:** (or adapt) we select found cases and alter their solutions in order to fix/adapt them to the current problem.
3. **Revise:** we verify a solution that resulted in the execution of the previous two stages.
4. **Retain:** in this stage, a built solution is brought to the case base forming a new case, and the process repeats.

Case-Based Planning applies this approach to planning. To this end, the general goal can be divided into a set of sub-tasks with the aim on speeding up planning by reusing the planning cases.

4   Method

4.1   Case Retrieval

In our approach, we define a *case* as an RL episode i.e. $\{(a_t, o_t, r_t)\}_{t=1}^{T}$ or contiguous chunk of the episode where elements of tuple stand for action, observation, and reward, respectively. We refer to the set of cases as the "expert" buffer. It holds behavior trajectories of the previously trained agent, which solve the task with high task-specific episode reward.

Each episode represents a solution to some task τ from the set of tasks $\mathcal{T}$. In general, tasks may come from arbitrarily different environments. We, therefore, assume that environments for each of the tasks are semantically similar to each other and represent different aspects of the domain. Tasks may differ in their own task-specific reward function R_τ and also in state transition distribution (e.g., for the robotic manipulation of objects with different shapes). In our case, we approach the problem of case-based planning by leveraging a mechanism that retrieves similar cases and uses them to accelerate the training of the reinforcement learning agent for the current task $\tau' \in T$. We emphasize that in general $R_\tau \neq R_{\tau'}$ where τ is the task of some case (trajectory) in the set of cases to which the agent has access. Therefore, we have chosen Model-Based RL as we may need to approximate $R_{\tau'}$ for a newly retrieved case from the set of cases.

For retrieving trajectories (each of which can be a contiguous chunk of the episode), we have chosen the learned similarity induced by a neural network, which compares the current trajectory from an agent's replay buffer $x = \{(a_t, o_t, r_t)\}_{t=1}^{T}$ with another trajectory M_j from the batch M extracted from the expert buffer. In particular, to retrieve the trajectory, we sample index j from distribution $q(j \mid x, M)$, which has the form:

$$q_\phi(j \mid x_i, M) \propto \exp(f_\phi(x_i)^T f_\phi(M_j)),$$

where f_ϕ is the learnable embedding of trajectory x or M_j parametrized by recurrent neural network with parameters ϕ. We implement f_ϕ as a recurrent neural network that consumes a sequence of actions concatenated with observation embeddings obtained from CNN. As the output, we use the last output vector of the recurrent network. In other words, we project trajectory x and each M_j into the embedding space, next, we calculate the inner product between the embedding of x and embedding of each M_j, and finally, we pass the resulting vector of inner products to the softmax, which gives probabilities for categorical distribution. We refer to f_ϕ as the retrieval model.

4.2   Case Revision by Training Case Retrieval Network

We consider several approaches for training the retrieval model. First, we feed each selected trajectory $M_j = \{(a_t^j, o_t^j, r_t^j)\}_{t=1}^{T}$ where $j \sim q(j \mid x, M)$ to the Dreamer and run its latent imagination procedure to obtain its value estimates $V_\lambda(s_t^j)$. Then we average the estimates over timesteps t and over batch indices

i and backpropagate gradients of the resulting scalar loss up to gradient w.r.t. weights ϕ of the retrieval model. We train the retrieval model to maximize the objective:

$$\mathcal{L}_V = -\frac{1}{n} \sum_{i=1}^{n} \sum_{t} V_\lambda(s_t^j)$$

To enable efficient gradient computation, we use a straight-through gradient estimator [3] to obtain differentiable samples j returned as one-hot vectors. We then multiply each of these one-hot vectors by a batch of expert trajectories M to obtain selection by index in a differentiable fashion. We refer to this method as a value gradient.

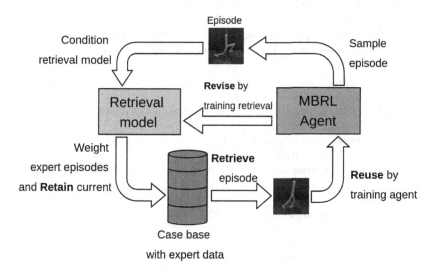

Fig. 1. The training cycle of the whole system.

Another approach for training the retrieval model is to use the REINFORCE algorithm [26]. For this, we sample $j \sim q(j \mid x, M)$ then we predict rewards of selected trajectory M_j using Dreamer's reward model: $r_t^j \sim p(r_t \mid s_t^j)$ and update the retrieval model to minimize the objective:

$$\mathcal{L}_R = -\mathbb{E}_{q(j|x,M)} \left(\sum_t r_t^j \right) \log q(j \mid x, M)$$

4.3 Case Reuse by Training the MBRL Agent

For training the Dreamer agent given a retrieved case, to accelerate the training, we modify the Dreamer's input batch as follows. Given training batch $X =$

Algorithm 1: Dreamer with retrieval model

Hyper parameters:

Sequence length	L	Collect interval	C
Batch size	n	Expert batch size	m
Initial episodes	S	Expert episodes	K
Expert batch probability	p	Expert fill fraction	β
λ-return parameter	λ	Set of prior tasks	$\mathcal{T}$

begin

    Initialize training buffer $\mathcal{D}$ with S random episodes;

    Initialize expert buffer $\mathcal{M}$ with K expert episodes each representing a solution for task from $\mathcal{T}$;

    while *not converged* **do**

        for *train step* $c = 1..C$ **do**

            `// Case revision`

            Draw n training sequences $\{(a_t^i, o_t^i, r_t^i)\}_{t=k}^{k+L} = x_i \sim \mathcal{D}$, $i = \overline{1,n}$;

            Draw m expert sequences $\{(a_t^j, o_t^j, r_t^j)\}_{t=k}^{k+L} = M_j \sim \mathcal{M}$, $j = \overline{1,m}$;

            Compute samples from proposal distribution for each x_i: $j(i) \sim q(j \mid x_i, M_j)$;

            Compute reward and value estimates $r_t^{j(i)}$, $V_\lambda(s_t^{j(i)})$ using selected expert trajectories $M_{j(i)}$;

            Backprop value $\mathcal{L}_V$ or $\mathcal{L}_R$ and update model parameters ϕ.;

            `// Case retrieval`

            Draw n trajectories $x_i \sim \mathcal{D}$;

            $\alpha \sim$ Bernoulli(p);

            if $\alpha = 1$ **then**

                Set input batch $b \leftarrow \{x_i\}_{i=1}^{\beta n} \cup \{M_{j(i)}\}_{i=1}^{(1-\beta)n}$;

            else

                Set input batch $b \leftarrow \{x_i\}_{i=1}^{n}$

            end

            `// Case reuse`

            Update parameters θ of Dreamer using batch b;

        end

        `// Case retention`

        Collect episode using Dreamer and store it to $\mathcal{D}$ and $\mathcal{M}$;

    end

end

$\{x_i\}_{i=1}^{n}$ and expert batch $M = \{M_j\}_{j=1}^{m}$, for each x_i, we sample $j(i) \sim q(j \mid x_i, M)$ (the expert batch is shared among x_i for all i as otherwise it would require $\mathcal{O}(nm)$ trajectories which is too much to fit into one GPU) and feed Dreamer with an updated training batch $\{x_i\}_{i=1}^{n} \cup \{M_{j(i)}\}_{i=1}^{n}$. Here it is important to note that the trajectory $M_{j(i)}$ may come from a different task compared to the task of x_i. For part of batch containing such $M_{j(i)}$, we turn off the reward model learning. We refer this procedure to as case reuse.

4.4   Case-Based Planning Process

We pose our method into a case-based approach in an iterative way. First, the MBRL agent samples an episode, which is then used to condition the retrieval model. The retrieval model scores the episodes in the case base with respect to the conditioned one. After that, it **retrieves** a new episode from the case base by sampling from the proposal distribution. The selected episode is then **reused** by training the MBRL agent. The conditioned episode is **retained** into the case base. After that, the MBRLagent **revises** the retrieval model (i.e., all next retrieved episodes) by training that model. The overall process is shown in Fig. 1 and summarized in Algorithm 1.

5   Experiments

5.1   DeepMind Control

We test our model on five visual tasks from DeepMind Control Suite [24] based on the MuJoCo physics engine [25]. Observations of an Agent are $64 \times 64 \times 3$ images, the actions range from one to 12 dimensions, the rewards range from zero to one, and the episodes last for 1,000 steps and have randomized initial states. The tasks include Walker Stand, Walker Walk, Walker Run, Hopper Stand, and Hopper Hop. These tasks represent different tasks within two domains, namely, Walker and Hopper. For each domain, we define a sequence of tasks with increasing difficulty. For the Walker domain, these are Stand, Walk, and Run. The multitask adaptation procedure will first solve Stand, then, with trajectories for the Stand task in the multitask buffer, solve the Walk task, and finally, having experience for the Stand and Walk tasks, solve Run. For the Hopper domain, the set of tasks consists of two tasks—Stand and Hop.

5.2   Experiment Setting

In all experiments, we implemented the retrieval model with the GRU cell [8]. We trained this model with Adam [15] optimizer using a learning rate of 0.001. We left all Dreamer-specific hyperparameters to be default [11], i.e. we trained model with batch size $n = 50$, each batch consisted of sequences of length $L = 50$. We trained the Dreamer and the retrieval model, each for $C = 100$ optimizer steps between the episode collection. We set λ-return parameter to be 0.95 and $\gamma = 0.99$. The probability of using expert data in training batch was $p = 0.5$, the fraction of the expert data in such batch was $\beta = 0.5$. The number of episodes for the initial pre-training was $S = 1$ (i.e., no pre-training on random episodes), and the size of the expert buffer was $K = 1000$ episodes. For DeepMind Control Suite environments, we trained each model for 2000000 environment steps.

5.3   Results

Currently, we have conducted preliminary experiments where expert data is formed by the same task trajectories but with a high episode reward. For this, we trained two baselines, namely vanilla Dreamer and Dreamer, with buffer initialized with expert trajectories. The first one indicates the default performance of the model while the second one shows how the model would perform with access to the expert data but without the case-based formulation. We report performance of two models, both with the same retrieval model trained with different loss functions. The first uses value gradient and the second uses REINFORCE loss described in the previous section. The results are shown in Fig. 2, each result is averaged over three runs. The model with a case-based batch retrieval constantly shows an improvement over both baselines, indicating that the model can benefit from the case-based formulation.

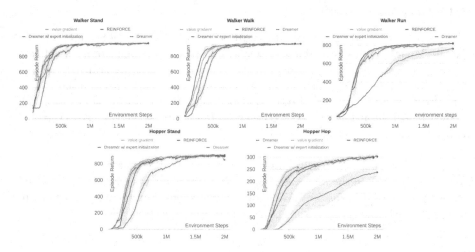

Fig. 2. Performance of different variations of Dreamer of DMC environments

6   Conclusion

Here we have presented a novel meta-learning algorithm that learns the retrieval model for a series of tasks in a lifelong fashion. For each particular task, it trains a separate model-based agent implemented with Dreamer algorithm. We consider the conducted experiments as first stage proof-of-concept experiments, which prepare the ground for full-fledged multitask experiments.

Importantly, current work is at the intermediate stage, and it contains several open research questions. The first open question in this work is whether the mix of x_i and $M_{j(i)}$ where $j(i)$ is selected according to the described distribution would indeed accelerate the training. Also, an open question is how the model explicitly defines and utilizes similarity between trajectories given that it is trained only with loss dependent on M.

Acknowledgements. This work was supported by the Russian Science Foundation (Project No. 20-71-10116).

References

1. Afsar, M.M., Crump, T., Far, B.: Reinforcement learning based recommender systems: a survey (2021)
2. Auslander, B., Lee-Urban, S., Hogg, C., Muñoz-Avila, H.: Recognizing the enemy: combining reinforcement learning with strategy selection using case-based reasoning. In: Althoff, K.-D., Bergmann, R., Minor, M., Hanft, A. (eds.) ECCBR 2008. LNCS (LNAI), vol. 5239, pp. 59–73. Springer, Heidelberg (2008). https://doi.org/10.1007/978-3-540-85502-6_4
3. Bengio, Y., Léonard, N., Courville, A.C.: Estimating or propagating gradients through stochastic neurons for conditional computation. CoRR abs/1308.3432 (2013). http://arxiv.org/abs/1308.3432
4. Bianchi, R.A.C., Ros, R., Lopez de Mantaras, R.: Improving reinforcement learning by using case based heuristics. In: McGinty, L., Wilson, D.C. (eds.) ICCBR 2009. LNCS (LNAI), vol. 5650, pp. 75–89. Springer, Heidelberg (2009). https://doi.org/10.1007/978-3-642-02998-1_7
5. Blundell, C., et al.: Model-free episodic control. CoRR abs/1606.04460 (2016). http://dblp.uni-trier.de/db/journals/corr/corr1606.html#BlundellUPLRLRW16
6. Bornschein, J., Mnih, A., Zoran, D., Jimenez Rezende, D.: Variational memory addressing in generative models. In: Guyon, I., et al. (eds.) Advances in Neural Information Processing Systems, vol. 30. Curran Associates, Inc. (2017). https://proceedings.neurips.cc/paper/2017/file/3937230de3c8041e4da6ac3246a888e8-Paper.pdf
7. Borrajo, D., Roubíčková, A., Serina, I.: Progress in case-based planning. ACM Comput. Surv. **47**(2), 1–39 (2015). https://doi.org/10.1145/2674024
8. Cho, K., van Merrienboer, B., Gülçehre, Ç., Bougares, F., Schwenk, H., Bengio, Y.: Learning phrase representations using RNN encoder-decoder for statistical machine translation. CoRR abs/1406.1078 (2014). http://arxiv.org/abs/1406.1078
9. Gorodetskiy, A., Shlychkova, A., Panov, A.I.: Delta schema network in model-based reinforcement learning. In: Goertzel, B., Panov, A.I., Potapov, A., Yampolskiy, R. (eds.) AGI 2020. LNCS (LNAI), vol. 12177, pp. 172–182. Springer, Cham (2020). https://doi.org/10.1007/978-3-030-52152-3_18
10. Ha, D., Schmidhuber, J.: World models. CoRR abs/1803.10122 (2018). http://arxiv.org/abs/1803.10122
11. Hafner, D., Lillicrap, T.P., Ba, J., Norouzi, M.: Dream to control: learning behaviors by latent imagination. CoRR abs/1912.01603 (2019). http://arxiv.org/abs/1912.01603
12. Hafner, D., et al.: Learning latent dynamics for planning from pixels. CoRR abs/1811.04551 (2018). http://arxiv.org/abs/1811.04551
13. Ibarz, J., Tan, J., Finn, C., Kalakrishnan, M., Pastor, P., Levine, S.: How to train your robot with deep reinforcement learning: lessons we have learned. Int. J. Robot. Res. **40**, 698–721 (2021). https://doi.org/10.1177/0278364920987859

14. Janner, M., Fu, J., Zhang, M., Levine, S.: When to trust your model: model-based policy optimization (2019)
15. Kingma, D.P., Ba, J.: Adam: a method for stochastic optimization (2014). Published as a conference paper at the 3rd International Conference for Learning Representations, San Diego, 2015. http://arxiv.org/abs/1412.6980, arxiv:1412.6980Comment
16. Kingma, D.P., Welling, M.: Auto-encoding variational Bayes. In: Bengio, Y., LeCun, Y. (eds.) ICLR (2014). http://dblp.uni-trier.de/db/conf/iclr/iclr2014.html#KingmaW13
17. Mnih, V., et al.: Human-level control through deep reinforcement learning. Nature **518**(7540), 529–533 (2015). https://doi.org/10.1038/nature14236
18. Moerland, T.M., Broekens, J., Jonker, C.M.: Model-based reinforcement learning: a survey (2021)
19. Pritzel, A., et al.: Neural episodic control. In: Precup, D., Teh, Y.W. (eds.) Proceedings of the 34th International Conference on Machine Learning. Proceedings of Machine Learning Research, 06–11 August 2017, vol. 70, pp. 2827–2836. PMLR (2017). http://proceedings.mlr.press/v70/pritzel17a.html
20. Schrittwieser, J., et al.: Mastering Atari, Go, chess and shogi by planning with a learned model. Nature **588**(7839), 604–609 (2020). https://doi.org/10.1038/s41586-020-03051-4
21. Skrynnik, A., Staroverov, A., Aitygulov, E., Aksenov, K., Davydov, V., Panov, A.I.: Hierarchical Deep Q-Network from imperfect demonstrations in Minecraft. Cogn. Syst. Res. **65**, 74–78 (2021). https://doi.org/10.1016/j.cogsys.2020.08.012. https://arxiv.org/pdf/1912.08664.pdf. https://www.sciencedirect.com/science/article/pii/S1389041720300723?via%3Dihub. https://www.scopus.com/record/display.uri?eid=2-s2.0-85094320898&origin=resultslist. https://linkinghub.elsevier.com/retrieve/pii/S138904172
22. Spalzzi, L.: A survey on case-based planning. Artif. Intell. Rev. **16**(1), 3–36 (2001). https://doi.org/10.1023/A:1011081305027
23. Sutton, R.S., Barto, A.G.: Reinforcement Learning: An Introduction, 2nd edn. The MIT Press (2018). http://incompleteideas.net/book/the-book-2nd.html
24. Tassa, Y., et al.: dm_control: software and tasks for continuous control (2020)
25. Todorov, E., Erez, T., Tassa, Y.: MuJoCo: a physics engine for model-based control. In: 2012 IEEE/RSJ International Conference on Intelligent Robots and Systems, pp. 5026–5033 (2012). https://doi.org/10.1109/IROS.2012.6386109
26. Williams, R.J.: Simple statistical gradient-following algorithms for connectionist reinforcement learning. Mach. Learn. **8**(3–4), 229–256 (1992). https://doi.org/10.1007/BF00992696

PySigma: Towards Enhanced Grand Unification for the Sigma Cognitive Architecture

Jincheng Zhou[1,2]([⊠])[ID] and Volkan Ustun[2][ID]

[1] Department of Computer Science, University of Southern California, Los Angeles, USA
`jinchenz@usc.edu`
[2] Institute for Creative Technologies, University of Southern California, Los Angeles, USA
`{jzhou,ustun}@ict.usc.edu`

Abstract. The Sigma cognitive architecture is the beginning of an integrated computational model of intelligent behavior aimed at the grand goal of artificial general intelligence (AGI). However, whereas it has been proven to be capable of modeling a wide range of intelligent behaviors, the existing implementation of Sigma has suffered from several significant limitations. The most prominent one is the inadequate support for inference and learning on continuous variables. In this article, we propose solutions for this limitation that should together enhance Sigma's level of *grand unification*; that is, its ability to span both traditional cognitive capabilities and key non-cognitive capabilities central to general intelligence, bridging the gap between symbolic, probabilistic, and neural processing. The resulting design changes converge on a more capable version of the architecture called PySigma. We demonstrate such capabilities of PySigma in neural probabilistic processing via deep generative models, specifically variational autoencoders, as a concrete example.

Keywords: Sigma · Cognitive architecture · Probabilistic graphical model · Message passing algorithm · Approximate inference · Deep generative model

1 Introduction

The Sigma cognitive architecture is the beginning of an integrated computational model of intelligent behaviors, with an end goal of becoming a working implementation of a complete cognitive system [13]. In service of this goal, four design desiderata have been in place to guide the research and development: (1) *grand unification*, that the architecture should span both traditional cognitive capabilities and key non-cognitive aspects – such as the symbolic, probabilistic, and neural processings – central to an intelligent agent, (2) *generic cognition*, that it should span both natural and artificial cognition at an appropriate level

© Springer Nature Switzerland AG 2022
B. Goertzel et al. (Eds.): AGI 2021, LNAI 13154, pp. 355–366, 2022.
https://doi.org/10.1007/978-3-030-93758-4_36

of abstraction, (3) *functional elegance*, that it should yield human-level intelligent behaviors from a simple and theoretically elegant base, and (4) *sufficient efficiency*, that it should execute quickly enough for real-time applications.

Sigma is implemented as a two-level architecture: a cognitive language level on top of a graphical architecture level. The cognitive language level provides a user-friendly interface for programming Sigma models by offering two essential constructs: `Predicates` that store and represent first-order relational knowledge and `Conditionals` that organize predicates into graphs and rules that enable deriving new knowledge and update existing memories. The graphical architecture level compiles the model written in the cognitive language into an *augmented factor graph*. This augmented factor graph inherits the essential semantics of the conventional factor graphs but augments them in several key ways to allow broader model capacity, such as allowing a variable node to represent first-order variables and introducing unidirectional edges. The actual computations then occur over a sequence of cognitive cycles by, within each, passing messages around this factor graph until quiescence (the elaboration phase) and then updating message contents in factor nodes as necessary (the modification phase).

Sigma's graphical architecture has successfully assisted in modeling a wide range of cognitive and non-cognitive abilities [13]. However, throughout the years of research on it, it has been apparent that the current implementation suffers from at least two fundamental limitations: difficulty in dealing with continuous variables; and lack of a critical cognitive capability for structure learning from experience; known as "chunking." In this article, we focus primarily on tackling the first limitation. We first propose a fundamental change to the message structure to efficiently represent continuous variables, accompanied by an enhanced design of the graphical architecture, message propagation algorithm, and inference/learning mechanisms. These changes ultimately converge on a new version of Sigma called PySigma that, by design, inherits all of Sigma's inferential capabilities and also extends them in significant ways. We then illustrate one of such extension regarding the support for neural probabilistic processing by demonstrating the modeling of a canonical deep generative model – the Variational Autoencoder (VAE) [8]. Finally, we briefly touch upon a potential future research direction inspired by the experience of modeling VAE that may lead to solutions to the second limitation.

2 Message Representation with Continuous Variables

The cornerstone of Sigma's graphical architecture is the *message*: a data structure that captures the first-order relational knowledge about certain facts. For example, the location of an object in the blocks world environment can be represented by a predicate `Location(O:object, X:value, Y:value)`, where variable `O` of type `object` refers to the specific object, and variables `X`, `Y` of type `value` describes the object's X-Y coordinate. The specific value of this predicate at any given time is then stored as a message with the same signature: `m(O:object, X:value, Y:value)`.

In Sigma, the message data structure leverages Piecewise-Linear Maps [13]. This implementation can approximate functions over continuous variables; however, it can get quite messy when learning the probability density function of a continuous random variable. For example, after multiple cycles of updating the piecewise-linear map, the messages tend to become too fractured and intractable to compute efficiently unless proper smoothing is applied.

To remedy this issue in PySigma, we recognize that a message is essentially encoding a *batch of independently distributed distributions*. Drawing inspiration from Tensorflow's distribution package design [4], we make the distinction between a message's variables that index the batch of distributions versus those variables that are their event variables. The former are called *Relational Variables* in PySigma, and the latter *Random Variables*. Then, to tractably encode the distributions, the Piecewise-Linear Map representation is replaced with two alternatives: the parameter and particle-lists format. A message assumes that the distributions come from a parametric distribution family and uses the parameter vectors to encode its distributions with the parameter format. With the particle-lists format, particles (or samples from the distributions) are stored rather than the parameters, allowing estimation of the statistics of the underlying distributions [3]. Under such formulation, any Piecewise-Linear Map message in Sigma can be effectively represented by a particle-lists format message in PySigma, enabling PySigma to be fully reduced to Sigma.

Because tensors can best represent components of both parameters and particle lists, we build PySigma's message structure on top of PyTorch tensors and implement PySigma's graphical architecture essentially as pipelines of tensor manipulations. Since PyTorch is a commonly used deep learning library, such design choices not only ensure the speed and accuracy of any tensor operation but also prepares PySigma for further integration with standard deep learning modules, such as deep neural networks [11].

3 Generalized Factor Graph, Approximate Inference, and Gradient-Based Learning

Apart from the new message representation and implementation, PySigma fundamentally changes several other aspects of Sigma's graphical architecture. First, PySigma cognitive models are compiled to an augmented factor graph that is further generalized, specifically in the factor node function formulation. In Sigma, a factor node function is formulated similarly to the tabular factor in a conventional factor graph and implemented as a Piecewise-Linear Map, which records every function value corresponding to each tuple of the function variable values. However, such a formulation needs exponential space when the number of function variables increases. PySigma relaxes this restricted formulation and instead relies on the following one, which defines two types of factor functions:

Definition 1. *An* n-*ary* **generative factor function** F *is a mapping* $\prod_{i=1}^{n} R_{V_i} \to [0, 1]$ *such that*

$$p = F(V_1, V_2, \ldots, V_n)$$

*An n-ary **discriminative factor function** G is a mapping $\prod_{i=1}^{n-1} R_{V_i} \to R_{V_n}$ such that*

$$V_n = G(V_1, V_2, \ldots, V_{n-1})$$

where $V_1, V_2, \ldots, V_n$ are the random variables, and R_{V_i} is the support set of the random variable V_i.

By doing so, PySigma admits arbitrary function implementations that conform to the above definition as factor node functions. Thus, for example, a deep neural network module can be used as a factor function approximator to resolve the issue of space explosion.

It should be noted that how PySigma integrates neural networks is very different from the previous approach in Sigma [12,14]. In Sigma, neural networks are reimplemented leveraging the existing components of the Sigma graphical architecture. What is done here for PySigma, on the other hand, extends the architecture to admit neural modules as the primary, inseparable components. Thus, compared to Sigma, PySigma is more deeply integrated with neural processing and hence, is prepared to take one step forward to bridge the gap between neural, probabilistic, and symbolic reasoning.

All of Sigma's message passing, inference, and learning mechanisms have been overhauled in PySigma to work with the new message structure and the generalized factor graph. PySigma still inherits the same two-phased cognitive cycles as in Sigma, but the implementations of both phases are fundamentally changed. PySigma also clearly distinguish between inference and learning: inference performs local updates on the predicates' working memory based on incoming messages to find the posterior distribution given the observations, whereas learning updates the model parameters to optimize a pre-defined objective function.

For message passing, the existing Sigma uses the Sum-Product algorithm, a form of exact inference algorithm, which suffers from tractability issues when facing continuous variables and generalized factor functions [13]. For PySigma, we have developed a set of generalized message passing rules to perform approximate inference. It is a combination of Particle Belief Propagation (PBP) [3,5] and Variational Message Passing (VMP) [2,15] on factor graphs. In the most general case, a conditional subgraph (the group of variable and factor nodes that a conditional is compiled to) expects all incoming messages from the incident predicate subgraph (the group of nodes that a predicate is compiled to) to be of particle-lists format. It then computes outgoing messages using the PBP message update rule on factor nodes [5]. However, if all of the incoming messages are also of parameter format and their assumed distribution classes are not only the exponential class but also conjugate to the factor function, then the VMP message update rule on factor nodes is used, which directly manipulates the exponential family distributions' natural parameters [15]. Such a hybrid message passing algorithm mostly produces the generalized particle-based approximate messages. However, the algorithm efficiently generates a parameter-based exact message when the incoming messages and the factor function share particular structures. Moreover, message passing in PySigma would be identical to the

Sum-Product rules if messages are discrete and the factor functions are in tabular format. In this way, PySigma can be easily reduced to Sigma, thus supporting all of the cognitive capabilities that Sigma's inference can achieve in principle.

For the inference update, we follow the PBP formulation so that particles are only sampled at the predicate subgraph, and a conditional subgraph does not alter incoming particles or sample new particles. This restriction is to prevent incoming messages to a predicate subgraph from having contradicting lists of particles [5]. We thus categorize PySigma's predicates into three types: the *non-memorial* type, the *variational memorial*, and the *Markov Chain Monte Carlo (MCMC) memorial*. The non-memorial type predicate is reserved for relaying messages from one conditional to another. The last two memorial types, however, actively maintain an internal message as their working memory and updates this message using the incoming messages. A variational memorial predicate explicitly assumes that a variational posterior distribution describes its memory and updates this memory by directly summing the incoming message's parameters if all of the incoming messages are of parameter format [2]. Otherwise, if any of the incoming messages are of particle-lists format, it resorts to the stochastic gradient update, similar to the update method proposed by the Reparameterization Gradient Message Passing [1]. Unlike the variational one, the MCMC memorial predicate does not make any assumption about the posterior distribution but relies on the MCMC method to iteratively update its memory particles [7].

Finally, learning is carried out in PySigma by gradient backpropagation, the same technique used for training deep neural networks. A PyTorch computational graph [11] that is automatically built when PySigma propagates messages in the elaboration phase of each cognitive cycle enables the gradient backpropagation. Although PyTorch automatically does backpropagation, PySigma actively controls the scope of the gradient flow to prevent one part of the graph from affecting the learning of another irrelevant part. Such a control mechanism also enables PySigma to choose different optimizers for each scope of the gradient and apply different fine-tuning techniques for each optimizer, such as early-stopping and learning rate schedules.

4   Deep Generative Modeling in PySigma

The expressive power of the new message representation scheme, combined with the generality of the generalized message propagation, inference, and learning algorithm, enables PySigma to capture an even more comprehensive range of models than Sigma, hence taking a step forward toward the ultimate goal of grand unification. Such increased capability can be best demonstrated by modeling deep generative models, a class of probabilistic models that takes strength from deep neural networks, which Sigma has difficulties modeling. To illustrate the deep generative modeling in PySigma, we will discuss one specific such model, the variational autoencoder (VAE), in detail [8], demonstrate how to model it in PySigma, and analyze the correctness of the resulting PySigma model.

4.1   Preliminaries

Variational Autoencoders are canonical deep generative models widely used for learning a smooth representation space for continuous data such as images and audio. It is a successful fusion between probabilistic modeling and deep neural networks: the model can be mathematically analyzed as a probabilistic graphical model at a conceptual level but relies on deep neural networks for the implementation and backpropagation-based stochastic gradient descent for optimization.

From a probabilistic inference perspective, VAE is a class of methods for working with the Latent Variable Model, a class of models where a group of latent variables is interlinked to explain the behaviors of the observed variables. Figure 1a shows the simplest possible latent variable model as a Bayesian network that consists of only a latent variable $\mathbf{z}$ and an observed variable $\mathbf{x}$. Figure 1b presents the factor graph representation of this model. The $p_\theta(\mathbf{z})$ factor node encodes the prior distribution over z, and $p_\theta(\mathbf{x} \mid \mathbf{z})$ factor node encodes the conditional distribution that determines the underlying dynamics between z and x. Throughout the following sections, we will concentrate on this simple model for illustration. We will assume a known and fixed prior distribution and call the unknown conditional distribution $p_\theta(\mathbf{x} \mid \mathbf{z})$ the *reconstruction model*. We will also assume the reconstruction model comes from a very general model family $\mathcal{P}$ for which exact inference algorithms such as the Sum-Product algorithm cannot solve in polynomial time. However, despite the generality, the reconstruction models can be parameterized by a parameter θ, and the probability density function of the model is differentiable with respect to θ.

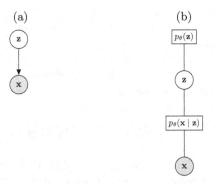

Fig. 1. Left (a): simple latent variable model as a directed Bayesian network. Right (b): the same model expressed as a factor graph.

There are two objectives of the above latent variable model that are worth pursuing:

1. **Inference:** with the reconstruction model $p_\theta(\mathbf{x} \mid \mathbf{z})$ fixed, find the posterior $p_\theta(\mathbf{z} \mid \mathbf{x})$ for the latent variable, given data $\mathbf{x} \in \mathcal{D}$.
2. **Learning:** to select a reconstruction model $p_\theta(\mathbf{x} \mid \mathbf{z})$ from the model family $\mathcal{P}$ such that the entire graphical model (prior + reconstruction) best fit the data distribution $\mathcal{D}$.

VAE approaches the inference task by introducing an *amortized* variational posterior $q_\phi(\mathbf{z} \mid \bar{\mathbf{x}})$ that is implemented by a neural network $f_\phi : \mathcal{X} \to \Lambda$ mapping a mini-batch of observed data points $\bar{\mathbf{x}}$ to the posterior distribution parameter λ that is then used to instantiate the variational posterior. This neural network is also known as the *recognition model*. Therefore, rather than iteratively finding a posterior $q(\mathbf{z})$ for multiple steps each time the reconstruction model $p_\theta(\mathbf{x} \mid \mathbf{z})$ is updated, VAE more efficiently obtains an approximated posterior through a single forward propagation of the neural network f_ϕ. Moreover, the inference task is converted into yet another learning task that is to update f_ϕ, and both the inference and learning tasks can be solved simultaneously by jointly optimizing the Evidence Lower Bound Objective (ELBO) for parameters θ and ϕ:

$$\mathcal{L}(\theta, \phi; \bar{\mathbf{x}}) = \mathbb{E}_{q_\phi(\mathbf{z}|\bar{\mathbf{x}})} \left[\log \frac{p_\theta(\bar{\mathbf{x}} \mid \mathbf{z}) p_\theta(\mathbf{z})}{q_\phi(\mathbf{z} \mid \bar{\mathbf{x}})} \right] \tag{1}$$

where $\bar{\mathbf{x}}$ is a mini-batch of observed data points. Accordingly, the updates are:

$$\phi \leftarrow \phi + \nabla_\phi \tilde{\mathcal{L}}(\theta, \phi; \bar{\mathbf{x}}) \tag{2}$$

$$\theta \leftarrow \theta + \nabla_\theta \tilde{\mathcal{L}}(\theta, \phi; \bar{\mathbf{x}}) \tag{3}$$

where $\tilde{\mathcal{L}}$ is the Monte Carlo estimate to the lower bound $\mathcal{L}$. Updating ϕ effectively solves the inference task, and updating θ effective solves the learning task.

4.2 VAE as a Message-Passing Factor Graph

With the VAE objective and optimization mechanics established, we now consider modeling the VAE as a factor graph to prepare for a PySigma implementation. VAEs, although inherently are directed latent variable models, are often optimized with a black-box optimization procedure (or end-to-end training in the deep learning context) in practice. In such a procedure, the model itself (including both the "reconstruction" model p_θ and the "recognition" model q_ϕ) is treated as a black box and optimized by first taking a global gradient back-propagation to the parameters of both models p_θ and q_ϕ with a subsequent joint parameter update to both θ and ϕ. This black-box optimization procedure, however, is very different from the design principles of a factor graph. The latter emphasizes breaking a global model into local pieces and relies on locally correct message update procedures to achieve the global optimization objective.

Fortunately, although modeling VAEs while completely conforming to conventional factor graph semantics is very hard, the task is simpler if we consider the augmented factor graph PySigma leverages. Figure 2a shows a modified version of the model in Fig. 1b, where a unidirectional message passing gadget is added alongside the original model, encapsulating the recognition model $q_\phi(\mathbf{z} \mid \mathbf{x})$. Figure 2b shows the actual compiled PySigma model, which will be analyzed in the next section.

To start, we notice that Eq. (1) can be expressed in the following factorized format:

$$\mathcal{L}(\theta, \phi; \bar{\mathbf{x}}) = \mathbb{E}_{q_\phi(\mathbf{z}|\bar{\mathbf{x}})}\left[\log p_\theta(\bar{\mathbf{x}} \mid \mathbf{z}) + \log p_\theta(\mathbf{z}) - \log q_\phi(\mathbf{z} \mid \bar{\mathbf{x}})\right] \qquad (4)$$

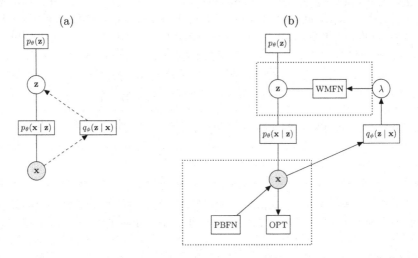

Fig. 2. Left (a): Latent variable model with conditional recognition factor. Note that the two unidirectional dashed arrows indicate that this model uses PySigma's augmented factor graph semantics. Right (b): Compiled PySigma model of the Variational Autoencoder. The nodes grouped by a dashed rectangle together construct a predicate subgraph.

At first glance, the three terms to be taken expectation seem to exactly map onto the three factor nodes in Fig. 2a, yet the subtraction sign before the third term indicates otherwise. Indeed, messages from factor nodes in a conventional factor graph will be taken product with at the variables nodes, leading to logarithmic summations in the overall probability density. However, this challenge can be overcome if we view $q_\phi(\mathbf{z} \mid \mathbf{x})$ not as a conventional factor, but as a *sampling factor*, from which particles of $\mathbf{z}$ are sampled. In this formulation, the term $p_\theta(\mathbf{z})/q_\phi(\mathbf{z} \mid \mathbf{x})$ as well as the term $p_\theta(\mathbf{x} \mid \mathbf{z})/q_\phi(\mathbf{z} \mid \mathbf{x})$ can be interpreted as weights of the particles drawn from $q_\phi(\mathbf{z} \mid \mathbf{x})$ that are *important weighted* against the distributions $p_\theta(\mathbf{z})$ and $p_\theta(\mathbf{x} \mid \mathbf{z})$ respectively.

To further illustrate the model's correctness under PBP, we break down the particle messages when the factor graph reaches quiescence, which is shown in Table 1. The "Particle Source" indicates where the particles of each message were originally drawn from, the "Log Sampling Densities" indicate the particles' relative frequencies, and the "Importance Weight" is the importance weight of the particles derived by dividing the target values by the particles' log sampling densities.

Table 1. Messages of the model in Fig. 2a when in quiescence state

Direction	Particle source	Importance weight	Log sampling densities
$\mathbf{x} \to q_\phi(\mathbf{z} \mid \mathbf{x})$	Data points $\bar{x} \in \mathcal{D}$	Uniform	Uniform
$q_\phi(\mathbf{z} \mid \mathbf{x}) \to \mathbf{z}$	Particles $z \sim q_\phi(\mathbf{z} \mid \mathbf{x})$	Uniform	$\log q_\phi(z \mid \bar{x})$
$\mathbf{x} \to p_\theta(\mathbf{x} \mid \mathbf{z})$	Data points $\bar{x} \in \mathcal{D}$	Uniform	Uniform
$p_\theta(\mathbf{x} \mid \mathbf{z}) \to \mathbf{z}$	Particles $z \sim q_\phi(\mathbf{z} \mid \mathbf{x})$	$\sum_{\bar{x}} p_\theta(\bar{x} \mid z)/q_\phi(z \mid \bar{x})$	$\log q_\phi(z \mid \bar{x})$
$\mathbf{z} \to p_\theta(\mathbf{z})$	Particles $z \sim q_\phi(\mathbf{z} \mid \mathbf{x})$	$\sum_{\bar{x}} p_\theta(\bar{x} \mid z)/q_\phi(z \mid \bar{x})$	$\log q_\phi(z \mid \bar{x})$
$p_\theta(\mathbf{z}) \to \mathbf{z}$	Particles $z \sim q_\phi(\mathbf{z} \mid \mathbf{x})$	$p_\theta(z)$	$\log q_\phi(z \mid \bar{x})$
$\mathbf{z} \to p_\theta(\mathbf{x} \mid \mathbf{z})$	Particles $z \sim q_\phi(\mathbf{z} \mid \mathbf{x})$	$p_\theta(z)$	$\log q_\phi(z \mid \bar{x})$
$p_\theta(\mathbf{x} \mid \mathbf{z}) \to \mathbf{x}$	Data points $\bar{x} \in \mathcal{D}$	$\sum_z p_\theta(\bar{x} \mid z)p_\theta(z)/q_\phi(z \mid \bar{x})$	Uniform

We can thus derive the marginal posterior for both node $\mathbf{x}$ and node $\mathbf{z}$. The former is simply the message $p_\theta(\mathbf{x} \mid \mathbf{z}) \to \mathbf{x}$, whereas the latter is the product of two messages: $p_\theta(\mathbf{z}) \to \mathbf{z}$ and $p_\theta(\mathbf{x} \mid \mathbf{z}) \to \mathbf{z}$.

$$post(\mathbf{x}) = \sum_z \frac{p_\theta(\bar{x} \mid z)p_\theta(z)}{q_\phi(z \mid \bar{x})} \tag{5}$$

$$post(\mathbf{z}) = \sum_{\bar{x}} \frac{p_\theta(\bar{x} \mid z)p_\theta(z)}{q_\phi(z \mid \bar{x})} \tag{6}$$

where $\bar{x} \in \mathcal{D}$ and $z \sim q_\phi(z \mid \bar{x})$. Here the notation *post* denotes that the values estimate the marginal posterior.

Looking back to the global ELBO Eq. (1), we notice that expressions (5) and (6) are both a Monte Carlo estimator to the ELBO, only with the former summarizing over variable $\mathbf{z}$ and the latter summarizing over variable $\mathbf{x}$. Therefore, if we optimize $post(\mathbf{x})$ with respect to the model parameter θ and optimize $post(\mathbf{z})$ with respect to the variational parameter ϕ separately, we recover the optimization procedures (2) and (3). Moreover, since both optimization on θ and ϕ are done separately and only using local incoming messages, we have achieved the goal of global optimization via local updates.

4.3   Model Implementation in PySigma

Figure 2b presents the schema of a compiled PySigma model that implements the variational autoencoder. It is an augmented version of the factor graph in

Fig. 2a with several PySigma's special purpose factor nodes added to complete the predicate subgraph.

At the bottom, the Perception Buffer Factor Node (PBFN) perceives a batch of data points at the start of each cognitive cycle and encapsulates the data points as message particles with uniform log sampling densities. The Optimization Node (OPT) calculates the loss value (5) by taking the product of the incoming message's particle weights. This loss value will then be used to back-propagate gradients to the reconstruction factor $p_\theta(\mathbf{x} \mid \mathbf{z})$ during the modification phase. Both PBFN and OPT, together with the observed variable node $\mathbf{z}$, construct the observed predicate structure.

To the right, the recognition factor node $q_\phi(\mathbf{z} \mid \mathbf{x})$, implemented by a neural network module, takes in the batch of data points and produces a batch of variational distribution parameters λ, which is then relayed through the variable node λ. The Working Memory Factor Node (WMFN) receives λ and instantiates a batch of independent variational distributions, from which particles are sampled with non-uniform log sampling densities. During the modification phase, it computes the loss value (6) and propagates gradients back to the recognition factor $q_\phi(\mathbf{z} \mid \mathbf{x})$. Both the WMFN and the variable node $\mathbf{z}$ together construct the latent predicate subgraph.

5   Future Work: Chunking

Chunking was implemented years ago in the Soar cognitive architecture, a predecessor to Sigma, where trees of rule firings could be summarized and replaced by single rules that are efficient to compute [10]. Unfortunately, due to the probabilistic nature of Sigma, summarizing Sigma's probabilistic logical rules is much harder, and there is yet to be a satisfactory solution. However, the modeling of VAE in PySigma provides an exciting lead. The recognition subgraph, in particular, might be generalizable in that it can be attached to any PySigma models to efficiently approximate the posterior of an arbitrary predicate given observations at some other predicates.

The implication of the recognition subgraph being an architectural pattern is far-reaching. For example, the parallel existence of a complex reasoning pathway with a simple neural approximator within a cognitive model can be related to the conception of fast and slow thinking in cognitive science [6]. Moreover, The ability of the architecture to automatically decide whether to attach such a recognition subgraph or an active control over the usage of the slow and fast message pathways are canonical metacognitive capabilities that are significant to the general intelligence [9]. Thus, it is worthwhile to investigate how well VAE can be further generalized in PySigma.

6   Conclusion

Sigma cognitive architecture and system results from decades of research on the integrated computational model of intelligent behaviors. Sigma has successfully modeled a wide range of capabilities yet faces a severe challenge regarding inference and learning with continuous variables. In this article, we presented several fundamental changes to Sigma's implementation that converge on a new version of Sigma called PySigma. We also provided a glimpse of the new capability these changes have unveiled, particularly the support for deep generative models. Overall, we demonstrated that PySigma is more capable than Sigma to unite neural and probabilistic processing, hence taking a step toward the ultimate desiderata of grand unification.

Acknowledgements. Part of the effort depicted is sponsored by the U.S. Army Research Laboratory (ARL) under contract number W911NF-14-D-0005, and that the content of the information does not necessarily reflect the position or the policy of the Government, and no official endorsement should be inferred. We also would like to thank Dr. Paul Rosenbloom for his comments and suggestions, which helped improve the quality of this paper. More importantly, we appreciate Dr. Rosenbloom's continuous and invaluable guidance in enhancing our understanding of cognitive architectures and the design choices for Sigma.

References

1. Akbayrak, S., De Vries, B.: Reparameterization gradient message passing. In: European Signal Processing Conference, EUSIPCO, September 2019 (September 2019). https://doi.org/10.23919/EUSIPCO.2019.8902930
2. Dauwels, J.: On variational message passing on factor graphs. In: Proceedings of the IEEE International Symposium on Information Theory, pp. 2546–2550 (2007). https://doi.org/10.1109/ISIT.2007.4557602
3. Dauwels, J., Korl, S., Loeliger, H.A.: Particle methods as message passing. In: Proceedings of the IEEE International Symposium on Information Theory, pp. 2052–2056 (2006). https://doi.org/10.1109/ISIT.2006.261910
4. Dillon, J.V., et al.: TensorFlow distributions (2017). http://arxiv.org/abs/1711.10604
5. Ihler, A., McAllester, D.: Particle belief propagation. In: van Dyk, D., Welling, M. (eds.) Proceedings of the 12th International Conference on Artificial Intelligence and Statistics. Proceedings of Machine Learning Research, vol. 5, pp. 256–263, 16–18 April 2009. PMLR, Hilton Clearwater Beach Resort, Clearwater Beach, Florida USA (2009). http://proceedings.mlr.press/v5/ihler09a.html
6. Kahneman, D.: Thinking, Fast and Slow. Farrar, Straus and Giroux, New York (2011). https://doi.org/10.1037/h0099210
7. Kim, H., Robert, C.P., Casella, G.: Monte Carlo statistical methods. Technometrics **42**(4), 430 (2000). https://doi.org/10.2307/1270959
8. Kingma, D.P., Welling, M.: Auto-encoding variational Bayes. In: 2nd International Conference on Learning Representations, Conference Track Proceedings, ICLR 2014, Banff, AB, Canada, 14–16 April 2014 (2014)
9. Kralik, J.D., et al.: Metacognition for a common model of cognition. Procedia Comput. Sci. **145**, 730–739 (2018). https://doi.org/10.1016/j.procs.2018.11.046, https://www.sciencedirect.com/science/article/pii/S1877050918323329. Postproceedings of the 9th Annual International Conference on Biologically Inspired Cognitive Architectures, BICA 2018 (Ninth Annual Meeting of the BICA Society), held 22–24 August 2018 in Prague, Czech Republic

10. Laird, J.E.: The Soar Cognitive Architecture (2018). https://doi.org/10.7551/mitpress/7688.001.0001
11. Paszke, A., et al.: PyTorch: an imperative style, high-performance deep learning library. In: Wallach, H., Larochelle, H., Beygelzimer, A., d'Alché-Buc, F., Fox, E., Garnett, R. (eds.) Advances in Neural Information Processing Systems, vol. 32. Curran Associates, Inc. (2019). https://proceedings.neurips.cc/paper/2019/file/bdbca288fee7f92f2bfa9f7012727740-Paper.pdf
12. Rosenbloom, P.S., Demski, A., Ustun, V.: Rethinking sigma's graphical architecture: an extension to neural networks. In: Steunebrink, B., Wang, P., Goertzel, B. (eds.) AGI-2016. LNCS (LNAI), vol. 9782, pp. 84–94. Springer, Cham (2016). https://doi.org/10.1007/978-3-319-41649-6_9
13. Rosenbloom, P.S., Demski, A., Ustun, V.: The sigma cognitive architecture and system: towards functionally elegant grand unification. J. Artif. Gen. Intell. **7**(1), 1–103 (2016). https://doi.org/10.1515/jagi-2016-0001. https://www.degruyter.com/downloadpdf/j/jagi.2016.7.issue-1/jagi-2016-0001/jagi-2016-0001.pdf
14. Rosenbloom, P.S., Demski, A., Ustun, V.: Toward a neural-symbolic sigma: introducing neural network learning. In: Proceedings of the 15th International Conference on Cognitive Modeling, ICCM 2017, pp. 73–78 (2017). http://www.doc.ic.ac.uk/~sgc/teaching/pre2012/v231/lecture13.html
15. Winn, J.: Variational message passing and its applications. Ph.D. thesis (2003). http://johnwinn.org/Publications/thesis/Winn03_thesis.pdf

Author Index

ited States
Publisher Services